IN THE RINGS OF SATURN

IN THE RINGS OF
SATURN

Joe Sherman

New York   Oxford

OXFORD UNIVERSITY PRESS

1994

Oxford University Press

Oxford   New York   Toronto
Delhi   Bombay   Calcutta   Madras   Karachi
Kuala Lumpur   Singapore   Hong Kong   Tokyo
Nairobi   Dar es Salaam   Cape Town
Melbourne   Auckland   Madrid

and associated companies in
Berlin   Ibadan

Published in 1994 by Oxford University Press, Inc.
200 Madison Avenue, New York, New York 10016

Oxford is a registered trademark of Oxford University Press

Library of Congress Cataloging-in-Publication Data
Sherman, Joe, 1945–
In the rings of Saturn / Joe Sherman.
p. cm.   Includes bibliographical references and index.
ISBN 0-19-507244-8
1. General Motors Corporation.
2. Saturn automobile.
3. Automobile industry and trade—United States.
I. Title.
HD9710.U54G47557   1994
338.7′6292222—dc20   93-12858

Grateful acknowledgment is made to the House of Bryant
to reprint four lines from *Rocky Top*, by Felice and Boudleaux Bryant, copyright © 1967 by the House of Bryant
Publications; and to Arcade Publishing, Inc., to reprint
seven lines from *Autogeddon*, by Heathcote Williams,
copyright © 1991 by Heathcote Williams.

9 8 7 6 5 4 3 2 1

Printed in the United States of America
on acid-free paper

For Andrew James

Contents

IN THE RINGS OF SATURN

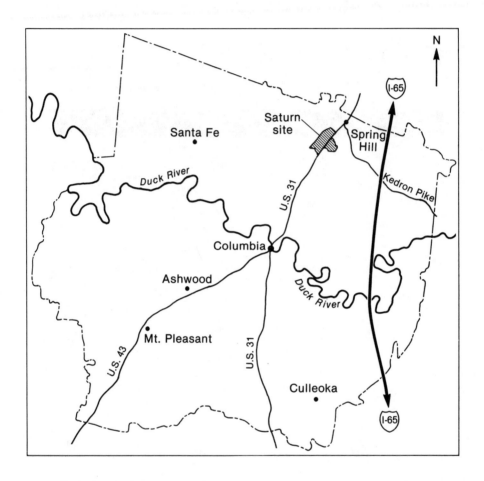

Maury County, Tennessee, 1985

Prologue

I've had years of cramped-up city life
Trapped like a duck in a pen
All I know is it's a pity life
Can't be simple again

Felice and Boudleaux Bryant, *Rocky Top*,
Tennessee State Song

I first drove into Spring Hill, Tennessee, in September 1986, four months after earthmovers had started peeling the loam off fields behind a six-columned *Gone With the Wind* style mansion a mile south of the village. Saturn, a wholly owned subsidiary of General Motors Corporation, had bought the mansion, called Haynes Haven, and a second mansion, Rippavilla, which sat across the road. Haynes Haven and Rippavilla anchored Saturn's 2,450 acres and it was here that the biggest corporation in America was going to have a small-car showdown with the Japanese. General Motors was finally going to try to build a high-quality, low-cost car that Americans liked.

I was in Spring Hill to write a magazine article about Saturn's impact on antebellum architecture. To date, not only Haynes Haven and Rippavilla had changed hands. A wild speculation whirlwind had swept through Spring Hill, through surrounding Maury County, and into adjoining counties in the wake of the official announcement, just over a year ago, that the largest one-time investment in the history of America, $5 billion, was going to be spent here. After the announcement, farms, businesses, homes, and thousands of acres were sold, along with more mansions.

That sticky Saturday afternoon in 1986, things in Spring Hill seemed quiet. I passed a two-story brick high school, slope-roofed bungalows with shaded porches. I drove slowly down the main street, literally a half-mile bump in the road with a few stores and another mansion clustered at the top of the bump, and a water tower jutting high overhead. Continuing south on U.S. 31, a Tennessee scenic highway, I soon passed Rippavilla, then Haynes Haven. A gap in the white fence running parallel to the highway marked the entrance to the Saturn site. A little gatehouse sat back from the road. Flags rippled on aluminum poles above its roof.

I continued twelve miles south to Columbia, the Maury County seat. A small city of twenty-five thousand, it too was picturesque and Southern, complete with brick storefronts encircling the courthouse square and a touch of American apartheid, a segregated warren of winding lanes east of town where most of the black people, who made up a quarter of the population, lived. That afternoon I drove up into the hills of Santa Fe, northeast of Columbia, where Jesse James had once hidden after a bank robbery. I cruised miles of back roads, passing row crop farms, dairy cows, tobacco barns.

Architecturally, the "dimple of the universe," as the region had been nicknamed a century ago, was a feast. From its mansions to its storefronts to its scattered churches to its surviving sharecropper cabins, Maury County fulfilled a visual legacy much of the New South had erased in the name of progress. Socially, as I soon learned, the region was also a throwback, a mix of mostly farmers, good old boys, blacks (most of them poor), and remnants of a once powerful Southern gentry holding on to vestiges of the past.

The coming of Saturn dramatically changed many of their lives. A few had gotten rich. Most had great expectations for the future. Some remained a little stunned even fourteen months after Saturn had detonated like a bomb, rippling psychologically, emotionally, and economically across the landscape. Why here, they still pondered. Spring Hill hadn't asked for Saturn. Maury County hadn't been ready for its demands. A thousand other communities—every single one of them better prepared—had wanted, had actively been competing for, Saturn. Nevertheless, now that Saturn was here, most natives sounded proud of it.

To me it seemed that the rural backwater, draped in history for decades, had suddenly been awakened from a long slumber. One day it had been dozing in the shadows of the nineteenth century, which had stretched slowly across most of this century. The next it found itself an outpost for the twenty-first. Practically overnight, the region became a microcosm of America's industrial future, a learning laboratory sited just outside the growth rings of a middle-sized, dynamic city. Here the country's biggest company was finally going to try to change the way it made cars—before it was too late.

The first car would not roll off the assembly line until 1990, however. The Saturn plant was going to take five years to get up and running because it was located on what urbanologists called a "green field site" and what local farmers called "damn good loam." It was going to be an "integrated facility." That meant the plant would do much of its own car making, from pouring its own engines and transmissions, to stamping its own fenders and frames, instead of simply assembling a car from parts manufactured all over the place. When the first Saturn appeared, it was going to be a great little car made by teams of caring autoworkers who had moved to this backwater and taken a cut in pay to start a different kind of company—a company that put engineering above accounting, people before machines, and quality right up there with godliness. And, of course, outsold the Japanese competition.

In 1986, that was the vision.

I had my doubts. Already the project had been downsized. It was going to cost $3.5 billion rather than $5 billion, employ 3,000 rather than 5,000, and build 250 thousand cars the first year, not 500 thousand, as first announced. Despite the ease with which GM had embraced the New Age rhetoric about teamsmanship, partners, and labor/management harmony, which Saturn was to personify, it quickly discovered that starting a new division from scratch, something it had not attempted since Chevrolet (in 1917), was going to be tough. And especially in a place six hundred miles from Detroit where the biggest event each year was the Mule Day Parade which, as one Southern belle confided, "draws more mules than you could ever possibly want to see."

That September, while writing my magazine piece, it didn't take long to deduce that Saturn was bad news for historic architecture— as well as for the region's farms, sense of hospitality, and Southern gentry, who found their power threatened. As for the car, I thought Saturn a doomed quest. It would probably be just another poorly made American steel box that advertising would lie about, another example of the double whammy of the American Century: the erosion of quality and the loss of place.

At the time I had the stereotypical cynical view of General Motors. I also had attended the University of Michigan Business School and had seen elements of the company up close: its hierarchy of white men, its narrow world view, its stodginess, its arrogance and power. I never owned a GM car; I bought foreign models: German, Swedish, Japanese. I seldom even test drove American cars anymore. Given GM's declining market share and the increasing gain by imports, most of them Japanese, my attitude toward GM seemed to be the status quo.

On the other hand I also wondered, could GM change? Could it become responsible to its customers, its labor force, this rural place? Or was Saturn Corporation, this much-ballyhooed rebirth of American know-how, going to be just another nail in the coffin of American industry?

Whichever way it went, I thought, the story would be a good one. It promised to touch many issues I was interested in: changing rural America, industrial renewal of the heartland, corporate responsibility for change, blue-collar workers with a voice in their company's future. And having lived most of my life in small towns, places with harmonious architecture, with people who knew one another, and with cows not far away, I felt some kinship with the people here. I felt their story was my story. So I decided I would witness the complicated tale as it unfolded, or observe it as much as physically possible. I wanted to feel the changes in Maury County, watch the construction of the integrated facility, understand the making of the little New Age car, which, after all, was the product most Americans would see and would ultimately determine Saturn's success or failure. Overall, I would compare what actually happened to the original vision.

Toward that end, between 1986 and 1992, I visited Maury County often, sometimes for a week, often for a month. I got to know some key players. I watched their attitudes evolve—toward Saturn, toward the county, toward their communities. I interviewed dozens of people, in offices, bars, and restaurants. I went to their churches, slept on their floors, hiked their hills. On numerous occasions I sat in my car and looked across fields of corn and soybeans at Saturn's in-process buildings lifting from a flattened plain behind the Haynes Haven mansion. I was occasionally allowed access to the site and was befriended by some Saturnites. In 1989 when the union work force began to arrive, I was impressed by their zealousness, commitment, and conviction that Saturn was different and so were they.

In mid-1989, after bouts of subjectivity that made me both anti-Saturn and pro-Saturn, I had a mild epiphany. We were all in the rings of Saturn, I realized. For if GM couldn't compete with all its resources and thousands of its best people being drawn here, if Saturn couldn't retrain and give workers more self-esteem, if it couldn't make a good cheap car, then America was in tough shape. Until then this truth had eluded me. I hadn't grasped just how telling this attempt at renewal was. The metaphorical coffin for American industry loomed out there ahead of us all—huge and dark and not a little scary—and much of American industry was in danger of falling into the coffin, along with workers, managers, suppliers, and even me.

After that I saw more clearly that GM was pulling out all the stops—its pride and future were on the line with Saturn. Maury County was no pristine backwater being taken advantage of by an indifferent Yankee giant. A rural leadership vacuum was perpetuating itself, fueled by a constituency that proved hardly more noble or less greedy than the big company and its newcomers. Meanwhile, the region was suffering protracted losses and had traded its farming and industrial past for a boomtown development model that was fizzling. Great expectations were turning sour, creating a reservoir of resentment instead of a pool of enthusiastic and supportive natives. The reasons were obvious: no locals got good jobs in the plant and Saturn's suppliers never relocated.

When the first Saturns started trickling out of the plant, rather than pouring forth as once envisioned, GM needed help badly. It was 1990 and the company was losing billions. Soon it would be closing dozens of facilities, laying off thousands of blue- and white-collar employees. No hype or appeals to patriotism were going to stem the flow of capital or keep the jobs. Only quality cars at good prices could do that. In five short years Saturn, the risky subsidiary on a green field site, had become GM's last best hope for a competitive future.

The big story, as it unfolded, broke into three smaller ones: Saturn becoming a quality car built a new way; the boomtown development model failing to revitalize the economy of Maury County; and, in the background, the woeful chronicle of GM coming unraveled economically and managerially as its newest division tried to succeed.

Several themes emerged. One was the importance of place in progress: how it is treated, how its leadership reacts, how national success can obscure local problems so they never get addressed. A second theme is teamwork with its many challenges. Teamwork of the kind Saturn aspired to in a culture of individualism proves a very high hurdle indeed, especially in a work environment that traditionally pitted management against labor. There are also questions about the success of teamwork undertaken between GM and the state, between the state and the county, and between the county and Saturn. A third theme is the pursuit of quality.

The word "quality" echoes throughout this book. From the plant to the car to the relationships, quality was Saturn's touchstone, its holy grail. Yet with all the emphasis on quality, one question I found myself repeatedly asking was, "Where has quality gone that we so desperately need to get it back?"

Throughout the late 1980s, it seemed to me that America so craved quality that it became just another buzzword. Despite the cheapening, quality itself remained—elusive, sought after, more longed for than ever. Americans cherished quality time for their children. We formalized quality networks in our businesses, longed for quality of life in our communities, overkilled quality the word in our ads. Yet collectively we were frustrated. We couldn't seem to get hold of quality as we once had. Without it America seemed destined to fall further behind in the making of world-class products, to stumble along haplessly down the yellow-brick road of mediocre education, to sit in handwringing circles and discuss quality, to form purposeful teams and pursue it—but to never quite recapture what had seemed so effortless and so synonymous with America just a few decades ago. That is, an ease and naturalness at making or being the best.

We knew we once made great stuff. Had we simply lost the knack? Had our standards remained static, or improved just a little, while the standards of other countries, such as Japan and Germany, both rising like phoenixes out of the ruins of war, defined some new epoch? A quality epoch that threatened to leave America behind?

Saturn became a quest for quality you could make a down payment on and drive home. And point to and say with pride, "Made in America."

The country needed that. As for actually capturing quality, that very notion, as Saturn management knew but had a hard time implementing, led away from true quality, which was a goal, not a place you actually got to.

There are some lessons in this story, both implicit and explicit. They emerge in the narrative, where I lean toward the anecdote over the summary, the quote over the generality. One is that big industry can change. Whether it can change quickly enough or thoroughly enough to compete in the global economy of the modern world is, at Saturn, still being played out. A second lesson is that if you're going to move a company into a rural region, you'd better hire some of the locals, or the backlash could undermine the gains. A third lesson is that teamsmanship builds quality, but to maintain teamsmanship the leadership has to be willing to part with some power and invest it in the teams, and workers have to give up some of their suspicions about management and commit themselves to the team and the product.

As for the question, "Is Saturn a success?" tentatively I can reply "Yes." But the story is complicated, the answers elusive, the jury (the American public) still out. In 1993, as this book goes to press, certainly by one yardstick—sales—Saturn is a hit. Americans everywhere want that car. By a second yardstick—profits—Saturn Corporation lost less its second year of production than it did the first, so movement is in the right direction. By a third yardstick—rural sharing of Saturn's prosperity—the project continues to be a disappointment. One final question—will Saturn continue to go its own way and escape the gravitational pull of GM, a company tottering dangerously close to disaster and undergoing managerial upheaval—I will deal with in the Epilogue.

Near the End of
Year One

1

A Fast Red Coupe

I laid eyes on my first Saturn, a red coupe with a blonde at the wheel, about thirty miles east of Nashville on I-40. It was mid-May 1991. The coupe zoomed by, doing about seventy-five. It slowed down when a Tennessee state trooper appeared on the other side of the interstate, then resumed cruising speed.

Staying close, I took a long look at the car. It was powered, I knew, by a 1.9-liter, double-overhead cam, 16-valve engine that put out 124 horsepower at the redline, 6,000 rpms. I had reserved expectations about the styling. But I had to admit—the coupe looked pretty sharp. It had a slightly raised rear, a passenger compartment whose low silhouette suggested the woman at the wheel was in a cockpit of a jet, and a downward sloping hood. After eight years of development and the opening ads of a $100-million promotion campaign, here was the small car that was supposed to show America could compete again, not just talk about it while naysayers muttered, "Have your kids learn Japanese." Given that America is in a recession, I thought, this little car has one big burden.

The next morning I drove south from Nashville on I-65 under an overcast sky. Middle Tennessee looked as green as Ireland once I got beyond Music City's sprawl. Punched into the green was the exit for Saturn Parkway, a five-mile connector built to link Saturn with I-65. Three car haulers loaded with gleaming new Saturns rolled along the other side, heading out and across America. Fields of knee-high grass bordered the highway. "For Sale" signs jutted above the still grass. The parkway ended at Saturn's security gatehouse. I checked through and drove about a quarter mile on the Donald Ephlin Parkway, named after the United Auto Workers leader most responsible for the Saturn labor agreement that attempted, with varying success, to soothe the enmity between management and labor. I wheeled into a parking slot in front of Northfield, the plant's administrative and training center.

Flags hung limply on thirty-foot poles. It was hot. I spotted a few Saturn coupes and sedans waiting for us media types to give them a spin later in the day. Climbing out of my dirty Dodge Colt, I had an awkward feeling of materialistic inferiority. My car was seven years old, Japanese-made, very small. Saturn Communications personnel, in white polo shirts, with *Saturn* emblazoned in red over their breasts, were there to greet the reporters pulling in. One of the Communications people, Jennifer Schettler, smiled and pointed toward a door in the two-story, gray complex with its circular drive and industrial style porte-cochere.

In the media center were coffee and donuts. Hardly had I drawn a coffee when a youthful-looking man with rosy cheeks and a Howdy Doody-like grin introduced himself as Jay Wetzel, Saturn's vice president of engineering. Chuckling, Wetzel said, "I was the first guy ever to get a ticket in a Saturn."

"Were you speeding?" I asked.

"Apparently I was a few miles over the limit."

Wetzel had been at GM's testing facility in Mesa, Arizona, with some production engineers. "We were all in Saturns. We had just driven out of our desert proving grounds and were headed up into the canyons. And in the bushes was a police car. I was about the third car. The first got his attention. He stopped me, told me I was going a few miles over the limit. I really think he wanted to see the car."

"Were these prototypes?"

"These were the original pre-prototype vehicles. Concept cars. This was back in 1985, and when I told him this was a '91 Saturn, he said, 'They'll never believe it at the station.' So he let me go."

Other vice presidents arrived, along with Skip LeFauve, Saturn's president. LeFauve, who had once been a Navy pilot, was a solemn man with the light blue eyes of a husky and spit-shined cordovan shoes. Neither LeFauve nor the vice presidents wore suits. They had on red Saturn polo shirts. The twenty or so reporters—from an edgy *Wall Street Journal* scribe who always seemed to have his opened notebook to somebody's chest, to a fountain-pen-using journalist for *The Financial Times,* to a television crew for NBC's *Nightline*—had a slight sartorial edge on their subjects, at least today.

The Saturn media event unrolled like script: continuous drama, lots of quick cuts, orchestrated. I noted that I was the only writer without institutional identity. *Freelance,* it said on my name tag. The term seemed to cause several Saturn vps to blink as they assessed its importance.

We rode buses to the plant, whose roof was visible from North-field. We toured the four interconnected buildings on little passenger trains, accompanied by the vps, a few visiting GM dignitaries who were in town to attend the GM annual meeting tomorrow, and the Communications watchdogs. We frequently passed beneath large American flags and big BINGO-like boards with *Teamwork Builds Quality* slogans on their bottoms, and under clicking conveyors carrying doors, drivetrains, and cockpits toward the assembly line ("vehicle systems" in Saturn lingo). Occasionally, the trains stopped for photo opportunities. Everyone piled off, snapped pictures, and talked to the executives or to autoworkers making cars.

Ed Killgore was driving one of the two media trains. Although I had never quite figured out exactly what his job was—construction superintendent, Saturn farm manager (a buffer zone surrounded the plant with seasonal crops, including corn, soybeans, and barley to soften its visual impact), or communications maverick—Ed Killgore had always been helpful. Since 1986 he had taken me on five tours of the site during various phases of construction. Usually we bounced around in a dusty Sierra 4 × 4, the no-nonsense Killgore in scuffed cowboy boots and a plaid shirt, his two-way radio crackling. With him I had seen "the most beautiful automobile plant in the world," as he once called it, evolve from a vast flat plain to a steel skeleton to a complex hive of machines, robots, systems, and people—all under one hundred acres of roof.

Today, perched at the front of a train, Killgore was watching a line of robotic welders. Sparks flew off the arms of the yellow robots as they danced, choreographed by computer, around galvanized steel spaceframes moving down the line in a kind of industrial ballet. Kill-gore had on his usual gear, along with protective eyewear. We all had been issued large clear glasses; they gave the media an otherworldly air. Killgore told me his present assignment was to set up an official tour of the plant, since a lot of people wanted to see it. But sure, he had time to give me a private run through. Just call him.

At another stop the *Nightline* crew, a reporter, cameraman, and soundman, filmed a technician installing headlights. The crew joined her on a skillet, one of Saturn's production innovations. A skillet is a wooden beltway, about fifteen feet wide, that moves along slowly so that technicians can work on cars as they and the cars move together, rather than having to walk alongside a moving vehicle. The reporter tried to get the technician, a black woman with a radiant smile, to say something interesting about teamwork. But she adroitly parried his queries about how well the teams worked, how coordinated the members were to date. Meanwhile, several Communications team members moved into position promptly. Monitoring the media, one member talked steadily into his recorder. When the *Nightline* crew walked off the skillet, he and the other red shirts visibly relaxed.

On the bus returning to Northfield, I sat by Bruce McDonald, or "Brewster," as he called himself, Saturn's vice president of communications. "Historically, we never asked people what they thought," McDonald said, referring to the training of the Saturn teams. "Now we empower them to really be an employee." A moment later, the high-strung man gripped my seatback with both hands and said intently, "What you're witnessing is the rebirth of American technological might. We're not here just to build a new car. We're here to reassert General Motors' might."

The rebirth theme had been a constant since Saturn's conception eight years ago deep within the sanctums of GM. Because the company had found it could not compete against the Japanese in the small-car market in traditional ways, the birth of Saturn as a kind of New Age flagship had been nursed along slowly, deliberately. The Saturn vision had included not only the wholly integrated plant, whose operation would resolve labor/management headaches, cut costs, care about the environment, and make a quality small car at a profit, but also the anticipation that the new satellite would "Saturnize" the rest of GM. That meant spreading enlightened labor/management ideas, teamsmanship, and Japanese concepts such as *kanban,* or just-in-time inventory, and *zaizan,* or continuous improvement, back through the moribund parent organization.

In the media center, McDonald moderated a perfunctory press conference. President Skip LeFauve told us that Saturn was selling all the cars being built, around thirty an hour, or six hundred a day. That was about half the number they had hoped to be making by now, ten months into production, but the figure was climbing. Vice president of engineering Jay Wetzel, when asked about Saturn's poor NHTSA (National Highway Traffic Safety Administration) crash reports, which had just been released and cast doubts on Saturn's safety relative to that of the competition, insisted that the car exceeded all "crash load management specifications."

Since people and their empowerment were the crux of change at

Saturn, the most pronounced difference between here and what Saturnites usually referred to as "the old world," or any other GM operation, I talked to Tim Epps, vice president of people systems, before everything broke up. A large, somewhat nervous man, Epps had just left an old world post as vice president of personnel, General Motors Europe, to join Saturn. He sounded as if he was still learning the lingo. "Using a model each semi-autonomous team learns conflict resolution techniques," Epps said when I asked how conflicts were handled. Team members who did not fit in could "de-select," he went on. But that wasn't happening much because they were "trickle hiring now, as opposed to ramping up."

To my question about how important language itself was to the training, Epps thought a moment, then said, "If you have a new expectation, don't use traditional words."

I wanted to ask him if the teams had real power. Could they hire, fire, and redesign themselves? Had they really taken control of decision making, or was management still calling the shots, but with language as a smoke screen? But Epps excused himself; he had to go. Call Communications for an interview, he advised.

2

Annual Meeting

The next morning, a few minutes before the start of GM's 1991 annual meeting, its eighty-third, I stood beneath a small, starched white tent by the Grand Old Opry at the Opryland Convention Complex outside Nashville and listened to a GM spokesperson explain how the airbag in a dark luxury sedan deployed. He was talking about the longitudinal component of an impact. Surrounding him and the car, at which he would often gesture, was a sampling of a disappearing America, relaxed upper middle-class white people. Most of the men wore suits and tie shoes, and had the casual stance of gentlemen not worried about paying the rent. The women, in pleated skirts and dresses, were usually hip-locked to their men.

Not a single black person in sight, I kept marveling to myself. Young people were rare in the crowd, too. General Motor's common stock, selling in the mid-thirties, was owned, if attendance here was a yardstick, by the same older Americans who loyally still bought its cars. I finally spotted a young couple. They were leaning over and peering through the window of a 1992 Cadillac Seville Touring Sedan. From a vantage point by the Cadillac's open hood, which presented a big 4.9-liter V-8 engine that got about twenty miles per gallon, I watched the procession of stockholders who had cleared security at this restricted affair. They wended their way through the display cars, stopping occasionally to pluck a donut from the piles or to draw a cup of coffee from one of many gleaming urns. In this setting it hardly seemed possible that America had had an acute energy crisis a decade ago, or that the earth was filled with finite resources whose depletion fueled cars. My gaze rested on a small red Saturn among the big cars, and the little sedan struck me as eminently sensible. Or at least as eminently sensible as any car could be in an age when, as the English poet Heathcote Williams puts it in *Autogeddon,*

Were an Alien Visitor
To hover a few hundred yards above the planet
It could be forgiven for thinking
That cars were the dominant life-form,
And that humans beings were a kind of ambulatory fuel cell,
Injected when the car wished to move off,
And ejected when they were spent.

"I'm so pro-GM, I'd buy anything they made," an older fellow told me a few moments later. Then he gave his wife a hand climbing out of the red Saturn. Once she was on her feet and pressing down her dress with both hands, he said he wouldn't take a road trip in such a little car, but he still might get one, just to drive around town.

I spotted GM's new chairman Robert C. Stempel walking briskly in our direction, a slight, almost Cheshire Cat-like grin softening his sharp features. Stempel wore glasses and had big shoulders. He went by with long strides. He didn't seem to have a bodyguard.

In the shade of a large portico, sprightly octogenarians handed out glossy folders filled with information to those of us heading to the Grand Old Opry's balcony. I took a seat and opened my blue-and-white folder. Two Saturns sped across the cover of GM's 1990 annual report. On the report's lower right corner it said, "Putting Quality on the Road." The financial summary showed GM had lost about $2 billion in 1990, compared to having made a profit of $4.2 billion the year before. In his "Message to Stockholders," chairman Stempel blamed some of the company's problems on the war in the Persian Gulf and the recession, which had taken consumer confidence down with it. But he also admitted it was time GM made big leaps forward in performance, cost reductions, and customer satisfaction. One positive note was that GM had been the only member of the Big Three to increase its market share in 1990. How it had done that and gone from a $4 billion profit to a $2 billion loss was one of those mysteries of big business that had brought a larger turnout than usual, around 1,700, to this annual meeting, held for the first time since 1966 outside Detroit, primarily because of Saturn.

A second drawing card was the list of items on the proxy statement. Of the ten items, GM's board of directors recommended the stockholders vote against eight. For instance, the board didn't think it ought to publish the names of executives making more than $100 thousand annually; it didn't want to divest from South Africa; and it didn't want to endorse the Valdez Principles, an environmental manifesto that mandated waste reduction, clean air and oceans, and conservation of energy. The directors argued that the salary disclosures wouldn't help stockholders make better voting and investment decisions, that GM had already sold its interest in General Motors South African to the subsidiary's employees, and the company had its own environmental principles, negating any need to adopt those linked, at least in name, to the disastrous oil tanker spill in Alaska in 1989.

Although it wasn't in the folder, I happened to have a copy of GM's first-quarter report for 1991, which had ended two months ago, on March 31. It carried more bad news. In the quarterly "Message to Stockholders," Stempel said it was "disappointing" to announce another loss, this one for $377 million. But not as disappointing, presumably, as it would have been to announce a $1.1 billion loss, which would have been the case without the sale of the GM Building in New York and some accounting changes.

The meeting opened with Stempel, GM president Lloyd E. Reuss, and four other top GM executives taking seats behind a long table on the stage. Stempel gave a short, upbeat speech in his stentorian voice. An articulate, forceful speaker, he declared, "We've got a home run with Saturn"; assured the stockholders that despite the recession GM was "not throttling back, we're accelerating"; but then cautioned them that even if the economy did rebound, it might be a while before GM rebounded with it.

After that, the meeting degenerated into a farce. The audience was filled with owners of the company, the GM board of directors, all the top managers, with the chairman wielding the microphone, yet the procedural rules of order printed on one of the enclosures were practically ignored. Three corporate gadflies in the audience, obviously aware of the unwillingness of GM's big shots to act tough in public, monopolized the proceedings. They pretty much commanded the microphones placed in the aisles meant for stockholders to ask questions. On several occasions one of the gadflies named Evelyn Davis informed the audience that she personally had brought GM's annual meeting to Nashville. Not the chairman or the board or anyone down at Saturn—she, Evelyn Davis, of Washington, D.C., had done this. A second gadfly, George Sitka, liked to point an extended finger toward members of the board of directors, including Stempel's predecessor, Roger B. Smith, and remind them, "You give general answers, not specifics!" The third gadfly, John Gilbert from Connecticut, whined even when giving a compliment, which he did not do often. Like his cohorts, Gilbert owned a few hundred shares of GM and was no stranger to these annual affairs. Stempel, Smith, and the others had sat through previous three-hour sessions with the same self-appointed hecklers.

In this circus atmosphere, a few financial questions did emerge and get answered. The audience learned that a forty-seven percent dividend cut was saving GM $722 million this year, that 300 of GM's 9,700 dealerships had gone out of business last year, and that the employee pension fund had assets of approximately $35 billion. But for the $400 thousand spent on it, the annual meeting was a token gesture, a lapsed opportunity for asking top management tough questions and trying to get answers. Later I asked several GM executives why management allowed such a farce to perpetuate itself in the name of an annual meeting. They tended to defend the gadflies, reminding me that stockholders had certain rights. Sure they did, but the exercise of those rights was ludicrously self-serving. I wondered why GM hadn't made changes to guarantee some kind of procedural satisfaction to more than three people. By playing to the gadflies, GM, as well as other large companies ("I'm a very big deal at Ford," Evelyn Davis bragged), guaranteed low attendance at annual meetings. Not that stockholders acting like a huge flock of well-dressed sheep didn't deserve some of what they got. It was hard to imagine how lethargic the meeting must have been in the years GM made a profit.

Stempel did mention Saturn's two recalls in response to one question. The first recall had been the previous February. A seat ratchet mechanism occasionally dropped an unsuspecting driver into the horizontal position. It had been replaced in 1,210 defective cars. The second recall had been announced only a week ago. Texaco had sent Saturn fifty-nine barrels of bad coolant. The coolant had eaten its way through the seals, hoses, and radiator cores of 1,832 Saturns before being discovered. Eleven hundred cars had been sold and the owners were all getting replacement cars. It was a costly screw up—about $18.3 million—but Saturn had turned a potentially huge embarrassment into a public relations coup by replacing the cars. Stempel said Saturn's handling of the recalls demonstrated "attention to detail" and "people doing their job."

I wandered out beneath the portico as a particularly loud groan from the thinning crowd greeted one of Mr. Gilbert's pompous questions. Elizabeth Murray, a reporter from the *Tennessean,* the state's biggest daily, was leaning against the railing. She told me she had sent several requests for interviews via GM messengers to Roger Smith and other board members, but they hadn't responded. "They're all sitting by the exit in the corner," she said, "so they can bolt out of here." In a column the next morning Murray would write, "It's not just in the movies that Roger B. Smith is inaccessible." She would mention Smith's cameo role in the hit documentary, *Roger & Me*, in which Smith continually refuses to visit Flint, the black hole in GM's galaxy, the place *Money* magazine named the worst city in America in 1988, to talk to workers laid off at GM plants.

Later in the meeting, a poised but exasperated Stempel told the shrunken audience, "I've tried to run a business-like meeting." A moment later he added, "This is a stockholders' meeting, and the stockholders have the right to express their opinions."

Those who did squeeze in good questions, and to their credit the gadflies did ask a few, didn't learn much new about executive bonuses, future company plans, or working conditions at GM plants in Mexico. The carnival atmosphere helped keep answers to those questions light.

Buses were available for those who wanted to see the Saturn plant and I rode one down. In a Northfield parking lot, lines of stockholders, some fanning themselves, waited to take cars on test spins. Others sat eating out of bag lunches beneath a huge tent. Several GM cars sat on display in the Northfield parking lot between the glass front of the building and the four flag poles. One was the futuristic HX3, an experimental hybrid powered by batteries and gasoline. The HX3 looked a lot like a giant slug on wheels with a glass head.

I did a loop in a SL2, keeping the transmission in second and third on the short test drive. My official escort was nonplussed about the tach touching the red line. Afterwards I was standing in the shade of the big tent when Stempel began making his way through some well-wishers, shaking hands, smiling, whispering into ears like a politician on the campaign trail. On impulse, I introduced myself. Stempel had a strong handshake that complemented his broad shoulders. He gave me his undivided attention, and after I told him I had been working on a book about Saturn since 1986 and asked for an interview, he gave me a name to call in Detroit.

"Tell him you talked to me," he advised.

Later in the afternoon I ran into Skip LeFauve. Wearing sunglasses and looking more relaxed than he had the day before, Saturn's president was walking past a Corvette on display in front of Northfield. He recognized me from a brief exchange we had had yesterday, removed his sunglasses, narrowed his light blue eyes, and said casually, "Got that book done yet?"

"No, not yet," I replied.

Over LeFauve's shoulder I saw Ed Killgore stacking Corvette literature on a table beneath a small tent. The afternoon had turned hazy, threatening. A few warm drops of rain began to fall. They spotted LeFauve's shirt, beaded on the glossy toes of his shoes. Standing in the pleasant drizzle I asked him his thoughts on the procedural shortcomings of the annual meeting, and he said he had left early. I inquired about Saturn's sales. Production, not a lack of customers, was determining the numbers, he said, as he had yesterday. LeFauve repeated that quality was the goal, not quantity. To my question about why Saturn marketing had not adopted a "Buy American" strategy in the wake of mounting national concern about America's industrial competitiveness and the war in the Persian Gulf, he said that unless the government promoted such a concept it never worked. Before he moved on, LeFauve agreed to be interviewed and assured me, "We'll help you any way we can."

On the bus ride back to Opryland I sat by Joe Virgo ("And I am a Virgo, too!") from East Tennessee. Virgo had bought some GM stock a few months ago because it was cheap. He grinned slyly when he said, "You know, all those Saturn folks give you the same line. I hope they mean it."

A week later, on a crisp morning with a breeze rippling the American, State of Tennessee, Saturn, and UAW flags in front of Northfield, Saturn Communication's Jennifer Schettler led me through long gray corridors with nothing on the walls unrelated to Saturn and into the executive area, which was subdued and quiet. Saturn's executives, except for LeFauve and the vice president of manufacturing, worked in Troy, Michigan, and traveled back and forth regularly by air. Schettler took me into the president's bright office in a corner of the building, natural light flooding in from two sides. Informally dressed in his red Saturn polo shirt, LeFauve pulled a chair out in front of his desk and sat. Schettler turned on her tape recorder.

Richard "Skip" LeFauve was Saturn president number three. The company's first president, Joe Sanchez, had died of a heart attack after three weeks on the job, back in February 1986. Saturn's second president, William Hoglund, had been the top executive for a year; most of his tenure had been in Detroit. General Motors had still been playing cat-and-mouse about whether Saturn was *really* going to build its manufacturing facility way down here in Tennessee. LeFauve, a youthful-looking man now fifty-six, had taken over in February 1986, three months before site work finally began.

"I was shocked; no doubt about it," LeFauve said, recalling his promotion. It had been announced in the Design Dome at the GM Technical Centery in Warren, Michigan. The dome, which looks from the outside like a gigantic upside-down wok and is normally a show-place for new models, easily held the four hundred or so people then assigned to Saturn. When the popular Bill Hoglund told the unsus-pecting audience that he was leaving the fledgling subsidiary, "There was this big moan," LeFauve said. "Then just dead silence" fell when Hoglund added that the guy beside him was going to take his place. The silence dragged on for so long, LeFauve remembered with a grin, that he had muttered under his breath, "Oh shit."

Not that he didn't want the job. He had been a people person his whole life and Saturn was putting people before machines. He was also an engineer, a hands-on kind of guy who had first caught "the car bug" as a Boy Scout back in Orchard Park, New York, when he and some other scouts had bought, rebuilt, and raced their own ja-lopy. And Saturn was supposed to be putting engineers in front of bean counters. But in early 1986 LeFauve's life had been complicated. He wasn't sure he could handle being president of Saturn. His wife had Alzheimer's disease; he'd have to move. Yet, with his commit-ment to GM and his manufacturing background (at the time, LeFauve had been vice president of manufacturing for the Buick-Oldsmobile-Cadillac Group) the longer he thought about it, the more he had realized he couldn't let the opportunity go by.

Eventually, although they hated to see Hoglund leave so soon—three presidents inside of thirteen months didn't bode well for a new company's future—the core group accepted him as the replacement, LeFauve said. It was a meaningful lesson. At Saturn the president had a different leadership role than at other GM divisions. He was not the most important person, LeFauve emphasized. The people designing, making, and eventually selling the car were more important; they just hadn't fully understood that yet.

Saturn was so different from the old GM world that during his first months on the job the whole project felt a little unstable, Le-Fauve admitted. There was no plant, no car. There was a strike threat. Labor and management were interpreting Saturn's radical new labor agreement. They were trying to forge some trust and openness, but making breakthroughs was tough, given decades of conflict. The chal-lenge was to get by the residue of cynicism from past failures at sim-ilar goals: teamwork, mutual respect, and shared decision making. The presence of a leader who didn't give orders, who was a kind of super consultant to teams that made decisions by consensus, took some getting used to. Especially since the executives, including Le-Fauve, had all matured in the old GM world where tenderness was a weakness, giving orders the sign of a man, and a veneer of toughness crucial to promotions. At the top LeFauve needed to act as a role model: he had to shed the old world's behavioral conditioning. He had to set the pace yet downplay his power. The intent was to flatten GM's traditional vertical pyramid of power, to make Saturn's pyramid more horizontal, more team-based. Ultimately, Saturn hoped to put much of the decision making right on the floor, where things would be happening. As an example, LeFauve mentioned Honda, where top executives worked in the plant, their desks often in the open in production areas.

In contemporary business language, Saturn was trying at the outset to become a "learning organization," a term from Peter Senge's *The Fifth Discipline,* which LeFauve said members of the top team were reading for future discussion. As the Director of the Systems Thinking and Organizational Learning Program at MIT's Sloan School of Management, Senge was one of the more prominent seekers of a new path for capitalism's future. His highly acclaimed book, a kind of zen of leadership, argued persuasively that the future of business was going to rely as much on the spirit of people as on capital, as much on going slowly and doing things right as on going fast and making mistakes, as much on a mind shift (*metanoia,* he called it, a transcendence into a whole new and deeper kind of learning than the corporate culture has known) as on old established thought processes. It was time, Senge said, for managers "to see the world anew," instead of resting on behavior from the past, which would not work in an increasingly competitive and global economy with twenty-first-century concerns.

Skip LeFauve also mentioned the irascible septuagenarian Dr. W. Edwards Deming. "If Japan Can, Why Can't We?," a TV documentary broadcast in 1980, had turned Dr. Deming into a kind of capitalistic folk hero overnight.

"Dr. Deming is such a powerful person," LeFauve said, smiling at some private recollection and glancing out the window. "You can be having dinner with him, and he's just chewing your ass—in a Deming way." LeFauve laughed. "Then you get up and you wonder if you've made him mad. He's not mad. He's very impatient with progress today that we're making in this country. At Saturn, everything we're doing is very consistent with what he says. For example, one of his principals is 'Drive out fear.' We work so hard to have people feel comfortable with anybody at Saturn. There are still people who are afraid of what they will say, or what they will do . . . or something."

At the end of the interview I asked LeFauve if I could spend a few days inside the plant. I wanted to see teamwork build quality, like the Saturn slogan said. I suggested joining the crankshaft machining team as an observer. The crankshaft is the strange-looking thing at the heart of the internal combustion engine, and I hoped to spend some time with the team at the heart of the heart of Saturn, so to speak. I planned to watch members interact with each other and with the robots and high technology at their command.

LeFauve thought a moment and then replied, "There're good things going on in powertrain."

Powertrain was the building in which crankshafts were made; they were cast by the lost-foam method and then machined before being installed in engines. LeFauve said he thought it would be OK if I joined the crank team, as long as the team approved. There was one caveat: no writing about the technical advances and patented processes that had put Saturn crankshafts on the cutting edge of engine technology.

For the next three weeks, I tried to follow up on LeFauve's go-ahead. But Saturn Communications, through which everything had to be arranged, gave me the runaround. Making a few inquiries, I learned that no reporters were getting inside the plant with the kind of freedom I anticipated being given with the crankshaft machining team. Saturn's media phobia was totally old world, observed one automotive reporter who had been following the story for several years, and was in sharp contrast with the attitude at the Nissan plant in nearby Smyrna, Tennessee. Nissan regularly invited him to the plant, urged him to write stories. "The tragedy is that Saturn's full of good news," he said.

At a luncheon at the Nashville City Club, where I went to hear Saturn's advertising manager, Luana Floccuzio, the guest speaker, I got an earful from Beverly Keel, the business reporter for the Nashville *Banner*. Keel, wearing an I-just-woke-up look and clutching a large yellow notepad, plopped down beside me a few minutes before Floccuzio, dressed to kill in a tight red dress and red high heels, with long red nails and a big black halo of teased hair, took command of the lecturn. Keel vented her ire with Saturn Communications and what she called its "bunker mentality." What bothered her most was all the teamsmanship and openness stuff encouraging the plant workers to talk honestly, yet how they could get in trouble unless Saturn Communications knew about an interview.

When I mentioned the possibility of interviewing Stempel in August, Keel livened up. She said she had interviewed Roger Smith twice. "It was like interviewing the Pope," she recalled, laughing. To get an edge, she had played the Southern belle. Sitting erect at our round table, Keel, twenty-five, tall and commanding, did a brief imitation. "Oh Mr. Smith, I'm Beverly Ka-eel, from the *Tennessee Bann-ah*," she said, pouring on the syrup. Smith had said sure. She'd gotten fifteen minutes, twice. She'd asked Smith if he had seen *Roger & Me*. He had. She told him some folks in Maury County were worried that what happened in Flint might happen there. Not to worry, Smith had assured her.

"We had a seven-week total flight," Floccuzio explained a few minutes later, describing Saturn's "rollout strategy" last fall. The car's introduction, or launch, had been preceded by eight print ads, Floccuzio went on. None of the ads showed a vehicle. They focused instead on the engineers and designers behind Saturn talking about why it was "a different kind of car" made by "a different kind of company." The print ads had generated over 100 thousand calls about a car people hadn't even seen, Floccuzio told us. When Saturns first hit the stores (in the new language a dealership was a "store"), print, radio, and national television commercials keyed to certain audiences appeared, this time with cars. Television spots ran, for instance, on "Twin Peaks" and "Cheers," and during the World Series. The ads played on sentiment and nostalgia, and emphasized quality at low cost.

Hal Riney & Partners of San Francisco had created the $100-million ad campaign. Writing in *New York* magazine not long after the launch, Bernice Kanner observed that the TV ads, which often featured the voice of Hal Riney himself reading the friendly copy, had "a front-porch style." They were "gentle, sentimental, down-home," with lots of mood music and "real" people who were actors.

Hal Riney & Partners had created the successful ad campaigns for Gallo wine and Perrier water. Moving wine and water, indispensable fluids for the chic and the health conscious, was different from moving metal, however. Convincing a consumer to lay down a dollar, or five, required a different level of penetration into human motivation patterns than getting the same consumer to take on three or four years of payments. The right water, after all, might suggest you were fashionable. And wine elevated the mood. But a car was, as they say in California, life itself. To the average American, the purchase of that car stood higher on his or her priority list than buying a house, having health insurance, or forging a good relationship.

Floccuzio assured us that Hal Riney's campaign was working just fine. She played a few of the TV ads on a video monitor. They were funny, informative, consistent.

To date Saturn was cutting into the Asian imports market, Floccuzio asserted. The average age of a Saturn buyer was thirty-eight, compared to forty for Asian imports. Seventy-three percent of Saturn's owners were college educated, as opposed to eighty-two percent of the owners of the Asian competition. Sixty-five percent of Saturn buyers would not have chosen an alternative General Motors vehicle. Of that sixty-five percent, two-thirds would have bought Japanese.

The idealized customer for the Saturn coupe, said Floccuzio, who seemed to fit the model, was a single female, around thirty-five, a woman who was image conscious and wanted "to make a personal statement with her car." The sedans were aimed more toward families. As for the connection between GM and Saturn, the ads purposely avoided the linkage, Floccuzio said, because Saturn needed to establish its own identity.

Floccuzio neither denied nor confirmed that the ads had been designed to subtly appeal to the "Buy American" streak just below the surface of many people worried about things like the national deficit, the trade imbalance, and Japan, Inc. One reason for not linking Saturn with GM, which she did elaborate on, was the perception problem the parent company faced. People didn't believe GM when its ads talked about quality. If Saturn was going to convince its prospective buyers that "quality" wasn't just another buzzword, that the company's response to two recalls had been genuine, it had enough hurdles to overcome without having GM stamped on every bumper.

3

The Zen of Quality

All the emphasis on quality begged a question: where had quality gone?

In *Zen and the Art of Motorcycle Maintenance,* published in the mid-1970s, a writer/philosopher named Robert Pirsig had tackled that question. His attempt to get a hold on quality tumbled Pirsig, then a professor of English at Montana State College, into temporary insanity. Rather naively, Pirsig admits in the now famous account, he set off through "the high country of the mind," a zone few entered and where "the harder you think . . . the slower you go." His mind came unraveled. The book both describes and reflects upon the unraveling during a subsequent cross country motorcycle trip with his eleven-year-old son as a passenger and Pirsig's BMW motorcycle as a metaphor for examining America's distancing itself from the hands-on-ness of quality.

Ultimately, Pirsig didn't successfully define what quality is, and concludes, I feel, that most of us fail to understand even the perplexity of the question, never mind achieve much personal quality in our work or lives. We have become too specialized, too focused, too compartmentalized to really deal with such a broad concept. Its essence is spiritual. It's as though we were clutching a handful of mist rising magically off a pond at dawn, intending to seize beauty, to clasp it to our breast. In a similar manner, quality, when grasped, eludes us, defies captivity.

Saturn had made quality, achieved with teamwork inside a learning organization, its highest goal. Saturn appeared to have few qualms about getting a hold on quality. Yet a good question seemed to be: did its management or labor know what quality was?

The quality disciple Saturn followed was not author Robert Pirsig, but the fellow LeFauve mentioned, Dr. W. Edwards Deming, the statistician/philosopher flustered with America's snail's pace competitiveness. To Deming, quality has some of the zen Pirsig attributes to it. Deming insists quality is not an organizational chart, a mission statement, or an ad campaign. It's a continuum. Though hard, if not impossible, to touch or see, quality can be measured along a continuum using statistical analysis.

That was one of the concepts that Deming, in the 1950s, had taught the Japanese. Little appreciated in America, where the economy had been booming, Deming had gone to Japan and helped lay the foundation for the evolution of "Made in Japan" from a synonym for junk to one of quality. Not that Deming taught the Japanese the essence of quality. From bonsai to the tea ceremony, from the martial arts to woodworking, the Japanese had a history of attention to detail. Deming focused that natural attention on industrial production and the refinement of process.

His message was that quality was an attitude—continuous improvement: *zaizan*—as much as a goal. It was omnivorous and self-perpetuating. The better a part got, or a company got, the more attuned it was to defects. In other words, you couldn't put quality in, you could only refine, tighten tolerances, make better measuring devices. And you must incorporate people with insight into the business, managers who had what leaders of the business renaissance of the 1990s called "mastery." Ones who knew that you never *reach* quality because it's like enlightenment to the New Age movement. And as Pirsig had learned the hard way, hiking in the high terrain of his own prodigious intellect, trying to get a firm grip on quality could drive you nuts. Yet continual movement in the direction of quality, maybe even glimpsing it, or thinking you glimpsed it, kept quality moving forward, god-like, misty, cherished.

In the 1950s, with his crew cut and his statistics, Deming must have seemed an odd bird on the four islands where the major product was still rice. He taught the Japanese they had to learn to think clearly first if they wanted to make quality anything. Then refine the thinking. Think and refine, think and refine—that was the mantra.

During the 1960s and early 1970s, when GM commanded more than fifty percent of the new car market in America, its top management had not done much thinking or refining. The managers put adequate quality into each model with engineering specifications. Then manufacturing locked in the level of quality on a massive scale, lowering unit cost. General Motors dominated the market by sheer might. The concept, as Deming knew earlier than most, became an invitation to an industrial beheading, samurai style. But American industry barely listened to him. Like some gruff backwoods preacher whose gospel from on high had been sneered at by his own countryman, Deming developed sort of an attitude. By the time he was embraced as a capitalistic visionary in the early 1980s, he was old and cranky. He had been preaching quality for so long he only wanted the pews of the Cathedral of Quality filled with CEOs, presidents, top dogs—in other words, with those highly paid, self-assured (though not as self-assured as they had been) executives he saw as pathetically out of touch with the real problem: themselves. They were the enemy. Quality needed to start right at the top if it was to do any good.

By the early 1980s, the American automobile industry was no longer overconfident and prosperous. Its managers no longer basked in the international recognition of their might and right; they had fallen swiftly. Only two decades earlier, American corporations, led by the auto firms, had personified what the French writer, J. J. Servan-Schreiber, in his best seller *The American Challenge,* called "the art of organization." Europe was dying economically, Servan-Schreiber wrote, and tens of thousands of European leaders agreed. The salvation of their continent, Servan-Schreiber had contended, lay in adopting American business practices.

But all things must pass. As surely as Servan-Schreiber attributed America's economic leadership to managerial superiority and intelligence ("American society wagers much more on human intelligence than it wastes on gadgets," he said), the underpinnings were wasting away. Education, beginning in the early 1970s, started slipping down the learning curve. Individual responsibility seemed to crawl into protracted hibernation. And the American automobile business, the industry whose impact on the economy dwarfed that of most other industries, drifted into a parody of leadership and a case of managerial paralysis just as the Japanese economic invasion shifted into second gear following the oil crises of the mid-1970s.

As a nation America had conditioned itself to believe it had a lock on quality. We based this belief on our national memory of the 1950s and 1960s, a brief, expansive era when America had set the international pace and the rest of the world played catch-up. Europe and the Orient were just getting back to speed from the damages of World War II. Eastern Europe and Russia were mortgaging their futures to compete in the Cold War.

But by the 1990s, we weren't so sure of ourselves anymore. We lacked confidence in our ability to get quality back in our goods, our schools, our lives.

Saturn had become a highly scrutinized attempt to shore up that confidence. Yet now that the first cars were on the road the quality question remained. There were recalls, problems with engine noise. Why couldn't the plant make enough cars? Saturn's parent organization was a master of denial and Saturn a kind of errant child six hundred miles from home. Had Saturn gotten a grip on quality? Was teamwork, the *sine qua non* of quality at Saturn, sprinkled liberally with Deming's philosophy and kept lean by *kanban,* doing its thing? I didn't know because I couldn't get inside the plant.

4

June in the Dimple of the Universe

It was June in Tennessee. Softball-sized magnolias weighed down the branches of trees. Cicadas keened. Fireflies, in the millions, hovered over suburban lawns at twilight, flashing and flying. And Saturn Communications still wasn't coming around so I decided to revisit several Maurians I had gotten to know on my previous trips.

Over breakfast one morning I talked to former Spring Hill Mayor George Jones. We were in Bucky's Family Restaurant, a few blocks from courthouse square in Columbia. George had the eggs and tenderloin, lathered in tan gravy. He sprinkled salt over everything until the gravy gleamed, cut his breakfast into a couple dozen bite-sized pieces, and listened to my questions. When I told George about my difficulties getting into Saturn after LeFauve had said it was OK, the volatile ex-mayor snapped, "It's a front. LeFauve don't give a damn about your book. He's telling you what you want to hear."

A few mornings later I visited James Lochridge, a farmer I had talked to half a dozen times the last few years. Lochridge owned the largest row crop farm in Spring Hill. His barns and farmhouse sat just over a knoll from the new Ryder trucking facility, which handled Saturn's cars and parts. Lit like a maximum-security prison from dark to dawn, the facility's yellow glow had just been extinguished when I pulled in Lochridge's barnyard.

James Lochridge was a tanned, handsome man in his mid-fifties who usually wore bluejeans and a bluejean shirt. Since it was summer, today the shirt had ragged short sleeves. Lochridge carried a round tin of chewing tobacco in his shirt pocket; it was the reason for his stained teeth. We talked for a while, then he walked over to his hired man, who was seated on a tractor, his leg in a cast. Swallows were swooping in and out of an open-sided barn over large round hay rolls, the kind the hired man would be collecting later in the morning. Once Lochridge sent him on his way he stopped for a minute. Spring Hill might still look the same, he told me, but the people had changed. "You get them more crowded up," he said in a voice that rivaled Hal Riney's for a smoky smoothness that relaxed you, "they're more interested in making money."

Lochridge was the seventh generation of his family to farm in Spring Hill. He grew mostly soybeans, with some corn, oats, and milo for his livestock. Unlike his son Randy, James Lochridge had never openly opposed Saturn. During the speculation whirlwind in 1985, he could have sold his farm for millions. Nowadays, ironically, he rented crop land at low rates from those who had bought farms but had not yet turned them over.

"Not but three people in this area are still farming full time," Lochridge said. He listed them: himself, John Campbell, and Bud Mitchum. And Mitchum had sold his farm for $3 million back in 1985; he was still working it for the new owner.

I asked Lochridge about the *Welcome to Spring Hill* video, a Saturn-sponsored shoot in which he, sitting in dappled light, talks about farmers being closer to God. He said he'd done it because Saturn asked him. He remained nonjudgmental about Saturn, though he knew, had known from the beginning, that the coming of the factory had changed farming in Maury County forever. It also had in some unfathomable way driven his boy Randy from the farm.

In 1985 and 1986 Randy, then in his mid-twenties, had gone through a year and a half of depression. An amiable bachelor with graying hair and bloodhound sad eyes, Randy had once told me about those days. "It was real hard to get up in the morning," he said. "It got late afternoon I wanted to go back to the house. I didn't have anything to work for." In 1987 he quit his father's farm. "I'd made up my mind I was going to stick with it, and then one day I heard this racket. I thought it was a tractor. I wondered who was using a tractor over there, across the road. It was a bulldozer. That's when I decided to leave. Something snapped. I'd been living in a daydream."

Randy had gone to work for the U.S. Department of Agriculture in Nashville as a trainee in the department's Agricultural Stabilization and Conservation Service. The job gave him a lot of one-on-one contact with farmers, and eventually, in 1991, brought him back home. Presently, he was the manager of the USDA office in Columbia and living in Spring Hill.

All along James had been supportive, encouraging his son to do what he felt was right. "Without that encouragement," Randy said, "I don't know if I would have made the change. It was that little nudge that did it." Not that he still wasn't bothered some by his decision. "It's going to end with me," he said, referring to the Lochridge farm. "It makes you feel inferior. It makes you feel like a loser."

I went with James Lochridge to his blue Toyota pickup. As we circled the garden, James said he still didn't think Saturn was going to turn out to be anything great, particularly for this area. "It's been a forced change," he said. "Force eventually loses."

We rode across a field behind the farmhouse in the pickup, a groundhog rifle wedged between the seats. A bucket of grain for feeding calves bounced in the truck bed. Circling fifteen or so calves, Lochridge parked, climbed out and in one smooth motion swooped up the grain and strolled toward the calves, singing out: "Calves, come on, come on, come on! Come on, babies! Calves, come on, come on!"

With him leading, the brown-and-white calves trotted across the sunlit pasture toward a gate by a shady creek. Arms out, I positioned myself between the pickup and the fence, blocking an escape route.

"Come on, babies! Calves, come on! Calves, come on!"

Blackbirds cackled in the trees as Lochridge swung the gate closed behind the frisky calves. They skittered alongside the ribbon of water.

"A farmer who farms for a living is the greatest environmentalist the country has," Lochridge declared back in the barnyard. "A farmer is close to nature, close to God."

Hanging around in the morning shadows of the barn, obviously anxious to get going with the rest of his day ("I've been putting in sixteen to eighteen hours the last few weeks; I don't even have time to visit my mother"), Lochridge recounted his tenure as a Sunday school teacher in the Methodist Church in Spring Hill. For seventeen years he taught grades ten through twelve, reading the Bible from cover to cover three times. Of all the biblical prophets and characters, the one he liked best, he said, was Solomon. Solomon had sought wisdom. "I'm a person in life searching for something greater than what I have," Lochridge said, staring into the middle distance and slipping a rugged hand into his shirt pocket for his tobacco tin.

Later that morning, as the heat settled in, I cruised the few back streets of Spring Hill, my windows down. To my eye the village looked only slightly changed from a year ago, or even five years ago, for that matter. The shady byways, with their vernacular houses, cabins, columned mansions, and contemporary ranches on an acre or more, still had the sleepy look city people associate, often incorrectly, with rural places, wanting them to satisfy some deep need for a peaceful retreat from urban life. Most of the senior citizens who had lived here in

1985 were still living here, I knew, in air-conditioned comfort. They had not yet been forced elsewhere by taxes or crime or the monthly charge for garbage pickup—one of the fees George Jones's foes had turned against him in 1989 when he had lost his bid for reelection as mayor. I slowed by Spring Hill High School, a two-story, 1930s classic. The school had a worn and tired look, as though it had been neglected. A new school was being built on fifty acres south of the plant, on land donated by Saturn. In the bump-in-the-road center of town, the McKissack mansion across from the village grocery had a "For Sale" sign on the lawn, as it had for six years. The bank and a gas station had closed. But the bank had reopened as a branch at Town Center, a development between the village and Saturn's northern boundary. You could get gas at a convenience store across from Town Center.

I drove north out of town. "There's no reason to fear shipwreck if Jesus is at the helm," the marquee of the Baptist Church declared alongside Scenic Route U.S. 31. Nearby, the little awning over the entry to the Hitchin' Post, the local bar, was more tattered than ever.

I ate breakfast at the Poplar House Restaurant, the place to hang out for rumors and good cheap food. A waitress told me that the former owner, the talkative and jolly Freeda Brown, had sold the business recently. Her husband had died of a heart attack. The new owner had installed a big TV, a nuisance if you like to eat in peace, in a conspicuous corner. Country singer Amy Grant, performing on MTV, serenaded a half dozen of us customers as we had our coffee, eggs, ham, and biscuits.

A few days later, on a sweltering afternoon, I visited Delilah A. Speed, a short-haired lawyer who specialized in divorce. No southern belle, Speed drove a red Dodge convertible with vanity plates (DAS), an American flag on the antenna, and a busted taillight. She had on penny loafers with no socks, khaki slacks, a flowery shirt, and horn-rimmed glasses when I talked to her in her office overlooking the Duck River in downtown Columbia.

"I'm very vocal, and it's caused me a lot of grief," Speed said, leaning back in a chair. "Right now we have a totally incompetent administration." The mayor, a former manager of the Holiday Inn who had done some public relations work, "does not have the fortitude to make a decision," Speed said. "She's a popular, sedate kind of person." Meanwhile, with no suppliers relocating, land prices still high, Saturn not hiring locally, and long-time industries folding, added to the national recession, Columbia was in a fiscal crisis. Bureaucrats hired to strengthen the infrastructure, but who weren't needed because nothing happened that they had planned for, were hanging onto their jobs. The hot talk in town concerned the new director of the Maury County Chamber of Commerce, a fellow named Tom Quinn, who recently proferred the expected platitudes about excitement and promise for the future at a "Business After Hours" meeting at Green Sporting Goods in Columbia. At the same time local officials seemed just as eager to stick their collective heads in the sand as their predecessors, Speed observed with bitter humor.

Speed had been on the five-member city council once before, in the mid-1970s, she told me. She'd run again in late 1986 because Saturn had made the position interesting. In some locals' eyes, perhaps a little too interesting. Although Tennessee had a long and colorful history of political scandal, Speed's private dealings since her re-election, which included supplying much of the stone for the Saturn Parkway from a quarry she owned and trying to get a development built outside Columbia, had smacked of illegalities. At present, she said, the state was investigating her having used some city help and equipment for personal gain. But she hadn't, she assured me. They'd probably just drop the whole thing.

Delilah Speed did have her defenders, one of whom was George Jones. In fact, George Jones and Delilah Speed seemed to be members of a mutual admiration society.

"The little guy loves George," she said. "He stood up and got more for his town than anybody." She was alluding to Spring Hill's lion's share of Saturn's in-lieu-of-tax money.

Recalling the pivotal tax negotiations, which had taken place hurriedly in August 1985, Speed said it had been a time when "even the powers-that-be seemed afraid to deal with Saturn on an intellectual basis." They had gotten in over their heads, saw Saturn as both a threat and a sugar daddy. As for Saturn "snookering our commission," Speed said, referring to the tax deal that had become the focus of sustained criticism (appearing in Columbia shortly after the deal had been made, Ralph Nader called it welfare from one of the state's poorest counties to one of America's richest corporations), she grinned, pushed her glasses back with one hand, and said, "I don't blame them; business is business."

"Who runs the city today?" I asked.

"Nobody. All of our past came to the present," she said, lighting a Winston. But the leadership wasn't forceful enough to get a handle on things. Now even the infrastructure they did have was crumbling.

The whole scene was rampant with irony, Speed elaborated, from the failure of the development model that was going to bring jobs and prosperity to the refusal of Saturn to acknowledge the value of the unemployed local work force. She recalled an unpublished meeting that she had pushed for last March with Saturn. At the time all the talk about partnerships had gotten to her.

"What about us?" she said, stubbing out her cigarette. "What about getting Columbia into a working partnership—that's what I wanted to ask them."

Despite the bad feelings, she added, most of the city council still wanted Saturn to succeed, still had hopes. If Saturn flopped, their reasoning went, it would flop right on top of Maury County.

The meeting was attended by the Columbia City Council, the previous mayor, and a few others with civic interest. Skip LeFauve, Communication's Laurie Kay, and some others Speed couldn't remember were there for Saturn. The meeting accomplished little. To the request for jobs LeFauve had responded with an anecdote, Speed recalled. He told the Maurians that at Packard Electric Division, where he started his career for GM, they had once faced a situation very similar to the one here. Packard had relented; it bypassed the UAW and hired local people. But then the locals who weren't hired had resented those who were. So, LeFauve had concluded, how could you win?

Speed planted her sizable elbows on her desk. "I told him, 'I think you have this backwards. Our people think they're better than your people.'"

Having handled their divorces, Speed knew a number of Saturnites pretty well, she said. None of the ones she knew liked the hostility, which was aimed mostly at their backs since in public, and face to face, Maurians treated the newcomers pretty well. The work force out there wants some local hires on the production line, she said. The refusal of management to hire qualified locals might be Saturn's downfall, she mused. From what she had seen to date, Speed didn't think the Saturnites with UAW roots were capable of making the quantum leaps in productivity and personal initiative Saturn needed to succeed. "They have allowed a previously institutionalized culture to make team decisions," she said. "They're experiencing a new freedom they don't know what to do with."

The conviction that a strong dose of Maurians into the unionized work force might improve it was spreading, I had heard from several sources. Yet LeFauve, UAW president Mike Bennett, and management were holding the line—seemingly an example of the old world reasserting itself. The Saturn teams weren't making the decision, but rather GM management and the UAW leadership together. In its defense, Saturn had hired cafeteria and janitorial help from the local labor pool, but wages were low. The plant also pumped a monthly payroll of approximately $6.1 million into the Maury County economy because forty-seven percent of Saturn's work force lived there. Some $20.5 million had also been paid in lieu of taxes to offset impacts on education, roads, infrastructure. As for the complaint about suppliers not coming as anticipated, Saturn had warned the county since day one that this might happen. Figures were also circulating that claimed twenty-seven suppliers had relocated to Middle Tennessee because of Saturn, employing around thirty-seven hundred. They weren't, however, in Maury County.

"The workers don't know who to trust, who not to trust," Speed said. "I think GM is making a big mistake by not encompassing all the people at hand." A moment later, after lighting up another Winston and staring at a big brown spot on the ceiling, she added as an afterthought, "It's no more them than it is us . . . but *us* doesn't think so."

Leaving Speed, I walked the few blocks to courthouse square, Columbia's architectural hub. The courthouse was a granite hulk with a cupola and a dark past (blacks had been lynched over the steps and shootings occurred inside). Streets went off in the four cardinal directions. Three-storied brick commercial buildings circled the square and lined the streets. Several housed that rarity of American commerce in the 1990s, the family-owned store. R.C. May, Jeweler, had a bright red, white, and blue sign, a neon cut-diamond on top of it and *Save, Save, Save* across an arrow pointing toward the door, each "S" in *Save* a dollar sign, and a touch of poetic alliteration, *Pay May Pay Day*. Helm's Jewelers, Ray Jewelers, and Goodman's TV all awaited shoppers. At Hancock Fabric, four months after Operation Desert Storm, patriotic yellow ribbon was on sale. Ted's, a sporting goods outfit a few doors up from Lucille's Restaurant, had a sign hung vertically over its entrance. "Ted's" was spelled upside down.

The black neighborhood in Columbia spread to the east of courthouse square. Its business district, called "Mink Town," was the site of bad race riots in the 1940s. Most of the residential area went by the name "East Hill." George Jones advised me that probably no blacks in East Hill would talk openly to me—they were scared or too indifferent. But he had introduced me to Charlene Ogilvie, a well-known preacher whose 8th and Woodland Street Original Church of God occupied a brick building on the edge of East Hill and whose free day care, the Non-Denominational Youth Crusade, was a couple blocks further east.

Charlene Ogilvie was a short, compact lady whose leeriness of a white writer, as Jones had forewarned, was palpable. Ogilvie did tell me that Saturn had been a big letdown for blacks in the area, and as of late "the disappointment has turned to hurt."

Her daughter, Rose Ogilvie, worked as a guidance counselor at Whitthorne Middle School in Columbia during the day, and a mortician at Roundtree, Napier & Ogilvie Funeral Home, which was attached to the 8th and Woodlawn Street Original Church of God, in her spare time. Rose Ogilvie being more talkative than her mother, I arranged to meet her in the brick, one-storied Non-Denominational Youth Crusade (NDYC) building a little before lunch time one sticky day in mid-June. A short woman with rosy cheeks, white glasses with one bow missing, and gold earrings, Rose Ogilvie helped out at NDYC when she could, like today, as thirty or so children, about a third of them white, played and then ate lunch at a long wooden table in the rectangular, cinder block-walled space.

What she had to say was that many blacks in the middle and lower classes in Columbia used to find long-range promise in the city and surrounding countryside. They could buy a home, a piece of land. Now prices were high, jobs scarce, and hopes low. Nobody in power seemed to care, Ogilvie said. George Jones might care, but he hadn't done a good enough job showing it during the recent election for county commissioner, the highest paid public position in Maury County. "George Jones never touched the handicapped," she said. "He never touched the projects. He spent too much time courting the voters who owed Sam Kennedy, didn't have any machinery in place. You can smile, shake hands, and grin all day; and you ain't going to win." She sounded vexed, though she smiled. "George wasn't dealing with a man; he was dealing with power."

That power was white, rooted, and didn't take real kindly to criticism from uppity blacks, she continued. "You talk to the wrong person around here, you could be out of work tomorrow. They take a person and make an example, ruin your life. You learn to say you don't know when you do. It's sad." Ogilvie called that the "fear syndrome." It had an accepting mindset: "There's no point in complaining because it ain't going to get any better."

Ogilvie sounded disappointed in Maurians for just taking what was happening to them, though Saturn wasn't responsible for it all, she said. Resignation and acceptance of the status quo had been around for decades. "There aren't ten strong people in Maury County," she said. Saturn's not hiring locals had stirred things up and now massive county layoffs added to the stewpot were threatening to make it boil over. Maybe that would get people speaking out and acting.

Although she didn't say so directly, I gathered from how Rose Ogilvie talked about her mother that she considered Charlene one of the few strong people in Maury County. There had always been eighteen, twenty kids around their house when she was growing up, Rose recalled. She'd thought they were her brothers and sisters, at first. In fact, they were orphans, street kids, runaways taken in by Charlene. She'd started a street ministry, then formed a church. Fifteen years ago, because too many kids were playing with each other sexually, Rose said, and getting in trouble, her mother opened this place. At NDYC everything was donated. About fifty-five kids, ages three, four, and five, came daily, beginning at 6:30 A.M. There were four teachers, a cook, and an assistant. The annual budget was $56,000, most of it from county funds and private donations.

As lunch broke up at the long table the conversations of the children had a *Jungle Fever* edge to them.

"What are you?" a little black girl asked her friend.

"I'm white."

"No you're not."

"I'm mixed."

High yella, macaroon, quadroon—here was the future of America right here in this room, I thought. The sisters had different daddies, Ogilvie said. "They'll never live in a brick house." NDYC tried to give them some self-esteem, taught them to cherish the will in their hearts, to see beyond often troubled and violent family lives toward a brighter future. A shy little girl wandered up and Ogilvie hugged and talked to her. She soon wandered away alongside the lime green wall, a shuddering air-conditioner accompanying her measured steps.

Just off courthouse square, above the Dollar Store, little arrows, the reflective, sticky-back kind you buy in a hardware store, directed me along a pale-walled corridor punctuated by half a dozen doors and into a waiting room best described as utilitarian. A voice shouted from an office that it would be with me in a minute. The voice belonged to Peter Frierson, a black paralegal for Maury County Legal Aid.

A rack in the waiting room was filled with brochures on topics like rehabilitation, unemployment benefits ("What If You Are Turned Down?" was a prominent title), child abuse. The brightest thing on the wall was a poster with starbursts. It proclaimed: "The Older Americans Art 1962–1990." Suddenly Frierson jogged out of his office and down the hall, papers in one hand. A minute later he jogged back, not looking at me. Several minutes after that he called me in.

Even Delilah Speed had pegged Peter Frierson "as kind of radical." Part of the problem was that Frierson wasn't real big on white supremacy. He wasn't docile, had taken on the Columbia Police Department at times, and had, he said, told black Saturnites he met, "You are a threat to the power structure." If they organized and acted, that is.

Peter Frierson was thirty-nine, light-skinned, with cropped hair and glasses. A Navy vet, he was presently second vice president of the NAACP of Middle Tennessee. Frierson had been the sophomore class president at the all-black Carver-Smith High School in 1968, the year Columbia high schools were finally integrated. Carver-Smith had not been far from where NDYC was today. "We got bussed," Frierson recalled. "There was chaos out there at Central High School from 1968 to when I left."

Listening to Frierson I was reminded that the Ku Klux Klan had been founded about thirty miles south of here, in Pulaski, Tennessee, that racism, violence, and victimization had been the legacy of blacks here for longer than most folks, himself notably excepted, cared to remember. After some run-ins with whites in power a year ago, Frierson had pretty much withdrawn from the public arena, he said. But he couldn't keep quiet. "I told my wife, 'I can't hide in the shadows. I got to get out there: the people need me.'"

Frierson said he didn't think many of the Saturnites had any idea of what they were getting into moving to Columbia and Maury County. "They came here, it was culture shock." They found a city with one black city council member, one black realtor, no black bank officers, no black lawyers. As we talked, Frierson kind of turned Columbia's welcoming motto: "New South Progress, Old South Charm," into "New South Greed, Old South Racial Prejudice." He mentioned the increasing homelessness that officials wanted to deny, overcrowded schools in which kids with Saturn parents had been mistreated, police departments right out of the classic southern stereotype—that is, manned by cops who liked to "intimidate the hell out of everybody," and always with a couple of "the typical 260-pound white police officers who will beat your ass."

One woman, Dieta O'Bard, the wife of a Saturn production worker, had refused to kowtow to a white cop in Columbia who continually hassled her, Frierson said. "She's just a strong dominant Afro-American that people around here aren't used to." But she can't get a job, he added. Every place she goes they tell her she's overqualified.

Dieta O'Bard lived in a comfortable brick house with her husband Mike, just off U.S. 31 a few miles north of Columbia. A solid, round woman she had a tranquility and self-possession about her. Mike O'Bard worked in the lost-foam foundry in the powertrain building at Saturn. The O'Bards fit nicely in the African-American middle class that had made it economically and socially, at least until they had taken up the offer to start a different kind of car company in rural Tennessee.

Dieta didn't make being black here sound as melodramatic as Frierson had. "It's a culture change for us," she said. "A little slower, a little laidback." Her introduction to the area had been rough, though. She had taken her four children into Columbia for the first day of school in September 1990, having been here only a week, and as they walked into school she heard someone shout, "Can't you read? Are you stupid or something?"

She looked and there was a policeman by her car. "I'm talking to you!"

"You're talking to me?"

He soon told her, "You're not welcome here," O'Bard said. There were more incidents with the same white cop in front of the school in front of her children. One day he said, "Give me your license."

"For what?"

"Give me your license!"

She got arrested for disobeying a police officer. Down at the station in Columbia, "We got in a heated dispute," she recalled. Out on bail, "I couldn't get anybody to represent me against a police officer." She had to get a lawyer from Nashville. The court dealt with the license issue, she said (she was convicted and paid a fine), but ignored her charges of police harassment. The press gave the story a lot of play, though. "I do feel that because of the press and the media, I do have some relief."

O'Bard said she and Michael were still considering a move to Nashville. They advise other Yankees who move here, whether black or white, to work on their southern drawl. But even before that: "Change your license plate."

One thing both Rose Ogilvie and Dieta O'Bard agreed on was, as Ogilvie put it, "The influx—nobody's ready for it," and O'Bard echoed: "If I have twenty-five people coming over for dinner, I start getting ready early."

5

A Peek Inside the Plant

Finally, Jennifer Schettler called. Bruce McDonald had given her the go-ahead. I could interview Tim Epps, the vice president of people systems who had told me at the end of the media day that Saturn's new way of doing things demanded a new language. I could talk to some members of the crankshaft team too, but it would have to be in Northfield; the plant remained off limits. When I reminded Schettler what LeFauve had said, she replied that manufacturing hadn't thought it was such a good idea to allow me on the crankshaft line. I told her that unfortunately I was leaving Tennessee in a few days, so could we reschedule in August? She didn't think there would be any problem. I pressed Schettler to get a hint why this customer of Communications felt so frustrated with her department's service.

"You wrote that article critical of Saturn way back when," she finally said, alluding to a piece I had done for *Historic Preservation* five years ago.

She was right—I had been critical. But not only of Saturn; I concluded that the company, the state, and local officials had all only halfheartedly safeguarded Maury County's antebellum architecture, tossing away the past for a dream future that had, as it were, turned into a partial nightmare for locals expecting work in exchange for giving up their former way of life. As for my having been put off for weeks, Schettler blamed her boss, McDonald.

"He's the hardest guy in the world to get hold of," she said. "He doesn't return calls."

Hanging up, I thought, this is all very *1984*-ish. Saturn Communications seemed a kind of parody of communications commanded by a one-star National Guard general named Brewster (McDonald had worked on press relations during Operation Desert Storm), with the front ranks of the force filled with "glorified secretaries," as one au-

Aerial view of Saturn plant in Spring Hill
(*Source:* Photograph by Ed Rode, Nashville *Banner*, October 8, 1990)

tomotive reporter described them. At the same time there was a steady complaint from Saturn about the press coverage it received.

I called Ed Killgore to see about the tour he promised me. A couple days later we rode away from Northfield in his red Sierra SLX. Killgore, the no-nonsense Texan, was wearing his cowboy boots, smoking a cigarette. He told me the plant was now in "acceleration mode." They had to get production up to sixty vehicles an hour, six hundred for each shift, twelve hundred per day. At a gate to the innermost ring of Saturn, Killgore inserted a card into a detection sensor. The gate lifted. We followed the roadway encircling the mile-long plant. Killgore parked by "body fab," as he called the northernmost building.

A blast of cool air met us as we entered a small door in a vast wall. At the far end of the building stood two Verson blanking presses. They cut steel into sheets, so it can go to the stamping presses, which hammer the steel into various shapes, depending on the dies being used. We passed dozens of coils of rolled steel, some six-feet high, resting on the buffed cement floor. Wedges kept the large coils from rolling down the long empty corridors between the press lines. Overhead hung huge yellow cranes. They lift the coils of steel and the dies back and forth to the presses.

At one of the blanking presses, which is over twenty feet tall, white, and as bulky as a dam gate, cut steel blanks from a coil rumbled out, one at a time, onto the arms of a forklift. Dies, as heavy as Krypton, dense and as sculptural as a piece from Henry Moore, line one side of the corridor. Stamped on their surfaces are their weights: twenty-five, thirty thousand pounds in several instances. As Killgore is explaining several features of a stamping press, which follows the blanking press in this, the press line, suddenly a garage-like door trundles down and closes off the interior of the stamping press. A red light flashes, a siren sounds. Through windows in the door I watch steel sheets being spit onto an orange material handler. The handler shifts horizontally five or so feet. The sheet, or blank, eases down on the lower die that has been installed. The upper die descends. They mate.

Mating dies emit a rhythmic sound, a five-note harmony followed by a sigh—the air compressor. The material handler lifts the partially shaped steel body part and shifts it forward to a second set of die. Simultaneously, the first die are reloaded with a flat blank. A car part made this way may be hammered into its final shape by as many as five sets of die, Killgore says. These dies and the presses that hold

47

them are expensive, costing tens of millions of dollars. The speed at which the dies can be changed, or "kicked off," as Killgore puts it, determines to a great extent how many cars can be assembled during a shift. This is especially true in a just-in-time inventory process where parts are not stockpiled.

Saturn's four huge stamping presses were manufactured in Japan, two by Komatsu Inc., and the other two by Hitachi Ltd. They traveled by ship to New Orleans. Three railroad cars and a dozen tractor trailer trucks hauled all their innards to Spring Hill. Here, Komatsu and Hitachi engineers and technicians installed each press, a process that took months.

The Komatsu stamping press is making roof panels now, Ed Killgore says. At the delivery end, two op techs wearing yellow gloves rub the curved, silvery surfaces of the panels, checking for defects. They carry each panel to a rack and slide it in, twenty-five roof panels to a rack. Their machine continues its five-note harmony, over and over again.

A rack of rear quarter sections, three feet high, gleaming, their curves thinning down almost like a waist, catch my eye. Grouped together they look like a piece of corporate art displayed on the buffed gray floor. Nearby is the strangest looking Saturn I've yet seen, a jester-mobile with a gray roof, blue door, green fender and hood. Killgore grins slightly and explains that the car is used as a test vehicle. A body part that is suspect, a little out of whack, will get fitted to see if the die is doing its job just right. By keeping the car here, workers can check parts more easily.

Also in body fab are twenty-four polymer injection-mold press lines. The injection-mold presses make the doors, fenders, and various panels, whereas steel goes into each Saturn hood, roof, trunk, spaceframe, and most interior panels. As opposed to having coils of steel alongside them, the injection presses are fed by pellets that are stored outside, in silos. Instead of pounding parts into shape, these presses combine heat and intense pressure to do the work.

We stop midway down one of the polymer injection press lines. A female technician named Lynda Woodward, wearing jeans and chewing gum, is all alone, dwarfed by the machinery. Woodward is handling polymer door panels, sanding blemishes, filling racks. Between her and us stands a big plastic tub called a reject bin. It's filled with panels Woodward found short on quality. She walks toward us, tosses another one on. The rejected panel feels warm to my touch, like bread just out of the oven.

"Don't say anything bad," Woodward urges me as I jot down some notes.

The good part is she's so concerned; the bad part is that reject bins are, if not rare in Japanese *kanban* systems, rarer than those here. Too many overflowing reject bins are not synonymous with high quality and they are a major reason why Saturn is in acceleration mode. Getting rejects, or defects, down to ten percent on each line has proven a formidable task.

The temperature is around seventy degrees, contrasted to ninety outside. Large blue ducts overhead snake everywhere, spewing out cool air, keeping the technicians comfortable, the robots operational, the machines content. Older auto plants typically have banks of windows that open and close, letting in not only fresh air but dust and dirt, which can speckle dies and foul machinery, demanding constant cleanup. We pass several fat-tired, three-wheeled bicycles chained to an upright steel column. The trade technicians who repair presses and machines when they malfunction, or fine tune them when they're a little bit off, ride the bikes around, their tools on platforms behind the seats. The bikes seem an odd throwback to another era, yet are very practical.

The die maintenance shop is adjacent to the press lines. It, too, looks like a throwback. For one thing, quite a few people are working here. Some tradesmen in greasy overalls hunch over dies. One is handrubbing a surface with polish, smoothing a blemish.

"Any defect you got on that die is going to come out on the part," Ed Killgore says before we stop by a particularly arresting die. Fluted, ribbed, and channeled, deeply recessed, the shiny die could be an Art Nouveau bathtub. Ed thinks it's half of the floor panel reinforcement set. If you had a crane, you could hang it in a gallery next to the rear quarter panels we passed earlier. It's quieter in the maintenance shop, too. Rock music is playing. From a distance come the rumblings of the stamping presses, the sighs of compressed air. We walk along in this oddly musical environment, Ed in his cowboy boots and me wearing protective glasses that someone before me smeared with greasy fingers.

Returning to Ed's truck, we drive toward the final assembly building in the middle of the plant. The manufacturing complex is basically four big buildings. Body parts come from body fab (more officially known as body systems) on the northern end of the complex, the end closest to Spring Hill. Engines and transmissions are made in the powertrain building, which is on the plant's other end and also houses the foundry. Between them are one smaller building, called vehicle interior systems, where cockpits are pieced together, and final assembly where, as Killgore puts it, "the action is." We pass the exterior silos of body systems filled with polymer pellets, a train car unloading more pellets from a spur. The plant's wood-framed cooling towers, which are located between the body systems building and final assembly, are enveloped in a thick and dripping mist. The towers look anachronistic, like something out of the nineteenth century.

Reject bins heaped with blue, black, red, beige, and other color fenders, door panels, roof panels, and other parts form a bright spot by a back door to the paint shop.

Killgore drives another quarter mile and pulls over by a little door in a wall that appears to stretch a half mile in either direction, a thin line of windows running horizontally along it to let in natural light. This is the eastern side of Saturn. The southern walls of the powertrain, final assembly, and body systems buildings parallel the roadway. A steel footbridge overhead connects the plant with one of many parking lots. A stairway with a yellow handrail descends to a large doorway. There is a major feeling of emptiness here. No one is on the footbridge, on the road paralleling the plant, on the other footbridges several hundred away to either side.

Cool air again exits as we enter. Neatly marked storage bins filled with cockpit parts line the floor. Overhead, clicking conveyors carry spaceframes, black from an epoxy electrocoat primer, toward final assembly. Several forklifts scurry by. There's a sign: *Quality Begins Here*.

On the first skillet in final assembly, when it's running, which it isn't at the moment, each spaceframe receives its hardware, cables, and shift lever. Then the spaceframe passes between a pair of robots. They caulk the firewall. The cockpit gets dropped in next, with its radio, instruments, motors for windshield washers and blowers, speedometer, and dozens of color-coded wires that make everything work.

The line in final assembly, the most crucial line in the plant, is down because there's a problem in the paint shop. This is not unusual. Lately, paint has been one of Saturn's production headaches. The waterborne acrylic chipped, bubbled, ran, looked flat. Last weekend Dupont flew some paint experts to Spring Hill to see if they could straighten things out. Maybe they hadn't been able to.

We pass the chassis work module where each chassis, riding down from above, gets bolted to its powertrain, which trundles in horizontally. Although the teams here are temporarily not working, behind them are Saturns that resemble a car as most people think of one. Or at least the skeleton of a car. There are no doors, no fenders, no seats, no steering wheel. Yet each Saturn could be driven, Killgore assures me, with a little ingenuity, if you added fluids: oil, coolants, gasoline.

The line starts moving again. Seats are being bolted in as a team swings into action. Members climb in and out of sedans, wielding bolting guns suggestive of the weapons actors blasted each other with in *Aliens*. Doors rejoin bodies. Fenders and hoods are going on. Fascia. The air has the smell of a new car showroom, that faint, not-very-good-for-you odor of glues, foams, paint, and plastic. The exterior body panels glide in from overhead. They look surreal, colorful cars held together by the momentum of their destinies, each skin draped in its finished configuration, a colorful epidermis of silver, red, gray, blue, glowing green.

In the final process area, a car gets coolants, fuel, a headlight aim, wheel alignment, and a dynometer test, which is a static drive by an operator in one of five bays. The operator runs through the gears, checking shift points, turns on the air conditioning and radio. Adjacent to the test bays is the repair area. There, two Saturns are on lifts. One's crankcase is being drained. Eight or ten other coupes and sedans sit around—all with defects. They are what Saturn is trying to eliminate: mistakes that demand personal attention between the end of the assembly line and the showroom floor.

In *The Machine That Changed the World,* published in 1990, a team of MIT professors compared the lean production system of the Japanese car makers with the fatter, more defect-prone systems in the plants of American and European car makers. The authors focused on final process and its repair bays at the ends of assembly lines. During their five years of observing plants around the world, the authors found the bays busy in most American and European plants (with the exception of Ford). Considerable time, attention, and money went into repairing defects in those bays. Whereas at Toyota, for instance, prevention of defects was a theme throughout every stage of the car-making process. Anywhere a problem appeared, workers had the authority to stop the line and fix whatever it was that caused defects. Stopping the line in a GM plant was the equivalent of handing in your notice.

The Machine That Changed the World claimed that mass production in the Henry Ford assembly-line mode was dying. The Japanese had devised a better method: lean production. Traditional mass production in auto plants meant shoving as many cars as possible down a line, always keeping the machinery running to cut costs, and fixing flaws in the repair bays. The method was outdated, wasteful of materials, and, more important, of people, the authors said. Lean production, by comparison, was flexible and saw people as crucial to its effectiveness. Lean meant keeping inventories low and communicating continually with suppliers, with the work force, and with dealers. It meant getting everyone along the process to think the *zaizan* way, the way of continuous improvement. And to have the confidence to do something to effect improvement with the assurance that one wouldn't get in trouble for it, to know it was better to get forgiveness than permission if you had the right answer to a problem requiring an immediate response.

Ultimately, in a lean system, the quality of a car as it was assembled was judged by those doing the assembling. They didn't pass their screw-ups along, with everything ending in the busy hands of the workers in the repair bays and, eventually, in the hands of dealers and car buyers.

Why had Ford become lean? According to these authors, Ford experienced a financial crisis in the late 1970s that woke up its management to the fact that it was change or else.

"Ford knew it had to make major changes in the way it operated," said one of the authors, James Womack. "But at that crucial moment, it didn't have the cash to invest in huge amounts of automation and new factories. So it did the only thing it could do: it modernized the way its people work." As for GM, Womack added, its "performance is really all over the lot."

Facing its own financial crisis, could GM be creative, get out the knife, and pare itself into the lean configuration the guys from MIT said was the only way to compete against the Japanese? At Saturn, the lean production system was supposed to have been built in. The Lynda Woodwards throughout the plant could stop their lines and not make it their last day on the job. Yet the stops had to be reduced. You couldn't constantly be halting the transmission line or the engine line or the crankshaft machining line. Eventually, the lines in powertrain, vehicle interiors, body systems, and final assembly had to be in harmony. It wasn't only people who worked in teams. All the smaller lines in the plant formed one big industrial team that had to achieve a certain degree of smoothness and continuity if Saturn was going to reach its goal of sixty cars an hour.

That hadn't happened yet. What I saw while walking around with

Ed Killgore—the down skillets, the delayed automotive nuptials of engine and chassis in the marriage/pre-marriage unit, the paint headaches—would continue to dog production throughout summer and fall. The production problems in turn made the work force, which had agreed to production bonuses to offset lower starting pay rates, want to return to the old way: higher wages hammered out annually during contract negotiations downplaying the importance of productivity.

Outside again, we stand by Killgore's red Sierra SLX. The shifts are changing. There are two ten-hour shifts, four days a week. It's a staggered arrangement, with workers on days for a week, then nights for a week. Physiologically, some bodies have had trouble adjusting to the schedule, I have heard. This may be a contributing factor to the production problems. Workers suffering from shift lag not only forget what day it is, and whether they're supposed to be at work tonight or tomorrow morning, but take that weariness and its mental cloud with them to work.

Four guys in shorts, carrying lunch pails and bantering with each other, hustle up the stairs and cross the footbridge. A black woman saunters upward, her hand on the yellow rail. A group of about fifteen exit final assembly, heading home after their shift. Approximately two thousand people are leaving the four buildings, and in the next half hour two thousand others will be coming in. Many of these Saturnites are in their twenties and thirties. They went through a long winnowing process to become team members of a different kind of company. They gave up higher wages, their homes and communities, and security in other GM divisions to move down to Tennessee to make a better car in what has become an increasingly hostile community.

One Saturnite, CTM Al Burris (CTM stands for "charter team member," or the first person hired for each of Saturn's more than 150 teams), had told me earlier that the situation wasn't good. Burris lived in Columbia with his wife and four kids. "There's a lot of negative impact," Burris admitted. "Blacks I know don't like us. People say, 'They got our jobs.' "

By "us," Burris meant the United Auto Workers. The UAW, in exchange for certain concessions to GM management in 1985, when the Saturn labor agreement had been negotiated, insisted on all the production jobs. This inside deal had not pleased the locals, who had expected jobs, but they had not complained loudly because thousands of secondary jobs were supposed to have rippled through the region. That hadn't happened. Meanwhile, Maury County's farming roots had been severed by land speculation, long-standing chemical and textile plants had systematically collapsed, and the backwater that had envisioned a giant leap to prosperity found itself instead in economic limbo. One conspicuous outcome was a visible cooling of most Maurians' hospitable attitude toward the Saturnites.

6

The Charlotte Store

On my drive north I stopped at Saturn of Charlotte, a store Skip LeFauve had spoken highly of. The first morning I was there all the professional automotive consultants, as they call Saturn car salespeople, gathered out front for a special training gig called a "ride and drive." Saturn Marketing had sent a three-person team, with a Mitsubishi Eclipse, a Toyota Corolla LE, and a Honda Civic DX, to Charlotte. The team was on tour to explain and point out the competitive advantages of the SC, SL2, and SL1 over their closest competitors. Carol Marcinkowski, twenty-four, freckled and ebullient, headed the team, one of several visiting all 108 Saturn stores that were now open. Marcinkowski told the dozen consultants, all but one wearing white Saturn shirts, that she was first going to "give them some thought starters."

As she talked, the whine of tires came from the blacktop of a busy four-laned Independence Boulevard. At Hillbilly Produce, next door to Saturn of Charlotte, birds sang in small trees. Marcinkowski soon introduced one of her cohorts, a young man in tan shorts, a black Saturn T-shirt, and white sneakers. He gave the Charlotte consultants the rundown on the Honda Civic versus the SL1.

"It's not much of a comparison car," confided the consultant not wearing a Saturn T-shirt. He nodded at the blue car. Dripping wet from having just been washed, it was still dirty because it hadn't been scrubbed.

Before she did the Mitsubishi/Saturn Coupe comparison, Marcinkowski recommended that the consultants find a copy of May's *Car & Driver,* and check out the good review of the SC. Mention it to your customers, she encouraged.

The Mitsubishi Eclipse looked better than either the dirty Honda or the maligned Toyota. It was bright red, clean, with sixteen-inch wheels. The engine, however, "was not as user friendly as the SC's." And Marcinkowski put a finger to a place where paint was chipping. Not good. At $13,130, base price, the Eclipse, with options, was going to cost a couple grand more than the SC, she added.

A few minutes later I was at the wheel of the SC, heading east on Independence Boulevard with Dexter Riffe, the consultant without the regulation Saturn shirt. A former mechanic and car salesman, Dexter Riffe wore the cuffs of his white shirt rolled up inside his sleeves and talked with a drawl. "This is a car town," he said as I went through the gears. "People come here and usually make a little money; they want to spent it."

I mentioned that I had heard the store sold a hundred Saturns last month. "Were many of those yours?"

"I didn't catch any of that fire," Riffe said.

He directed me to some recently laid asphalt awaiting its subdivision. "I bring folks here who really want to drive," he said.

I managed a squeal from the 195/60R15 steel-belted radials on the empty swath of future street measuring about a quarter-mile. At the street's end I wheeled the coupe around, curb-to-curb and gave it another shot back the way we'd come. Then I suggested to Dexter Riffe, who struck me as the kind of guy who had left his share of rubber signatures on various highways in his past, that he give me a demonstration of how well Saturn could lay rubber. We exchanged seats. He wound up the horses, gave them a calming second at 4,000 rpms, popped the clutch, and smoked for about thirty feet. Shoving the stick of the world-class transmission into second, Riffe got another short burn, then was in third and doing seventy.

A few moments later, the red Mitsubishi Eclipse turned onto our mini-track. Riffe smiled and tailed it. The Eclipse veered around where the street ended and so did we. I fingered my window down. In the Eclipse sat two Saturn automotive consultants, a black guy and a white guy, both wearing their "Saturn of Charlotte" short-sleeved shirts.

"Which one's faster?" the driver, the white guy, asked out his window.

His passenger, leaning forward slightly and grinning, held up his arm and tapped his watch.

"There's only one way to find out," Riffe told them. Suddenly he popped the clutch. Tires crying, we wailed forward for about two hundred feet. Then backed up. Rubber smoke drifted through my open window, borne aloft by sticky North Carolina humidity.

"How'd you git that thing to burn rubber?" The driver of the Eclipse sounded perplexed. Leaning forward, both hands on the wheel, he stared at Dexter Riffe through his aviator glasses.

"It's a standard," Riffe said. Plus, of course, the 195/60R15s had already been warm.

After a little muttering about how they didn't have a chance in an automatic, the black professional automotive consultant, eyes on his wristwatch, executed the classic countdown. We screeched off, straight and smooth. I saw the Eclipse in my exterior rear-view mirror. Dexter Riffe topped a crest, going fast. A van sat crossways in the street, trying to turn around with a turning radius far greater than that of either the coupe or the Eclipse. As the van scurried toward the curb— evidently the driver heard us coming—Riffe flew by with a little bounce over some dirt marking a utility line. He flashed me a grin, then tapped the brakes. I pitched forward into my shoulder harness, flushed with adrenaline and pleasure.

Back at the store, I talked with Riffe's team leader, Al Hendershot, a short balding fellow in tassel mocs and a beige suit. Hendershot had been on board since the second week the store opened. He'd left a job as a marketing consultant in West Virginia, motivated by Saturn's call for unusual sales people, "people who wouldn't have sold cars because of the stigmatism associated with it." He moved to Charlotte with a new bride. "I kissed her and said, 'Pick up this box,'" he joked. At the store, "It was crazy. We had so much synergy when we started." Seven months later, though, he echoed the sentiments of Delilah Speed: "I think Saturn needs to give everyone another commitment fix."

A thoughtful and articulate guy, Hendershot described Saturn as "basically a socialistic company." He said, "We're following a socialistic philosophy." He explained that this store was not built exactly to Saturn's specifications. It had previously been a Saab dealership. Saturn bent a little with Rick Hendricks, the owner, because of his clout in the region: Hendricks owned thirty-six car dealerships in the Carolinas and was said to have been the inspiration for *Days of Thunder,* the film starring Tom Cruise about a race-car driver. The gray store did have the Saturn portico and tight interior. A receptionist sat by the door behind a curved counter. A cutaway Saturn ("That car there sold more cars here than any salesman, I assure you," Dexter Riffe had said), several sedans, and a couple beckoned on the floor. There were a few wall displays, and the consultants' open cubicles scattered between the showroom models. Parts and service were in back.

What had most surprised Hendershot when he started at Saturn were the customers. "Bright, educated pacesetters" intrigued by the idea of a "smart car" was how he described them. He was a little disappointed, he confided, that Saturn's marketing people hadn't picked up on the smart car/bright people theme. "They've ignored the intellectual potential of the market."

As for the consultants, he felt that indoctrination into the Saturn philosophy, the people-teamwork-quality thinking, was crucial. "The biggest theory with Saturn is the mental change. We get a lot of good salespeople who can't make that transition." The reason for the mental transition was simple, he continued. "There's not that much difference in the cars. So we need to make customers feel like part of a new movement. America wants to return to greatness. Saturn is one of those hopes for greatness. If you have that belief, you go through the day easier."

Hendershot even thought Dexter Riffe would come around. "Dexter's new. He's a great guy. Eventually, he'll come our way, but it's going to take a while. Dexter 's trying to change us."

The store opened on a rainy night last October. Only ten SL2s, all red, had been on the lot. Yet people had swarmed into the place.

"It was overwhelming," recalled Gary Porter, the general manager. "We were overrun."

"I never knew so many people knew about Saturn," seconded Linda Penland, the sales manager.

Sales, of course, had been zilch. Saturn of Charlotte didn't have cars. In fact, because production at the plant was so behind, the fifty stores that opened nationwide had to be reimbursed for losses.

"Finally," Penland said, "SL1s, SL2s, and SCs started to arrive and people just kept coming. Five hundred in a week. It had a touch of Disneyland to it. It was like nothing I've ever experienced." There was a lot of cheering, she recalled. The war in the Persian Gulf had started and folks felt patriotic. Maybe not patriotic enough "to be ready to give up their Honda or Toyota," she added, "but they would love to buy an American car with quality in it." Penland got so tired at the store, she said, that she usually went home and soaked in the tub every night to get the cramps out of her legs.

Penland knew car sales. Her father was a Ford dealer in Florida, her brother a car salesman. She had been selling cars all her life. Saturn had caught her attention six years ago, she told me. She liked it because it wasn't flashy. "Fast, flashy cars were trendy in the eighties," she recalled. "The nineties generation car buyer is the most conservative I've ever seen." And she definitely hadn't switched to Saturn from the BMW/Land Rover/Porsche dealership she had worked for because she was a General Motors fan. "I worked with [GM] once," she said, "and they were the most insensitive, indifferent company I ever heard of. They've ruined Pontiac. If they had just taken care of their customers." Instead, "they totally lost all common sense, and all humanity."

Now eight months after the memorable opening, sales were strong but Penland needed cars. She had only seventy vehicles in inventory. Fifty were supposed to go to a satellite store being opened in Hickory, North Carolina.

The following day, standing in the shade of the Saturn canopy and listening to the birds next door, I surveyed Saturn's competition: Toyota City, Honda, Mitsubishi, Nissan, and Mazda, one after the other, their signs lined up on the other side of Independence Boulevard in the clear blue-skied morning. I headed across the four lanes of traffic.

"I don't think it's built very professional," Brian Barry, the twenty-seven-year-old sales manager at Toyota City, said about Saturn. "They should have sunk more time and pride in it."

Honda displayed a 1970 yellow coupe and a 1971 green 600 on the showroom floor. They looked like toys: ten-inch wheels, chrome bumpers the size of towel racks, chopstick-sized windshield wipers. A courteous salesman named Bob Wilson, white haired, avuncular, told me the old models were powered by motorcycle engines.

It occurred to me that in some ways Honda had gone backwards. With their little vent windows, incredible mileage, and easy service, the two little sedans on the floor epitomized a true user-friendly car of a kind you couldn't buy anymore. Nothing on the road nowadays was as efficient, practical, and light on resources.

At Mitsubishi, Greg Shadrach liked the looks of the Saturn coupe. "Their commercials are great," he attested. But then he repeated a sentiment heard across America: "I don't carry much faith in American cars anymore. Saturn isn't going to restore my faith, I'm sad to say."

David Itoop at Mazda had actually driven the Saturn. "I liked it," he said, "it's a good car." Not as good as a Mazda, but then few vehicles were. Take the Miata here, for instance, the native of India said, smoothly leading me along. "It's a rich man's toy, or a poor man's dream." Mazda was experiencing what Itoop called "positive growth," conducting training programs to improve selling skills. One thing that puzzled him about Saturn, Itoop admitted, was the no-bargaining position. "I don't think American people are willing to accept it. It's a nice philosophy, but it's going to take more than one car maker to change it." In India, he said, "there is no negotiating for a car. They say car is twenty thousand rupees, car is twenty thousand rupees."

Quality, the buzzword of car sales, was repeated by most of the eight sales people I talked with. Their cars had more of the q-word than Saturn, they assured me. Brian Barry at Toyota even told me a story to back up what he meant by Toyota quality. A prospect had come in, Barry said, claiming Saturn was a high quality car, just like Toyota. She couldn't make up her mind which one to buy. To show her, sales manager Barry changed from his white shirt, tie, and chinos into a tank top and shorts, hopped in a car, drove her across Independence Boulevard and into the Saturn lot. Surreptitiously, he had his prospect pull hard on a Saturn bumper, pointed out a flawed body fit. He didn't have to finish the story, but he did. "She bought a Toyota."

Undoubtedly, in the world of car sales, as in love and war, the standards of fairness depend on the combatants, but the perception of quality, on the other hand, has a constancy to it. American cars, as validated by the 1990 sales of the Big Three, had major quality problems, both real and imagined. The Brookings Institute, a Washington, D.C., think tank, had just verified this fact with a survey of car owners' buying histories over several decades. Much to the surprise of nobody, least of all the salespeople, consultants, managers, and mechanics who sold and serviced vehicles across America, devotion to cars manufactured in this country had been in steady decline. And regard for Japanese cars had been on the rise. Poor quality had cost the Big Three their best sales tool: brand loyalty.

The Origins of
a Different Kind
of Company

7

The Fall of Big

Since its creation in the 1920s as an amalgamation of such long-forgotten auto companies as Oakland, Rainier, Ewing, and Carter Car with those still recognizable seventy-five years later—Oldsmobile, Pontiac, Cadillac, and Chevrolet—General Motors had made big cars. The problem with small cars was their lack of profit. The company's recent history included a few footnotes dedicated to small cars, called "import fighters" and "contemporary cars," and most recently "sub-compacts," yet until Saturn, GM never seemed to want to build a truly good small car. Making a quality small car was just as challenging as making big cars—even more so since the company had never been good at anything small, particularly small volume—but required commitment. Without that commitment, especially given the continuous improvement in quality of the competition in the 1980s, any attempt at a small car, no matter what it was called, was doomed from the outset.

Bigger had been better for decades not only because big cars made better profits, but because big cars conferred more status, they were synonymous with America, they were a metaphor for GM itself. At GM you were a *big* car guy, period. From the boardroom to the shop floor bigness had been a kind of abstract god that ruled over most decisions.

But bigness tumbled from grace. The tumble had taken several decades, cost GM billions, and, more important, lost the out-of-touch company the faith of millions of buyers, including that controlling bulge in American demographics, the Baby Boomers. The Baby Boomers' faith in big American cars had started to wane during the 1960s, when the VW "Bug" became a counterculture institution, but truly shifted into high gear after OPEC's energy wake-up call in the mid-1970s, a call that GM, along with Ford and Chrysler, tried in vain to ignore. Even when Saturn was going through its small-car birthing pains in the mid-1980s, the vision of America returning to the big car days of the past haunted GM's top management, most of whom had come of age during the era of the two-ton land yacht and harbored in their hearts a hard-to-let-die attachment to all that chrome, rubber, and power.

After all, GM's founder Alfred P. Sloan, Jr., had himself decreed big was better. Sloan had still been chairman in the early 1950s, when the first invasion of small cars, mostly British marques such as Hillman, Austin, Jaguar, and MG, along with the exceedingly expensive Rolls-Royce, which was not small, started appearing on America's growing network of roads. Sloan's genius at organization, the big is better credo, and planned obsolescence, which introduced new models every year to shove the old out of fashion, had made GM king of that road.

In those days GM had also been right: Americans didn't like small cars. Not much, anyway. Dodge Firearrows, Chrysler Windsor V-8s, Ford Fairlanes, Chevrolet Impalas, and Oldsmobile Golden Rocket 88 Holidays, to name a few of the popular models, were more their style. These cars were symbols of America's intoxication with bigness. From the vast virgin forests of the nineteenth century to the skyscrapers lifting above Chicago and New York in the 1920s, to the scope of FDR's New Deal and the destructiveness of the atomic bomb, America and big went together. And in the 1950s America felt *really* big—industrially, politically, militarily. Disposable incomes were rising rapidly—almost sixteen percent annually. Incomes would rise another sixteen percent a year during the first half of the 1960s. The Great Depression and World War II had created a pent-up demand for products and goods of all kinds, which helped make the postwar years a brief, bright, materialistic era the likes of which the country had never known, one that future decades would misconstrue as the historical norm. It was a time when America was practically a self-contained economic system. Cars, refrigerators, clothes, shoes, furniture, and foodstuffs were made in one region of the nation and transported to others. During the 1950s total imports were only around three percent of the gross national product. Much of the rest of the industrial world, including Japan and Germany, was still trying to regain its balance from the ruins of World War II. Those countries had to think small. Not America.

In America, even if you started out small—in a Chevy, say—in a few years you could move up to a Packard Four Hundred, or to an Imperial, or Cadillac with fins that looked like they would help you soar right to the top of the economic ladder. The unspoken but powerful presence of that ladder overshadowed your life, especially if you grew up in the 1950s, as I did, in a working-class town where my dad drove Oldsmobiles. It was rare for anyone to pull into the driveway behind the wheel of a Cadillac. If they did, kids came running. Adults sidled over, checked out the chrome, the fins. They were usually impressed. The whole little drama equated power with bigness with Cadillac. And the fellow behind the wheel—it was seldom a woman—was *somebody*. Not your basic Chevy or Olds-driving textile worker, but a big deal in a big car with a big future. Yet adults also never talked much about the status that went with a Cadillac. That was taboo.

Cars led the unspoken, unacknowledged, and powerful "keeping up with the Joneses" syndrome psychiatrists and social theorists were starting to talk and write about. Cars infiltrated the psyche's longing for status; they mocked a supposedly egalitarian world and exposed its hypocrisies and longings. Like jewelry that not only glittered and sang, but inside of which you could make love on sumptuous sofas with ashtrays on both ends, the large, glitzy sedans captivated the eye with their body-like curves in a decade proud of big busts and rolling hips. They placated, somewhat, the wanderlust spirit during the ascent of golf, the Cold War, and Elvis.

Rich oddballs, closet Anglophiles, and snobs drove foreign cars—that was how most Americans saw it. And how GM saw it too, although in public corporate executives called them nicer names, like "nonconformists." Who else would pay half again the price of a good American sedan for, say, a Rootes Motors Hillman Minx, a fuel saver with a sorry 37-horsepower engine in a nation of V-8s? Americans bought cars like they bought meat. By the pound, not by the foreign name.

In retrospect, it seemed natural enough that the British led the first foreign car invasion. We had been fighting partners during the war. In the early 1950s, "things British" were perceived as high class, the opposite of the trickle of manufactured junk, mostly toys, coming from Japan. Rootes Motors, Sunbeam-Talcot, Morris, Austin, and Jaguar had a residue of goodwill neither yen nor marks could buy. But the British rather quickly exhausted it. Their expensive little cars too often left puddles of oil on garage floors, proved exasperating to get fixed since few garages—or dealers—stocked spare parts, and at trade-in time taught owners a humiliating lesson in accelerated depreciation. Forty years later, in the 1990s, if someone used the term "British invasion," few Americans, middle-aged or younger, were likely to conjure up memories of the Hillman Minx, or of the tiny Austin, even though both were mildly popular in 1954. More likely, the phrase "British invasion" evoked nostalgic images of the Beatles singing "I Want to Hold Your Hand" on the *Ed Sullivan Show* in 1963, or of the Rolling Stones singing "Satisfaction"—"I can't get none." Yet a decade before music from Liverpool and London became such a huge hit, British cars had led a less heralded, and much less successful, attempt to penetrate the nationalistic American marketplace.

By the early 1960s the British car invasion retreated from whence it came: small, scattered car factories in England where hand craftsmanship endured, the steering wheel was on the right-hand side, and where one part would seldom do if an engineer could figure out a way to do the same job with two. British sports cars, Austin-Healeys, MGs, and Triumphs, did manage to hold onto a number of enthusiasts, yet they were a different breed; scarves, Irish caps, and goggles were identifying elements of their attire. Sports car enthusiasts formed loose fraternities that never seemed to tire of sharing adventure stories about the high drama of the road, often featuring breakdowns in the snow and parts hunts across numerous contiguous states in search of something like a TR-3 throwout bearing.

Therefore, if GM's management murmured assuredly from the 14th floor of the General Motors building in Detroit, "Americans don't like small cars," the reasoning seemed sound. Yet the failure of British imports to penetrate the American market was something GM's management would remember long after it should have, for the small foreign cars really didn't test the accepted truism that Americans loved only big cars. Instead they simply demonstrated that Americans were smart enough not to buy small cars of low value.

Volkswagen, despite strong anti-German sentiment in the states because of the war, pulled away from the other small car competition during the late 1950s, primarily by learning from British mistakes. First, VW built a low-cost, fun-to-drive car a home mechanic could tune with a screwdriver. Second, the company established a dealer network synonymous with Teutonic reliability. Volkswagen's meteoric rise (sales went from practically nothing in 1950 to 177 thousand, or three percent of the new car market, in 1961), although far from unnoticed by GM, Ford, and Chrysler, was greeted with the reassuring refrain: "Americans don't like small cars."

The prototype for the VW bug, which became the best selling car in the world, had been developed before World War II by Dr. Ferdinand Porsche at a Wolfsburg factory. Adolph Hitler had even visited and taken a spin with Herr Doktor in a VW convertible not terribly dissimilar in style or engineering from VWs driven along the back-roads of America thirty years later by acid-headed flower children. Initially, in the eyes of most Americans, the VW was a weird little car. Not a few of the curious, upon popping the hood, scratched their heads and wondered, "Now, where in the . . . ?"

It was in the rear: air-cooled, horizontally mounted, and about the size of an air-filter on a Cadillac. Those who took a VW for a drive were in for another surprise. Robert Sobel, a business historian whose book *Car Wars* details VW's ascent from a car American dealers wouldn't touch to a fad whose drivers started clubs, tooted at each other, and loved to talk about their cars, summed up their impressions: "Compared with American sedans, the VW Beetle seemed a nimble, precise, jewel of a car." The message was "that economy, lower price, and size didn't have to imply cheapness or loss of status." Most unusual of all, VW didn't change its style. The bug looked virtually the same not for two or three years, but for twenty. Disdaining planned obsolescence design changes, VW opted instead for small engineering refinements and a holistic vehicle whose running quality, a product of total integration of design and engineering, took priority over looks.

As VW sales exposed a flaw in the big-car logic, one manufacturer, American Motors (which combined Nash and Hudson in an attempt to survive 1950s consolidations in the auto business while other members of the so-called "Little Six," Studebaker, Packard, Kaiser-Frazer, and Willies, floundered), did come out with a smaller car, the Rambler. The brain child of George Romney, a folk hero of the American auto industry, the Rambler was rather nondescript, small, and low cost. But it sold surprisingly well. Clever, industry-challenging ads ("Why should a 110-pound woman need a two-ton car to take her three blocks for a package of bobby pins?" one asked), a late-1950s recession, and the charge by a small segment of society, personified by the Beats, that Americans were greedily materialistic and wasting the country's resources by making things like dinosaur-sized cars when little ones like the VW worked just fine, helped sales a lot.

Meanwhile, the Big Three held fast to their claim that no money was to be made in small cars even as imports, with VW leading the surge, were about to capture more than five percent of sales and with the Rambler continuing to sell well. Somewhat begrudgingly, and in unison, in 1959 the Big Three finally geared up three "import fighters," the Chevrolet Corvair, the Ford Falcon, and the Plymouth Valiant, to teach VW and American Motors a lesson.

With its technologically advanced air-cooled, rear-mounted engine and its jaunty styling, the Corvair appealed to Americans who liked the idea of owning a sports car in the British tradition but wanted their roadster easier to get fixed. The Corvair caught on—not as well as the Falcon, which was a real throwback to simplicity, but better than the Valiant. The accountants at GM, however, did Corvair a disservice. To fatten thin profits, they eliminated a few things, including a stabilizer bar, which was standard equipment on a true sports car. As a consequence, Corvair's performance often contrasted with its sporty appearance. The car tended to wobble on fast corners and flipped all too easily, especially if an outside tire dropped over a soft shoulder. Busted steering columns—actually iron shafts, with flimsy steering wheels attached—occasionally impaled drivers. In addition, the cooling system frequently leaked and wafted carbon monoxide into the interior, lulling late-night cruisers to sleep.

A young lawyer named Ralph Nader rose to national prominence documenting the dangerous performance of the Corvair. In his book, *Unsafe at Any Speed*, Nader spelled out the deaths and tragedy wrought when penny-pinching for profit was a priority over sound engineering. Nader lambasted not only the Corvair, but GM and the entire auto industry's indifference to driver safety.

General Motors didn't take kindly to Nader's attacks. Management denied cutting corners. They hired detectives to tail the lanky crusader, hoping to uncover some dirt and besmirch his reputation. But GM was no CIA. As the bumbling gumshoes hassled Nader, the press got on the case, and soon GM's attempt to sully Nader's credibility looked even sloppier then the shortsighted manufacturing decisions behind the car he so ridiculed. The efforts backfired. Not only did GM further erode buyer enthusiasm for what might have become a fad automobile if it had had the handling and safety features its target market needed for its driving habits, but its paranoia cast a shadow over the whole industry. Eventually, Nader sued GM for its attempted character assassination and won. General Motors Chairman James Roche made a public apology to Nader, but it was a little late now that it was common knowledge that engineers at Chevrolet had suggested improvements on the Corvair, only to be overruled by the accountants who saved an average of about fifteen dollars a car. Nader's crusade against GM in particular, and the American automobile industry in general, helped invoke the industry's worst fear: regulation, most notably the National Traffic and Motor Vehicle Safety Act of 1967.

The Chevrolet Vega was small-car footnote number two in GM's history. The project got rolling in 1968, again as a so-called "import fighter" in the "contemporary car" class.

Nineteen sixty-eight was the year after the "Summer of Love" in San Francisco, which introduced Americans to LSD and free love, as well as to the Tet offensive in Vietnam and psychedelic-painted Volkswagens. In this atmosphere the computer-designed Vega was supposed to shore up GM's strength in the low end of the market where Volkswagen had carved out a niche with its strong dealer network and Germanic pride in engineering, and where the Japanese were starting to make inroads. Vega debuted in showrooms in September 1970. Its European-sounding name, the Vega 2300, was similar to the BMW 2500 and the Alfa Romeo 1750 Berlina of the same era. Chevrolet soon dropped the "2300" when American buyers, more in tune to nameplates alluding to animals—the Mustang, the Cougar, and the Barracuda— and to power—the Tornado, the Grand Prix, the Imperial—got confused; many seemed to think the engine-size designation, which identified the cubic centimeter displacement, was the price.

All in all, the Vega was uninspired and uninspiring. Not that its main American-made rival, the Ford Pinto, did much to stir the hearts of car buyers either. Hastily engineered at Ford, the Pinto had a gas tank so close to the rear bumper that it sometimes exploded in fiery rear-end collisions. The Ford Pinto soon surpassed the Chevy Vega as the worst-made car in America, according to several polls.

In a myopic sort of way, GM, more than Ford and Chrysler, did have a defense for its protracted embrace of bigness. In the early 1970s GM still commanded more than fifty percent of the new car market in America, and profits were impressive, around $2 billion annually, or almost seven percent of sales. Small imports remained an irritant, nothing really that menacing to the power makers ruling boardrooms in the Motor City. Then, in late 1973, OPEC changed the rules.

Even when GM decided to compete in what it saw as the fringe market with the Vega, the big money had gone not into engineering, but advertising. General Motors felt its reputation would lure import buyers back into domestic models because Americans wanted to buy American. The flaw in the logic was its disdain for the q-word, quality. When the Vega had appeared, both the Japanese and the Germans were manufacturing tight, run-to-drive, well-appointed cars whose small power plants maximized limited horsepower. More important, the attention paid to detail by Toyota, Datsun, and the newly arrived Honda, put the domestic rivals to shame.

Nevertheless, again GM's rationale about Americans buying habits was not totally off base. Initial sales of the Vega were encouraging. It sold 323 thousand cars the first year and 370 thousand the second. Yet a prophetic honor came Vega's way when *Motor Trend* magazine named it "Car of the Year" (Corvair had received it a decade before). Predictably, Ralph Nader jumped on the Vega, claiming the cost-efficiency experts—from the financial wizards in top management to the stylists who had skinned the car to the marketing staff who spent millions trying to make the Vega literally a member of every family that had a TV—had once again squelched the engineers.

In April 1972 the recalls began. First, 130 thousand owners received letters telling them a carburetor and/or muffler problem might ignite their gas tanks. A month later 350 thousand more Vega owners learned their gas pedals might jam on the highway. In July, notices went out that the rear axle might be short, causing a wheel to roll off. With the third recall, ninety-five percent of all Vegas manufactured before May 1972 had critical safety flaws, and the car had transcended its place as a footnote in GM's history and was on its way to becoming a chapter. As Emma Rothschild noted in *Paradise Lost: The Decline of the Auto-Industrial Age,* the Chevrolet Vega was "an extreme case in its capacity for inspiring and then dashing consumer expectations."

What really distinguished Vega, however, was a strike. In the Lordstown, Ohio, plant where the car was made, GM had special hopes of eliminating some labor headaches between labor and management. Toward that end the company hired mostly young people with little or no experience in factories, convinced they would be less troublesome. The young work force did not like being excluded from decision making any more than its older union brethren in other GM plants. Criticism of management and suggestions for improvements on the assembly line and elsewhere were neither encouraged nor welcomed. The oppressive atmosphere rubbed the work force the wrong way, primed as they were by slogans of the 1960s—"Question authority!" "Do your own thing!" "Don't trust anybody over thirty!"

Plant management, in sharp contrast, came from another era. Lordstown was part of GMAD, the General Motors Assembly Division, which had been formed in 1965, partially at least to defuse the threat of the federal government, spearheaded by then Attorney General Robert Kennedy, busting up GM because of its monopolistic size. Managers at GMAD were steeped in toughmindedness. One of their credos, an idea whose popularity within management circles had become as entrenched as the belief that bigger was better and small meant marginal profits, was that high production and strict discipline went hand in hand. Toughmindedness helped you win, toughmindedness meant you were a leader, toughmindedness filtered down through plant managers and to the foremen on the line who said, in effect, "Hey, you guys and gals torquing bolts and installing seats can't solve the problems here."

Behind management's philosophy was the attitude that factory workers had little to give. If allowed to participate in change, or in defining their jobs, they might want to participate more, eventually making participation an expectation, a kind of sharing of control and power that GM management did not want to share. The notion that cooperative, appreciated, and listened-to workers might build higher quality cars that cost less, if considered at all, was quickly rejected. It was a radical idea whose time, at least in American plants, had not yet come.

The situation at Lordstown was just one more turn of the thumb screw on the hand of labor. Almost since Henry Ford's Model-T plant had opened in Highland Park, Michigan, to great fanfare on New Years Day in 1910, only to be parodied by Charlie Chaplin in *Modern Times* in the 1930s ("Don't stop for lunch." "Be ahead of your competitors."), assembly lines had been called graveyards for the brain, Faustian tradeoffs of the soul for money. Both labor reformers and social theorists lambasted them. Along in the late 1960s and early 1970s another element, robotics, had been introduced to some auto assembly lines. Seen as cost-cutting machines that didn't talk back or demand vacations or pensions, robots were often placed in plants with little attention to how machines and people might work in harmony, or to the threat they posed to union membership. Labor unions hated robots—they claimed they stole human jobs. Management loved them—they said robots lowered production costs.

At Lordstown, GMAD executives pointed proudly at twenty-six robots that welded body parts placed in the same spot again and again by human hands. Hands that had to be quick. The production quota at Vega was 102 cars an hour, contrasted with 60 at a Chevrolet Impala factory. But the Impala was a standard-sized car, with predictable profit margins and sales. Vega, on the other hand, was small; it had to be made efficiently by toughminded managers to wring even a little profit from each vehicle.

In the summer of 1972, ninety-seven percent of the work force at Vega voted to strike following a disciplinary "get tough" move by management to combat absenteeism, slowdowns, and sabotage. Management claimed the workers were destroying the cars. One spokesman blamed the "youth rebellion" of the 1960s, with its defiance of authority. Vega UAW members shot back that the working conditions were bad, discipline resembled that at boot camp, and cars were shipped riddled with defects because production goals overshadowed all other considerations. Their complaint was that no one in management was willing to stop the botched system and attempt to repair it.

Neither labor nor management showed a willingness to wrestle with the root problem: a lack of mutual respect. Management fixated on events it had set in motion decades ago and now expected, with toughness and discipline, to hammer back on a profitable course. Labor got angry and wanted to get even.

The strike lasted three months. What GM labeled "an entirely new concept of assembly" looked like a plant caught in a time warp, a time-and-motion nightmare orchestrated by Frederick Taylor, father of the stopwatch efficiency now synonymous with automobile manufacturing. The media had a picnic. It depicted a classic young liberals versus old conservatives brawl: flesh-and-blood people refusing to be integrated with steely superhuman robots. Frustrated managers defended themselves—they were just doing things the way they always had, they protested. Between labor and management stretched an abyss of misunderstanding, with efficiency on one side and the eternal hungers of the human spirit to do a good job, to feel challenged by it and appreciated for it, on the other. The deadlock weighed heavily on management's shoulders. With necks rigid from the stress of toughmindedness, they snarled, "Those sons-of-bitches will do what we say or they'll be out on the street!"

Nowhere in GM's past had the breakdown between efficiency and spirit come to a head so quickly. Organized on mass production principles forty years old and peopled by a force fueled by the liberating hungers of the 1960s, Lordstown seemed fated to fail. And it did. The Vega, the strike, the intransigence were symbols of the autoworker's alienation from a numbing job and a sign of tough times ahead for GM if it didn't recognize that automation didn't make cars: people did.

To a detached observer, GM's efforts to manufacture a good small car verged on the farcical. They suggested a practical joke, behind which smirking executives were chuckling because, in fact, they had decided to make trick cars, little Corvairs and Vegas better suited for Hollywood studio lots than for the highway, what with their eagerness to roll over, explode, or have a wheel just veer off and head up an exit ramp, leaving the startled driver to handle the challenge of pulling over and getting help. Compared to the Vega, the Pinto, and the larger, more popular American cars, Volkswagens, along with newly arriving Toyotas, Hondas, and Datsuns still seemed like drivable toys. But toys, as hard as it was for many people to believe, that lasted.

So, was GM worried?

Not yet. In the early 1970s management was fretting a little, but the world's love affair with the car kept sales good around the globe, factories humming, bonuses climbing, the UAW placated, if not fulfilled. The accountants in Detroit held the engineers in check.

In *The Fifth Discipline,* Peter Senge relates a parable that summed up GM's response to its looming predicament. It's called the "Parable of the Boiled Frog." An alert amphibian is placed in a pot of water. The pot is put on the stove. The heat is turned up quickly and the frog leaps out to safety. Then the frog is returned to the pot, to the heat, and the temperature is turned up slowly. Feeling warm and cozy, the frog relaxes, and gradually boils to death.

In the 1970s, Senge says, the Japanese were warming the water gradually. Management at GM sat, contented and toughminded. The temperature was rising, but "the frog's internal apparatus for sensing threats to survival is geared to sudden changes in his environment, not to slow, gradual changes." When GM finally felt the heat in the early 1980s, Japanese car sales in the American market had topped twenty percent. By the late 1980s, when Saturn was well along on the drawing board, the Japanese share of the market was almost thirty percent.

Notes Senge: "It is still not clear whether this particular frog will have the strength to pull itself out of the hot water. . . . We will not avoid the fate of the frog until we learn to slow down and see the gradual processes that often pose the greatest threats."

In 1978 GM unveiled the first of its alphabet cars in response to tighter federal mileage and pollution regulations. The X-cars, which included the Chevrolet Citation and the Buick Skylark, had V-6 engines, were small by big-car standards, and were welcomed by an inflation-battered public, millions of whom were still reluctant to buy

Japanese but who could no longer afford standard and luxury-sized cars. The X-cars didn't lure many import buyers back to GM, however. They disappointed the high expectations of those who had switched to Japanese imports with their distinctive road feel and amenities, cannibalized GM's big-car divisions, and drew some customers away from Ford and Chrysler.

In 1981 came the J-cars. They included the Pontiac J-2000 and the Cadillac Cimarron, characterized by auto analyst Maryann Keller in *Rude Awakenings,* her version of GM's stumble from greatness, as "nothing more than a Chevrolet Cavalier with leather seats and a luggage rack."

So much for being *somebody* in a Cadillac. It was the 1950s reversed. But now you were as foolish to buy the overpriced small Cadillac as your uncle, the one who loved to reminiscence about his war escapades in London and had been coughing up the extra cash for a Wolseley Six Eighty back in 1950. The big difference was that at least with the Wolseley your uncle had acquired a little status.

The alphabet cars repeated the pattern: hyped expectations followed by disappointment. They also introduced two new manufacturing processes called downsizing and badge engineering. Downsizing meant, in effect, "Honey, we shrunk our old standard model, but we're charging just about as much for it." Badge engineering was a kind of assembly-line shell game in which powertrains, body panels, and interiors got shuffled around between various GM divisions, making models look new when they weren't.

Anyone comparing a 1982 Honda Accord with a J-car "wasn't going to take the J-car very seriously," Maryann Keller wrote. Especially at a time when gas was selling for well over a dollar a gallon and fears were widespread that it might climb to three times that. A sluggish vehicle with a throwback engine, a modified four-cylinder introduced two decades earlier, rather than a high-revving, torque-strong power plant like those in most imports, did not seem the ideal way to take advantage of the situation. But the new J-car had other disadvantages as well. Badge engineering made it a look-alike, feel-alike, drive-alike car that broke down a lot and irked the heck out of dealers and owners alike. Badge engineering wasn't really engineering at all, but rather a process that was hurting pride in individual GM divisions and making their cars characterless.

In 1981, GM announced its first loss, and a year later the economy dropped into a recession. General Motors' new chairman Roger Smith found himself at the helm of America's largest company during the economic doldrums. Since 1978 GM's car sales had dropped from 5.3 million to 3.1 million. Truck and bus sales had taken a similar dive percentage-wise. The company had lost not only loyalist buyers of its mainstay big cars, but alienated converts to its alphabet cars, locked horns with the government over clean air, safety, and economy standards, and, in general, refused to accept how drastically the world had changed.

As Smith strategized for the company's future, obviously big changes were needed. But surrounding the chairman was the same old corporate culture, the same one Smith had matured in as the protege of Thomas Aquinas Murphy, a personable and well-liked chairman who had run things during some tough years, 1974 to 1981. General Motors' highly paid, coddled, and secure top executives were seldom critical of one another, and had lost their cutting edge. The corporation had become a parody of "the art of organization," which French writer J.-J. Servan-Schreiber had ascribed to its pacesetting style in *The American Challenge,* his 1969 best seller that captivated business executives, politicians, and bureaucrats in Europe while describing a model for them to follow. Instead of internal balance between car guys and so-called bean counters, the bean counters at GM now kept their heels on the engineers' fingers. Committees, whose role was to make policy and set direction, had become rubber stamps for decisions made by the chairman. Smith's two predecessors, Richard Gerstenberg, or "Old Gerstenberg the bookkeeper," as he called himself ("I am like an ant on the front of a log heading downstream toward a treacherous bend, and all I can do is stick my foot in the water to steer us clear and yell, 'Whoa!' ") who was chairman during the first turbulent oil crisis, and Thomas Aquinas Murphy, also convinced that events were bigger than he was ("The job controls me and not vice versa"), did little to change the corporation's direction. Murphy actually became a vehement opponent of regulation, railing against the very standards the Japanese seemed to have little trouble meeting and blaming those standards for GM's high production costs.

After getting himself settled in as the boss, Roger Smith, a shrill-voiced accountant with the ego of a prima donna, was determined to change things. And one of the first things he changed was the latest small-car project. He killed it.

Scheduled for a 1985 launch as yet another alphabet model, Chevrolet's S-car had been earmarked to compete against the Japanese at the entry level. But a six-week study conducted at Isuzu (GM had owned part of the small Japanese car company since 1972) said that

Chevy, then under Bob Stempel, should forget it. The figures—hotly refuted by a few executives—claimed that Chevy would have to spend $5,700 to make the same car Isuzu could build for $2,800.

In Smith's mind the message only validated his instincts. He was sure the future lay in high technology, lower labor costs, and acquisitions of pace-setting companies whose advances could quickly disseminate throughout GM. He was already courting the mercurial Ross Perot, founder and main shaker and mover behind Electronic Data Systems (EDS), in the first of several high-tech affairs that he would get excited about and spend a fortune on. Eventually, GM bought EDS and its 13,800 employees, who integrated into GM's 800,000, for $2.55 billion. Neither the GM board of directors nor top executives with access to Smith's ear argued forcefully against the chairman's lopsided high-tech agenda, which soon included the acquisition of Hughes Aircraft Corporation. Roger Smith felt sure that EDS and Hughes would leapfrog GM not only out of the hot water it had settled lethargically into, but over the not-so-well capitalized competition too.

Yet doubt circulated in the corporate ranks. That GM was losing its cachet to American buyers was becoming troublesomely clear. It was also clear that instead of ignoring the Japanese, management had better start scrutinizing them closely. Toward this end, during the next few years, a number of managers toured Japanese plants both in America and abroad, including the just-opened Nissan plant in Smyrna, Tennessee. The factories were not sets from *Star Wars,* they discovered. Robots weren't all over the place. In fact, the plants didn't look or operate a lot differently from GM's older plants, the very ones the high technology thrust was closing. That the Japanese made high-quality cars in plants that weren't out of the future or some high-tech nirvana that GM could reach with large enough expenditures on machines was mystifying. That they did it for less money than GM was distressing. But that the Japanese cars made in the less-than-futuristic factories also *exceeded* buyers expectations was downright mindboggling. Some GM managers were beset by the unnerving conviction that the Japanese "possessed a secret strategy that went far beyond technology," Keller wrote. The managers desperately needed to put a finger on "the *tangible, technological* evidence of mastery" that the Japanese possessed, she added. But they couldn't.

So when Roger Smith killed the S-car, confidence within GM that a good small car was feasible was an all-time low. Numbers and attitudes both said, "Forget it."

Alex Mair, a vice president of advanced engineering at the GM Tech Center in Warren, didn't want to forget a good small car. A rarity at GM, Mair was known as a guy who spoke up about what bothered him. And the longer he mused about the decision to drop the S-car, the less he liked it. Mair again scrutinized Chevy's estimated costs for the car and again compared them with Isuzu's. He had a mild epiphany—or a mild epiphany for the closed ranks of GM. The company's system for developing new cars was a mess, Mair realized, and the only way to compete with the Japanese was by starting entirely fresh, with a blank sheet of paper. All he had to do was convince the already intimidated hierarchy, which was psyched out by *nippon-do* (the Japanese way), by *zaizan* (continuous improvement from the bottom up rather than the top down), and by *karoshi* (a willingness to work to the death for one's company in the samurai tradition) that a new way of creating a car was possible.

One sure way was to scare them, to demonstrate that the small-car market itself wasn't the threat. It was the whole market that GM was in danger of losing. If Chevrolet couldn't compete with a small car today, why should Oldsmobile be able to compete in the intermediate models a couple years down the road, once the Japanese moved in there? Or Cadillac in the luxury models once the Japanese started making expensive cars?

Mair went to Roger Smith and the GM Executive Board, which then included the seven top managers in the company, and personally pleaded his case. Garnering their approval, in June 1982, Mair pulled together what is known as a "skunk works," an unofficial but sanctioned project where engineers and designers could bounce around new ideas. The skunk works was put under the wing of Advanced Product Manufacturing and Engineering at the Tech Center and assigned some office space.

That September Reid Rundell, then heading GM-Holden Limited in Australia, got a call "out of the blue," as he remembered it. Headquarters wanted Rundell to return to Detroit and be the skunk works' executive director. For Rundell, the transfer was welcomed. The two years he had lived in Australia, "we were getting killed in the small end of the market," he said.

Back in Warren, Rundell assumed control of what now became the "no name project." He had a staff of around sixteen. America was still in a recession, car sales were terrible, and more than ever GM needed a popular car at the entry level. Nevertheless, internal forces within the corporation wanted to torpedo the no-name car before it even saw the light. The project angered some executives. Being territorial, they wanted it placed under the direction of an existing division, not independent and competing for tight funds. Others ruefully pointed at the S-car figures and muttered that with American labor costs and inefficiencies, a profitable small car was a pipe dream. Despite the opposition, the no-name project gathered momentum. The idea had force, the tenacity of necessity. Roger Smith wanted to create a trademark small car, it soon became clear. Recalling this crucial incubation period, Rundell said, "Alex [Mair] provided all the protection we needed from internal forces at GM."

How serious Roger Smith was about incorporating Japanese methods into the company's future became apparent in March 1983. Against unusual and vocal internal opposition, Smith endorsed and pushed through the board of directors a joint partnership with Toyota to manufacture a small car in California. Called NUMMI (New United Motor Manufacturing, Inc.), the GM/Toyota partnership would prove to be a key tactic of a larger strategy, in which Saturn was the *coup de grace*. Fighting the Japanese head-to-head was suicidal, Smith had concluded. NUMMI, located in a converted older plant in Fremont, California, promised to be an alternative to trade barriers and protectionism, defenses many of the chairman's auto world contemporaries wanted the government to erect high to guard them from the Japanese.

At NUMMI, the argument went, GM managers would witness close up how the Japanese operated, how their management and labor got along, how teamsmanship worked on the floor, how quality got put in and costs squeezed out. Smith argued persuasively that NUMMI would buy both know-how and time for a made-in-America, cutting-edge facility where a competitive small car could be manufactured. Of course, crawling into bed with the enemy, whatever the long-term strategy, drew a wrath of criticism. But like the famous ducks in the lobby at the Peabody Hotel in Memphis, where he would soon meet Tennessee governor Lamar Alexander, often referred to as "the best salesman Tennessee ever had," Roger Smith had a gift for weathering storms.

8

People First Labor Contract

While Roger Smith's larger corporate strategy might have looked to some like a sellout to Toyota, over at the Tech Center Reid Rundell's team had more practical things to worry about. For instance, what should the no-name car look like? How should it be manufactured? Who would sell it? And, of course, a name—it needed a name. It soon got one, Saturn, in honor of the National Aeronautics and Space Administration's Apollo program. It was a linkage lost on the majority of nonrocket-scientist Americans. They heard the word Saturn they still associated it with the romantic planet with the rings around it. As for Saturn's design and how the car would be manufactured, about all Rundell's team knew for sure at this stage was that they couldn't do things the old way or they'd end up with another S-car.

Alex Mair's conclusion that GM's new-car process was old and outdated quickly became Saturn gospel. A New Age car couldn't be a consequence of GM think, with its bureaucracy, decision-making niches, and long lead times.

Gradually, three main thrusts moved Saturn away from GM's pull and into its own unique orbit. These were: (1) a commitment to advanced technology; (2) an acceptance of the need for integrated business systems; and (3) a belief in enlightened people relationships. It also soon became obvious that the new business systems and people relationships had to be priorities. Technologically, GM was in good shape. Then the people challenge leapfrogged the business systems one. If Saturn was going to succeed, the new company might not have to reinvent the wheel, the reasoning went, but it absolutely had to reshape labor-management relations and the workplace so that the people making Saturns cared about them.

Tackling the people problem first, Saturn recognized the long-simmering feud between labor and management throughout the organization. It had persisted for decades, heating up during contract negotiations, cooling down during good years, flaring again when plants were closed or strikes occurred, as at Vega. The adversarial relationship was wasteful and draining, it eroded mutual respect. Yet it was also defended. It not only identified toughminded managers and helped their promotions, but also buttressed the UAW's tough-guy stance as defender of blue-collar workers at the mercy of an indifferent giant. In other words, adversity between management and labor had become a weighty piece of process. Yet "there was no way that the Japanese, who worked together for a common goal, could ever be beaten by people trying to kill each other," observed Neil De Koker, director of business systems at Saturn in the early days.

Enter, stage left, Donald F. Ephlin. Often called a renegade and a visionary, Ephlin, fifty-eight, was director of the UAW's General Motors Department, which numbered 350 thousand members. Ephlin's goal in life was to get managers and engineers to understand working people.

Ephlin had climbed up the hierarchy of the UAW in much the same way executives worked their way up the ladder at GM—through dint, perseverance, and seniority. As a gunner on a B-24 bomber, he had flown twenty-seven missions over Germany in World War II, returned home to Framingham, Massachusetts, and found a job building a nearby GM plant. "The day the plant was done, I went to work inside it," he said. He was a millwright. The plant assembled Buicks, Oldsmobiles, and Pontiacs, three strong sellers. "In those days management was pretty bad," Ephlin recalled. "All the union had to do was pass out the cards."

And pass them out Ephlin did. He rose through the union ranks quickly, became president of his plant's Local 422, and, in 1960, was appointed to the UAW International, the twenty-six-member governing body. In the early 1970s he was administrative assistant to then UAW president Leonard Woodcock during precedent-setting negotiations with the Big Three. Since then, Ephlin had become known as a union progressive. His main concerns were for greater worker participation in decision making and for workplace improvements. In 1983, Ephlin was a little leery about Saturn when Al Warren, vice present of industrial relations for GM, told him about the small-car project. Shortly thereafter, Ephlin got his first official briefing.

Reid Rundell and several other members of his team sat down with Ephlin, a solid, white-haired fellow who didn't lack for a sense of humor, at the GM Tech Center. They told him they wanted to bring labor in on Saturn during the development stages, something that was unheard of in conventional new-car starts. But when one of them said the UAW ought to name three representatives and GM name three, and that the six could come up with a magic pill for the labor/management headache, Ephlin laughed. "I know the union doesn't have one or two people who are smart enough to do this," he said. "And neither does GM. So why don't we open it up?"

From that came the momentum for the Group of 99, Saturn's first visible giant step away from its parent organization. Members of the group were chosen from fifty-five GM plants in seventeen divisions. Forty-two were UAW plant personnel, thirty-five were GM plant management, and the rest came from the staffs of both the corporation and the union. A Saturn Study Center was established and a mission statement—"To identify and recommend the best approaches to integrate people and technology to competitively manufacture small cars in the United States"—formalized. The driving question was, "If we started over from scratch now, what would we do?" And the fuel to propel the group toward its mission was Alex Mair's earlier observation about GM's new-car process: "The entire system is a mess."

Oddly egalitarian for a large, hierarchical corporation, the Group of 99 got together for its first meeting at the Weston Hotel in downtown Detroit. All the talk about change and vision notwithstanding, it was deja vu: GM guys in suits huddled together; UAW guys, in shop jackets, clustered with their female peers. Trust? What in hell was that? You mean, between us and them?

Although the hotel was located in what was euphemistically called Detroit's Renaissance Center, the meeting was not a miracle session. Cynicism ran deep. There had been numerous new beginnings of one kind or another the last decade or two at GM. Now, sitting together for the first time, the UAW and GM loyalists listened to speeches about how great teamwork was, how wonderful a world it would be if only everybody could be quality partners in quality circles making quality cars that Americans loved. Questions followed. Coming down to earth, someone asked about the group's budget.

"Whatever you need," came the answer.

A shop foreman asked, "Where do we go?"

"Wherever you need to."

"How do we dress?"

"Casual."

Travel plans were made. Teams were organized to reflect the various pieces of the new car-making pie: trim and hardware, paint, body, assembly, and so on. Annoying tokens of status and separation, such as the GM guys having telephone calling cards and not the UAW members, were eliminated; everybody got a calling card.

Not everybody approved of the Group of 99, however. One vocal opponent was none other than Alex Mair. He didn't think this was the magic pill for the labor migraine, and in particular didn't like the size of the pill the small-car project was being forced to swallow. Mair "was resistant to the idea of the ninety-nine," De Koker recalled. "He wanted it to be a very small team of people and he was upset that we had let this thing grow, and especially upset with me for having these ninety-nine outsiders from the UAW and other divisions doing something that maybe ten or fifteen people could have done."

It did seem, at the time, rather farfetched, almost naive: sending people from sides that had trouble even speaking to each other openly into the corporate hinterland on a cooperative mission. Giving the Group of 99 this much rope was a sign of just how unsure GM was about how to proceed. Notes Maryann Keller in *Rude Awakening,* "It was in the early 1980s, a rare experience in corporate America, and almost unthinkable at General Motors, to set a group of people free to run with their vision."

But off they went, armed with calling cards and credit cards and a *carte blanche* to ask the impertinent question, "What if?" The ninety-nine attended seminars of both domestic and Japanese car manufacturers, visited suppliers and dealers, met and talked with academics about the future of the car business, toured forty-nine different GM plants, made seventy-five trips to sixty non-GM companies that included Volvo in Sweden and Hewlett-Packard in California, traveled more than two million miles, and put in around fifty thousand hours. A catalyst for transformation, the Group of 99 was one of those fanciful, costly, enlightening experiments that only a company with the resources of General Motors could pull off—all to find out whether the stillborn S-car hadn't said everything there was to say already; that is, going head-to-head against the Japanese, you're dead.

During this period, which spanned the winter and spring months of 1984, from being practically a nonentity within the company, Saturn began energizing its own glow. Proselytizers emerged. One of them was Neil De Koker. About the rarefied atmosphere surrounding Saturn in those days, he told Keller, "The emotions, the tears, the whatever it took to really create a team and a culture and a commitment—I could never fully describe it. I get emotional now, just thinking about it. It was like being part of an evangelistic organization—

we were the Bible-wielding 'Southern Baptists' carrying our Saturn philosophy around."

In the spring of 1984, following the Group of 99's travels, a plan was written at the Saturn Study Center based on the findings and conclusions. It was submitted to the UAW leadership and to GM's Executive Committee.

"I thought it was kind of utopian," Ephlin remembered. "I didn't feel it all could become a reality. Perhaps we could use pieces of it."

The GM Executive Committee shared few of Ephlin's reservations. The committee went along with the recommendations that Saturn be a wholly owned subsidiary of GM but reshaped beyond the parent's recognition. The committee also urged total integration of all systems of the business, a separate union/management agreement, and a from-the-ground-up new car—not a patched together marque with a lot of hype.

Roger Smith had gone public briefly with Saturn some months before, in November 1983, boasting that the project was of "cosmic proportion." But now the final report from the Group of 99 received the imprimaturs of the GM Executive Committee.

At the Tech Center, the Saturn team began to grow. One new-comer was Billy Joe Horan. A native of Tennessee, Horan had left the South in the 1950s, worked at AC Spark Plug in Flint, became a troubleshooter for a group called Teamstudy at the Tech Center (Teamstudy solved tough manufacturing problems), and then, along with several other Teamstudy members, had been assigned to the blank-sheet-of-paper skunk works that was now Saturn. "They told us far and away more than on any other job I had ever worked on," Horan said. "You were privy to information you never dreamed you'd have access to."

Horan helped build the original prototypes. By July 1984 they were welding body panels by hand, he recalled. For once, design, engineering, management, and labor were all working together, in harmony. There weren't too many chiefs, even fewer titles. Rundell was the boss. They worked six- and seven-day weeks. By September, eight drivable Saturns had been fabricated from scratch and four months later Roger Smith drove one of them around at the official announcement in Troy.

For the UAW, however, the question remained, as Ephlin put it, "How to hell do you implement the plan?"

In his estimation, the plan as conceived by the Group of 99 and

stamped by GM management "was the most advanced human relations system" GM and the union had ever come up with together.
"Bits and pieces of it occurred all over the place. But in total I don't
know anything like it." Initially, two things about the plan worried
him: the plant location and the labor contract. But they were both
resolved during the 1984 bargaining session when GM agreed that
the Saturn plant would be built in the United States and that a labor
agreement would be worked out consistent with the Group of 99
report.

For such a sophisticated human relations system, some precedents
did exist. Ephlin had witnessed a couple of them himself, in Sweden,
at Volvo and Saab, during the early 1970s. Both companies developed
incentives that included giving up some decision-making power, letting workers determine to a greater degree how to get their jobs done,
and generally heightening self-esteem throughout their factories, to
keep Swedish blue-collar workers from leaving for better-paying and
more satisfying jobs elsewhere.

The task of writing Saturn's labor contract fell to a six-man committee, with three members from the UAW and three from GM. The
men first met at Marygrove College in Detroit in April 1985. "At this
time everything was secret," Jim Wheatley, one of the UAW representatives, told me years after the fact. "We worked over there for about
three weeks. All the news media was trying to get information. They
found out we were over there, so we left and went up to Bay Valley
[a resort in Bay City, Michigan] for four weeks. In about thirty days
time we did the whole Saturn agreement.

"When we started, and everybody crossed their heart that it was
true—and, of course, it wasn't, but everybody said it was—we were
not to have any outside interference from anyone. No one was to tell
us what to do. We were supposed to do the whole thing, and after
we got done they could knock out what they wanted to. But otherwise, forget where we came from and who we represented. . . . Back
in those days anyone who had any authority in General Motors, or
the UAW, too, with the exception of Ephlin, they pretended we didn't
exist. And what we was doing, we were funding all this out of the
Human Resources nickel money, so nobody was having to approve
the expenditures. We did everything by consensus."

Wheatley and his GM counterpart Richard Huber wrote the pay
and incentives package. It said Saturnites were going to be hired for
life, but with lower wages than their counterparts in other GM factories—at least initially. That was where production bonuses came in.

The bonuses were a motivating carrot to get wages equal to, or higher than, those at other auto plants when Saturn's production met or exceeded certain goals.

The Saturn Memorandum of Agreement, the official name of the labor contract, even included a clause called the "Saturn People Philosophy Summary Statement." It said, "We believe that all people want to be involved in decisions that affect them, care about their jobs and each other, take pride in themselves and in their contributions and want to share in the success of their efforts."

One sticky question was not resolved by the labor contract committee: who gets the jobs? Wheatley said he had known then that this could become a real sore point once the plant opened. "I was born and raised in Tennessee," he told me. "I'm aware of the outlook of local Tennesseans. I never realized how dumb and illiterate we was until I came back here after being away for thirty years. The high school system and everything is not up to par." However, he added, "The best technicians we could get would be some of these boys off the farm who had worked with machinery and equipment. They don't have someone tell them what to do. If the plow breaks, they fix it. My argument was that the best thing we could do was we could sprinkle these guys throughout the plant. In other words, each team could have one regular guy from the community. The team, production-wise, would be better than having everyone from General Motors. They'd bring something new. And from the community relations standpoint, these would be the best ambassadors that we could have."

Wheatley's give-the-locals-a-few-jobs logic did not prevail. Ephlin, for one, didn't like it. He had too many thousands of UAW workers on layoff not to give them first shot at Saturn's five thousand new jobs, he felt, even if that meant moving them all down to Tennessee from other GM locations. When it came time for the UAW International Board to ratify the labor agreement, the board changed the ratio to one hundred percent UAW production personnel and zero locals, shoving a powder keg under the great expectations Maurians had for future jobs.

There were several other problems with the farsighted accord. One was that it represented a yet-to-be-hired labor force, so there was nobody to vote for or against it. Another was that Tennessee was a right-to-work state, which meant you didn't have to join the union even if the factory you worked in had one. Lower starting wages with production incentives didn't set well with some union higher ups, either. Nor did the whole concept of shared leadership. Wasn't it management's job to lead—not the union's? Wasn't this co-mingling the responsibilities the union and management were built on? It sure was. That was what the Group of 99 envisioned. The threat, of course, was that this would ruin the union.

The ruin-the-union argument was an old saw. It had been trundled out at NUMMI where GM-UAW teams were going through a shaky transition period to forge a partnership with Toyota. Teamsmanship, it was muttered by some opposition union leaders, was just another way of laying people off.

Nevertheless, the Saturn agreement was ratified by the UAW International and announced by UAW president Owen Bieber on July 27, 1985, the weekend Spring Hill was declared the plant's future home. "We have made some vast strides here," Bieber declared. "The agreement is innovative, it's new." For the first time in UAW history, workers were "going to have a great deal of input into how that plant is operated. The union will be a full partner in all decisions," Bieber continued, "from the shop to top management. No decision can be made, no action can be taken without an agreement by the workers. That is a degree of co-determination never before reached in U.S. collective bargaining." At the same time the union held on to the right to strike, to binding arbitration, and to grievance procedures.

In mid-1985 NUMMI was already putting into motion some of the vast strides Bieber attributed to Saturn. Teams making cars there had recognized that people made automobiles, not technology. The results were that NUMMI was manufacturing good cars, output was high, waste low, and much of GM—especially old-line managers struggling to be competitive under the old system—was annoyed at, as one manager put it, "All that NUMMI talk."

To GM conservatives NUMMI was a little too much New Age lingo, sensitivity training, and Japanese cooperation all under one roof in California. Saturn sounded as if it was going to be more of the same only in Tennessee. Toughminded managers seeing capital siphoned off from their pet projects didn't want to hear any more about *zaizan* or about how, at NUMMI, attention was devoted to details, plant politics was secondary, and everyone, from welders to assembly-line foreman to white-shirted executives felt what it was like to realize their full human potential.

A NUMMI backlash radiated through GM as Saturn was coming into being. Roger Smith, who had initiated both NUMMI and Saturn, didn't seem to know what to do about it. While NUMMI joined a number of other strategic efforts going forward simultaneously, including Saturn and the integration of EDS, as Maryann Keller wrote, "There was a lack of coordination among the many efforts, and no central system for evaluating them."

Saturn as a takeoff from NUMMI in the area of labor relations was firmly refuted by Ephlin. He noted that the NUMMI labor agreement predated Saturn's by only a few weeks and that the Saturn agreement really had come from the report of the Group of 99, not from Toyota precedents. Actually, NUMMI seemed to have run interference for the level-playing field project that followed it by absorbing some of the anxiety of UAW leaders who were real nervous about teamwork and trust and human potential undermining their power. Like some of their contemporaries in management, the conservative UAW branch wasn't convinced that all the New Age hocus-pocus and the Japanese partnership would do much except leave them standing there in their underwear, facing a reduced UAW work force. The message then would be, they grumbled, that "teamwork" and "partnership" were just another way of saying "layoff" and "getting screwed."

Ephlin understood their anxieties. Yet sometimes heads had to roll and he preferred that they dropped from white collars rather than blue. But that couldn't be guaranteed. When the big guillotine of competitive ineptness started falling regularly, as it had for years now, watch out—no one knew for sure where the blade might cut next.

The NUMMI experience spotlighted a weakness between the UAW leadership and its rank-and-file. Here you had union members being offered breakthroughs unimaginable only a couple years before, the workplace involvement and the voice they'd been clamoring for, and union leadership waffled about endorsing them because the changes threatened their power. Yet, given the labor cost disparities between Japanese car makers and their American counterparts, unless the UAW and management cooperated, whether they had to lighten their numbers and link pay to profit or not, they weren't going to be making cars in America much longer. From the individual's point of view, the making of quality cars in a NUMMIesque work environment promised a better sense of well-being, of self-worth. As things stood, Ephlin said, in most GM factories, "You hate to come home to your children and have one of them ask, 'Whatdaya do, Dad?' And you say, 'I build junk'."

Not that NUMMI or Saturn humanized assembly lines, he added. But they did improve them. Saturn in particular hoped to stir long-dormant enthusiasms for work. It would still be hard work and often boring. But, Ephlin once told me, "It's like the guys at NUMMI say, 'We're working harder but we like it better.'"

After the Saturn labor contract was ratified by the UAW International, the fight wasn't quite over. The Right to Work Foundation filed a complaint with the National Labor Relations Board and tried to take Saturn to the mat over the right-to-work issue. Tom Harris, chairman of the National Right to Work Legal Defense Fund, argued that his organization did not see the labor deal as cheerfully as GM, Saturn, and Tennessee officials did. Harris called the agreement "a shocking example of big business and big labor teaming up to deny workers their rights under the law. . . . This coercive sweetheart deal at Saturn has a chilling effect on the right to work."

The challenge was not upheld, but it still bothered Ephlin. "Our labor laws were created for a different era," he said. "Here we were, doing what everybody said we should do and it's darn near declared illegal. The U.S. has got to get its act together if we ever want to be competitive internationally."

As Ephlin saw it, during President Reagan's administration the auto industry became expendable. "There was this belief that somehow we didn't need manufacturing," he said. "We were going to be in the high-tech business." This was part of America's denial of its declining industrial competitiveness, Ephlin felt. Meanwhile, Japanese-financed and managed industries not only in Japan, but in Taiwan, Hong Kong, Bangkok, Singapore, and elsewhere across the Pacific Rim, were winning an undeclared but ongoing economic war with the sluggish and overconfident West. Standards of living and expectations were rising in the emerging economies as they produced one product after another better and more cheaply than Americans. Televisions, electronics equipment, copiers, cameras, automobiles—"Once you've lost stuff," Ephlin lamented, "once it's gone, it's a helluva lot harder to get it back."

9

Gut Feel and Car Smarts

Saturn's first official management team, a president and five vice presidents, was announced in January 1985. Their initial challenge was one of forgetting. To create the so-called "business of the business" for a factory of the future in some green field site no one had yet identified, they had to forget much of what they had learned in other divisions of GM.

None of the vice presidents or the president, Joseph Sanchez, had worked together before, so the first week or so was spent getting to know one another. John Middlebrook, in charge of marketing, was forty-three. Born in Michigan, Middlebrook had started his career at Oldsmobile when he was eighteen. Guy Briggs, forty-six, was in charge of manufacturing. He'd gone to work for GM in 1961, while still at the University of Michigan. Tom Manoff, vice president of finance, was also forty-six. Manoff had ascended through the ranks of the bean counters. James Lewandowski, forty-seven, was the head of human resources. He had started out at Cadillac in 1955, then branched into the often troublesome area of personnel, and now had a job of immense importance, given the radical shift from people as the problem to people as the solution. J. Jay Wetzel, II, forty-five, rounded off the leadership team as vice president of engineering.

If one of the vps had an extra load to carry, it was Wetzel, the sole engineer in the group and the guy destined to pick up Saturn's first speeding ticket. Up to this point in his career, Wetzel had had a blessed, one-division record. He was a Pontiac man. He had been since 1963, when he graduated from the University of Michigan with an engineering degree. "Big enough to be significant, but small enough to be family," as he described it, the Pontiac Motor Division was physically removed from Detroit, had taken the name of its city, and prided itself on cars made more by "gut feel and car smarts." At Pontiac, Wetzel had thrived. He wended his way through the close-knit organization, attended MIT as an Alfred Sloan Fellow in 1972, and, ten years later, became Pontiac's chief engineer. He was in charge of eleven car lines, including the popular two-seater, the Fiero, another small-car project that had died. When GM reorganized in 1983 and 1984, sowing discord throughout the divisions, Pontiac had been pulled apart and Jay Wetzel had found himself with the newly formed C-P-C Group temporarily. But in May 1984 he had been given a special assignment, to assess the Saturn small-car project at the GM Tech Center.

Wetzel spent seven months on the assessment. In December 1984 he reported that Saturn seemed to be off to a good start in every area except one: the car itself. Saturn had to be "productionized"; that is, design and manufacturing must be integrated from the beginning. The prototypes, the original concept cars, also were not competitive stylistically, he concluded.

Discounting that troublesome fact (Saturn was already two and a-half years old), the GM Executive Board, headed by Roger Smith, gave Saturn Corporation the official go-ahead. During the first weeks of 1985, while the final decision was being made as to exactly where Saturn would fit in the GM galaxy, financing was put on hold, though. "It was humorous at first," Wetzel remembered. "We paid for everything with our gold American Express cards. My wife did the books at home." At the same time, if Saturn was going to be fundamentally different rather than just another GM footshuffle or accounting abracadabra while market share continued to plummet like a Cadillac tossed from a high building, it was pretty obvious it had to stand apart from the parent company. Yet letting go was something GM found excruciatingly hard to do.

Then three weeks along, with many decisions still up in the air, Saturn had its first casualty. President Joe Sanchez died. Sanchez, a Brazilian with a broad and deep hands-on feel for all aspects of the automotive business, had been working hard. After all, here was the opportunity of a lifetime and adrenaline levels among the members of his team were at race-track highs. Sanchez was trying to bring the men together and developing future strategy with Reid Rundell, who had remained as executive vice president in charge of strategic planning, a position he would fill for the next year. Wetzel, Briggs, Manoff, and the others were going over the labor agreement concepts in the Group of 99 report, and were wrestling with the old bugaboo: just who were these millions of Americans who bought Japanese cars and *why* did they buy them? They were also rearranging their desks.

At Saturn, even in its temporary quarters at the GM Tech Center, the one man/one office organizational architecture was gone. Now the furniture shuffling reflected the new philosophy of teams and partnerships. For instance, Wetzel and Briggs, product and process, faced each other across an oval table, their work stations to their respective rears. They were physical evidence that product and process had to harmonize right at the beginning, had to be like the front wheels on a car, turning together, accelerating together, slamming on the brakes together. But then, as all this was going forward, the new president, tired, his head crammed with information, had driven home to Lansing and suffered a heart attack.

Saturn found itself leaderless. On the recommendations of the vice presidents, William Hoglund, a lanky, smooth, financial-side guy whose father had been a GM vice president and whose brother was a GM vice president ("Hoglund was kind of born to be a vice president of General Motors," Ephlin once quipped), took Sanchez's place. Hoglund was fifty, headed for the highest echelon in the GM hierarchy. Yet even after he assumed command, an "I think this is for sure, but I'm not sure" attitude prevailed, Wetzel recalled. The chief engineer was feeling a little of that ambivalence himself. One day it was, "God, I've got a chance to start a new company." The next it was, "Holy mackerel, we're betting the farm on it in a big way."

Once Hoglund took charge, money began to flow. The new business systems were determined, defining processes and creating structure. The vice presidents scrutinized GM's past and borrowed or modified what they could use and tossed out the rest. During the spring of 1985, while giving structure to the engineering piece of the picture and integrating it with the process of conceiving a plant that built high-quality cars with less floor space, less material, and less energy, Jay Wetzel found himself working harder than he ever had in his life. His career was on the line.

"We had an all new team, all new business systems, everything new. Boy, it got complicated in a hurry. I didn't realize in the beginning how complicated it was going to get with the all-new this, the all-new that."

Just how crucial engineering would be at Saturn was strikingly apparent, and Wetzel was responsible for much of it. Engineering, after all, was what the car would *be*: how it looked, how it performed.

In early 1985, however, there was no car and there was no edifice. And like Jay Gatsby sixty years earlier, Saturn needed its own edifice. Edifices, to be exact: a plant *and* a headquarters.

In October, several months after the official announcement that Spring Hill had won the site contest for the plant, the executives cleared out of the Tech Center and moved into Saturn's new offices in Troy, a fifteen-minute drive north. It was a hectic, exciting time. "Seat-of-the-pants decisions" were being made, Wetzel said, decisions reminiscent of the gut-feel Pontiac school of automobile making. He and Guy Briggs decided that Saturn would have a steel spaceframe as a skeleton. Spaceframes, which could be difficult to weld, had been used a lot in aerospace work, but not for cars. A combination of steel and plastic would form Saturn's skin. And the new plant was going to have its own foundry, a rare feature in the specialized world GM had adopted for its other divisions. In the foundry Saturn would cast its own engines by the lost-foam process. Lost foam, a sophisticated, but again untried process, at least on this scale, would eliminate waste and milling operations found at more traditional foundries. As new systems and intuitions merged and synergized, Saturn seemed on its way to fulfilling a hope, a hope that it would be a learning organization flying across the corporate sky, all systems go.

Even "the backup," another GM tradition, was eliminated. The conviction was, Wetzel said, that "as long as we have a backup we'd tend never to put all our energy in the primary objective."

In the new offices, the organizational layout continued to distinguish the emerging new world of Saturn, as it defined itself day to day, from the old world at GM. Team leaders occupied workspaces in the middle of floors. Their teammates who were being hired, trained, and indoctrinated in the Saturn philosophy, could see them and talk with them. Low-walled, modular partitions created semi-permanent spaces in which the new Saturnites worked but couldn't hide. Wetzel and Briggs continued as partners at an oval table. And, "no matter where you sat," Wetzel recalled, "to make your way to either the coffee machine or the cafeteria, you had to bump shoulders and talk to people." There were also numerous small conference rooms. Each had at least one wall of glass so that the new Saturnites walking past could glance in, register from the faces or charts or visuals what was going on, and, if they thought it necessary, do an about face, open the door, and take a seat.

Each month around 150 new people joined Saturn. Their enthusiasm was infectious, but training them presented another challenge. "You're trying to explain who does what, when, where," Wetzel said. "It became very confusing."

To ease the confusion they developed "success enablers," little aides like an internal Yellow Pages that identified what individuals at Saturn did and where they were in the purposeful chaos. Circles of responsibility were established, with meetings often held in the round. The most important circle was the Saturn Action Council, or SAC, which included the vice presidents and a baseball cap with an S on it. Whoever called the meeting wore the cap first. Each speaker in turn put on the baseball cap. There were a number of "strokes of simple street smarts" Wetzel claimed—for instance, the name and model designations. Most car names evoked thoughts of prestige, spirituality, animals, or, in the case of some European marques, numbers "to confuse anyone who doesn't really own one, like the BMW 535i." They decided to call all Saturn models simply "Saturns," with designations keyed to their differences: SL1, SL2, SC.

Wetzel got to handpick leaders of his product development teams, or PDTs. They were the engineers in charge of specific parts of the car: the engine, drivetrain, transmission, the spaceframe, the interior, the cockpit, the skin. They also built a Saturn technical center in Madison Heights. Officially called the Saturn Pre-Production Design and Build Center, and unofficially "Twelve Mile" by some and "the sandbox" by others, the facility was where prototypes got built, bodies made and scrapped, engines created and tested. Once it was up and running, seventy-five or so technicians, working with the drawings and directions of hundreds of engineers and designers both in the sandbox and at the GM Technical Center, could build six prototypes in a week, if they had to.

Each product development team was responsible for its slice of the car. Each slice had to relate to all the other slices in order to capture what had been missing for too long from American cars: a single design voice. A single design voice, Wetzel said, was Henry Ford and the Model T, Gordon Buehrig and the Dusenburg, Dr. Ferdinand Porsche and his sports cars, Zora Arkus Duntov and the Corvette, Lee Iacocca and the Mustang. "Cars that changed the course of the industry," Wetzel called them, but cars mostly the product of one man. At Saturn, by contrast, "we needed to capture that single genius in a team environment—what a conflict!"

Ultimately the goal of all systems was unity of purpose, achieving that single design voice of old and creating modern teamwork. The toughest challenge for him, Wetzel said, was protecting the character of the car itself, while maintaining unity of purpose and keeping harmony among his teams. All the forces that had derailed other cars in the recent past had not disappeared. Plus everything was new at Saturn. Accounting, manufacturing, people systems—all made their demands on the car. But if engineering lost its focus on making the best car it could within the cost parameters, which were established at the outset, the game would be lost before it even began.

Coming to
Tennessee

10

The Site Sweepstakes

The Peabody Hotel in Memphis is famous for its ducks. They waddle along a red carpet to the fountain in the lobby, then spend afternoons swimming to entertain the guests. In March 1985, Roger Smith went to the Peabody Hotel for a conference. A good friend of his, Howard Baker, a former senator from Tennessee and soon-to-be White House chief of staff for President Ronald Reagan, arranged for Smith to slip away from the conference long enough to meet Lamar Alexander, the governor of Tennessee. Lamar (practically everyone in Tennessee called the young governor by his first name) wanted to tell Roger Smith why the Saturn plant, which dozens of states were after, should be located in Tennessee.

The meeting was scheduled in a modest room, with no heavy-duty visuals. An easel was set up, charts prepared. Informality was the key, but salesmanship was foremost in mind. The setting of the scene was a bit like the creation of a Jack Daniels' Sour Mash ad, one in which some oldtimers in overalls talk about how "ricks" of charred hard maple give the mash a better taste, or lean back in their rocking chairs and soft-sell how sipping good their whiskey is. The arrangements had that down-home flavor, yet, in fact, rigorous attention was being paid to every folksy detail.

One detail was the easel. It stood too high for Smith, a short CEO. The charts Lamar intended to talk about, charts about Tennessee's central location, strong work ethic, Better Schools Program, and low taxes, might give Smith a stiff neck as he looked up at them. So Ted Von Cannon, the deputy commissioner for Tennessee's Department of Economic and Community Development, hustled out to the Memphis streets, located a hacksaw, and trimmed down that easel.

Afterward, everything went down as smooth as sipping whiskey. Lamar Alexander, a governor who liked to walk among the people in plaid shirts to assure them he was a common kind of guy, and Roger

Smith, an older grey-suited corporate hero who had temporarily steered America's largest company out of the economic doldrums (from a record-setting loss of $763 million in 1981 to a record-smashing profit of $4.5 billion in 1985), even seemed to like each other. Lamar waxed eloquent. Smith, escorted by only an aide, didn't ask many questions. Maybe he was impressed by how informal and self-assured the governor was, or by the fact that Lamar had never flown up to Detroit, like so many other fawning governors had to present their cases. Or by the fact that Lamar had declined, after the National Governors' Conference in Washington the month before, to appear on the "Phil Donahue Show" with more governors to talk about why their respective states were ideal for Saturn. Or maybe Lamar, a recognized wordsmith and budding author ("He's almost an intellectual!" Von Cannon once exclaimed), caught Chairman Smith off guard with his oft-quoted "level playing field" metaphor.

The quote went something like this: "U.S. automakers have been saying that if they could get the Japanese on a level playing field, Roger, 'We can beat them.' Well, you'll have a level playing field in Tennessee."

The exact phrasing has been lost because no one thought to bring along a tape recorder to the Memphis meeting. Regardless of linguistic nuances, Roger Smith knew a challenge when he heard one. It was obvious that his old buddy Howard Baker had led him into this informal but controlled environment, and the opportunistic young governor had tossed the gauntlet down. If GM really wanted to take on the Japanese, Lamar was telling him, Nissan Corporation was making 250 thousand cars and trucks a year just thirty miles southeast of Nashville. Was GM ready to go head-to-head with the manufacturer of the best selling small American "import," the Nissan Sentra?

Roger Smith knew he had better be ready. Since 1982 he had been nursing Saturn into being. Smith might lack empathy for tens of thousands of GM workers laid off from idled plants, but his mothering instincts for new projects with huge expenses and mega doses of high technology was legend. And Saturn was his baby. He'd officially announced it only two months before. At a news conference in Troy, Michigan, he had said, "We are adding a new automobile operating unit—Saturn—to our passenger car lines of Chevrolet, Pontiac, Oldsmobile, Buick, and Cadillac. Not since 1917, when Chevrolet joined the General Motors family have we added a new nameplate." He'd gone on to proclaim 1985 the "Year of the Saturn," a year to "reaffirm that American ingenuity, American technology, and American productivity can once again be the model and the inspiration for the rest of the world." Then he'd gotten to the heart of the matter. A huge, new integrated facility was going to be built. "A learning laboratory," he called it. A New Age kind of factory that would use less materials, less energy, less manpower, and less floor space than other plants, and produce a low-cost car better than those of the Japanese.

To auto industry analysts this was good news. Finally, GM recognized it had to face a crucial question: why couldn't it make a good small car Americans liked better than the competition?

But could the titan of American industry pull off this feat? For years buyers had sneered at GM's entry level cars, refused in ever-increasing numbers to even give them a test drive. Then, when they traded, they didn't look at GM's intermediate or standard or luxury models, either. Falling market share told the story. From a high of fifty-two percent of the market, GM's share had, by 1984, slid to forty-six percent (it would plummet to thirty-six percent over the next five years). Ford Motor Corporation controlled nineteen percent of the nation's new car market, Chrysler Corporation ten percent, and the imports, the majority of which were Japanese, eighteen percent. Saturn meant GM intended to reverse a trend.

After his speech, Smith slid into a Saturn prototype so photographers could take some pictures. For three years select technical, manufacturing, and marketing staff had been working on the little car at the Tech Center. Admittedly, modern restraints—most notably coefficients of drag—had dampened their design options, making the "slippery" look a must. But they might as well have called the prototype a Toy-Hon-Zu. It looked like the various body panels of several popular Japanese imports riveted together. A car virtually indistinguishable from its future competition seemed a peculiar way to reaffirm American ingenuity and inspire the world.

Of course, GM was only doing what dozens of other American corporations had done, or were doing, lately: entering an emulation mode. After decades of raids by the Japanese on American technology and know-how, here was the ultimate counterattack: copying them back.

In the mid-1980s new car introductions weren't what they'd once been either: glamorous, creative, and often delightful events that forecast exciting times ahead on America's roads. The winged-Chevys of the early 1960s, the robust family sedans of the 1950s, and the parade of chrome-bedecked box-mobiles of the 1940s—arrogant, fuel-hungry status machines that slammed the wind out of the way instead of slicing through it—were all memories. Saturn's introduction merely confirmed what some observers had been saying ever since OPEC had almost quadrupled the price of gas twelve years ago. The golden age of the automobile was over.

Although the majority of Americans probably wouldn't have agreed with John Keats, who wrote in *The Insolent Chariots,* "Automobiles are overblown, overpriced monstrosities built by oafs to sell to mental defectives," or have gone along with Winston Churchill, who once opined: "I have always thought that the substitution of the internal combustion machine for the horse marked a gloomy milestone in the progress of mankind," in 1985 many would have agreed that no matter how much advertising tried to convince them otherwise, cars cost too much, they polluted the environment, and they strangled cities in ugly littered ribbons of asphalt. Drive-by shootings in Los Angeles, thousands of dead animals left behind whirling wheels, and 40 thousand traffic deaths a year from 34 million accidents made dents in the auto's popularity as well. Nevertheless, cars also remained incomparable yardsticks of status, sleek pleasure machines, libido strokers with leather seats. They moved you around and sometimes even made the movement thrilling. Yet the bottom line was impossible to refute. Cars weren't magical anymore. They had become sleek, high-tech necessities of ambivalence. Their real power lay in the fact that they created something America desperately needed: jobs.

Press releases following Roger Smith's announcement confirmed that Saturn was not about style (maybe that would come later, some observers thought, and the first Saturn would roll off the assembly line in 1990 looking entirely new and exciting, a car style-conscious American drivers would slide into with a smile). No, Saturn was about change. Saturn was a confession couched as a boast that GM had to change the way it made cars. The company needed to transform its toughminded managers into team players, give assembly-line workers a renewed sense of self-worth, demonstrate that it could build the best car-making facility in the world—all the while making a profit that pleased stockholders.

The timing seemed good. A strong national economy had bred an attitude of optimism after the pessimistic 1970s. Americans were again buying new cars. Yet many buyers seemed to believe that quality had become intrinsic to the Japanese models, like health was intrinsic to dark bread. General Motors' white-bread kind of automobile had lost its appeal to their appetites. As long as total sales of new cars kept climbing, as it had been, GM could probably still make a profit even while losing market share. But the situation could change from year to year. Ultimately, GM was going to have to exert itself. Saturn, a revolutionary new flagship that would lead the corporation into the twenty-first century, said that it was preparing to do just that.

"I'm not a guy who likes change," Chairman Smith conceded. "But we have to change."

Figuratively down in the boiler room, wearing his United Auto Workers hat, Donald Ephlin warned, "If Saturn fails, America is in big trouble."

In early 1985 any way you looked at it, Saturn was a big deal. At inception it was the largest one-time investment in the history of the United States, $5 billion. Six thousand jobs were going to be created in the plant, with an estimated fifteen thousand spinoff jobs at suppliers, many of whom would locate near the plant, or so it was presumed. The future location of the integrated facility, the learning laboratory that was going to help teach the rest of GM how to be competitive, remained a complete mystery, however.

The fact that Saturn was going to be "not too close and not too far away from Detroit," as GM cryptically put it, turned the site hunt into a kind of cloak-and-dagger industrial development tale. It captured unprecedented media attention and generated the kind of hype and drum beating usually associated with national elections and multistate lotteries where no winner emerges for weeks and weeks.

Exactly where was "not too close and not too far from" Detroit, anyway? New York? Missouri? Tennessee? Kentucky? Minnesota? What about the Rust Belt areas of Ohio and Indiana, or even Michigan itself? Throughout the spring of 1985 rumors of large land transactions in any one of several dozen states prompted calls to Argonaut Realty, GM's land-buying office in Detroit. Meanwhile, like country girls vying for a date with the richest guy in America, hundreds of rural communities primped and packaged themselves to tantalize Saturn. Encouraged by enthusiastic industrial development officials, the communities refined their appeals. Rural places competed because few cities had the twenty-five hundred acres GM said the plant would need. Across the Midwest, in dozens of small cities and towns, reporters badgered real estate agents and politicians. Were they in touch with Saturn, they wanted to know, hoping to break the story wide open.

All the hype, exaggeration, jobs, and money made for a quick forgetting that, at least initially, the way Roger Smith had conceived it, Saturn was about process, about how GM had to change the way it made cars in order to remain competitive—not about how crazy Americans can get over a contest.

The first official entry in the site competition was Ohio. Within weeks of Smith's January announcement, its department of development sent in eighty-three possible sites to Argonaut Realty for consideration. Illinois followed with sixty, including a video of one town, T-shirts from a second, and three hundred letters from unemployed folks in a third. Missouri sent in thirteen prospective sites. Governors began flying to Detroit to see Roger Smith. Some promised to pay for the land, others for the highway leading to it, others for job training, others for everything that all the other governors had promised. Missouri's Governor John Ashcroft even left a billboard behind in Detroit. On it was a picture of the ringed planet with some hokey copy: "Saturn, Give Us a Ring."

Eventually, thirty-eight states and a thousand communities entered the Saturn contest. Youngstown, Ohio, even sent a high school band to march in a parade in Detroit. Golfer Arnold Palmer could be heard on Motor City radio talking about the attractiveness of Pennsylvania—at least until annoyed listeners turned the dial.

Spearheading Tennessee's recruitment strategy was Bill Long, the state's Commissioner of Economic and Community Development. Lantern-jawed, hawk-nosed, and "clueless," as one investigative reporter described him, Long was a retired Marine colonel who liked pressure and hated the slow crawl of bureaucracy. Long's command, ECD, had a staff of around 250 and a budget of $11 million. Typically, ECD dealt with clients looking for five, ten, maybe twenty acres. Saturn was in another league. And probably would locate in another state—that was the sentiment inside ECD between the January announcement and Lamar's meeting with Roger Smith in Memphis that March. The sentiment had good cause: the Nissan coup of four years ago. No betting man would have put a case of Jack Daniels on Tennessee's odds of winning Saturn too. Until Lamar pitched Roger Smith personally, that is. Immediately thereafter, the governor directed Bill Long to go for it: two auto plants in Tennessee would definitely be better than one.

To land Saturn, Long flanked standard operating procedure and mobilized an "operation center," a military strategy. The strategy was necessary because, Long explained, "Something of this magnitude, this hot, it moves fast." The operation center enlisted select personnel, including Long's deputy, Ted Von Cannon, used code names for authenticity, and maintained a hush-hush atmosphere.

The operation center worked out of Long's suite of offices in downtown Nashville. The small staff put in long hours, gathering, sifting, and polishing information about taxes, infrastructures, roads, schools, sewage potentials, and water resources of different communities. They sent the information along to Argonaut Realty's offices on Grand Boulevard, across from GM headquarters in Detroit. Long made it a habit to call Argonaut every Friday afternoon at 2 o'clock. He asked how things were going. If Argonaut expressed some interest, say, in a community outside Knoxville, the following week field staff gathered information about the place, the operation center distilled and organized it, and Ted Von Cannon often hopped on a plane to fly north to Detroit. Sending a good-ole-boy courier like Ted Von Cannon, like the informality of the Peabody Hotel meeting, was vintage Tennessee industrial recruitment strategy. A big, friendly, loose-limbed redhead who put callers on hold with an informal, "Can I give ya a holler back," Von Cannon was a good ole boy in a suit. "I kind of bird-dogged Saturn," he once told me.

Hundreds of competing proposals, brochures, T-shirts, videos, and letters found their way to Argonaut's offices. But Tennessee was the only state that regularly hand delivered all its stuff. One day, while Von Cannon was sitting there in a secretary's office with Tennessee's latest report, the secretary, who recognized him by now, glanced around at the stacks of materials. "I knew we were going to get a lot," she confessed wearily. "But not *this* much."

During his trips to Detroit, Von Cannon usually dealt with Argonaut Roger Boelio. Boelio, a five-year veteran of Argonaut Realty's special assignments section, was Von Cannon's counterpart in their respective hierarchies. Von Cannon showed up ready to answer any questions but there were few, which surprised him. The Argonauts seemed to know almost everything about a location before he even arrived with the information. They had obviously done their homework. "Mostly," Von Cannon deduced, "what GM learned from ECD was how it would be treated by government agencies."

Argonaut Realty's official duty, according to Roger Boelio, was "to provide a cost-efficient real estate service to General Motors Corporation." It had been doing that since the 1920s by acquiring land for new plants and expansions. Argonaut's biggest purchase, Boelio said, had been during that first decade of its somewhat clandestine history.

The office had bought ninety square miles of Louisiana timberland to be used in car frames and truck platforms at a time when wood constituted a major component of many vehicles. In contrast to those distant and relatively hassle-free days, Boelio recalled having been at a recent land signing in Wentzville, Missouri, where helicopters hoovered overhead so photographers could take pictures. Below harried land owners were signing options. Wentzville now had a plant that assembled Buicks, Pontiacs, and Oldsmobiles. Like Spring Hill, Wentzville lay just beyond the growth ring of a city, in that green zone demarcating suburbia from country, a region where fertile farm land was sold for development at high prices.

Argonaut's decision to focus exclusively on Tennessee was made in April 1985. Three to five Argonauts worked in the state at any one time. Two made decisions, the others did the leg work. Bill Long and ECD had come up with some good sites, Boelio said, but GM was not too concerned whether the state found the site or not. At a certain stage in the land game, GM usually sent in its own people. Entrusted with the responsibility of seeding corporate growth, often in old corn and hay fields, the agents had special status and were well trained. If they failed at a mission, the biggest economic force in America, aside from the government, wasn't coming in.

That had happened in the spring. For Saturn's future home Argonaut's sights had originally been set on some land outside Lexington, Kentucky. But Ed Houlihan, president of the Lexington Chamber of Commerce, together with Lexington's mayor, a fellow named Scotty Baesler, had said no to Argonaut's request to have a large tract of land discreetly rezoned. Houlihan, apparently cut from different cloth than most chamber of commerce directors, stunned the Argonauts by informing them that the farm land they desired "God wouldn't be able to get for a halo plant." Such metaphorical quotability went hard against GM's grain. Offended by Houlihan's jibe, GM management directed the Argonauts to shift their attention to the next state south.

That a region, or state, would turn aside an overture of development by GM, or any large firm, was rare. Oregon had a reputation as a "no growth" state, and in the East, Vermont passed a first-in-the-nation environmental control law, called Act 250, regulating growth. But such political assertiveness had not caught on. Even its contemplation was villified in the South, where growth was typically lubricated by a willful compliance to the wishes of industry, along with the marginalization of those who criticized those wishes. So in Lexington, when Ed Houlihan uttered his halo quote, adding that Kentuckians also weren't overjoyed about the prospect of thousands of laid off Detroit autoworkers disturbing the tranquility of horse country, it was an unusual and courageous stand. And, as events soon showed, possibly a one-man stand, with a diminishing number of supporters. In 1986 Toyota announced that it was going to build its new Camry plant in Georgetown, just north of Lexington, off I-75, smack in the middle of blue grass country.

At any rate, Argonaut shifted its attention further south. In Tennessee the agents stayed undercover, rented non-GM cars, changed hotels, but did not, Boelio insisted, resort to false credit cards, as some sources claimed. As for the future site, the Argonauts found Nashville "topographically difficult." So they spread out. In the north rail service seemed limited. West of Nashville was too rugged. At this stage in the hunt the Argonauts were still guided by Saturn's original "primary criteria," the ones a thousand communities had tried to fit: twenty-five hundred acres of land, a railroad line nearby, reasonable access to an interstate, adequate water and sewage, and a community "with a good quality of life . . . large enough to accommodate any transferees." But they couldn't find a tract to fit the criteria.

"When people drive through an area looking," Boelio explained, "whether it's an urban area or a rural area with a lot of spaces, they think you can put something here, there, that there are a lot of possibilities. Whereas, in reality, there are not." General Motors' identity as the possible buyer had to be kept a secret because, if word got out, prices would change dramatically. "People fasten on price," Boelio said, "particularly if it's a large company that they think has a lot of money. All of a sudden you're being asked prices that do not make the project feasible." When Argonaut did pick a site it would bring incredible intensity to bear on the property. "Essentially, what Argonaut is doing is collapsing twenty or thirty years of land transactions into a space of a few weeks," Boelio said.

Argonaut's power to transform a place had an almost mythical potency, a potency derived not only from GM's money, might, and connections, but from the expectations created in the aftermath of the announcement that the largest company in the world was coming to town.

Finally, a site in Tennessee presented itself.

"I've got a couple of maps with something like eight thousand square miles of Tennessee between the border of Alabama and the border of

Kentucky," Boelio recalled. "Spring Hill sticks out like a sore thumb. I was driving the car the day we found Spring Hill. It was a nice warm sunny day in Middle Tennessee."

Probably only in America could so many places have wanted something so badly, and gone to such extremes to get it, only to have it end up in a place completely unprepared for it. Spring Hill lacked access to an interstate, had neither adequate water or power, and was far from being a community capable of handling thousands of transferees. Exactly why the decision was made to buy twenty-five hundred acres of rolling farmland adjacent to a bump-in-the-road-town south of Nashville remains a mystery.

The land buy began one day in early May, when Saturn general counsel, Edmund J. Dilworth, Jr, a large, furtive fellow worried about the press tailing him, showed up unexpectedly at the office of Nashville attorney Jim Neal. Neal had become somewhat famous during the Watergate scandal as one of President Nixon's defenders. Dilworth asked Neal, whom he knew, for a little help.

Jim Neal called Maclin Davis of the prestigious Nashville firm of Waller, Lansden, Dortch & Davis. But Davis happened to be out to lunch. When he came back to his office, he returned Neal's call.

"Mac, I've got a man in my office who represents a big corporation," Neal said over the phone. "He wants you to do something for him. But if you don't accept the deal, you have to promise never to tell anyone."

"We were so curious," Davis recalled. "We were dying to find out who it was."

Davis, silver-haired, suave, in his sixties, and a second senior partner, Lawrence Dortch, waited impatiently for the mystery client to appear. Davis represented the state Republican Party, of which Governor Lamar Alexander was the titular head. Dortch was a native of Columbia, the only city in Maury County, twelve miles southwest of Spring Hill. Both attorneys had helped Lamar bring Nissan to Tennessee five years earlier.

Dilworth soon lumbered into their lobby on the twenty-first floor of One Commerce Place, identified himself, explained his mission, and reemphasized what Neal had said. "Absolute secrecy" was a must. And if Davis and Dortch couldn't swing the deal, everything was off.

"We felt like we were CIA agents or something," Davis said.

Dilworth even had a map. It identified a romantic stretch of the Old South just outside Spring Hill. General Motors wanted the stretch:

rich loam, rolling fields, mansions, farmhouses, silos, white fences—the works. Dilworth asked Dortch and Davis if they could option it.

The Nissan land buy had not prepared the twosome for anything quite like this. First of all, the Japanese auto giant announced publicly that it was coming to Tennessee. Then, negotiations for the eight hundred acres in Smyrna, about twenty miles southeast of Nashville, remained in the open, with constant communication between the Japanese, the Nashville lawyers, the locals, and the state bureaucrats who pulled everything together. General Motors was different, however. Despite its intentions of cultivating a new era of teamwork and improved self-esteem in the factory, the land buy was to remain very nineteenth century—which is to say, secretive, with clandestine intermediaries and a front. Secrecy was the key, and paying as little as possible was the goal.

Dilworth had come to the right duo for the job. Lawrence Dortch was not only a native of Columbia, but he knew the Rasbury family that had just inherited Rippavilla, one of the two desired mansions on the tract. Dortch's daughter had gone to school with Martha Lagerquist, who owned Haynes Haven, the second estate on the tract. Haynes Haven, with its eleven hundred acres, more or less, was the key to the whole deal. For his part, Maclin Davis knew the absentee owner of one of the smaller farms adjacent to Haynes Haven, as well as the woman who owned several parcels of land on the border of the tract. Both Davis and Dortch knew the gentleman farmer who owned the four-hundred-acre farm just north of Haynes Haven. His name was J. Ross Cheshire, Jr. Cheshire was an old colleague of theirs, and his son Jimmy happened to be a lawyer in the firm. Finally, making the whole deal seem preordained, the trust that managed Haynes Haven for Martha Lagerquist was located next door to the lawyer's offices, in the Third National Bank. Dortch and Davis simply had to take the elevator down, walk around the corner, and enter the building where acquaintances, totally unaware, were key to the whole deal.

A recent addition to the Nashville skyline, the bank had a cap that aped the Parthenon, a replica of which stood in nearby Centennial Park. Its base copied some of the geometry of an Egyptian Revival style church, the Downtown Presbyterian, that was across the street from the bank's main entrance. The bank and the church were significant polarities in an evolving Nashville. In 1985 Music City was not, as many Americans imagined, a low-rise capital filled with honkey-tonks, cheap hotels, and fuzzy-cheeked singers plugging their amps into gas station outlets so they could croon to the tourists. It had been a little like that twenty years ago, when the Grand Ole Opry was packed with music fans on Saturday night in Ryman Auditorium, the Confederate Gallery with gum two inches thick on the bottoms of its pews. You slid your hands under there and it felt thick and convoluted, like brains. The new Nashville, with its Opryland theme park, suburban sprawl, and delapidated downtown, boasted a number of postmodern skyscrapers while developers and preservationists competed for the future of historic buildings and neighborhoods. Downtown was acquiring what most on-the-rise cities seemed to acquire: tourist buses masquerading as old trollies, restaurants with ferns in the windows and signs on the sidewalks, the homeless shoving their carts, and even a sushi bar along Second Avenue, the city's lineup of Italianate warehouses converted into shops, eateries, and offices. Overlooking all of it was the Third National Bank in which one found the trustees of Haynes Haven.

They knew each other, the bank officials and the lawyers. Nashville remained an old-fashioned city that way. They constituted what James Huhta, a professor at Middle Tennessee State University in Murfreesboro, called "an informal aristocracy of power." Many had attended Vanderbilt University, or graduated from Vanderbilt Law School. An old chum system rooted in a common university and a certain unspoken sense of pedigree made it easier to get things done. As Maclin Davis succinctly put it, "Friends are easier to deal with than strangers, especially when secrecy is demanded."

The power of the informal aristocracy was eroding, newer Nashvillians assured me, yet it still remained formidable.

Even among friends, Argonaut's presence in Tennessee in May of 1985 had to be absolutely "hush hush." Some word might sneak out, especially with so many reporters on Saturn's trail. Davis and Dortch promised to do everything within their power to plug leaks, insure secrecy, and protect the client's identity. Disclosure would skyrocket land prices and if they lost the options, GM didn't want word of a failure here to sour its chances in the states still hoping Saturn might land in one of their corn fields.

A five-man legal team of Davis, Dortch, Dick Lansden, Wil Johnston, and Wes Shofner was hastily pulled together and went to work. Keeping the other thirty-odd partners in the dark wasn't easy, Davis said, but when a client made you feel like you were a CIA agent, not telling your associates what you were up to only increased the flow of adrenaline.

Argonauts Ted Soley and Marilyn Nix initially stayed with Dortch and his wife in a Nashville suburb. Soley and Nix drove a Ford Lincoln Continental. Other Argonauts like Roger Boelio flew down and rendezvoused with them and with different members of the five-man legal team, varying meeting places, times, cars. Dortch led the forays into Maury County, and when he and the other lawyers began showing up at the recorder's office in Columbia, they didn't bring along Dilworth or any of the Argonauts.

Sliding the cloth-bound volumes of land transactions out of their display niches, and whirring the microfilm spools and staring at the display screens as dozens of deeds blurred by, the visiting lawyers did cause some commotion. Local lawyer Robin Courtney thought his old classmate Dortch (as teenagers during the Depression they had marched together to classes at Columbia Military Academy) was checking out his agrarian roots before he retired. Then Courtney realized Dortch had too many of his high-priced colleagues with him for that—after all, Courtney thought, Dortch hadn't been *that* deeply rooted in Maury County. Courtney, a small man with fluffy white hair and the quizzical look of a bird, didn't ask questions though, and the lawyers volunteered no information about their purpose.

The visiting attorneys were lucky in a way. Until a couple of years ago, county land records had been stored in the courthouse basement. The records had been moved across the street to the spacious, well-lighted ground-level floor of the courthouse annex following a restoration project. Moving them out of the bowels of the courthouse and into the new annex had demonstrated renewed respect in Maury County for its most valuable asset: land—as well as a reviving, if modest, appreciation for the county's wealth of nineteenth-century architecture.

Most of that wealth had accumulated slowly, well over a century before, when Maury County had been an agrarian stronghold in the emerging South. Columned mansions had headquartered vast cotton kingdom plantations. Columbia's own James K. Polk made it to the White House championing America's sense of "manifest destiny," the idea that this was a benighted republic, a nation of destiny just beginning to flex its muscles. During Polk's term, and throughout the 1850s, Columbia and Maury County had been significant on the national scene. The Civil War changed all that. As a key transportation corridor, Maury County switched hands five times during the conflict. Death, skirmishes, and the sad and tragic Battle of Franklin marked the region south of Nashville irrevocably. "I wish there was a river of fire between North & South that would burn with unquenchable fury for ever more & that it could never be passed, to the endless ages of eternity by any living creature," wrote Nimrod Porter about the devastation and cruelty of the war in the wake of the retreat from Nashville in late 1864. Reconstruction proved to be a protracted, humiliating ascent, not back to normalcy, but to a new, Northern-enforced way of doing things. At the end of the nineteenth century the discovery of "stink rock," or phosphate, at least renewed the moribund economy. The mining of limestone-based lodes beneath the county's topsoil made a number of Maurians rich and provided hundreds of jobs. But by the 1980s, the phosphate mines were mostly exhausted and the processing plants had closed. General Electric and Union Carbide were the major employers in Columbia. Each had about seven hundred employees. Out in the countryside soybeans had become the major farm crop. Tobacco was still intensively cultivated, although acreage, which was mostly in burley, had decreased over the years because of the labor expense involved in its growing. The cultural highlight of the year was the Mule Day Parade in Columbia, which took place on the first weekend of April.

The antebellum architecture, especially out in the rolling countryside surrounding Columbia, where the real wealth had been, continued to make a powerful visual statement about a heritage and way of life that had been, for the most part, abandoned. The well-known showplace Rattle and Snap, located in Ashwood, had been restored. Other columned brick mansions stood in various stages of neglect, crumbling tokens of an agrarian, slave-powered system. For better or worse, Maury County languished in the shadows, dreams, and romantic tales of its pre-Civil War period of great promise. Something equally grand or equivalent had never come along to take its place.

Whether Dortch or his associates had feelings of sympathy toward the colorful past of Columbia and Maury County is not known. But this was a unique American backwater, a place on the northern rim of the Deep South only begrudgingly edging into the twentieth century. Looking out from the courthouse annex in Columbia at the historic courthouse with its violent past, at the sauntering blacks with their obsequious manners, and at the white gentry chatting through changes of color at the stop lights, gave you a sense of that. Strip-style America had laid down a little of its handiwork between courthouse square and the countryside, but the sole fast-food franchise within a half dozen blocks of the square was an old Dairy Queen. Even it was historic, according to preservation planner Richard Quin, since Lyndon Johnson had eaten there during a visit in the 1960s, when Lady Bird Johnson dedicated the local community college.

After Lawrence Dortch and his associates slid the big land books back in their niches, clicked off the microfilm machines, pulled on their jackets, picked up their briefcases, and departed with their copious notes on the trails of deeds, mortgages, transfers, and encumbrances that are the history of a tract, a stir remained in their wake. Something big *was* coming into Maury County, no doubt about it. Throughout the spring rumors had been circulating about an Arab sheik or a Long Island millionaire buying land, a defense contractor building a plant, and, of course, about Saturn. High-priced lawyers from Nashville didn't drive down here repeatedly and buff the chairs in the recorder's office with the seats of their expensive trousers for nothing.

Cynics scoffed about Saturn coming in—old Lawrence Dortch and his dark-suited cronies were nothing but smoke and mirrors to throw the media off the real location, they said. Reporters thought otherwise. In the *Tennessean,* Nashville's morning daily, they wrote that Maclin Davis's firm was negotiating land options on sizable parcels in northern Maury County for a client the firm would not disclose. But it was probably GM.

"Is it GM, Maclin?" the reporters repeatedly asked the silver-haired and dapper Davis.

"I can't tell," Davis replied in his smooth and drawl-free voice.

A few of the oldtimers who spent their afternoons in the shade of Columbia's courthouse square had a notion mules might be coming back to a region once famous for them. Davis picked up on that. He used the return of the mules as a humorous foil when attacked by too many questions. Sure, it was mules, he said. The mystery client was going to raise jacks and jennies here and ship them to the Third World.

Good ole boys in their pickups spit out a few choice possibilities about the area's future, usually strung together with four-letter epitaphs riding arches of tobacco juice they let fly out their windows. At Lucille's, a popular restaurant in downtown Columbia, businessmen, farmers, reporters, and those with time on their hands kicked all the rumors around while washing down turnip greens, okra, black-eyed peas, Southern fried chicken, and barbecue, pit-style, with coffee or iced tea. They tended to agree that something big was coming in, no doubt about that.

11

Buying the Farms

The pivotal meeting between Lawrence Dortch and the Rasburys, the family that had just inherited Rippavilla, took place in late May in Nashville's Marriott Hotel, the one out by Opryland. Accompanying Dortch was Ted Soley, a tall, pale Argonaut who claimed he was a realtor from Chicago. Soley and Dortch teamed up in a loose alliance to option Rippavilla as Dortch alone had been making little headway.

Until the previous February, an eccentric divorcée named Hesta Petty Munns owned Rippavilla. Munns had died suddenly, leaving the mansion and its twenty-eight acres to her sister, Joy Rasbury. It was well known within the family circle, though, that Trish Rasbury, Hesta's favorite niece, would eventually own Rippavilla. That had been Hesta's wish.

Trish Rasbury, an aristocratic young woman with a musical lilt in her voice and a fondness for cigarettes and coffee, was the curator of education at the Tennessee Performing Arts Center in Nashville. The several times we talked about the sale of Rippavilla in late 1986 and 1987, she remembered that Soley had worn cheap jewelry and a polyester suit to the Marriott. He had a cool professionalism about him—no sentimentality at all—and reminded her of the Prospector, a character in *The Mad Woman of Chaillot,* by the French playwright Jean Giraudoux. The Prospector wants to tear down Paris and replace it with oil wells; he utters such memorable lines as: "Civilization gets in our way all the time." And "the real estate people—you can always do business with them. It's human sentimentality. How can you do business with that?"

Trish Rasbury had been under considerable emotional pressure in the spring of 1985. Her fiancé was ill with terminal cancer, her aunt hardly in her grave, and now these two men, one of whom had been partners way back with her granddaddy in a phosphate mine, were putting the squeeze on her mother and her father. Soley did most of the talking. He told them that the rumors they had been hearing were true. All their neighbors had signed options with the mystery client he and Mr. Dortch represented. Rippavilla was surrounded. Now, if Joy Rasbury would suggest a reasonable price, "We can get in with the package."

The word package annoyed Trish Rasbury. Rippavilla was no package. It was a landmark, an icon, a remnant of history standing on the last of its original several thousand acres. Hundreds of Civil War soldiers had bivouacked on the lawn, generals had eaten their last meals in its dining room.

Within a few years Trish wouldn't want to live in Rippavilla, Soley cautioned. What was coming wasn't real neighborly.

Joy Rasbury asked, as she had at previous meetings with Dortch alone, if the client couldn't go somewhere less fertile and historic. Dortch and Soley demurred; the site wasn't their choice. They were just doing their job. And part of that job was to assure the Rasburys that the mystery client would do whatever they wanted, within reason, to buy Rippavilla.

Breakfast ended with Joy Rasbury promising, "We'll think about it."

But really, Trish asked, what was there to think about? They were surrounded. Her parents were dairy farmers with sizable land holdings in Columbia and Spring Hill. They had never had to deal with pressure tactics or with a mystery client who had front men and deep pockets. Rippavilla had only been in the family's hands since 1961, she said, but they had grown attached it it, felt a sense of stewardship. Trish vividly remembered her first visit to the mansion. She had been six. Aunt Hesta, a stylish woman who had grown tired of Nashville society after a third divorce, had just bought the "historic white elephant," as she called it, from Ruby Davis, the best bootlegger in Maury County. With her mother and father, Trish had driven north from Columbia and into a circular drive lined with trees. "I just remember it being so cavernous," Trish said about the house. "So incredibly huge. They were trying to get the old owner out and the new owner in. I just remember it being awfully cold because it was December, I think, when they were closing on the house. But it was also just wonderful, almost castle-like because there was so much of it. And the rooms were so big. And I also remember some of the prior owner's decorating—how appalled we were with the yellow and purple tile in one of the bathrooms, which we later undid."

A surviving symbol of the romantic South, Rippavilla had Tower-of-the-Wind capitals on top of white columns you could not wrap your arms around, chimneys jutting high above the roof, imposing bulk, and a Greek Revival front. Inside, the ceilings were high, the fireplace mantels Italian marble, the main staircase curved. If the decorating scheme left a little to be desired, it was because Tennessee bootleggers were better known for the smoothness of their moonshine than for the quality of their damask wall coverings.

Throughout the 1960s and 1970s Hesta Munns lived there by herself. Or almost by herself. The ghosts of five Confederate generals killed in the Battle of Franklin in November 1864 were rumored to be in there too. It was classic Civil War ghost lore: eccentric socialite comes home to manse occupied by the heroic dead. The story was wonderful. On November 30, 1864, the generals had eaten breakfast as guests of Susan Cheairs, the wife of Major Nathaniel Cheairs, a French-Huegenot perfectionist who had built the mansion in the 1840s. The generals' commander, the neurotic General John Bell Hood, berated them for having allowed a trapped Union army to have marched unmolested straight through their lines and through Spring Hill the night before. The subsequent day was a tragic farce, a predecessor of the theater of the absurd, yet all too real for Generals Cleburne, Stahl, Granbery, Adams, and Gist. They led about twenty thousand troops in a suicidal charge at Franklin late that afternoon. Hood, one useless arm strapped to his body and one leg amputated, watched from a nearby hill.

One hundred and twenty-five years later the exact legend associated with Rippavilla and the Civil War was a little hazy. Trish Rasbury insisted the spirit of Major Nat Cheairs roamed the manse. Others claimed the five Confederate generals stalked the stairs and jangled their spurs and shouted accusations at Hood for sending them to early graves.

"Civil War kooks," as Trish called them, coveted Rippavilla because of these legends. Other passersby, even if unsympathetic to Civil War ghost stories, were usually impressed by the grandeur of the Greek temple facade amidst the trees.

Hesta Petty Munn had grown old in Rippavilla. She had money, stocks, and she shunned the local limelight. Once beautiful and elegant, with elongated Latin features and jet black hair ("She was like an Auntie Mame," Trish remembered fondly, "totally unabashed about just being herself"), Hesta seemed to shrink with age. "You saw this giant car going down the road and no one driving," Trish said with a smoky laugh. "That was Hesta!"

After she died in February 1984, Rippavilla stood empty the rest of the winter. Meanwhile, the telephone at the Rasburys home farm south of Columbia began to ring. Joy Rasbury listened to preservationists, realtors, and Lawrence Dortch telling her they wanted to buy Rippavilla. Grieving over her older sister's death and reluctant to be rude, Joy took the intrusions to heart. The main difference between Dortch and the others was that he was a family acquaintance, and had owned the mine with Trish's grandfather.

Following the Marriott meeting and the notice that they were surrounded, "The whole thing began to be this psychological charge," Trish said, "especially to Mother." The scuttlebutt around Columbia made it sound like their recalcitrance might squelch a big opportunity for Maury County. "You get to a point," Trish said, "where you say, 'We can consider doing this.' We have no desire to do it. But it's unnerving to think that two thousand acres around you have been sold to God-knows-who." In June, the Rasburys hired a lawyer and began negotiating for what Trish called "corporate responsibility for the structure." They didn't want it razed, or historically bastardized. Because of its uniqueness, the price for the mansion was negotiated separately from the land. "It was a windfall, in a sense," Trish acknowledged, but one that left her and her mother a little scarred. "It hurts every time you drive down the road," Trish said of her trips past Rippavilla after the sale. A bitter Joy Rasbury, who spent some time in a hospital for stress during the negotiations, added, "They came in here in a ruthless manner and put a boot on our necks."

A quarter of a mile from Rippavilla and on the other side of historic U.S. 31 sat Haynes Haven. With six columns, third-story dormers, and spacious verandahs, Haynes Haven had an ersatz *Gone With the Wind* grandeur. Locally, though, it was best known for its horse cemetery, the final resting place for Haynes Peacock, who had thrown off a plow to become a champion; Napoleon Direct, who had broken the two-minute mile; and Billy Direct, Napoleon's foal who had bettered his sire's time and whose record remained unbeaten to this day. Some idea of the stature these horses attained in Maury County can be better appreciated by recalling Napoleon Direct's funeral in 1914. The procession started at courthouse square in Columbia. The bell in the tower had tolled as wagons and riders wended through the city streets past harness-racing fans, past shoeless kids musing over the perplexing question of just how you buried such a big dead thing, past women with parasols and men wearing hats. The procession traveled the twelve or so miles north and encircled the large hole in the ground. As with Lamar's speech in the Peabody Hotel, no record of the eulogy given Napoleon Direct survives, sad to say.

One thing was certain. By mid-1985 little remained to remind a passerby of the legacy of Haynes Haven's harness-racing days. The mansion stood empty most of the time. Martha Lagerquist seldom stayed there. Horses boarded in the stables, but they weren't hers. Despite its two-hundred-head dairy farm with five barns, and several silos on eleven hundred acres, Haynes Haven was not a home. As signs in kitchens around America proclaim, "It takes a lot of living to make a home." Haynes Haven was a metaphor. It was a romantic, unlived-in monument to faded horse-racing glory managed by a trust located in a postmodern skyscraper thirty-five miles away. It contrasted sharply to its older neighbor, a place definitely old South: worn, closed, and lonely looking, waiting for God-knew-who to move in there with the ghosts of those cranky generals.

A rake-thin fellow named Elmer Holt was the caretaker of Haynes Haven. His wife, Gladys, was the housekeeper. Gladys cleaned the mansion, vacuumed the Orientals, and changed the sheets regularly on all the beds, just in case Lagerquist showed up. Holt mopped the floors, made small repairs, and did, as he put it, "anything that came up."

What came up mostly was the grass. Cutting the grass and doing odd jobs, with no real boss to speak of, Holt assumed a mildly proprietary air toward Haynes Haven. In the subtle chemistry of transformation, it seemed to Elmer Holt that by the time the mystery client appeared, he had become as much the master of Haynes Haven as anyone else.

Of course, Holt's attachments were purely sentimental. Lawrence Dortch did not call Elmer Holt to talk about a deal. He called the lawyers for the trust at the Third National Bank. Just how much success he was having with them became news in early July when the *Tennessean* told its readers that the Nashville heiress, Martha Lagerquist, through her trust at the bank, together with the owners of eight or nine contiguous farms and parcels, had all signed options with a mystery client.

By then, Maclin Davis, teaming up with Ted Soley, had worn down Nashville insurance man Jack Brandon. Brandon owned one of the smaller farms. "Come back tomorrow," Brandon said he told the insistent duo, "I'll either tell you to go to hell, or I'll give you a price on my farm."

Davis and his sidekick also tied up Elizabeth Love's ninety-plus acres on the southern edge of Haynes Haven. "They came in here and offered her a price," her husband Dinning Love said about the sale, which took place shortly before Elizabeth Love died. "We got a lawyer," he told me. "It left a bad taste in my mouth."

J. Ross Cheshire, Jr.'s farm was optioned by Dick Lansden, another senior partner at Waller, Lansden, Dortch & Davis. Cheshire had known Lansden for fifty years, ever since they'd gone to Vanderbilt Law School together. Initially, Cheshire told Lansden he wasn't interested in selling. He'd owned his farm, a total of four hundred seventy-one acres, for fourteen years. An operator ran it, raising tobacco and Black Angus beef cattle. But then Lansden had called again and asked to come over to Cheshire's office. He brought along Lawrence Dortch, whom Cheshire also knew, and a realtor from Chicago named Ted Soley. Leaning heavily on the persuasive authority of the informal aristocracy and offering Cheshire, who had a reputation as a shrewd negotiator, a price above market, the deal was consummated. "I got what I asked for," Cheshire told me a couple years after the sale. So he'd parted with the land, the farmhouse with its hardwood floors and L-shaped porch, the barns, the tenant house, the shop, and the outbuildings. He hadn't wanted to let everything go, he repeated, but he'd known Dick Lansden for a long time, and he got a replacement farm, up in Springfield, Tennessee, as part of the deal, reducing his tax bite.

Cheshire showed me an album of photographs of the Spring Hill farm, noting that everything had been razed except for the trees standing by the farmhouse porch and his old red tobacco barn in sight of U.S. 31. "The only reason they left it there is they had told the Spring Hill people they could see rural scenery," he said.

I asked Cheshire if he had been bothered by the lack of disclosure. He said no. It wasn't unusual, and Dick Lansden had told him the client needed a large tract because he wanted to build something with a buffer zone around it, a zone free of beer joints, cheap motels, and places like that. One thing had surprised Cheshire, though, and that was to learn later that Soley never had an office in Chicago. He worked for GM out of an office in Detroit.

"I don't want to say anything about Dick Lansden and Lawrence Dortch," Cheshire said. "But they sat there and let him tell me he was from Chicago. Misrepresenting facts could be considered unethical in any profession."

Ultimately, of course, the Saturn land buy didn't depend on

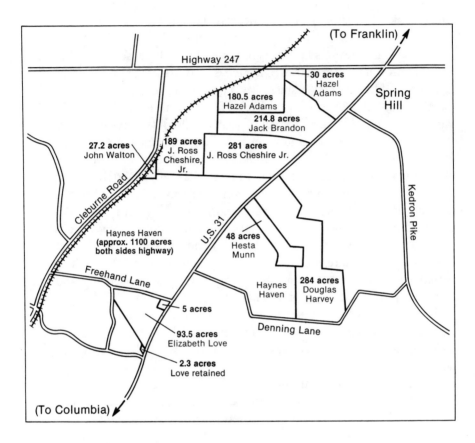

Farms and acreage of Saturn land buy in 1985

Cheshire's cooperation, or on the Rasbury's giving in, or on Elizabeth Love signing her option before she died. The three sales were important, but they were peripheral to Haynes Haven. Its acquisition, ironically, was the easiest of all.

Like the Rasburys, Jack Brandon, and Ross Cheshire, Martha Lagerquist also initially balked at the offers to buy her place. But a sentimental heiress proved a rather unformidable foe for the two persuasive and powerfully connected front men, Maclin Davis and Lawrence Dortch. Lagerquist soon let her lawyers cut the deal. One of them, Vance Berry, had written her father's will and was a co-executor of the estate.

"Martha did not want to sell," Berry told me. "She was very anxious for us to retain the property. And would be very happy today if we had not sold. And if she were the only person we had a duty to we might not have sold the property. But we had duties to both Martha and the people who will succeed her. We had a duty to the remaindermen [people who inherit a piece of an estate after the main beneficiary dies]. . . . We had to look at that obligation as well as our obligation to the income beneficiary. She finally acquiesced. At some point we probably would have seriously considered selling the property over her objection."

At his death, her daddy, Jesse Stallings, left no thunderous directive that Haynes Haven not be sold and had given the trustees broad discretionary authority. "Mr. Stallings was a trader," Berry reminded me. "He had no long-term sentimental attachment to this property."

In 1985 the dairy farm was not making much, if any, profit, so, from an income standpoint, the property was not a good trust investment, Berry went on. Yet Lagerquist had wanted it. She didn't need any more income, but she wanted something to hold onto from her past. "When her mother died, the home place in Nashville had been sold," Barry said. "And this property was the only tie she still had to her parents. And for purely sentimental reasons, and having no need for the money, and no desire to see a commercial development on the property, she didn't want to sell."

"Then why did she?" I asked.

"She got tired of listening to us. You know, their offer got up to a point that Mr. Smith [first vice-president and trust officer for the Third National Bank] and I felt, looking at our responsibilities to all the beneficiaries, including the ones who would succeed Martha, that we were not sure we could defend our position in refusing to sell. We had appraisals. Offering prices were substantially in excess of appraisals."

Berry said he had felt no pressure from governor Lamar Alexander nor from ECD to close the deal. The fact that he had known Maclin Davis since high school and Lawrence Dortch since he had been practicing law also had no affect on him, Berry contended. "We still made them produce the client for an interview. And after listening to that client, and this was before the story broke—and they gave me a fabricated story of what they were doing—I had some misgivings about whether these people were for real or not. I had felt better about it before I met the client."

When I called Martha Lagerquist, she didn't want to talk about the sale. Her trustees had received a big offer they couldn't refuse, she said, and that was that.

According to caretaker Elmer Holt, there was a little more to it. "Whenever it came to pressure, she wasn't to make those decisions," he recalled. "She just walked away from it. She was very miserable."

Holt remembered the day he had been mowing the lawn by the verandah of the mansion and Lagerquist was meeting with some lawyers inside. She'd run outside, he said, and just grabbed him. "Mr. Holt, the bank's forcing me to sell," she bawled, putting her head on his chest. "I don't want to!"

Holt's idyll on the estate ended not long after that. Trust manager Smith ("Whatever he said went," Holt said) gathered the caretaker and the farm hands in the small office of the horse barn. He told them Haynes Haven had been sold. Holt had a few weeks to vacate the caretaker's house he and Gladys lived in on the road linking the stables to the dairy farm.

"Her trust took her to the cleaners," was Trish Rasbury's assessment of Martha Lagerquist's sale. "She backed the Mercedes up to the front door, rolled up the Orientals, and drove off."

12

A Speculation Whirlwind

The weekend of July 27, 1985, Saturn officially came down to Spring Hill and the eleven hundred women, children, and men in the village were swept up in a whirlwind beyond their wildest dreams. For days "For Sale" signs seemed to rain from the sky, and soon outnumbered the school children. Strangers appeared behind folks mowing their lawns and made them outlandish offers for modest homes. A Texan strolling through the village, a beer in hand, was spotted by a Spring Hill policeman. He approached the man and informed him, "You can't drink in the street here, sir."

The brazen stranger looked at the cop like *he* was from outer space. "I'm here to buy!"

"Not For Sale" signs began to appear.

One real estate company set up shop in the McKissack place, the biggest house on Main Street. It had once been the home of Jessie McKissack Peters, a Southern belle whose charms had proven irresistibly fatal for Confederate General Earl Van Dorn over a century ago. Jessie's husband, Dr. George Peters, had shot Van Dorn in the back of the head in another mansion down the street, then escaped through Union lines. Quite often speculators could be seen leaning against the white columns of the McKissack place, eyeing the traffic cruising Main Street. Across from them, chain smoking Camels in his cinderblock deLaval dealership, was John Campbell. He hated the speculators. He saw greed written all over their faces. A 1941 graduate of Spring Hill High School, Campbell was a proud and conservative farmer who milked Jerseys at dawn and dusk, and operated his dairy hardware business in between. Reporters eager for a little outspokenness, which was hard to find in the stunned community, tumbled regularly through his door and into a chaos of used and new parts, catalogs, and junk. "A year ago, I believe the people who lived in Spring Hill were happy," Campbell told one reporter from *Automotive News*. "They seemed to have enough money for what they needed. But once this thing broke, nobody had enough money. The money has changed people."

The speculators could have cared less about John Campbell. They wanted land. If agents inside the McKissack place didn't have any to suit them, they could deal with dozens of other real estate agents who had set up temporary offices in restaurants, rooms, and houses around town. One guy even worked out of cardboard boxes arranged in the trunk of his car.

If you wanted a piece of the action early, you had to be quick. You needed cash or good credit. And it didn't hurt to be up to date on land-option contracts, either, and not so beholding to religious rituals that you put off an appointment in order to go to church. Columbia realtor Cyril Evers learned this financial truth the first weekend. A call at 7:30 Sunday morning on July 28 caught Evers by surprise. Over the phone he learned that a car dealer and a retired banker, both from Sherman, Texas, after hearing that the Saturn plant had come down in an unheard of village thirty-five miles south of Nashville, had driven through the night to get here. They'd apparently picked Ever's name out of the phone book once they'd arrived.

"We want to buy!" one of them informed him.

"Well, I go to church," Evers replied. "Meet me at my office at noon."

Expectations high, after services Evers drove the two wired Texans north from Columbia on U.S. 31. A little over a mile south of Spring Hill they passed six-columned Haynes Haven on the west side of the road and then the forlorn-looking and vacant Rippavilla on the other side. In and around Spring Hill, Cyril Evers stopped here at a farm, there at a house. Dozens of other cars, including several Mercedes with Texas plates, were churning up the dust along the back roads. Eventually, it dawned on Evers: "The smart boys, they spent Sunday morning picking up options."

Late Sunday afternoon Evers and the disheartened Texans returned to Columbia. It didn't seem right somehow that they had missed out on the land-buying opportunity of a lifetime because Cyril Evers was a God-fearing Christian. The Texans immediately pulled out, heading back the way they had come. After they got home, one of the men fired off an angry letter to the Columbia *Daily Herald*, complaining about the ungodly pyramiding of land prices around the future Saturn site. Reading between the lines, what really offended the men was·the fact that smarter boys had teamed up with quicker-at-the-draw realtors and beaten them to places like Kedron Pike, which passed through large farms to the southeast of Spring Hill, and John Lunn Road, which dog-legged east off Kedron Pike and was rumored to cross over land on which the Saturn Parkway would be built. When one of the smart boys spotted Joe Farmer barreling down a dirt lane in a pickup, he pulled behind and followed that pickup to a porch, or a tobacco barn, or a field of soybeans. He enticed Joe Farmer with a hard-to-say-no-to option. Often Joe Farmer heard he could even stay on for one dollar a year, if he wanted, operating the farm until the new owner said it was time to go.

Prices spiraled upward wildly—$1,000 an acre, $5,000, $13,000 and higher. You could buy options at inflated prices if you were willing to deal with the smart boys, a few of whom began flipping their properties before banks had even processed the paper. "Flipping" was a way to multiply profits by arranging for a quick appraisal at an inflated figure, then borrowing against that figure and selling the land; the end result was often a tidy profit before the original Joe Farmer owner even had time to buy a new pickup.

Land at key intersections, or where speculators convinced themselves key intersections would one day be, sold for as much as $25,000 an acre. For many land owners the big question was, "Do I sell now or hold out for more?"

"It was mentally confusing," James Lochridge said of the whirlwind period. "You never wanted to sell, never had any idea of selling. But you got to thinking, Am I the only one gonna be left?"

Randy Lochridge added, "You went to church, that's all people talked about—who got what for his land? You couldn't see anything coming down the road for the dad-gum 'For Sale' signs on the corner."

The speculators angered James Lochridge. He felt they were strangers who didn't give a damn about Spring Hill, and who were making more money off a farmer's land in a few weeks—or even in a few days—than the farmer had working it for years. Not that farming wasn't on the decline in Maury County before July 1985, both Lochridges conceded, but all of a sudden, as James put it, "The temptation was always tugging at you to sell. Say you were satisfied, had no intention of moving—what would you do, you were offered ten, fifteen times what your property was worth?"

Randy's rural world flipped upside down and it would take years for him to get over it. Shortly after the announcement he had gone to a meeting organized by a distraught John Campbell and aired his opinion that cities and farms don't mix. The feelings just leaped out of his heart, he said, and reporters must have scribbled them down. None of them knew where he lived, but the next day he glanced out the window and there, pulling in, was a car from a local TV channel. Twenty-two, Randy Lochride had never ridden a subway. He'd never seen a homeless person crumpled in a doorway (a prospect, he once told me, that made him feel terrified). Suddenly he was on national television, in America's major newspapers. He'd become the spokesman for the farmers who somehow felt betrayed.

James Lochridge tried to keep his son's feet on the ground. But the swirl and roar made Randy's mind spin. When reporters from the *New York Times, Chicago Tribune, Wall Street Journal,* and several television networks all contacted Randy on the same day, "the circuit breaker kicked," he said. He fled to the Duck River and went fishing. Gradually, as the months passed, it dawned on him that Spring Hill was giving up an entire way of life. At a public forum he asked Saturn president William Hoglund what they were getting in return.

Modernity, was Hoglund's answer, jobs and progress.

"I got to the point where I thought, 'I'm the only one saying this,'" Randy recalled of that hard time. "I lost my drive. I thought I ought to just sit down and shut up." But staying quiet depressed him. He began seeing the farm as an heirloom.

Meanwhile, investors and speculators tied up thousands of acres. Maury County's pride, its big farms, suddenly became its vulnerable underbelly. There were no braking mechanisms in place to slow a speculation whirlwind: no capital gains taxes, or land trusts restricting development, or open-space easements creating legal assurances that property, as it passed from owner to owner, would stay open. In Maury County at large no zoning whatsoever existed, although plans were set in motion to change that.

During the whirlwind, farms along main roads and near intersections bucked the highest winds, with the intensity diminishing the farther away one lived from the epicenter of Spring Hill. In short order agriculture as a way of life in Spring Hill accelerated into oblivion, leaving some dirt farmers, like Miller "Bud" Mitchum who pocketed $3 million, rich. Mitchum seemed to have a hard time keeping from grinning. To him and some other farmers the whirlwind suggested a gift from a merciful God. After all, the mid-1980s were a bad time to be living the Jeffersonian agrarian ideal. Many nights you could watch episodes of the protracted tragedy of the American family farm on the evening news. The much talked about economic safety net of Reaganomics, which promised to keep the poor from hitting the ground as social programs were dismantled, didn't seem to be catching farmers. A SWAT team had to go in after an obstinate one wielding a shotgun from behind his overmortgaged combine in Kansas. Grandfather's pistol eliminated one in Vermont out behind the woodshed because he couldn't free himself from the humiliation of bankruptcy. Suicides, stress counseling, and land auctions replaced pull-yourself-up-by-your-bootstraps independence, Grange get-togethers, and church across much of rural America. Tall Harvestore silos, eagerly bought a few years before, stood like blue tombstones above flapping tin roofs. Country singer Willie Nelson started something called Farm Aid, funded by concerts. Musical culture heroes like Nelson and Waylon Jennings sang to raise bucks for farmers so they could eat, exert political action, get legal advice, and handle the angst of bankruptcy.

The Saturn whirlwind flipped things upside down in Maury County. Many normally worried farmers suddenly felt lucky. For them, Saturn meant good weather, equipment that never broke down, bountiful harvests, and high market prices all coalescing out of a crazy tempest into the warm smile and friendly handshake of a stranger with paper and pen in hand. A number of farmers eagerly took that pen and signed their names. Those who didn't, like James Lochridge, often wondered if they should have.

The maelstrom of change offended dairyman Campbell so much that he became the nucleus of that American institution, the Concerned Citizens Group. There, Randy Lochridge made his media debut. Group members met weekly at the elementary school and often talked about the elusive variable called "quality of life." They doubted their children and grandchildren could afford to buy land in Spring Hill anymore. They both praised and criticized the flood of strangers. They questioned Saturn's "need to know" information policy, wondered why there was no construction timetable, and were appalled at the awful, incessant greed.

That fall some figures about the future plant's impact proved easy to come by. The state kept boasting about them in the papers. Saturn intended to employ more than five times Spring Hill's total population. Saturn's annual payroll would be $200 million. The local share of tax revenues was estimated (before the in-lieu-of-tax negotiations) as $4.6 million for the first year. Some $2.3 million was going to be paid in state taxes. Saturn production workers would earn $13.45 an hour and its skilled trades workers $15.49 an hour in a county where the average factory worker made $7.20 an hour. The industrial appetite of the plant would be staggering: eighty megawatts of electricity, five million gallons of water, three million gallons of waste water, all per day.

Amid all the general euphoria about the future, no one, except John Campbell and Randy Lochridge, at least publicly, seemed to feel that preserving the family farm might be just as important to rural economic development as making cars to compete with the Japanese.

For weeks, from dawn to dusk and often well into the evening, the tables and booths of Spring Hill's two small restaurants were packed. Entering the fifty-odd seat Cedar Inn, you might see a cluster of Century 21 Realty brokers wearing their trademark gold jackets and sitting around their regular table. One day a Nashville song writer strolled in. He had penned a little song about a little place nobody had ever heard of becoming a boomtown of twenty-five thousand. "Looking for someone to back this up," he declared, and sought out a record producer among the crowd.

At the Poplar House Restaurant, Freeda Brown beamed at her customers. Before Saturn announced its location, she just happened to have scheduled an auction of her business. "I guess the Lord was just shining on us," Brown proclaimed.

It appeared He was.

The morning of August 8 the two rooms of the Poplar House were jammed. The parking lot was full. Parked cars lined U.S. 31 in both directions. Just like Freeda Brown and her partner Edna Hadley had stipulated in the contract, the Poplar House stayed open during the auction. Freeda and Edna didn't think any auction ought to inconvenience their regular customers. They served a pile of fried chicken, a parcel of fried catfish, and more barbecued ribs than you could count. They sliced dozens of pies, poured gallons of coffee and iced tea. When the auctioneer's gavel came down, they found themselves suddenly $450 thousand richer. David Chen, a speculator from Dallas, was the winner, or loser, or whatever it is you call someone who just spent that much money on a one-level brick square whose menu carried nothing on it for over four dollars.

Chen slipped out a side door. A spokesperson told the media his boss felt all the publicity surrounding this auction had hampered other deals he had in the works. Locals stood around shaking their heads; real estate agents gloated. Not sharing Chen's reservations about speaking, another Texan, who had been the sole bidder against Chen, told reporters, "I'm going to let him have all the high-priced stuff. There's plenty here for everybody." He added that he was moving to

Spring Hill, into the 1870s house he had bought two days before for a quarter of a million dollars.

In the kitchen, Freeda Brown, fifty-four and a lot richer, smiled and propped up her legs. Now that the auction was over, she felt a little ambivalent about the sale. It was going to be heaven not to get up every morning before the sun rose. Yet she was going to miss the farmers and all this latest craziness. Her husband, Clint, he liked to socialize—what was he going to do with all his free time?

Think about buying back the Poplar House, probably. For within a year, the Browns would have their restaurant back, paying a lot less than Chen had given them. By then a popular joke around Spring Hill would go like this:

Question: "What's the difference between a Maury County cotton field and a developer from Texas?"

Answer: "The developer from Texas is easier to pick."

But in August 1985 prices were not yet falling, and the whirlwind continued, implacable, unabated, unpredictable, crazy. The whirlwind fed on itself, on media hype, on human greed. Unknown strangers flew, drove, and hitchhiked into Spring Hill. There were speculators in their Mercedes and Cadillacs, map-reading realtors from nearby towns. There were TV crews and where-can-I-find-a-phone journalists, seven alone from the *Detroit Free Press*. Poor outcasts from other towns showed up high on hope, bureaucrats with too many pens in their pockets came for the state, planners arrived with their visionary schemes no one wanted to hear, often accompanied by experts always from more than fifty miles away. The curious came with their insatiable questions, the concerned with their worry, the politicians because it was good to rub against such an experience in anticipation of the future. Vanguard Saturnites showed up from Detroit, promising, "We want it just like you!" This motley mob with its wants and desires, promises and dreams, swept through and around and back through again, a force of change doing its work on the bump-in-the-road town with its grocery store, bank, gas station, two restaurants, library, and surrounding houses and farms, all identified by a water tower proclaiming this to be SPRING HILL: HOME OF THE RAIDERS.

Two meetings welcomed Saturn to the dimple of the universe—one national, optimistic, and expansive; the other local, skeptical, and anxious. The "Maury County Town Meeting Honoring Saturn Corporation," held on Tuesday, July 30, crammed media, dignataries, and a thousand spectators into an auditorium at Columbia State Community College. Following the National Anthem, Lamar Alexander took the podium. He claimed that GM was a pioneer leading America back to "worldwide industrial greatness," and that Tennessee was providing the new environment for the greatness. Saturn president Bill Hoglund promised that the company would "preserve the quality of life and natural beauty that attracted us here in the first place." Local author Peter Jenkins (*Walk Across America*) reminded the audience how he'd spent five years stalking across the country seeking the ideal place to live and praised Saturn for making the same choice as he had: Spring Hill. Jenkins advised the folks about to move there because of Saturn to learn local customs and traditions, like picking tobacco, so they would fit in, not mess things up.

" 'Picking tobacco?' " one local scoffed after the meeting. "Sounds like Jenkins needs to stay here another three years."

Tobacco is cut and pulled from the plant. Its cotton that gets picked.

Having Jenkins deliver Spring Hill's response to Saturn irked a number of folks in the auditorium. But they weren't really surprised that much. They were no strangers to the fact that few state or local officials understood or respected small-town dynamics and sensibilities. A simple phone call to somebody like Mattie Laura Harris, who had lived on Main Street in Spring Hill her whole life and was loved by just about everyone in the town, would have put a genuine spokesperson up there. Most people in Spring Hill, the truth be known, didn't think much of author Peter Jenkins on his two-hundred-acre farm. He might have a national reputation and even be a good writer, but as for representing Spring Hill, that would take a lot more than three years on two hundred acres and being Lamar's media pal.

The second meeting occurred in Spring Hill because a number of townspeople, including John Campbell, demanded it. Two deputy commissioners of ECD, including the affable redhead Ted Von Cannon, and Lamar's press secretary drove down from Nashville on the order of their bosses, who decided to sit this one out. In a freewheeling and hectic session before four hundred citizens and journalists crowded into the elementary school cafeteria, the underlings made it sound as though the state knew little more about Saturn's plans than you could read in the *Tennessean*, or see on Channel 5 "Eyewitness News." Two remarks from the audience, both by farmers—"What we need here isn't a factory—we need a good rain!" and "I don't want my son working in an automobile plant with beer joints all around it"—eased the tension while at the same time touching important issues. All in all, Von Cannon and his cohorts left Campbell and most everyone else with few answers and a disquieting feeling that those stirring up probing questions at this early date were rabble rousers. For Campbell, the idea that he was some kind of radical just because he wanted answers made him madder than before.

To a few observers, it began to appear that Saturn, rather than a masterfully planned and skillfully executed coup, as the state proclaimed, might have simply fallen into Lamar's lap. A thousand places had prepared for Saturn, but Spring Hill had not been one of them. Now the state, having steered Saturn there in a way, was scrambling to get all the primary criteria into place that GM had said were so crucial. About the only element firmly in place was the already well-documented willingness of state officials, and the seemingly equally cooperative willingness of local officials, to do whatever Saturn wanted. Spring Hill had little input into whatever was going on even though several critical issues, including an in-lieu-of-tax agreement, zoning, water, sewage, and utility questions, job training, and the path of the Saturn Parkway, had yet to be resolved.

The first week of August, Lamar helped write copy for ads boasting about Saturn. He mentioned Peter Jenkins, country singer Minnie Pearl, and *Roots* author, Alex Haley. The full-page ads ran in the *New York Times,* the *Wall Street Journal,* and *USA Today.* Lamar listed his phone number. Investors "looking for a home" were invited to call him.

All this time, in its public statements, GM repeatedly insisted that the Spring Hill site for Saturn was "tentative."

Lamar named a twelve-member Saturn Cabinet Council to ease the impact. A Maury County Task Force was established to coordinate between Saturn, the state, and the locals. Planning, zoning, and building code regulations were hammered out at special meetings to which opposition forces came in good number, fighting restrictions limiting their freedom to do what they wanted with their lands. Territorial feuds erupted between Spring Hill and Columbia as both towns wanted to annex the county property separating them.

Throughout these tumultuous months, the majority of Spring Hill residents were neither attending meetings of the Concerned Citizens nor selling their land for millions of dollars. They were going about their business. Many hoped Saturn meant better jobs and learned that being in the fast lane for a brief while was exciting. Just about everyone in America now knew where bump-in-the-road Spring Hill was, and they felt proud about that.

Spring Hill's blacks, practically all of whom lived out past White Hall (another mansion in town, one in which Jessie McKissack had

brushed past a startled matron and rushed up the stairs to first introduce herself to General Van Dorn) in a neighborhood called Newtown, seemed more stoic than the whites about the future. Speculators weren't making a fuss over their houses, their trailers, or their
gestures at the kind of agriculture that some politicians liked to equate
with "yesterday's values"—a few chickens or goats or hogs in the yard
to tend when the owner came home from work. For blacks, Julia
Haddox, a housekeeper, seemed to sum sentiments up. Haddox told
radio interviewer Lin Folk, "One say this, one say that. It's comin',
it's comin'—that's the way I look at it. Good or not, there's one thing
we can't do. That's stop time and change."

Spring Hill's Mayor George Jones agreed. Newly elected and unpaid, the mayor found himself short of cops, short of sleep, and short
of answers to all kinds of questions his constituents were asking. Mayor
Jones had had an inkling months ago that Saturn was coming to Middle
Tennessee, but he didn't have the faintest idea that it was going to
land right outside his living-room window.

13

The Mayor

His Honor Spring Hill Mayor George Jones was at the wheel of his blue 1979 Lincoln Continental, a relic of an age when cars weighed five thousand pounds, had four hundred horses under the hood, and powered along the asphalt on big tires, snouts high, downing a gallon of gas every few minutes. Three radios crowned the drive-train hump, with little red blips flowing horizontally across one of them like flashing jewels. Blueprints and maps were heaped on the back seat, like so many wallpaper samples. When the mayor pulled into one of his spec houses (he built George Jones Custom-Built Homes to make ends meet), left the baby blue dinosaur in gear, and ran down the drive, white socks showing, I reached down and slid a box of .22 revolver ammunition from under my seat. Was the mayor armed, I wondered. He hustled back up the drive and hopped in. He made it clear he was a little aggravated at the crew that had prepped the drive for the asphalt coming later today. They hadn't done it right, he said. We backed out, went up the street to U.S. 31, and headed south toward Columbia, smoothly, gaining power.

It was November 1987, more than two and a half years after Saturn had landed in the mayor's village. I was spending time with him to see how things were going. The first Saturn was scheduled to roll off the assembly line in thirty-two months.

We drove to Discount Builders Supply, a warehouse and small retail outlet the mayor owned on the strip outside Columbia. He slipped into one office and talked design and numbers with a young fellow and his wife, and I chatted with Roy Caruthers, the manager of Discount Builders Supply, in a second office. Caruthers recalled that two years ago George had hidden right in here. He had been dodging reporters and TV crews, Caruthers said, after GM had threatened to pull Saturn out of Tennessee because George wouldn't go along with them on a rezoning issue.

It had been late August 1985, a time of angst, excitement, and frustration for the mayor. Folks in Spring Hill were badgering him with questions. Neither GM nor the state was providing him with the information he needed to give them sensible answers. With only two months of public office behind him, Mayor Jones found himself being sorely tested. "You had told me this was going to happen," he had admitted to me earlier, on the drive here today, mentioning the speculators, the traffic, and the worry about everything from crime to taxes to busloads of blacks just pulling in from Detroit and unloading, "I would have run as fast as I could in another direction, I never would have thought I was qualified."

He sure hadn't stayed on the job for the money. Initially an unpaid position, once Saturn landed, the aldermen voted the sum of $500 a month for the mayor. Mayor Jones put in sixty to eighty hours a week. Under pressure, overworked and underpaid, he made a few discoveries about himself. For one, a certain tenacity lurked deep in his soul. Being in the limelight didn't bother him much either, since he was kind of a showman at heart. The mayor also developed a simple and effective strategy with which to negotiate deals: "Get all you can up front because we don't know what tomorrow's going to bring." He had an equally simple tactic to accomplish his strategy: "Use the same damn tactic back on them they use on you, and their fuse will burn out."

So, as Roy Caruthers recalled the story, when Saturn had approached George and the Spring Hill aldermen with a request for a discreet rezoning of the site from agricultural use to industrial, the mayor saw his chance to exert some power. And he took it.

It was just a fluke that Saturn had to seek Spring Hill's approval for anything. The site was legally in Maury County where, as of yet, there was no zoning. However, Spring Hill had just established something called a "regional planning area" to help it handle development overspill from Williamson County to the north, the fastest growing region in Tennessee. The move gave upstart Spring Hill serious zoning muscle. Its jurisdiction now extended for a five-mile radius around the village borders, and Saturn clearly fell within its authority.

At Saturn's first rezoning hearing, Mayor Jones and the eight aldermen said no to the company's request. Then the mayor informed the media that he and the board were considering annexing the Saturn site to Spring Hill, which was something they could legally do.

Well, Mayor Jones might as well have stuck some matches between the toes of a giant and lit a couple. The big fella finally looked down. Oh yeah, there was a village of eleven hundred folks right by his feet, wasn't there. A little stumbling could do a lot of damage.

Recalling his role in the ensuing George Jones versus the giant standoff, Roy Caruthers grinned and said, "It was fun."

Once the story hit, Caruthers went on, George became the prey of a massive media hunt. Reporters wanted to question him. Television crews wanted to video him. Why was the giant crying, claiming the little town didn't like it? In Spring Hill, newsmen and crews parked in sight of the mayor's house, watching for him. They cruised by the temporary Town Hall. They drove down to Columbia and scouted out Discount Builders Supply. It was sweltering hot, a Saturday, the media wanted George bad. Headlines the day before and reports on television had shocked Tennesseans, informing them that Saturn might pull out. So the public's expectations had been set on edge. Folks were muttering, You mean all those full-page ads Lamar just ran in *The Washington Post* and *The New York Times* and *USA Today,* bragging about how Tennessee has thrift, excellence, choice, competition, yesterday's values and tomorrow's jobs, all within easy reach of three-quarters of the rest of America, were for naught? Come on, Mayor Jones, what's the story? This ain't no horse and pony show, mayor. You got Saturn talking a sudden pull out? You got the giant from Detroit all upset over Tennessee's hospitality?

Well, you don't know half the story, George would have told them, if he hadn't been hiding out to make the giant sweat a little, to toss a little of Saturn's need-to-know policy back in its face. You don't know how things have had to be done in a brutal, forceful way, how the lifestyle of Spring Hill has been shot to hell. You don't know the downside, and it's time Lamar and Saturn and General Motors did know it, started paying us some attention. The folks in Spring Hill have had to give the most, live with Saturn the most, have their lives changed the most. And what have we gotten for it? Damn little but traffic, greed, and a lot of unanswered questions.

"Hid right here," Roy Caruthers said, glancing around the little office with the girlie calenders on the wall. "Was avoiding reporters. But they found him."

That's when George phoned Caruthers at his house. Said, "Roy, I'm stuck in the store. The news media is at the door. They're banging on the door."

Roy had promptly headed over to help his boss. The plan was for him to get the key to the Lincoln, which George had stashed in a hiding place outside Discount Builders Supply, and then lead the media off on a wild goose chase. But then, on the way over, Roy spotted Mavis Jones, George's wife, and Naomi Derryberry, a newly elected alderperson, on the road. Roy waved Mavis and Naomi down and filled them in on the car-switching scheme. They liked it and followed him. Roy parked his Datsun below Discount Builders Supply in a lot, climbed in with the women and rode up here, got out, and watched them drive off. There didn't seem to be anyone around, he said, so he let himself in the building.

George was behind the mirrored glass, in the office he was using right now to hustle a house sale. His jaw was working some Redman Chewing Tobacco. Frown lines made vertical furrows between his eyes.

"George, there's no one out there," Roy told him.

"They must have just left."

Roy went back out, found the keys, and approached the Lincoln Continental. It was not the one George and I were using today, but its predecessor. It too had bristled with antennas for George Jones never knew when he would need to get in touch with the state highway patrol, county law officers, ambulances, rescue vehicles, City Hall in Columbia, or with his own police officers who not only had radios in their cars but carried walkie-talkies with them wherever they went. Now, hiding out, the mayor was removed from his four-wheeled, two-and-a-half ton communications center. On the road it would have been as conspicuous as a hippopotamus among pigeons. Sitting out there in the sweltering heat, it might as well have been in Texas.

Roy Caruthers slammed the door shut on the hot interior and had barely inserted the ignition key when a young lady with a driver pulled alongside in an "Eyewitness News," Channel 5, sedan.

"Mr. Jones?"

Roy eased down the window. "No way. I just came to pick up his car."

Cruising off, Roy called George on the car phone, told him the "Eyewitness News" team had been hiding out by U-Do-It-Rental. They'd gone back there now.

George quickly snuck out the rear door of Builders Discount Supply, which was out of sight of U-Do-It-Rental, jumped the fence, slid in Roy's Datsun, and drove home.

The media couldn't find Edmond Dilworth, Jr., either. The tough-minded Saturn general counsel had gone up against the feisty mayor who thought his town was getting the shaft, and there had been a communication breakdown. Dilworth's job was to make breakthroughs, which he had been doing steadily until now, not to allow breakdowns.

Dilworth, fifty-four, was under tremendous pressure, no doubt about it. Crucial questions about water, zoning, sewage, roads, planning, local involvement, schools, and infrastructure improvements remained unresolved. General Motors seemed to presume that the state would handle these details as it had handled them for Nissan five years earlier. Yet the two projects were very different. Smyrna was larger, had known Nissan was coming, and worked with the state and the company to iron out the complexities. Spring Hill, on the other hand, was a stunned backwater with a part-time mayor. Maury County as a whole seemed to have little idea of what had hit it. Faith in the state to step in and facilitate things was misplaced, according to Ron Cooper, principal planner for the local planning office of the Middle Tennessee Region of ECD.

"There was never any real understanding about what planning is in Tennessee," he said. Cooper felt that neither the state nor GM knew what they wanted to see happen in Spring Hill and the area. Tennessee's planning efforts basically boiled down to a rent-a-planner, hands-off policy, and GM kept a veil of secrecy over any vision it might have had of the region, a vision Cooper became convinced was non-existent. The state, which had the chance to coordinate some innovative planning on an unprecedented scale, put all its energy into creating a false illusion of control and authority. The real responsibility for handling local problems fell on the shoulders of local officials who were woefully unprepared. Only one of them seemed to rise quickly to the occasion. That was George Jones, whom Cooper characterized as "a feisty little son of a bitch," adding, "I shudder to think if George hadn't been there."

For Ed Dilworth, dealing with Nashville lawyers where secrecy was insured by friendship and avoiding reporters had been a kind of game were a lot different from dealing with local yokels like Mayor Jones. Or, for that matter, the intransigent dairyman John Campbell. Campbell had gotten under Dilworth's collar so irritatingly one day that Saturn's spokesperson, Laurie Kay, had to pull the huffing attorney away from the irate farmer before the two of them went at it. Now, with Saturn's location public knowledge, all eyes in the upper hierarchy of GM were on Dilworth. He had to keep his cool, maintain a blanket of secrecy over Saturn, and walk the tightrope of negotiations with state and local officials. All in all, Ed Dilworth was attempting to be that paradoxical man, the toughminded team player, the kind GM hoped to produce in great numbers at Saturn, and finding it stressful and exasperating, if not downright impossible.

General Motor's position on Saturn at the time, as one inside observer noted, was "a muddle puddle." So Dilworth had cause for some anxiety. Although close attention was being paid to the development of integrated technology, business systems, and enlightened people relationships within the future plant, what went on outside the gates, with the exception of U.S. 31 for a few miles, where Saturn was endorsing a scenic preservation corridor, was given scant attention. Having unleashed forces of change, which were severing the region from its past and knocking it into a psychological and economic limbo, the company, in concert with the state, talked a lot but did little. Behind the scenes the locals were fending for themselves and GM was struggling to make itself competitive with the Japanese. The troubling immediate question—who was accountable for the future here—wasn't being addressed. The prevailing attitude was that the rural backwater was becoming modernized, whatever that meant. Certainly it meant jobs. Surely it meant progress. Obviously it had something to do with quality of life, but which way the quality would go was only mildly debated. In the impending shadow of imagined economic gains, bothersome worries about place just weren't very important.

Given GM's history of plant construction, most of this seemed totally predictable. Typically, a new GM plant meant a six-hundred-acre site alongside a thruway with a chain-link fence around it. General Motors didn't worry much about things "out there." But now, with Saturn, GM was taking great pains to protect the environment inside its gates and declared it no longer wanted certain undesirable elements, like fast-food franchises, junk yards, message parlors, and bars, messing up the rolling rural landscape. John N. Costonis, the dean of Vanderbilt Law School and a nationally respected planner, was hired to guide the scenic preservation corridor. Yet, having had little experience in responding to place, GM proved incredibly naive about the complexities involved. For one thing, GM took no time to learn about the history of Maury County. It didn't bother to hire a local business person to act as an intermediary, which would have eased communications between Saturn and the local communities. As Argonaut had come down from Detroit to find the land, GM people newly assigned to Saturn came down to do what needed to be done. They learned, sometimes very slowly, as Ron Cooper pointed out, "There are all these little fiefdoms down there." Third, GM never grasped the degree of hostility that lurked in the hearts of many local land owners toward planning of any kind whatsoever. And fourth, of course, they didn't know that some feisty little local named George Jones would light matches between a giant's toes, if he had to, to get some attention.

From Saturn's vantage point, the mayor just didn't see the big picture. He was too local, too provincial, too worried about his little one-star town and what it was going through. He couldn't understand that Saturn was going to make life better for thousands. He just wasn't cheering loudly enough over new jobs, more money, growth, and progress.

During the last week of August, with the rezoning vote and Spring Hill's annexation threat still unresolved, Dilworth and the dapper Maclin Davis went to Columbia to meet with not-so-dapper Mayor Jones and Robin Courtney, the elfin-eyed lawyer who represented Spring Hill. Dilworth was not at his best negotiating with a guy who didn't wear a tie and talked with a nasal twang a bluegrass singer might have envied. All efforts to reach an agreement failed, and polite gestures of diplomacy disintegrated.

"They were trying to wear me out," George recalled.

Finally, a flustered Dilworth said, "Mr. Mayor, I don't think you understand. If you don't agree to rezone, we're going to pull the plant out of here."

George fired back, "I don't give a fuck what you do. We didn't ask you to come here in the first place."

Robin Courtney said he was a bit startled. But then George always had a way of summing things up. As for Dilworth and Davis, Courtney had never seen two lawyers turn so pale. Negotiations for that day were over.

Afterwards, George called a reporter and the next issue of the *Tennessean* said Saturn might pull out. "They're tearing our town inside out," the mayor protested in print. "They're tearing the guts out of it." He said he had been requesting a meeting with officials from Saturn, the state, and the UAW, but nobody listened to him. They were only interested in the dirt, he said. And he was obligated to find out "what we're getting out of this besides the traffic. They owe us that much."

Promptly, Channel 5 sent its "Eyewitness News" teams looking for George Jones. Lamar Alexander tried to reach him by phone. But George wasn't answering. The governor's press secretary told reporters: "He was surprised to hear about this. The governor will try to call again in the morning."

George advised Roy Caruthers at the store, Mavis at home, and his staff at the Town Hall to just let Lamar leave messages. Finally, having given the Governor a taste of the state's own medicine, George returned a call. Lamar said he wanted to come down.

"No, I'll come up," George replied.

The next day he drove to the governor's mansion in Nashville and told Lamar that Spring Hill shouldn't be paying the bills and handling all the turmoil caused by Saturn, a plant it hadn't even asked for. In exchange for the mayor agreeing to cooperate with the rezoning, Lamar promised to help with the turmoil. As a gesture of atonement, the governor also invited the Spring Hill board of aldermen to the mansion the following day, Labor Day 1985. Most of them went. He treated them to cake and coffee, which Naomi Derryberry said was awfully hard to keep balanced on both knees while listening to a pep talk.

Within a week ECD head Bill Long showed up in Spring Hill to appraise the traffic. Lamar arranged for Charles Frazier, who had designed Hilton Head off the coast of South Carolina, to come to Spring Hill as a temporary consultant. Another public meeting was announced, this one with the A-team rather than the underlings. Lamar, Saturn President William Hoglund and UAW Vice-President Don Ephlin faced an overflow crowd in the Spring Hill Elementary School cafeteria. Lamar tried to ease worries and stroke concerns. Commenting on the tax issue, which seemed high on the list of people's concerns, he said, "The best thing you can have as a taxpayer is a big friend to pay most of the taxes." Answering a question about Saturn's prolonged "tentative" status, Hoglund admitted that GM wasn't sure Maurians wanted the plant; until the corporation was sure, construction would be delayed.

It sounded like Lamar had GM on his level playing field, but now the giant was procrastinating about kicking off. By this time Mayor Jones and the Spring Hill aldermen, the legitimate representatives of the people, had relented about the rezoning request and Saturn had its approval.

Today, more than two years later, William Hoglund was gone, Lamar was gone, Don Ephlin had turned his attention to other matters, but George Jones remained mayor of Spring Hill. The big guys had started things moving, then left them for the little guys like the mayor to deal with the consequences. One consequence was deflated expectations. Roy Caruthers told me this was his last day at Discount Builders Supply. "I had visions of bonuses, commissions," he said.

"Then nothing happened." He was going to work for the U.S. Post Office.

After George finished talking with the couple in the other office, we climbed into his Lincoln and headed back to Spring Hill. Fifteen minutes later we passed Saturn's entrance. Over the rolling crop land jutted the tips of several cranes. After Rippavilla, movers were peeling topsoil, getting down to a limestone bed for the Saturn Parkway. George turned east on Kedron Pike, then onto John Lunn Road, went beneath the limbs of a big ash, and gestured out his window at a field. "Here's where I want to put one of my fire stations," he said. We passed a few grazing Hereford, fields of green winter wheat, black birds reeling overhead. The fields were James Lochridge's. Soon George pulled his dusty dinosaur over. We sat there, staring out the window.

A round moon hung low in the twilight sky, stripes of pink cloud scattered before it like a designer rug. Earthmovers were silhouetted like scorpions against the sunset. Blazing red piles of coals marked where trees had burned all day. The wind was behind us so the sound of machinery could not be heard. Without sound, the scene seemed surreal. As the light faded, George drove to the new sewage treatment plant. We sat there in the idling car, looking at this modern maw for treatment of waste. When I asked what it had been like negotiating with Ed Dilworth, George said, "He's an asshole."

The mayor was staring at me, I thought, as I wrote that down.

"You know the difference between a Yankee and a damned Yankee?" he asked.

"No."

"A Yankee comes down here and goes home. A damned Yankee stays."

The last two years had been an easing back down to reality. It was as if Spring Hill, and parts of Maury County, like a helium balloon whirled up to great height, had sprung a leak and slowly drifted back to earth. Options on farms and properties expired without being exercised. Businesses started in anticipation of growth disappeared. Doomsayers began muttering:

"Saturn's a sham."

"It'll never be built."

"Edsel."

Yet the entrance had appeared off U.S. 31, with its flagpoles and lights, Ross Cheshire's farmhouse and outbuildings were razed, and in 1986 big yellow earthmovers started creeping over the landscape behind Haynes Haven, working around the clock, flattening knolls, removing topsoil. The machines suggested huge insects at work, and at night, when the row crops were ready to be harvested in the buffer zone, their lights grazed the golden tops of the corn stalks, sweeping them again and again. Toward the end of the year, thirty or so Saturnites were out there. They came and went regularly from Troy, Michigan, where design and manufacturing work was proceeding apace.

Saturn's visible representative in Maury County was Laurie Kay, the company's community relations manager. Accommodating, reserved, loyal, Kay had an office in the northeast corner of Haynes Haven. Twice she allowed me inside Rippavilla. We walked around the chilled rooms. Once I examined window panes in a parlor, hoping to find the initials allegedly scratched there—a dusty war legend claimed the five generals had sealed a suicide pact. This gullible Yankee found only clear glass. Kay said Saturn's plans included making Rippavilla a tourist center. But nothing was firm.

Despite Saturn's laboriously slow start, press releases insisted everything was "right on target."

In October 1986, without notice, however, one cutback had already been announced. Skip LeFauve had broken the news that Saturn would employ only 3,500 the first year, and manufacture 250 thousand cars, rather than employ 6,000 and manufacture 500 thousand cars. The $5 billion investment was now $3.5 billion, he said, with the expenditure being spread over a longer period of time.

The cutback fueled speculation:

"Saturn's packing up and heading home."

"General Motors's worried about its other divisions."

"Vega!"

Laurie Kay repeatedly declared, No, no, we're staying; GM's commitment to Saturn is as strong as ever.

Yet there was no denying it. Like a new star that had flared temporarily in a brilliant display, by late 1987 Saturn had cooled off. Its magnitude diminished. Tennessee's new governor, Democrat Ned Ray McWherter, no longer could refer to Saturn, as Lamar had, as the biggest one-time investment in the history of the United States. The cutback also slowed the momentum of local planning in Maury County. In late 1985 zoning laws and building codes had been passed against staunch opposition. A year later, the opposition again rose defiantly. Why do we need all these anti-American controls with Saturn cut in half, its spokesmen asked. The planners pointed out that although Saturn might be on its way to becoming just another auto plant, albeit one surrounded by corn instead of chain-link fence, real estate prices had not plummeted from their heights, and thousands of newcomers would be arriving, beginning in 1989. Traffic, school, tax, and development pressures would still be tremendous, the planners argued. Their reasoning prevailed, though their credibility was somewhat undermined.

By November 1987, some things seemed back to almost pre-July 1985 normalcy. For instance, Freeda Brown was in the kitchen of the Poplar House Restaurant again. Her husband Clint was at the tables, socializing. Most of the get-rich-quick speculators had left town. The McKissack place still stood empty, but no speculators leaned against the columns. Across Main Street John Campbell had cooled off a little too. Yet Spring Hill had imploded commercially. The hardware store had closed, the farm supply business had closed, the Cedar Inn had closed. New owners who had paid top dollar were waiting for something to happen. Meanwhile, you wanted a pound of sixteen penny nails, some Bag Balm for your Jerseys' udders, you had to drive to Columbia. Despite the deflated economic atmosphere, most locals I talked to thought things were getting ready to bust open again. Argonaut Realty was setting up a house search bureau for transferees. Realtors were getting calls. On the site steel was going up. One project practically everyone mentioned as a harbinger of the future was Town Center Development, located between the Spring Hill Elementary School and Saturn's northern boundary.

One dreary morning I met Mayor Jones at the temporary Town Hall in front of the elementary school across from Town Center Development. Bright-eyed and bouncy, the mayor was in a hurry, telling me to hop in his van. He drove out into the middle of U.S. 31, handed a walkie-talkie to one of his police officers directing early morning traffic, then wheeled around and cut past some hay bales and onto the thick black asphalt of Town Center's main drag. We passed the fifty-two-room Steeplechase Inn, which was nearly completed and scheduled to open early next year. A mini-mall, including a grocery store four times the size of the one across from the McKissack place, a bank, and several fast-food outlets facing U.S. 31, were on the drawing board, along with five hundred apartments. The apartments were going to be ready when the UAW workers and their families began arriving in late 1989. Architecturally, Town Center would have a Colonial Williamsburg look. The Colonial Williamsburg look was a bland blend of brick and gable ends with cursory allusions to the past.

In the distance, on a knoll, men were shingling the cupola on the roof of the future Town Hall. Seemingly big enough for a small city, it included a weight room, a courtroom, offices, the police department, and a community room in the basement. It was being paid for by Saturn's in-lieu-of-tax dollars, which the mayor had been responsible for negotiating.

We drove to Columbia. En route, the mayor said "go-by-the-book" inspectors had been enforcing the new building codes too strictly, making life difficult for small contractors, including him. The inspectors were bored since no big projects had come on line yet, where their skills would be needed, he theorized. Town Center was pretty big, he conceded, but Gateway, for instance, would be real big: a thousand homes, forty-two hundred apartments, an industrial park, and a shopping center. Gateway was going alongside the Saturn Parkway not far from the James Lochridge farm.

In Columbia, we parked a block from courthouse square, just around the corner from the historic Dairy Queen where LBJ had once eaten, walked into Oldham's Fine Foods, and joined a boisterous group of boosters seated around a large wooden table. All the important news and spicy rumors in Maury County originated at this table, I was informed as I got introduced to a mechanic, a radio station manager (WMCP: Maury County Progress, 1280 AM on your dial), a used car dealer, an ad manager, a retired cop, and an accountant from Jackass Junction, a place "they've pretty much ruined," he said with a laugh—"They've paved two roads."

A Yankee from Vermont, the whitest state in the Union, I was unaccustomed to hearing the word "nigger" sprinkle the conversation as regularly as sugar went into coffee and as casually as honey coated biscuits. The men denigrated blacks with a practiced nonchalance, which I couldn't decide was innocence or insensitivity, or some combination of both. I wondered how they would react when black United Auto Workers and their families, blacks with more money in their pockets than these men were used to seeing most blacks make in Columbia, moved into the dimple of the universe. De facto segregation remained an unwritten rule here. Kids attended school together and blacks rode where they wanted on the bus—although that, too, was an image of the past since public transportation was practically non-existent.

Back in the van, George left historic downtown Columbia and entered the fringe world of franchises: a Kwik Sak, an Auto Shack, a Kentucky Fried Chicken, a Catfish Delight, U-Do-It-Rental. We were

Anywhere-Outside-a-Small-City-USA. One arm on the wheel, chewing some tobacco, he said he was worried that none of Saturn's suppliers had located around here yet. He wondered if they'd ever come.

Already it was easy to forget that only two years ago official pronouncements had made it sound as though every man, woman, and child between Jackass Junction and Culleoka, every down-on-his-luck redneck driving a battered pickup, every high school graduate who couldn't read, every housewife who wanted to earn a little fun money— all could find good jobs if they wanted to. Maurians had gradually accepted that the union had a lock on the jobs inside Saturn, but there were going to be all those rings, just like the planet. And with the just-in-time inventory Saturn was copying from the Japanese to cut costs, it made sense that most of the spinoff jobs ought to be within a short drive of the loading docks. In Town Center's industrial park, for instance. Out there at Gateway. And then those jobs were supposed to spin off more jobs, in service and construction. The mere "tip of the iceberg," Tennessee Senator Jim Sasser had called Saturn after the official announcement. Now, here it was, November 1987, and seven hundred men were working on the site, yet not a single supplier had broken ground in Maury County. The thing that had seemed so clear during the whirlwind had been the fact there would be all these jobs. So where were they?

With three years to go, the mayor said, a lot could happen. On the other hand, suppliers might never flock here as anticipated. Lawrence County to the southwest, where unemployment hovered around twenty percent and where land was real cheap, was linked to Saturn by good roads. Why wouldn't the suppliers, when and if they did come, locate there, instead of in Maury County where prices were so high?

After a stop at Discount Builders Supply, where business was real slow, George drove east and by the dry Columbia dam, which sat off to one side of the Duck River. Bleached white from the sun, it suggested a monstrous leviathan with a spillway for a mouth, washed mysteriously onto dry land. We turned southeast, heading toward Bryant Station to check on a spec house he was having built near the Marshall County line.

Sporadic drizzle splashed the windshield from a low gray sky. George chewed tobacco and perched his left foot on the dash, scrunching his knee against the door. He steered with one hand, occasionally taking a Hardee styrofoam cup from between his thighs and spitting brown juice into it.

There was no traffic. Gray fin-like shapes, seams of ragged lime-stone, jutted from wet fields on either side. The limestone underlay had accumulated when Middle Tennessee had been under an inland sea. The risings and fallings of the sea over millennia had layered its bed with the shells and bones of mollusks, crabs, and other creatures containing lime and phosphate. The layers had, through the pro-tracted workings of geology, become brown phosphate blanketed with soil that drew its nourishment, like some rich agrarian sponge, from the creature-rich substrate. About a century ago a stonemason named Bill Shirley had discovered the extensive underlayment, spotting fins such as those we were passing today in an old Union breastworks a mile and a half south of Columbia. Going home Shirley happened to run into the poet John Trotwood Moore. A practical poet, Moore advised Shirley to contact a man he knew in Birmingham; he might invest money in a phosphate mine. Little came of Shirley's efforts to get a backer from Birmingham. But he persevered and soon helped get a phosphate company capitalized. Stink rock, as phosphate was called, was on its way to making a number of Maurians rich, employ-ing thousands, and polluting a great number of American creeks, riv-ers, and lakes on behalf of markets for fertilizer, pig iron, and slag, which railroads used as track bed. Nowadays, Monsanto Chemical Company and Occidental Chemical Company were the last large op-erations mining, washing, and processing limestone in the county and both were going out of business.

We swung southeast after Rock Springs. I asked the mayor about his past. He was born in Erwin, up in east Tennessee, he said, on a hillside farm, the second oldest of seven: four boys, three girls. His parents raised and sold pigs, raised and sold strawberries, kept some cows. To my suggestion he must have hunted and fished a lot, the mayor chuckled.

"I never even had time to go huntin' and fishin'. Daddy always had something for us to do when I was a kid. When he died [George was thirteen], I definitely had to work then. We didn't play sports, things like that. We got out of school, came home and worked. Lots of kids got to stay and play ball.

"We raised our own food, took our corn to the mill, swapped it out. Grew wheat and everything for our flour. Lard—we rendered our own lard when we killed our hogs. We bought sugar by the hundred pounds to make jelly, apple butter. We'd go to the orchard in the fall of the year after crops were in, up in the mountain area. And they would let you pick them up yourself for a dollar or two a bushel.

We'd go up and pick up a truck load, take all the kids, then bring them back and make apple butter, and then we'd have apples to eat all winter long." They kept the apples in a dirt-floored cellar with walls of "old round creek rock. My daddy built the house probably in the early thirties. Built it himself.

"As of October 29, he's been dead thirty years. And it's hard, really, to remember a whole lot. I done what he said. He was a very strict person . . . I felt like. He died with cancer. He was fifty-two years old."

Sitting in an abandoned meadow across from a not-very-prosperous-looking farm was the spec house. Nailed together two-by-tens buttressed the little pediment in front, awaiting replacement by columns. The roof was capped, the windows in. A mason and his crew were laying up brick. An insulation crew was supposed to be here. They weren't.

Cows grazed in the field across the road from where the front lawn would go. A deteriorating farm sagged in the distance. It occurred to me that this would have been a good spot for Saturn: flat, not so fertile, not very historic, just as accessible to I-65, the limestone closer to the surface. It may have been just the spot Joy Rasbury had been thinking of when she had asked Ted Soley and Lawrence Dortch why the mystery client had to own Rippavilla.

"Why they had to built it on the most beautiful farm land around, I'll never know," Matty Laura Harris, an elderly resident of Spring Hill, once said.

Heading toward Spring Hill a little later, George and I passed scattered tall, elongated houses with chimneys on both ends and a simple elegance of line. They occupied a rung on the architectural ladder below the mansions and above the small, slope-roofed cabins once inhabited by tenant farmers and their families, a number of which also appeared here and there by streams, by gray tangles of tree trunks, and on knolls. Most of the tenant cabins were surviving examples of a rural building tradition. Simple, side-gabled homes with usually brick or stone chimneys at one end, they were made of wood or logs, and were mostly empty. Trailing out of the occasional chimney, like a squirrel's tail waving in the rain, came the smoke of a wood fire. We passed through Culleoka, once a large, prosperous settlement. It looked bleak, closed down, inhabited now by what the mayor alluded to as "people who worked a long time for a low wage."

We returned to Spring Hill. Hardly had we entered the temporary Town Hall when an excited woman bustled in and declared, "I'm looking for my husband." Mayor Jones told chief of police, Phil Lovell, a huge beefy man who swelled his blue shirt to bursting, to help her out. Otherwise, the mayor added with a grin, "Come on back, and I'll help you find him myself." While the chief talked to the lady, a fellow in his late twenties, wearing a shirt and tie, came in. He was with the gas line company and wanted to know where the supply line should T off the main to the new Town Hall. A map got spread on the floor. Forming a semicircle around it, the town building inspector Billy Ingram, the gas man, the chief, and the mayor stood there, all staring down, eyes shifting. The mayor stepped backwards, propped himself on the Coca-Cola cooler, unhitched his tape measure, and extended the blade out about eight feet so it hung there, threatening to break its curvature. He eased the tip down to the map.

That was that.

Shifting to a desk, the mayor flipped through town ordinances. Then he had a phone conversation with a builder about what he could and could not do on his property. Since Spring Hill and Maury County were both zoned, a builder needed a minimum of a sketch of the house on the lot and percolation tests for sewage to start construction. Letting the phone dangle from his hand, the mayor walked to a wall of the double-wide and scanned a zoning map. To his right, at his desk, Bobby Ingram was clipping his fingernails. Chief Lovell had plopped into a seat, his elbow on the desk. The lady with the missing husband had left.

"It depends what kind of wild buyers you git," the mayor said into the phone. He listened. "It's hard to take another dummy's move."

Neither the chief nor Bobby Ingram moved. Yet the expressions on their faces changed subtly, as though they both agreed.

The mayor talked big figures: a million dollars, two million, two point five million dollars. He glanced around, eyes glinting mischievously. He advised the builder to check at the courthouse in Columbia to make sure the figures were right.

The head of Spring Hill Sewage and Light, loose-limbed and cheery-eyed R. L. Hogan, came in. The town secretary, young, thin, and shy, talked with Chief Lovell, then with Mayor Jones. Ingram eased up off his chair and peered intently out the window toward U. S. 31. The atmosphere in the Town Hall had a restrained but almost palpable edge of anticipation. The unasked question was what in the world's going to happen next around here? Something new or strange or interesting was going to occur in the next minute. Or at least by lunch time, which was fifteen minutes away. No one stayed still for more than a few moments. R. L. Hogan and George soon got into a conversation about a lady who kept bothering R. L. last week about getting her water hooked up. R. L. said he finally told her, "Git you a couple five gallon buckets, lady." Grinning, George spit into a styrofoam cup he'd picked up. The lady had called him afterwards, he told R. L. "I smoothed her feathers," he said.

We drove to the Poplar House for lunch. George grabbed a table. Immediately, Clint Brown joined us. Clint's voice was gravelly, his cheeks lined with red veins. A number of steelworkers and construction workers in boots and flannel shirts sat around tables and in booths. Next June their number would increase to over twenty-five hundred.

"Saturn's the best thing ever happened to Tennessee," Clint told me.

George laughed. "Clint's a Yankee. He worked up in Michigan for a while."

"Had to leave Tennessee because I couldn't get a job in Tennessee."

Clint handed me his card. It said the Poplar House Restaurant was open seven days and evenings, served Sunday dinners, welcomed truckers. He invited me to eat here whenever I was in town. Once the waitress took our order, Clint said, "George, you're the best public official we got."

The mayor blushed.

Jim Wheatley, one of the six authors of the Saturn labor contract and now the UAW International rep on site, stopped and chatted. Other men stopped, shook the mayor's hand, asked him how work on the Saturn Parkway was going, when Gateway was getting off. The mayor's replies were positive, optimistic. One guy asked if he'd been deer hunting. No, not yet. Our lunches arrived. The mayor had the fried breaded pork chop with pinto beans, cabbage, and applesauce. I was having the salisbury steak with beets, coleslaw, and applesauce.

The conversation shifted to the subject of the new office George would soon occupy. Clint Brown said it would be odd, George having an office. For the last two years, he said, "You could tell it was George driving down the road because he'd be in the middle of the seat, like a mailman."

"For two years I've had my office in my car," George said, laughing.

Early that evening I found myself back in the temporary Town Hall, killing time. Buddy, a patrolman, sat at a desk. Darkness pressed against the small windows. I was looking at aerial photographs of the town, waiting to meet Naomi Derryberry. I walked over to Buddy and we talked. I commented on how much historic architecture there was in Maury County.

Buddy gazed up. He said he lived in the same bend in the river that his grandaddy had lived in. Was restoring his grandaddy's house. "Putting dog houses on the roof." On a sheet of paper Buddy sketched the house, a vernacular dwelling with gable ends. He added a bay window, showed how he had moved a door "to balance it." By then I understood that by "dog house," Buddy meant what I called a dormer.

A part-time policeman, Buddy's interests included geography and local history. The subjects had fused when archaeologists from the University of Tennessee had recently finished a dig near the Saturn Parkway, he said. They found artifacts left by nomadic Indians from the third and fifth centuries. Relating this, Buddy was animated. He gestured with one arm.

"When they started excavating for the Town Center here, the treasure hunters went nuts," he said. "They had those metal detectors."

Clasping both hands, Buddy swung his arms back and forth over the desk. "It made you wonder if there was ever that many troops over there," he said. "They found a lot of stuff, though."

A door opened and Naomi Derryberry bustled in. She was an attractive bleached blonde in her mid-thirties with big, squiggly-framed glasses and a substantial amount of blue eye shadow behind them. She sat on the edge of a folding chair and was immediately as forthright as George Jones.

She was divorced and in love with Spring Hill, she said. Raised in Nashville, she still worked there, car pooling on alternate days, but her heart was here in Spring Hill. Her social life revolved around civic duties, a seventeen-year-old son named Blair, and five sets of grandparents she had adopted on her street.

When I asked about her political ambitions, Derryberry laughed. "I wanted to be the first woman mayor of Spring Hill, " she said. She had settled for alderperson instead, after considerable soul searching. Her husband had been a man who did not like his wife doing anything that upset the status quo, she went on. When they had divorced, that conditioning had taken a while to break. Since then, she had not returned to her maiden name, Berry, but remained Naomi Berry Derryberry.

Having run for the first time when George Jones had, in May 1985, Derryberry said she was surprised she had won. Like George, she originally hoped that while she was in office Spring Hill might attract some light industry and link up with I-65. It had done both of those all right. Nowadays, she hoped she didn't look stupid sitting up there in front of the town's citizens, she admitted. And she did feel stupid some times, she insisted. But that was probably because she was a woman.

Presently, her big concern was the school. Tremendous pressure was building to go regional, to lose the high school because of Saturn and anticipated growth. Derryberry had graduated from a large high school in Nashville, she said, and Blair would graduate with his class of fifty here in 1988. She thought bigger schools warehoused kids. "They need to be individuals," she said, about ten inches away from me. "They have to do something drastic to get attention in those big schools."

The school question had emerged as *the* issue of late. A special meeting called for later tonight would decide whether the town would offer its new recreation park as a site to keep the high school in town.

As I talked with Derryberry, citizens started filtering into the Town Hall. The metal walls occasionally rattled with the wind. Naomi Derryberry smiled at some of the people and occasionally waved, exchanging a few words in her Southern drawl. When she first moved to the village, she told me in a hushed tone, she had been told, "Single men and jobs are about the same in Spring Hill; you have to wait on a death to get one." Now that that was no longer a truism, she didn't know if she liked it. "It's frightening to think Spring Hill has to depend on General Motors," she added. "For Spring Hill, this has been a tragedy they had to deal with. The town was going to change, but not like this." She said she wished there was something she could do to make the future more reassuring for the elderly couples on her street. They were worried about taxes, about living on fixed incomes. She really did feel, she told me earnestly, that the place had struck a chord in her heart. "The people here have been good to me. A bleached blonde from Nashville, they've accepted me."

By this time a dozen people had come in. Buddy remained at his desk. Chief Lovell filled the doorway as he entered. Town attorney Robin Courtney was there. The mayor rushed in, smiling, greeting folks. Naomi waved at him. In a low voice she told me that one of the things that worried her still was how men perceived her. "Some men don't take me seriously," she practically whispered.

As if on cue, an old farmer loped over, bent down and pecked her on the cheek, then talked to her using a tone of voice usually reserved for adults sharing wisdom with a child. She listened politely, then glanced at me as the farmer headed for a seat, her eyes flashing behind the big glasses.

The meeting began with the town officials at two tables butted together in front of the audience, which numbered about twenty-five, mostly older folks. Discussion was brief, all of it relating to hopes that the recreation park site, if donated to the county school board, would help keep the new high school in Spring Hill.

Alderman Billy Kinnard seemed to sum up the feelings of just about everyone in the place when he said, "As much as we hate to lose the park, we hate to lose the school more." There was some conjecture that the school board might relent in its opposition to a Spring Hill site because the county commissioners, who appointed the school board members but were powerless to overrule their decisions, did not like the proposed school site south of Saturn (actually in Columbia since the process of annexation had extended the bigger city's boundaries considerably) much better than those here tonight.

When it came to a vote, the aldermen unanimously approved offering the recreation park to the school board.

Naomi Derryberry then stood and reminded everyone that the 150th anniversary of Spring Hill was coming up soon. A big Christmas party and celebration were planned for December 17, including the installation of a large Christmas tree whose boughs would hang heavy with bells. The names of the families in Spring Hill would be on the bells. There was going to be a slide show of the town's history as well, Christmas caroling, and the official ribbon cutting to open Town Center, where the tree would stand. All the churches in town were donating the ingredients for the huge birthday cake, Derryberry added, her eyes bright and a grin showing her teeth. "George, with all his hot air, can blow the candles out."

That December, watching Naomi Derryberry and several other women organizing the 150th birthday party, I realized that at least the center was still holding in Spring Hill. But for how long?

The "For Sale" signs were still numerous enough to create a feeling that the whole place was up for grabs. Mayor Jones definitely had his share of critics. Some resented all the publicity he had received. Others didn't like his one-man leadership style. Still others opposed the sign ordinance, or the grandiose Town Hall, or complained about the size of the police department, which now numbered seven officers, all white.

No one seemed to be articulating specifics about the town's future, except for developer Larry Atema. Ironically, the birthday party was going to honor the village's past while symbolically transferring its future to Atema's development. From the audacity of its name to the width of its asphalt, Town Center Development promised to be as much a new world for Spring Hill as Saturn was for GM. The big difference was that Saturn was going to be a learning laboratory, whereas Town Center consolidated design elements that had been gutting towns in rural America for decades. Town Center was going to be disconnected from the true village of Spring Hill not only architecturally, but socially, economically, and as a pedestrian place. The town, including the mayor and the aldermen, seemed to be going along with the developer's vision, unwittingly participating in the destruction of their village's vitality.

The village still had its rural look. The streets were shady, appealing byways down which to bike or stroll. The rolling meadows west of town were still dotted with gray barns and white farmhouses. Blackbirds wheeled over green fields of winter rye. Black Angus foraged in the tarnished meadows.

Newtown, the black community east of the high school, also remained untouched. I drove past its small houses, shacks, and junk cars one evening with Naomi Derryberry as my passenger. "A goat lives in that house," she exclaimed excitedly. "Can you believe it, a house with a goat in it?"

Three days before the party, a freak storm blew through the village, flattening the Christmas tree in Town Center and ripping most of the specially made banners off the telephone poles. Awakened by the wind, Derryberry pulled on some clothes, rushed out of her bungalow, drove to the tree and futilely tried to do something to keep it upright. Fortunately, it was tethered. The now horizontal cone, hung with hundreds of bells somewhat horizontal in the wind, did not blow away.

The afternoon of the 17th the weather turned cold. I arrived early at the Spring Hill elementary school, where the event was to begin at 7:30. A birthday cake the size of a small aircraft carrier, with 150 candles arranged in Vs on the landing deck and the number 150 high on the bridge, was being rolled down a hallway to get it out of reach of stray fingers. Derryberry, wearing a mid-calf skirt slit high, bustled around. George Jones's wife Mavis, a local named Jane Watson, and Judy Smiley, who worked for Town Center Development, were the other organizers. When Smiley arrived, she lifted her knee-length skirt, revealing long underwear. She was ready for the outside ceremonies later in the evening.

John Campbell attended the party, as did Randy and James Lochridge, both looking freshly scrubbed. Before the activities started, George Jones announced that Skip LeFauve had called him that afternoon and said he was sorry, but he couldn't make it tonight. Spring Hill's TV celebrity, Bill Hall, the weatherman on Nashville's Channel 4, did come and served as one of the hosts. A solid, happy-faced man with an emotional delivery, Hall stood in front of the enthralled audience and recalled how he would never forget the days he had walked down Duplex Road from Newtown, smelling the honeysuckle, no shoes on, jeans ripped, probably no shirt on either now that he thought about it. He loved it here, he said. He loved the country, the people, the smells. He regretted that his children, growing up in Nashville, couldn't experience some of the wonder he had.

A brief narration of the town history prefaced a slide show the four women organizers had pieced together. The cake was wheeled out, its candles lit and blown out. Gleeful children held plates high for a piece. Then almost everyone pulled on their coats to go outside for the official opening of Town Center Development.

By the entrance off U. S. 31, Mayor Jones flipped the switch for the Christmas lights on the telephone poles lining the main road of the development. Then the tree lit up. About 150 adults and children had braved the chill to witness and take part in the official opening. Several small children clung to their parents' legs. Candles had been passed out inside and now people tried with various degrees of success to light them in the cold breeze. Flickering, and dripping on hands, the candles cast light on faces as the high school band played "I'm Dreaming of a White Christmas." Everyone sang "Silent Night." Larry Atema gave a little speech, thanking Saturn, complimenting the mayor and other town officials for their planning ordinances, and for the roads they were building and the utilities they were laying to serve the future. Then a ninety-seven-year-old citizen of Spring Hill and a lady farmer who had once tilled the acreage owned by Town Center Development cut two ribbons across the development's access roads to the patter of polite applause.

The townspeople started walking en mass toward the glowing Christmas tree in the distance. It was a bizarre scene. Some people still held candles. To our right the Steeplechase Inn was in mid-construction. Naomi Derryberry was smiling, her arms wrapped around herself as she walked. Children burst ahead, laughing. The scene sticks in my memory as a high-water mark of sorts, a night of joyous optimism erected on the past and linked to a future as tenuous as the flames of the candles.

14

Lost Opportunities

Spring Hill deserved to be commended for trying to assert its will concerning the future high school and for celebrating 150 years of small-town history instead of simply giving in to the forces of bigness and growth buffeting it like a leaf in a storm. It helped that many of Spring Hill's citizens were deeply rooted there, and that relative newcomers like Jones and Derryberry had taken the village to heart. Collectively, the townspeople seemed to want Spring Hill to have its own future, its own high school. They were proud of its history. The mayor and the aldermen had also committed the village to planning the future to some extent with zoning, subdivision regulations, and a sign ordinance to stem visual blight.

Saturn's position on planning, meanwhile, had gone from one of concern to indifference. Initially, in 1985, Saturn had encouraged planning. "We want planning, we want zoning, we want the whole schmeer" was the message Saturn had broadcast then, according to Mort Stein, planning director for Williamson County at the time. The corporation endorsed county-wide zoning and wanted a scenic preservation corridor established to limit eyesore development for several miles along scenic U.S. 31 between Spring Hill and Columbia. But despite having Vanderbilt Law School dean John Costonis to lead Saturn's effort, something had gone wrong. Whether it was the local groundswell of opposition to the scenic preservation corridor itself, or the general clamor about private property rights, or simply the realization by Saturn management that they had enough to handle inside the plant let alone outside it, once the scenic preservation corridor proposal was cut from Maury County's proposed zoning bylaws in early 1986 Saturn withdrew from the planning debate. The corporation adopted a head-in-the-sand attitude toward what was going on outside its gates, at least publicly.

In retrospect, spurning Saturn's concern about the visual look of the neighborhood was a big mistake. The Maury County Planning Commission, which had only been established in August 1985, had alienated GM, a company not known for taking sides on something as politically volatile as planning, rather than drawing the company into the process. By cutting Saturn's proposed scenic preservation corridor idea from the bylaws, the commission may have helped get zoning passed, but it also lost the biggest player in the planning game for a short-term gain. Subsequently, Saturn hunkered down behind its white fences and refused to assert any planning agenda, or to even participate in planning.

Why did Saturn withdraw?

Once the scenic corridor idea died, "They were afraid of rocking the boat," Mort Stein said. The "need-to-know" policy stiffened, he added. Power was wielded from out of sight. Saturn's spokespersons parceled out useful information as though it were water during a drought: if you got a little, be happy. As for Maury County's long-term planning woes, Saturn gradually adopted the classic private enterprise defense: it's none of our business. Yet, according to Stein, "Saturn was playing off the state, the county, and the City of Columbia. Trying to get information was practically impossible."

Whether I talked with planners, politicians, community leaders, or private citizens, with rare exception they agreed with Stein that getting information from Saturn was tough. The "need-to-know" policy led to an erosion of trust. There was endless headscratching as officials speculated about the information they couldn't obtain. Feuds broke out between county planning and anti-planning factions about the philosophical *right* to plan. One truth was self-evident: when Saturn withdrew behind the relative safety of its fences, Maury County and the region lost the most influential player in the whole messy planning process.

Whether Saturn sat inconspicuously on a green field site behind Haynes Haven, or on an asphalt slab shadowing U. S. 31 and encircled with barbed wire, it was the undisputed nucleus of change. That change was bringing children to educate, traffic to handle, sewage to dispose of, infrastructure needs to envision. It send ripples of anticipation not only through Maurians' budgets and schools, but through their Southernness and dreams and fantasies. The ripples were unmitigated by the slowness of the plant construction and, once unleased, they produced a rocking, sloshing, protracted transformation in the dimple of the universe, while the force creating the ripples pleaded *nolo contendre*.

Saturn planned well and with environmental sensitivity within its boundaries. The insensitivity toward what was happening outside the gates provoked frustration and led to hard feelings. As a precedent for gigantic rural redevelopment projects in pristine backwaters, the we're-not-getting-involved defense left much to be desired. Nevertheless, Saturn kept insisting it was a good neighbor.

In *The Experience of Place,* a book about altering how we look at and deal with rapidly changing cities and rural regions, urbanologist Tony Hiss writes: "No one can previsualize the effects that large-scale rebuilding will have on the experiencing of an area, because this means trying to previsualize the cumulative effect on a place of years of change and redevelopment." Typically, Hiss claims, even when predictions have been made about development, they are frequently wrong, bringing "widespread distress—after the fact—about the loss of a valued experience." No doubt, if Saturn's management had put forth an agenda after the failed scenic preservation corridor try, any previsualization of cumulative effects would have been a formidable challenge. On the other hand, didn't the corporation have a responsibility to at least cooperate with the region that had not even asked it there but now had to previsualize to the best of its ability what the future might look like? The corporation accelerated several decades of normal change into a few years in the same way that Argonaut Realty had accelerated decades of land sales into a few weeks. Yet no obligations were recognized. Saturn avoided that tough partnership. From Skip LeFauve on down, management held the company line: what goes on out there is none of our business; that's why we pay all those taxes, so local officials can deal with it.

State planner Ron Cooper thought there had been a major internal battle as to whether Saturn should have any external involvement or not. "When Skip LeFauve became president," Cooper said, "they began to look only internally. They had a bigger tiger by the tail than they thought, and they had better pay attention to what was going on internally."

And they had. Inside the gates, control and planning and clear strategies remained priorities, fostering teamwork, trust, and quality. One question went begging for an answer, though. Was Saturn contributing to a repeat of a pattern of mistakes outside the gates whose cumulative impact on people, a region, and on other rural development projects that would look to this one for guidance, dwarfed those positive changes going on inside?

An insight into how planning eventually did make its mark on the region was given by a remark historic preservation planner Richard Quin made while talking about local imbroglios. "Around here," Quin said, "feuds take precedence over all other considerations."

Feuds about planning became endemic. Spring Hill and Columbia, with Mayor Jones and Mayor Buddy Morgan butting heads, went at it over water rights, over the "bigger cities rule" (Tennessee law allows the bigger of two cities to annex land two municipalities are fighting over), and over the site of the future Spring Hill High School. The high school, given growth projections and Columbia's use of the bigger cities rule to expand north to Spring Hill's border, would serve families in both towns, as well as parts of the county neither town had annexed to date. Of course, planning of any kind in a region where people still hotly debated the right to plan could be expected to incite a little drama. Both sides on an issue sometimes preferred to sidestep the legal talk and procedural niceties altogether, and, as Quin once told me with a laugh, "Just charge in with a Rebel Yell."

Having cooperated with GM to bring Saturn to Maury County, the state now pretty much washed its hands of the nitty-gritty details of planning for the aftermath. Planners like Ron Cooper were available for a fee. The way it worked, Cooper explained, was that each county or city or town could contract with the planning office in its region and rent a planner. As you might expect, Cooper said, a planner was often called in urgently at the last minute to resolve a problem that had been months in the making.

"Were there ever conflicts between the development and planning arms of ECD," I asked Cooper in late 1987.

"No," he'd replied. "In fact, there's hardly any communication at all between the two."

"Why not?"

"There's no leadership."

Because of this lack of communication between ECD and the local communities, and the absence of leadership, instead of being a planner's dream, Saturn became a planner's nightmare, Cooper said. He witnessed the failed opportunity firsthand.

Cooper was hired by Columbia in early 1985 to define the city's probable growth patterns, showing officials where to extend city services, including water, sewage, electricity, better roads. Saturn landed and immediately the squabbles started with Spring Hill. Then Saturn curled up tight after the scenic corridor letdown, the state didn't do anything, and Maury County took a licking in the tax negotiations that would, to a great extent, determine its ability to meet future capital expenditure and infrastructure needs. "The poor bastards were stupid enough to think they could go head-to-head with GM," Cooper told me, disgustedly. "That's one of the saddest commentaries on the whole thing. Ed Dilworth spent his whole career beating down the unions."

The going-it-alone route became the modus operandi for the county, Spring Hill, Columbia, and, to a lesser extent because of its distance, Mt. Pleasant, the third municipality. They each had planning commissions, rented planners, cooperated some, feuded. Various types of impact fees were debated. Columbia even hired a full-time planner, along with engineers and inspectors. Capital expenditure budgets were passed and growth management studies paid for to generate fiscal projections on limited information and to anticipate the social problems of growth. One bothersome fact that kept coming up was that Saturn, for the first ten years, would be making flat tax payments that added up to $70 million below what it would have owed if taxed normally. For the next thirty years, from 1995 to 2025, Saturn would be taxed on only twenty-five percent of the plant's assessed value, reduced by depreciation and losses. "For GM, the Saturn represents another step in the ongoing experiment to discover just how far it can lower its tax obligation," Anthony Borden wrote in *The Nation*. "Yet no one in Tennessee seems to have contacted any Michigan politician or community group for advice on the tax agreement." It looked like small businesses, farmers, and property owners—together with the suppliers, if they ever relocated—would be footing the difference.

By late 1987, with the boom still a bust but with zoning regulations in place and inspectors at the ready, the anti-planning forces regained some strength. They pointed at the salaries of engineers and planners, and questioned if planning itself was not the reason suppliers had stayed away and development hadn't taken off. It appeared that the boomtown development model, to which so many expectations of growth and jobs were strapped, was sputtering to a standstill. Planners, developers, politicians—all had accepted the power and truth of the model. Its appropriateness was neither questioned nor analyzed. As Saturn had come out of the blue, the reasoning had gone, so would suppliers, construction companies, new businesses, malls, and, of course, all those jobs. The model had taken on a powerful life of its own. And like anything a place puts its faith in, the model proved hard to let go.

What was lacking was an overall vision of what the future around Saturn should be—or should try to be. What did Maurians want?

Modernization of a rural backwater was the nebulous goal. But the region was giving up its agriculture, its phosphate plants, its distinct Southernness, and its other options. And for what? No one could articulate that. "Progress" and "jobs," two buzzwords of modernization, were the vague catchalls. Maurians were not encouraged to say what they wanted. Little about anything could be confidently previsualized without Saturn's participation. In the atmosphere that prevailed, planning as a concept, as a possible route—albeit a hard one— toward a vision, did gain a little altitude. But it couldn't stay aloft, not without the help of Saturn and the state.

Suspect from the start, "planning" became just another bad word, edging right up there with "union," "Yankees" and "taxes" as something worth feuding about.

Maybe good planning was doomed here from the start, Mort Stein reflected years after the question was moot. "The planning needed to have been in place before Saturn hit," he conceded.

Yet how could it have been, given all the secrecy and fronts demanded by economic development competition? Most corporations were not going to immediately change the way they bought land— that was certain. Planning before things happened still was considered un-American in many states. But pulling together after something happened? Economically, 1985–1987 were strong years to have made headway in that direction, it seemed to me. The truth of the matter was that in Tennessee the political leadership was unwilling to bring pressure to bear on GM or Saturn. The partnerships Saturn was developing internally and with its suppliers and retailers had no equivalent in state politics between the government in Nashville and that on the county level. Ultimately, the absence of planning was a failure in leadership of a tremendous scale, a scale America needed desperately to get some kind of handle on. Without leadership, no broad vision existed. A "window of opportunity" to try to create a new rural redevelopment order had opened. But nobody jumped through.

It was easy to blame Saturn, blame Lamar, blame ECD's planning process that Ron Cooper described as a "circuit-riding attempt at planning." You could blame the car industry, a powerful scattering of companies led by the Big Three whose lack of foresight was the stuff of legend. Or blame the victims, lately a popular way out of bad situations. Sure, blame the Maurians and their rural leadership vacuum and their feuding. After all, they hired the wrong experts, didn't answer the right questions, didn't have the right stuff.

Ultimately, all three parties—Saturn, the state, the region—shared responsibility for not seizing a great opportunity. But Saturn and the state were the main players, at least initially, when the potential was the greatest. The model Saturn was trying to forge inside its plant—emphasizing people, participation, trust, and partnerships—was just as applicable outside its gates. But the company never preached or sold or even encouraged it there. After the scenic preservation corridor bombed, it never preached much of anything to the place it had changed forever. Except trust us—we want it just like you.

One person who did have an alternative economic vision for Maury County, albeit a modest one, was Richard Quin, the region's historic preservation planner. Quin didn't reject the boomtown model, but earlier than most he saw that it wasn't going to work as well as most people presumed. Much of the Saturn-related growth was going to take place to the north of Maury County, he figured, where there was more culture and prosperity, and to the south and west where cheaper land would attract working families. All of which was fine with Quin because he wanted Columbia and parts of Maury County to develop what he called a "Natchez kind of economic base." He wanted the region to turn its historic resources, its architectural feast and colorful history filled with characters even a Faulkner would have had trouble making up, into tourist dollars and jobs that protected the resources they promoted. A major hurdle to his vision, however, was something Quin readily admitted: "Only a few people ever understood the idea."

In early December, a couple of nights after the meeting about the site of the future high school in Spring Hill, I had found Quin in his nineteenth-century Victorian house in historic Ashwood, a few miles southwest of Columbia. Sipping really dark bourbon called "stiff" in the light of his computer screen, Quin was half working on a building nomination for the National Register of Historic Places. You could hear loose tin slapping the roof of his barn and the branches of a large magnolia tree rising and falling on two sides of the house simultaneously. Quin wore a suit, his glasses perched on his head. He turned pensive as he told me he was scheduled to talk to thirty or so wives of Saturn executives at a newcomers seminar sponsored by a local bank eager to get their business. Sounding baffled, he said, "I can't relate to people who will change locations for economic reasons. I can't think of a single thing to say to those women." Quin popped a few hard red candies into his mouth, finished his drink, and got up from his chair. He headed into the parlor for the sideboard, glass in hand.

A postmodern Southern gentleman, Richard Quin was then thirty-one. Born and raised in Columbia, he had grown up in a Tudor bungalow across from the Athenaeum, a city landmark built by a Confederate from Vermont before the Civil War. The Reverend F. G. Smith had used the building as the rectory for his Columbia Athenaeum, a school that drew young ladies from all over the South. During Quin's boyhood in the 1960s, the historic rectory, with its Moorish lines and castellated roof, became a museum. Quin used to cross the street and play on the porches. He had also traveled often with his mother, whose roots were deep in Maury County, on various history missions.

"I was in school," Quin once reminisced, "she was president of the Polk Auxiliary, ran the Polk Home. I used to hang around there all the time." A friend of his mother's was director of the division of archives and history in Mississippi. Quin went on, "She had a job in history where they actually paid her to do interesting stuff. I'd never heard of something like that."

A succession of coaches (athletic coaches who taught history were a tradition across much of the nation in those days) supplemented Quin's knowledge of history in the local schools. Then he attended the University of North Carolina and the University of Tennessee. He was interested in historic preservation but at that time neither school had such a program.

"People didn't even know what that was," Quin recalled. "I had to kind of pick classes that would help me in that later. I came back to Maury County in '79 and started working on a Masters degree at Murfreesboro [which did have a program in historic preservation]. At the time I got a job in Williamson County, doing historical survey work. I worked on that for a while until they got a grant here in Maury County to do the same thing."

Quin became the preservation planner for the South Central Development District just as a state preservation plan was being shaped. Grandly conceived and poorly funded, it allotted him thirteen counties to take care of. All of them were rich in historic resources few people cared much about. He managed to add two more historic districts to Columbia, which had one, lobbied successfully for a city ordinance protecting buildings in the districts from being torn down without a hearing, and spent quite a bit of time on the road in the other twelve counties under his jurisdiction. The scope of the job was grand and impossible, but Quin liked it. He brought a refreshing attitude toward preservation's formidable tasks in a region where humidity seldom let old wooden structures rest. Some of them just had to rot, he felt; that was part of the mystique and romance of the South. Save those that you could.

Before I went to sleep in Quin's back parlor, I made my way through his study, down a dark hallway, past tall windows in the front parlor, and outside. Big dry magnolia leaves scurried across the ground. In the wind tin still banged on the barn roof. Two of his cats rubbed against my ankles. About a mile away, but practically invisible because of the shifting trees and the darkness, stood St. John's Church, where several generals who had eaten their last breakfast at Rippavilla on November 30, 1864, had been buried after the Battle of Franklin. St. John's was one of the places that lent Quin's Natchez-like idea both spice and feasibility.

A week or so later Quin and I went to a High Tea at the Carnton House in Franklin. Carnton was where four of the dead generals had been laid out on a verandah after the battle so their soldiers could walk by, paying last respects. Inside the boxy, rather austere mansion, were gathered some blue-haired ladies, white-haired gentlemen, a few younger people, and several students from a local college. The students, all female, wore hooped gowns to lend the tea authenticity. Maneuvering in the gowns was a challenge that made several of them repeatedly blush.

Quin and I found ourselves in the dining room sipping sherry and port. Our conversation was heavy with war lore. Quin told anecdotes about the hospitality Southerners showed the Union officers, about the wealthy burying their silver in front lawns to keep it from being stolen, about the hunting after the war—with most of the able-bodied men gone for four years, game had multiplied. In his dark suit, hair over his forehead, Quin glanced around merrily; he was in his element. Then he suddenly veered away from history and recounted his first meeting with R. B. Toone, George Jones' predecessor as mayor of Spring Hill. Feeling that it was his duty as the region's preservation planner to introduce himself to Mayor Toone, Quin said that one afternoon he had driven to Spring Hill and located the former Town Hall, a two-room cinderblock building in the village. The door had been wide open. An older gentleman was mowing the lawn.

"It was kind of unusual," Quin said, "pushing a lawn mower in your bare feet. I went up to him, and I asked if he could direct me to the mayor. 'By cracky, you're talking with him,' the fellow said." Quin chuckled. "By cracky," he repeated, enunciating sharply, dimples deep and eyes sparkling, "I hadn't heard that one in a while."

After Quin left the High Tea, I strolled around Carnton in the moonlight. I peered at a replica of slave quarters. I crossed a meadow to the Confederate cemetery, entered the slightly agape gate, then passed through a second gate. There, fifteen abreast on either side, were the graves of the unidentified dead from the Battle of Franklin. I counted ten rows as I walked, each tombstone a small thing about a foot high and not two feet from its neighbors on either side. I counted forty more rows and I reached the end of the cemetery.

Generals Cleburne, Adams, Granbury, and Stahl had all been buried here, then disinterred later, their remains moved elsewhere. General Patrick Cleburne, the highest ranking Irishman to fight in the Civil War ("Men seemed to be afraid to *be* afraid where he was," one of his captains said), had been moved first to the graveyard at St. John's Church. Later, in 1879, he'd been dug up a second time and transferred to Helena, Arkansas, where he had lived since immigrating to America from Ireland at age twenty-one, back in 1849. The remains of less-honored privates and captains and boy drummers were still in this ground, knuckles occasionally touching, knees probably interlocked in places, their lives as dim in the minds of humankind as those of the dogs and pigs that had scattered when the shooting had begun well over a century ago.

An historic marker attached to a post was readable beneath a buzzing security light. Two lights actually, both buzzing loudly. The moon had lifted over them, a third beacon to help my reading. One thousand four hundred and ninety-six men were buried here, the marker reported. And now cars were pulling out with folks in them who had nibbled the wine and crackers and sipped the eggnog and sherry at the High Tea. Radials crunched on gravel. I walked back the way I had come.

I next saw Quin in July 1988. We ate lunch at Lucille's Restaurant across the street from his office in Columbia. Quin, wearing a tan summer suit, a tie, and deck shoes, made a few comments about how Maurians' patience toward Saturn was starting to stretch thin. We crossed the street in the hazy heat just below the courthouse. In his office Quin showed me some newly painted signs for the city's historic districts. We then went out to his car, parked behind the South Central Development District's offices, where you had a view of the dilapidated and mostly abandoned black commercial part of Columbia. He cleared folders and books off the passenger seat of his small Chevy Nova, crammed half a dozen film canisters into the glove compartment, and told me to get in.

The car was an oven. It cooled as we left downtown, passed the Polk House and the West Sixth Street and Mayes Place Historic District, sliced through the encircling ring of franchises, banks, and malls, and entered the verdant countryside. Quin kept nursing the Chevy (Nummi-built, it had a Fisher body, Toyota interior) up to forty-five, but the front end wobbled alarmingly. A sheepish grin on his face, he said, "My tire's got a dish in it. Good tire, though."

We were en route for a tour of the proposed Ashwood Historic District, the centerpiece of Quin's Natchez-like economic vision. The district, in Quin's words, "reflected the height of the antebellum plantation system in the upper South." It included St. John's Church, three intact plantations, eight antebellum mansions, the settlement of Ashwood, and dozens of other significant buildings and natural features spread over twelve square miles of rolling countryside threaded by winding roads. Driving those roads, Quin pointed to tree lines. They defined boundaries, he said. He indicated several trailers and George Jones-style modern ranch houses that were "non-contributing members."

"What are the chances of getting this district on the National Register?" I asked.

"It's going to be tough," Quin said. Most land owners within the district were sympathetic to the nomination. State and national preservation officials endorsed it. But skeptical local officials and developers opposed it as a threat to property rights. If he could swing it, this would be the largest historic district in Tennessee.

Seventy-five percent of the district consisted of the surviving farms and land of the once powerful Polk and Pillow families. According to popular legend, the five Polk brothers divided a five-thousand-acre land grant their father had won in a gambling game called "rattle and snap" from the governor of North Carolina in the early 1800s. The brothers erected St. John's Church as a spiritual anchor near the center of their farms ("They did not call them plantations," Quin rejoined). The Polks played an instrumental role in Columbia's rise as a city of consequence. Their power peaked when cousin James, who lived downtown, went to the White House. The Pillows arrived in this lush and fertile frontier about the same time as the Polks. A military family, they likewise built mansions and farms. They bought slaves. Nowadays three Polk mansions still stood. Clifton Place, home of general Gideon Pillow, retained its quarter of row houses where the slaves had lived, and a dozen outbuildings. An archaeological survey of one of the outbuildings, the necessity—known also as the outhouse or privy—recently unearthed 8,655 artifacts, including pottery, china, flatware, and personal items from over a half a century.

Quin passed by Big Bigby Creek, named from the Indian word *tombigbee,* or *maker of coffins,* and slowed so I got a long look at a couple of mansions. Each had once centered its own world: farm office, kitchen, smoke house, carriage barn, ice house, spring house, play houses, greenhouses, and servant quarters, not to mention necessities. Hamilton Place, built by Lucius Polk in the Paladium style, had a particularly attractive Tuscan colonnade leading from the rear of the house to a detached kitchen, a popular feature that kept heat out of the main house during the summer. Rattle and Snap, built by George Polk and named in honor of the lucky game, was "so ostentatious it would have appalled Hadrian," Quin joked. The house's ten-columned portico loomed at the end of a long driveway framed with white picket fence. Ashwood Hall, built originally by "the fighting bishop," General Leonidas Polk, and later enlarged into a grand manor house set in groves of oaks had unfortunately burned in 1873. A ginkgo tree, at 18' 10" the largest in Tennessee, stood near the former manor house site.

St. John's Church, Quin explained, was still used once a year by the Episcopalians for Whitsunday, the first Sunday after the first full moon after Easter, commemorating the descent of the Holy Spirit on the apostles. Vines gowned the church's central tower. Its famous cemetery now also functioned as the burying ground for the bishops of the Episcopal Diocese of Tennessee. Inside the austere structure, faint shafts of light dropped from lancet windows. The pews, Quin told me, had been fashioned from trees felled nearby. A balcony, where slaves once listened to the deacons below preaching to their white masters, creaked beneath my feet as I climbed up.

We ended the tour in the settlement of Ashwood. Quin directed my attention to abandoned commercial buildings, granaries, tenant houses, a railroad station, then to the Canaan School, built for black students in 1915. A few minutes later he pointed out sixty acres adjacent to his house in the proposed district. Percolation tests were in process on the land for a possible development, he said.

Because of such development pressures and less than enthusiastic county officials, the idea of showcasing the past in a Natchez-like way had not gathered much momentum. In a way this idea was radical common sense: using what Maury County already had rather than attracting the new from somewhere else.

"The crux of the issue," Quin said, "is that historic resources are in the way of economic development." It was a perception that made Quin's job often less than comfortable for him. His belief that an alternative economic vision had a place in Maury County, and that its creation would give people a better feel for continuity, kept him going at what often must have seemed a thankless job.

As for actually establishing an alternative economic base in Maury County, he was skeptical it would ever happen. "I always maintained we had the historic resources of Natchez," he said, but those resources weren't like stink rock; they couldn't wait patiently to be discovered. By the late 1990s Quin warned, without protection and awareness of their uniqueness, many would be gone.

Although he often joked about Saturn, Quin was only mildly critical of the project. He recognized that the plant was a boon and appreciated that its impact on what had been a sleepy place draped almost suffocatingly in its own history was gradually making people appreciate the preciousness of what they had so long taken for granted.

Late that July afternoon we drove to Spring Hill along back roads. On both sides trumpeter vine and prairie coneflower bloomed. Quin kept inching close to forty-five, then slowing down to stop the wobble of his Chevy's front end. Sweeping a hand toward some ox-eye daisies on the roadside, he said, "They aren't indigenous. Union soldiers probably brought the seeds in the fodder they lugged south."

By Mayor Jones's brick ranch, Quin turned right onto the black asphalt of Town Center. He veered up toward the columned new Town Hall. He had seen Mayor Jones on TV last week, he said, dedicating the large brick building.

"He didn't look happy," Quin said.

We passed the intersection where the Christmas tree had almost blown away before the 150th anniversary celebration of the town and approached the Steeplechase Inn. Slowing, Quin brushed the hair off his forehead. "Spring Hill has a richer heritage than any place you could imagine," he said sarcastically. "And they built shades of Inigo Jones." He was alluding to the exaggerated formality inappropriately adopted by Town Center and comparing it to the courtly style of Jones, a seventeenth-century English architect.

The New Plant and
the Newcomers

15

One Hundred Acres Under Roof

During much of 1988, if you had climbed to the white cupola perched on the roof of the new Spring Hill Town Hall, you could have seen, about a mile to the southwest, a red steel frame being sheathed in blue. It was the powertrain building, where Saturn's engines and transmissions would be made. Powertrain was going to be the first of the four buildings completed in the complex.

That January the building had had something called a "topping out," a party of sorts, celebrating the web of steel finally covering 1.1 million square feet of rock. The last beam of the massive frame had been lowered into place by a crane and bolted, then steelworkers in thick overalls had lined up behind a pleased Skip LeFauve and some of the construction management for a photo opportunity. Above their hard hats, lashed to one of the beams, was a small fir, a traditional builder's symbol for good luck.

In March 1988 the first powertrain machinery, a die-casting unit, arrived. A forty-two-wheel truck hauled it down I-75 from a factory in Michigan. A furnace to melt aluminum soon followed so casts could be poured. Lamar's successor, Ned Ray McWherter, a heavy-set fellow with rural roots in West Tennessee, led a junket down to see the plant that March as well. A Democrat who had bragged during his campaign that he ate Vanilla wafers and washed them down with coffee for breakfast, Ned Ray McWherter was a guest of CSX Transportation, which had built the Saturn spur off its tracks. Legislators, lobbyists, and reporters received CSX engineer caps and whistles for the ride from Nashville. Once the train rolled onto the site, the dignitaries and reporters were bussed to the powertrain building. There Ned Ray looked around and declared, "Saturn is building a massive, massive plant."

By this time the Saturn Parkway—cost: $27 million, paid for by the State of Tennessee—had taken rough shape across five miles of farmland. Tall TVA electricity towers stood in a line leading to the horizon. Powertrain had reached sixty percent of completion; it needed to be up and running first because much of its state-of-the-art equipment, including the risky lost-foam foundry, was going to need lengthy fine-tuning.

Now Saturn had the money to make sure the fine-tuning occurred. The so-called "high-risk period," the years 1985–1987, during which Saturn's future seemed, despite constant reassurances from GM, anything but guaranteed, were over. In December 1987 GM's board of directors had finally committed $2 billion to construction and development. Later that month Skip LeFauve publicly acknowledged that the Toy-Hon-Zu Roger Smith had driven around in 1985—a car that "looked like the guy who designed the front didn't talk to the guy who designed the back," LeFauve joked—was being redesigned. LeFauve referred to the redesign as a "phantom car." It wasn't something Batman might want to hop in, but an imaginary vehicle being pieced together in the minds of the design staff, a vehicle that consolidated all the latest and best features of the competition. In other words, a much-improved Toy-Hon-Zu.

On March 1, 1988, Saturn's Recruiting, Application, Screening, and Selection department, known as RASS, officially kicked off the hiring campaign at a plant in Willow Springs, Illinois, the first of 136 UAW-affiliated GM factories to be visited. The curious got brochures, saw a video, and had a question/answer session with the RASS reps.

No company had ever relocated this many blue-collar workers before: three thousand initially, with thousands more to follow once production began in 1990. The RASS reps emphasized that Saturn was a great opportunity, but not for everybody. Both active and laid-off UAW members could apply. Applicants had to pass a screening process, be interviewed, and undergo an orientation, all the while demonstrating they could accept more-than-traditional responsibility levels and work as team members. It sounded like a big change from the way most workers had been hired at GM, which typically required only a breathing test: you were breathing, you were in. Those who were hired would leave their seniority behind and accept a lower base pay, but with a reward system linked to production. Saturn would have no hourly rates and no time clocks—a dramatic change—and there were only two job categories: operating technicians whose starting pay was $27,976, and trade technicians whose starting pay was $32,219. Although wages were twenty percent lower than for similar work in other GM/UAW plants, the benefits, including pension plan, health insurance, and paid vacations, would be much the same.

If good people made good cars and if Saturn was going to elevate people above technology, obviously hiring the right people at the beginning was crucial. Especially given the fact that Saturn, in exchange for new work rules, greater expectations, and lower starting pay, was also guaranteeing a lifetime job for those willing to take the leap.

Keeping with the Saturn philosophy, RASS was a partnership between GM and the UAW and went about its work in a new way. The main hurdle, again, was GM and the past. Because RASS had to hire from within GM, every prospect already had a good dose of the old world, with its work rules, grievance procedures, and time clocks, as well as occasional in-plant sabotage, alcohol and drug abuse, and an often distressing indifference to quality. Spokespersons from RASS emphasized that at Saturn training was a priority and would continue as part of the job, as *zaizan,* or continuous improvement, to create a different kind of work force.

In Maury County the prospect of Saturnites actually arriving rekindled talk that the boom was about to begin. Of course, with over two thousand construction workers already on site, Spring Hill looked pretty busy anyway, especially in the mornings and late in the afternoons. A few thousand construction workers leaving a dusty site during a drought had a powerful thirst, so the parking lot of the Spring Hill market, the best place to buy beer, was extraordinarily busy.

The UAW also got a lot of press in Tennessee that hot dry summer of 1988. Union organizers in Smyrna boasted they'd have the Nissan plant organized before Saturn opened. All summer long, accusations flew back and forth between the union and Nissan management about lying and pressure tactics. The feuding awoke old suspicions and resentments many Maurians had about unions and union members. The feud reminded some folks that these newcomers moving in weren't only Yankees, they were union Yankees.

There was also a lot of grumbling about Spring Hill's becoming a speed trap. In July alone, the village cops gave out nearly seven hundred speeding tickets, justifying the reputation.

At Fox's Barber Shop next to the Polar House Restaurant, Larry Fox, the proprietor for twenty-one years, regarded the goings on with a somewhat jaundiced eye. Fox recalled the real whirlwind days, the greedy speculators, the wild expectations, the unrealized predictions, and the long-festering disappointments. "You can't look into the future," he observed. "But a lot of people are trying. It's got people all mixed up." Recounting the subtle but pervasive changes in the village, including the loss of its commercial vitality, the closing of the single gas station, the long wait that had gone on for how long now—three and a half years?—for something to happen, Larry Fox was less than impressed. "Things seem to have gone backward instead of forward," he said.

Realtors begged to differ. Things were heating up, they insisted.

Judy Langsdon, Maury County's community development director, urged caution. "We expect growth to be incremental, not boom-type," she said. "I think we were all overly optimistic in the beginning."

Argonaut Realty was back in the county. The special office that had acquired the site had been contracted by RASS to relocate the Saturn work force, both union and non-union types. Prior to moving people, Argonaut sent letters to realtors, advising them it was seeking quality agents to sell land and houses. First, though, an agent had to attend a training session and some agents weren't big on that.

"Shit, after thirty-five years I didn't figure I needed any training," Cyril Evers said. By mid-1988 the realtor and small-time developer who had missed out on the initial land buy the weekend of July 27, 1985, was even more pessimistic about Saturn. Now, if Evers endured a training session and was a quality salesman, Argonaut Realty was telling him it was going to pass along prospects—all Evers had to do was pay a twenty-five percent commission on every sale. He refused.

One Saturnite who received a free overnight stay at the Holiday Inn in Columbia, paid for by a realtor who showed him around, was Billy Joe Horan, the technician who worked on the first Saturn prototypes at the GM Tech Center in 1984. One of the first transfers South, Horan bought a new home in the Stirling Heights section of Columbia. To his dismay he discovered there were two price lists in town. "Soon as they learned you were from Saturn, they went to list B," Horan said. "Too many people around here thought the Saturn people were rich."

Claudia Dunavant, a former community development programs manager for the South Central Development District, was hired to assist with the relocations. Dunavant located over a hundred Saturnites, but got into a feud with UAW International Representative Jim Wheatley and eventually lost her job. A native of nearby Giles City, she had landed the rare inside job for two reasons. First, she had gotten to know Saturn's Laurie Kay in her official capacity as community programs manager, and second she had good contacts in the region since she had been a reporter at the Columbia *Daily Herald* before going to work for SCDD. When Dunavant had first met Kay, Saturn's community liaison had been accommodating but reserved. Kay's job was to deal with the media. She also made speeches to civic groups in and around Maury County. In 1986 the two women spent quite a bit of time together promoting Tennessee's Homecoming celebration. "We were famous in our region," Dunavant recalled. "Every little wide spot in the road knew us."

Knowing officials and being known in wide spots of the road eventually brought Dunavant to the attention of Argonaut Realty. Two Argonauts showed up at Dunavant's office at SCDD, she recalled, and made her feel important because she was familiar with the region's elected officials, media, and power brokers. Charmed, "I helped them waltz right into communities," Dunavant said. She was surprised to learn, however, that Argonaut had little experience relocating union, or "rep" workers; it usually worked with "non-reps," or executives. Yet the special office had bid the job of relocating the most blue-collar workers in industrial history and had gotten it. According to Dunavant, few of the Argonauts in Tennessee seemed to understand who they were moving as rep workers, or where they were moving them to.

To remedy their ignorance a little, Argonaut offered her a job because she knew the ropes. In early 1988, she accepted. Once Dunavant took the job, she found out it had been offered over Jim Wheatley's objections. And he, she once told me, was "a BMOC, a big man on campus." Wheatley had definite ideas of who should be working the front lines of the relocation effort, and it wasn't her. The UAW International rep wanted some women he knew in Detroit to be doing the job.

Dunavant went to work in one of the RASS trailers on the site. Many Saturnites whom she relocated did not fit the image Maurians had of their future neighbors, particularly in terms of their affluence. Early publicity about some of the executives, and about the RASS people who had moved to the area, had been misleading, she felt. The early arrivals had been management, made more money, had different expectations. On the other hand, the union members Dunavant found herself talking to had often been laid off for years. They lived in places like Flint, Saginaw, and Detroit, where selling a house to get some cash to make a down payment in Maury County was unrealistic. For many of them "the thrill of getting the job was outweighed by the fear of moving here," Dunavant said.

Former journalism colleagues kept calling Dunavant for an inside story about Saturn. Having signed a secrecy pledge as a condition of employment, she begged off. Although there was some movement within Argonaut to improve the relocation process, to broaden it and make it better, Dunavant said that basically the view Argonaut had of the South, and of Maury County, was racist. They put blacks down and didn't think much of southern whites either.

Wheatley had considerable power and soon managed to have some women from Detroit who knew nothing about Maury County join the relocation team. "He didn't want the people relocating people to have knowledge," Dunavant recalled. There was some infighting going on at Argonaut about how to treat future Saturnites, but gradually the emphasis on Dunavant's job shifted to control and limited information. Hard questions were supposed to be given soft answers, answers that in her mind set the newcomers up for future disappointments. Dunavant said she started feeling trapped in her job. She had no one to talk to and felt barraged by warnings from Saturn Communications not to say a word to the press about anything—remember, you signed a pledge. An occasional unauthorized interview appeared on bulletin boards she walked by daily, "Don't do this!" was penciled in large print next to the text. Those who talked without authorization were tracked down by Saturn Communications, reprimanded, and shamed. Dunavant kept her mouth shut. But she kept having clashes with Wheatley and was feeling heavily stressed. Finally, in October 1988, she got called into the office and was summarily fired. Jim Wheatley and several human resources people told her they were terminating the Tennessee leg of the relocation program. As far as Claudia Dunavant could determine, she *was* the Tennessee leg. "I told them, 'People hate you guys!' " she said. But the experience intimidated her. Years after the fact, when she discussed the circumstances with me she said she had needed therapy afterwards. "I'm still afraid of those people," she confessed.

Although Jim Wheatley got his way with Claudia Dunavant, he was having a hard time adjusting to the new world, even though he had been one of the six men who defined it back in early 1985 up in Bay City, Michigan. Things had gone sour for him slowly despite his enthusiasm for Saturn.

When Wheatley had first arrived in Spring Hill in 1986, he had found, in his words, "People loved Saturn, they hated the UAW." He took it on himself to become a UAW spokesperson. He started attending dinners, giving speeches, trying to create some goodwill toward the UAW. "He thought he was Walter Reuther," his boss Donald Ephlin said. "He wasn't."

Two years later, with Saturn's massive relocation program well underway, Wheatley's vision of what Saturn was going to be, and what reality was had substantially veered apart. "Argonaut would never listen to me," he said bitterly. Eventually, clashing with Ephlin and others, he was transferred back to Detroit.

While Claudia Dunavant and Jim Wheatley, ironically, both Tennesseans, were disagreeing over the extent and helpfulness of the information provided to Saturnites about their future homes in the dimple of the universe, the plant itself continued to go up smoothly. I visited Ed Killgore several times during 1988 to observe its progress. I met him at the Facilities Group headquarters, a cluster of temporary trailer-like units abutting a white board-and-batten barn behind the Haynes Haven mansion. Inside the trailers, packed as tightly as the pens in Killgore's pocket, were work cubicles and offices. A few harried but good-natured secretaries handled the orders, requests, and construction-site banter with aplomb and good humor. On a bulletin board by the door I once read a Xerox copy of a little ditty that summed up a popular view of their importance.

Chairman can leap tall buildings in a single bound.

VP leaps short buildings with a running start.

Department head barely clears quonset huts.

Project architect runs into buildings, talks to walls.

Secretary lifts buildings and walks under them, kicks
locomotives off the track, catches speeding bullets in her
teeth and eats them, freezes water with a single glance.
SHE IS GOD.

Killgore's desk—not that I could ever see it—was covered with folders, maps, and blueprints to a mean altitude of about eight inches. A series of snapshots taped to the wall depicted the stages of an explosion, circa June 1986, a time when drilling crews, their insect-like machines veiled in dust, had been preparing limestone for dynamite. Dropped into the drilled shafts and detonated (windows rattled unceasingly in Spring Hill that summer), the dynamiter's art had been

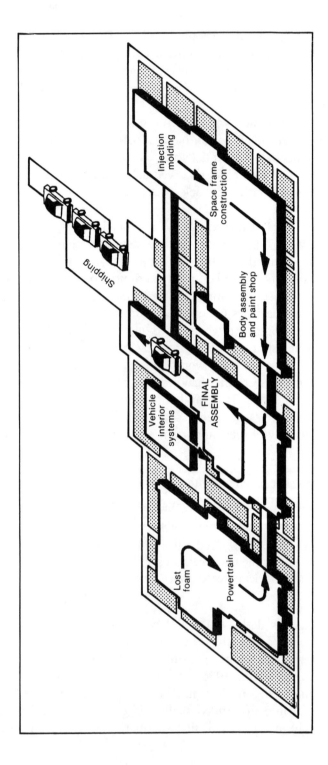

Production flow—Saturn manufacturing complex

captured by amateur time-lapse photography. The first shot showed a little gray cloud erupting out of ground that looked chewed. Then a cloud billowed. There was a plume. It dissipated.

One bright clear morning in July 1988, Killgore told a secretary he would be out on the site for the next hour. We climbed into a dusty red Blazer and drove off. Crossing the future Saturn Parkway, we stopped on a plateau destined to become a parking lot. Below sprawled the plant.

The previous December powertrain's skeleton had been up. A mile to the northeast body systems had been partially erected. In the middle final assembly had been an in-process. Now, seven months later, powertrain was sheathed in blue, its roof mostly on. Body systems was mostly skinned as well. Between them, final assembly remained in the steel erection stage.

I counted eight cranes jutting above roof lines. Big yellow trucks hauling crushed rock from the on-site quarry navigated dirt roads alongside and between the buildings. A cement truck, its cone rotating, disappeared into powertrain. Small yellow pickups were kicking up dust here and there; they looked like toys. Killgore drove down an earthen ramp. A few minutes later, having encircled the powertrain building where the smell of roofing tar was strong, we reached the far side of final assembly. He slowed by "inspiration point," a small door through which finished Saturns would roll in twenty-four months. A handmade sign read: "Shipping point for the best cars in the world."

"We've done a lot of things differently," Killgore drawled. "That's one right there." He pointed to a pond. "It's a fire protection reservoir, but stocked with fish." General Motors never would have done that before, he continued, nor have left the trees out there either. As we drove off he said they were not planting buffer crops on this side of the plant so as to make security easier. An intruder would have to climb the fence, come over the railroad tracks parallel to Cleburne Road, skirt the pond, cross open ground, then somehow gain entrance to the plant without being spotted.

We drove along several of the new roads being graded on the plant's back side. Inventory was going to be stored out there, with deliveries made around the clock. Everything would come via the Saturn Parkway as the main artery, then branch onto the appropriate secondary lane to loading docks. We passed some sun-scorched corn. Killgore said the Saturn farm, originally conceived as a profit maker, was now more of a cheap way to maintain the site; crops were easier to plant and harvest than grass to tend and mow.

He showed me the wood-framed cooling tower, the new waste-treatment facility with its five tanks, the largest of which held half a million gallons. Sludge would be the big effluent; Saturn would treat it, then pipe it to Columbia's municipal sewage plant.

A while later, with the radio crackling and sunlight playing in dust devils far down the road ahead, we drove alongside the future paint shop where construction was proceeding slowly to "maximize process refinement," as Killgore put it. That meant finalizing everything as late as possible to make sure the process was cutting-edge. Killgore said he couldn't talk specifics about the paint shop ("It's a trade secret"), but in it steel, using primers, epoxy electrocoats, waterborne acrylics, and polyurethanes, would be painted somewhat differently than with polymers. The paint technology for achieving luster, along with a protective surface, was changing so rapidly that by delaying the paint process, it would ideally be the latest thing. And Saturn would have it.

One thing not a trade secret was the Tennessee sky look of Saturn's acres of exterior wall. Bluish gray, with a Kalwall strip of opaque fiberglass running horizontally about fifteen feet up to let in light, and with glass windows at human height occasionally set in rows where people would be working, Saturn did blend into the weather pretty well. On blue skied days like today the skin looked blue; on rainy days it seemed gray.

Although there was no evidence left of it now, a fascinating discovery had been made under the future paint shop during preconstruction borings. When core samples had been drilled to check the integrity of the limestone rock pad beneath the loam, an ancient marine riverbed had been found. Once the loam and dirt were removed, a canyon thirty to forty feet deep in places had been revealed. Stalactites jutted from the floor and squidlike invertebrates had left their imprints in the prehistoric river's banks. Geologists had been called in to investigate. They climbed down, poked around, removed some fossils, and determined that a river had probably flowed through there during the mid-Paleozoic Era, about four hundred million years ago, when the large lake covering much of what would one day become Middle Tennessee had drained. Today, the river was filled with crushed rock.

In December 1988 I returned to the site with Killgore when construction was at its peak. More than twenty-five hundred people were working to complete the job. To fight the December chill, standard uniforms now included extra flannel shirts, one-piece worksuits, and gloves. All the structural steel was up, and most of it skinned in Saturn gray/blue. Machines and pieces of equipment were arriving by truck and rail. They were lined up by doorways the size of billboards. Installers, a few of them chattering away in Japanese, were putting various machines in place, working with Saturn engineers and team members already hired by RASS. In the row of trailers lining the rim overlooking the hectic complex, dozens of new charter team members (CTMs) were thumbing through RASS' application files, screening their future teammates.

This day, after descending to the plateau and driving next to powertrain, final assembly, and body systems for a mile, Killgore turned left, went about a quarter mile and parked by the solid north wall of body panels, the tallest section of the building. We walked through a small door and onto a cement floor that spread in front of us like a gunmetal lake. Again, as on previous tours, it struck me how few people you actually saw working here. Not that Saturnites weren't around, but the complex was so vast and sprawling that even with thousands here you often felt as if you were practically alone.

"That's one of the presses," Killgore said, pointing.

On first glance, it suggested a galactic spaceship moored on the set of *Star Trek* or *Star Wars*. It had been made in Japan, Killgore said, by Komatsu. Japanese technicians had traveled to Spring Hill to advise on its installation.

On closer inspection, the guts of the stamping press suggested the view beneath an automobile hood, albeit a huge one. Hoses of varying diameters, wires of different colors, and shiny metal parts were everywhere. I asked if maintaining a press like this was difficult. No, Killgore said, it came with diagnostic equipment built right in; the equipment told the operator what needed to be fixed.

To the north of the press, between it and the loading dock doors through which the rolls of sheet steel would arrive twenty-four-hours a day, stood a Verson blanking press and a smaller decoiler. "You load a coil of steel on the unit," Killgore said, nodding at the decoiler. "It feeds it into the blanking press, which blanks off the section pieces for whatever size you need for the parts you're making in the press line. This section will operate just to feed what is required in the other parts of the plant."

"How does the blanker cut the steel?" I asked. "Is it like a knife, a laser?"

"No. Basically it's like a press; it shears."

Walking back along the press line, I was amused by the colorfulness of the large space. Big HVAC ducts overhead were silver gray. Ninety-foot yellow cranes that had been outside on my July visit now hung high overhead, cables dangling from their horizontal booms. Everything up there was bolted to red steel beams. In total, the body panels part of body systems suggested a color scheme for first grade, as did the shapes: monolithic, blockish, round, rectangular.

We stopped by a rectangular hole in the floor. It was about twenty-five feet wide, ninety feet long, and fifteen deep. It was a press pit. A second Komatsu transfer press probably traveling our way right now on a dozen oversized trucks out of New Orleans would sit on the thick concrete pad in the pit and tower thirty feet over our heads. On a previous visit Killgore parked beside this pit when it had been just a big hole in the ground. Looking down I had seen a jungle of matted rebar and vertical reinforcing rods. Several crews totaling around forty men had been working, many of them guiding the tip of a cement truck hose, a dense stream of aggregate flowing from it and around the rebar. Layer upon layer of cement had been built up to make the pit incredibly strong—strong enough to endure the constant, tremendous pressure exerted by the press and the dies that went in it, dies often weighing over twenty thousand pounds. The more successful Saturn became, the more crucial it would be that each press pit, which was basically a cement pad blasted and poured into a rock pad, held up.

"What's it like breaking in these presses?" I asked.

"That's the tough part; putting the building up isn't the tough part."

A hundred feet further along the floor, which was pocked with holes and squares and small rectangles, some with wires and tubes spewing forth, the future hookups encircled with yellow caution ribbon, we reached the body fabrication area. Here welders, mostly robotic but a few human, would put spaceframes and body parts together in a medley of movement and sparks. It was an area of car-making Killgore knew well. He had begun his career for GM as a spot welder in Arlington, Texas, when he had been twenty-one, he had told me. He'd soon traded his big welding gun for a pencil and become a spec writer for process, designing machinery installations for new factories GM was building in the late sixties. He'd moved to Detroit by then and joined GM's Facilities Group, which built the structures process had to fill. He joined the overseas arm of the group in 1975 and went to Australia, Korea, Columbia, Taiwan, Portugal, Germany, and England, working on wholly owned GM plants and on joint ventures. When I once asked him which assignment had been the most interesting, he said this one—Saturn. Otherwise, it had been the two years he spent in Iran. He'd worked on an assembly plant for the Shah before the Ayatollah Khomeini assumed power in the mid-seventies. Called a CKD operation, for complete knock down, the factory received crated Cadillac Sevilles and Chevy cars and trucks, and put them together. "We were over there during the good times," Killgore noted nostalgically.

Back in his Blazer, he plucked the radio mike from its cradle and called one of his superintendents. He told him he had seen an engineer hanging dangerously over the side of the new press.

"What was that location on him?" came the reply.

"Well, it's . . . the second press in from the north side. It's the one on the south side, the one they're putting in there."

"Ten four. Where you at?"

"I'm on the north side of body panels."

Although safety was always important, ever since the death of Calvin Davis in this building a year ago, it had become a fixation. Davis, fifty-one, had been testing bolts up high. Safety nets had been strung for the steel monkeys, as they were called, but Davis, leaning out beyond a net without tying himself off to a beam, had a bolt snap. He took a fifty-foot nosedive. Davis's death was a black spot on an otherwise good safety record for a project this size.

On the job, drug use or drinking were causes for immediate firing. There was random drug testing. Whether that would continue once the plant was up and running had not been decided yet. Although vigorously pushed by Saturn management, this was one area where the partners couldn't agree; the UAW opposed drug testing.

In 1988 a knowledgeable observer told me after requesting anonymity, "GM is obsessed with its drug problems." General Motors was on an anti-drug crusade, he said. After years of denial, management had finally accepted that it had a substance abuse subculture: drunks on assembly lines, lines of cocaine on machinist benches, roaches in the johns. At Saturn, he confided, whenever you heard "work ethic" it probably meant "no dope." Other sources validated his assessment. I heard about workers on older assembly lines openly drinking beer, how the smell of marijuana floated pungently in the oily din. Some time later, after Saturn was running, a CTM confided to me that in his old plant, "We used to do lines on the roof. Or we'd spread them right out on the desk. Hell, we even did acid, then had to pound out doors. I had a general foreman who would cover my ass. All I had to do was make sure that when he returned from lunch, his sixteen-ounce cup was half filled with liquor."

The safety infraction of the engineer having been reported, Killgore drove around the northwest corner of body systems and headed by a row of loading docks. From this perspective the plant did possess a certain visual appeal. Part of it was its sheer immensity, the newness of the paint, that it blended into the sky. Saturn was certainly a long ways from early twentieth-century automobile factories like those designed by architect Albert Kahn in Detroit. Yet Saturn's layout—the delineated process areas, the long and unobstructed spaces for machining and assembly lines, the merger of utility and industrial beauty—was similar to what Kahn had designed for Henry Ford, Chrysler, and so many others almost a century before.

Although the plant lacked such design wonders as Palladian-inspired smokestacks standing on the roof like Kahn had put on Ford's Model-T plant in Highland Park, a sort of sculptural quality distinguished the cooling towers and bag houses on the periphery of the powertrain building. The towers would cool fluids used in machining operations and the bag houses would filter dirty sand so it could be reused. Roughly the size of a one-car garage, each elevated bag house had a roof shaped like a funnel with its spout snipped short. Ducting connected each bag house to the interior of the powertrain building. The houses, clustered together, gave the otherwise monotonous facade a playful look.

Parking not far from them, we walked through the foundry area where iron and aluminum would be cast into crankshafts, blocks, heads, valves, and other engine parts. Tall vertical containers against one wall looked like something you might have seen storing grain in a barn. Instead, these would hold sand, Killgore said. It would be packed around styrofoam molds before iron or aluminum was poured in, vaporizing the molds and forming parts. Then the sand would be shaken away, cleaned, and recycled.

A couple hundred feet away, in the future transmission machining area, cement trucks were pouring their loads while crews steered the cement around and over flumes channeled beneath the floor. The flumes would handle coolant for machining. A backhoe bucket tamped the ground nearby, readying it for cement. Although Killgore had mentioned that women were working on the crews, except for several directing traffic on the flat plain years ago, I hadn't noticed any until now. Two, their frames slight in blue sweatshirts, were sliding sheets of plywood from the bed of a black pickup. Nearby, cement trucks beeped, backing up, their cones turning. Large overhead lights gave the vast space an otherworldly glare. A third woman, her braided ponytail dangling from the rear of her hard hat, lugged a hose. Two young guys were guiding the serious end of a crane. One of them momentarily dangled from the hook, making his friend laugh. He was lucky Killgore didn't see him.

A few minutes later we were watching a solitary die-casting machine make valves. The machine was brilliantly lit. A single robot lifted each cast piece, swiveled, and eased the piece onto a table. A man wearing gloves and eyeglasses examined each stem, then piled them on a second table. Recording the scene was a photographer and his assistant. There was a fellow, the first person I'd seen in here wearing a suit, taking some notes. Killgore said they were working on the die-casting machine training manual.

Outside, Killgore drove up a long slope on a paved road toward an intersection with the Saturn Parkway. He turned left and headed for Northfield, the administration building, which was also in process. Suddenly, the new Spring Hill Town Hall popped into view, the new and bigger Spring Hill water tower alongside it. Off to the west, I caught a brief glimpse of Cleburne Road, of rolling fields still worth lots of money on the books of their speculator owners. Killgore dropped me at my car, and a jogger huffed by along the dirt land connecting the temporary facilities complex to the Saturn Parkway. There was also a SOVRAN bank sign, and an arrow pointing toward a restaurant serving breakfast and lunch. It was in a trailer. So you can eat here, get your money, and work, I thought. Saturn was becoming its own little world.

16

Changing of the Guard

That December I saw George Jones on several occasions. The mayor didn't look good: drawn around the eyes, heavier around the middle, tired. Discount Builders Supply in Columbia had folded and he had taken on a sizable contracting job, overseeing the construction of a fifty-thousand-square-foot textile factory on the outskirts of the city for a local developer named Eugene Heller. That was in addition to the thirty to forty hours a week he was still putting in as mayor.

Meanwhile, P. D. "Pete" Boyd, a well-liked former mayor of Spring Hill and a volunteer coach for the Spring Hill's pee-wee baseball and football leagues, had announced he was running against Mayor Jones next May. "He may be serious competition," Naomi Derryberry said.

Boyd's campaign had several themes. One was that Spring Hill had not boomed. A second was, as he put it, "I want Spring Hill to git back to that little friendly community where everybody knows everybody, and everybody loves everybody." Pete Boyd also opposed two changes Mayor Jones had instituted: the sign ordinance and garbage pickup fees. Boyd promised voters he'd get rid of the garbage charge if it took him and two others in a rented truck to collect the garbage.

Five months before the election Boyd already had plenty of supporters. One-time George Jones fans who had jumped the fence included Clint and Freeda Brown at the Poplar House Restaurant. I sat down with Freeda Brown in the restaurant one day between meals and asked why her allegiance had switched.

"George was a country boy," she said. "Now he's like a banty rooster and he wants to crow loud."

At the big round table in the corner by the door to her kitchen Freeda Brown recalled how George had said he wanted to keep Spring Hill like it was. But now they were losing everything to Town Center—the post office, the bank, some of the restaurant trade. She didn't resent Larry Atema, she interjected, nor did many other people in town. But reasons she never clearly articulated, both she and many townspeople blamed George for what Atema's development was threatening to do. Then Freeda suddenly declared, "Downtown Spring Hill will always be where it is!"

Flushed, she sighed. She glanced with understanding at a tired waitress who dropped in a chair on the other side of the table. The aldermen just followed George around in a pack, Freeda lamented. "Something is wrong when he makes the suggestion, brings it up, and they all say yes, or all say no together. You can't take eight people from any place in the world and get them to agree. He's being a bully. He's God. You treat him like a king, and that's it!

"It's sad because we supported George in everything he did, and considered ourselves good friends." Now they couldn't even talk, she said. Only two of the eight aldermen came into the restaurant regularly any more.

"What do the Saturn people say about Mayor Jones?" I asked.

"They want to get rid of him; they laugh at him behind his back."

The Poplar House Restaurant sign, leaning against a post outside—she couldn't put it up, she complained, making a sweeping and dismissive gesture with one hand toward the front windows facing the highway. "It violates the sign ordinance."

A tanned farmer in a cowboy hat eased into a seat by the waitress. Joining in the conversation, he recalled that a Kwik-Sak convenience store planned to locate in the village, then hadn't. He blamed the sign ordinance. "You can't git a better business than a convenience store," he assured me.

I asked him who was going to get elected mayor.

"George."

As if someone had slapped her in the face, Freeda Brown rolled back from the table. Her eyes widened considerably. "Why, he's the first person I've heard say that! But then he's honest."

A few minutes later, leaning forward again, she sounded perplexed. "If George could have just kept his level head, he could have gone places."

After the first of the year I arranged to travel around with the mayor one day, hoping that I would get some fresh insights into the workings, or non-workings, of his campaign. I went to the new Town Hall at 7 A.M. Building inspector Bobby Ingram invited me into his office. Sitting behind an oak-veneer desk, Ingram explained that his office had become sort of the conference room by default. That was why the coffee makings were in here rather than in the real conference room, which seldom got used. He was around the Town Hall the most, he said, so it was natural for everyone to just kind of congregate in his quarters.

The office was spartan. A few brand-new bookcases held rolled blueprints. A filing cabinet filled a corner. On a table were the coffee fixings: instant, Cremora non-dairy creamers, sugar packets, stained plastic spoons, all lined up in front of a Mr. Coffee.

Suddenly Police Chief Phil Lovell burst in. He tossed a newspaper on his desk and said disgustedly, "Why don't we have crime like this? Look at that front page!"

Murfreesboro, a small city thirty miles west, had six robberies in the last ten days, the article said. The very idea of all that crime stirred Chief Lovell's adrenaline. His biceps bulged, straining the short sleeves of his shirt. He glanced out the window, at me, at Ingram's cigarette perched between two fingers. The mayor strolled in.

"George, we're doing something wrong," the chief said, jolting the mayor a little. "Look at that!" A big finger aimed at the newspaper. "Six armed robberies in ten days! I was traveling through Franklin yesterday and they were having a robbery in broad daylight!" The chief sounded like he'd been on a low-crime diet for too long and had to get off it. "I took a drive over to Murfreesboro a couple days ago," he confessed. "Just to be in the vicinity of some good crime."

Smiling thinly but not responding, George dropped into a chair, and deposited his heels on Ingram's desk. He launched into the Gateway project. It weighed more heavily on the mayor's mind than his town's lack of good crime. Although he had always praised Gateway before, now the mayor made it sound as if he had been suspicious of what he called "the Pettigrew bunch" from the beginning. "They're shady," he said.

Ingram listened, made a few remarks. The chief kept his eyes on the newspaper, vicariously taking the Murfreesboro robberies in. He wasn't about to let the conversation get stuck on the shady Pettigrew bunch when there was crime to talk about. Finally, George gave him some attention. Yet mention of the time last summer when the chief had chased an escaped prisoner into a garage on Main Street didn't brighten his mood. George Jones and Bobby Ingram took turns reminding the chief of more recent brushes with wrongdoers that he had enjoyed right around here. For instance, there was the guy they had shot.

That memory did evince a slight smile. The chief lifted his eyes from the paper, where they had seemed to have become fixated. It was a domestic quarrel, he said for my benefit. "He was trying to cut her up with an ax." They had chased the guy down a dirt road for miles. In service to the truth the chief said, "The officer that was in pursuit with me shot him."

The mayor chuckled, spit into the oak-veneered waste bucket by Ingram's desk. Two more Spring Hill policemen and R. L. Hogan came in, and went directly to the Mr. Coffee. George said we had to roll.

We headed toward Columbia in a beat-up Chevy truck. On the drive George talked bitterly about the ongoing battles between Spring Hill and Columbia. The latest one involved a lawsuit over the relocation of water lines necessitated by the Saturn Parkway. At issue was which town was going to pay the $125 thousand for the relocation. According to George's interpretation, this was just a surface issue. The real issue was water itself and who controlled it. He said that Columbia, from which Spring Hill got most of its water, wanted to reduce the flow, which an existing contract guaranteed, because officials in Columbia didn't want Spring Hill to grow. They also didn't like it that Spring Hill was selling some of the water to Williamson County. Then he elaborated a little more about the Gateway project. The two topics, water and Gateway, were heavy on his mind and throughout the day he would make allusions to them. They were development issues and political ones that intertwined, pulling him down. Without water there couldn't be development, and without development George's stature as a politician would take a dive. The Pettigrew bunch had a Texas lawyer in Tennessee now, he said, and were no longer playing either by the pages of the twenty-page agreement worked out eighteen months ago, or by other rules he was familiar with. Gateway, if it was built at all, was now going to proceed in stages. The fire department, recreation facility, and sewage plant expansion, all of which George had planned to pay for from fees agreed upon in the original agreement, were in doubt. He said he was still working to get the fees up front, but he didn't sound convinced that would happen. His by-the-seat-of-his-pants, office-in-the-car approach to administration was getting stretched thin.

After coffee and biscuits at Oldham's Fine Foods with the boosters, who were in a rare racist and sexist good humor this morning, we visited the in-process textile factory George Jones, the builder, was overseeing. It was a steel-framed, cinderblock building being laid up by the same mason I had met a year ago at Bryant Station. Grinning as he had then, but now wearing a ballcap with a propeller on the top rather than a ski tuque, he told George a few jokes. At Columbia Garden Apartment, where we stopped next, George talked with Eugene Heller, the factory owner. George had also built this apartment complex for Heller a few years back. A bright, somewhat absent-minded businessman, Heller had jumped into real estate wholeheartedly after Saturn had been announced. He owned about twenty-five hundred acres, much of it around Spring Hill. To date, he hadn't sold an acre.

In Heller's offices, located in one of the apartment units, a large map covered an entire wall. Heller's holdings were framed in colored magic marker. One tract was adjacent to I-65 at the Saturn Parkway exit. Eight hundred acres surrounded Big Oak Lake, three miles southwest of Saturn. The lake had once been open to the public for fishing and swimming. Now it was a No Trespassing zone.

Heller's office manager told me the locals were unhappy about the Saturn-related job situation, but nobody was doing anything to change it. Impatient to leave, I found George in Heller's dark office, talking on the phone and sounding exasperated. "How'm I gonna do the financing?" he was saying to someone. "It comes time to pay them, I'm going to write them a check!"

We ate lunch at Lucille's Restaurant and the mayor turned on the charm whenever someone sat to exchange a few words with him. Between visitors, though, he complained that the garbage fee had been twisted into a big issue in Spring Hill and insisted that he couldn't back down on the fees now—it wouldn't look good. Late that afternoon we had a couple cocktails at the American Legion, the only place in Columbia that served hard liquor by the drink, then drove north, joining the stream of red tail lights. Ten minutes later we passed Haynes Haven. Lights glowed in the windows. We went by a dark Rippavilla, then a Saturn Parkway bridge loomed ahead, crossing U. S. 31. Huddled together in the median were two Spring Hill patrol cars.

Spring Hill's reputation as a speed trap was also harming the mayor's popularity. Since there was not enough crime to keep seven officers occupied, speeders had to do. They gave out hundreds of tickets every month. The officers were also extremely well armed, just in case something serious happened, having recently turned in their six-shot .357s for fifteen-shot 9 mm pistols, the semi-automatics drug dealers preferred. The firepower and crime focus did strike some citizens as excessive and paranoid. Pete Boyd was making the management of the police department an issue in the election.

Mayor Jones defended the department almost religiously. Drugs were viewed particularly fondly ("Eighty-five percent of all crime is directly related to drugs," I once heard Chief Lovell say, not identifying the source of this exaggerated statistic) because their confiscation resulted in additional funding from the state and federal governments. With the money the department could arm itself better. The ax-wielding husband had been shot by one of the new semi-automatic 9 mm pistols. So, presumably, would any drug dealer caught in the village of Spring Hill.

"You guys don't go to sleep back there," George said into his radio.

Given the long pause that followed, I wondered if the heavily armed officers were already sleeping. Finally one of them asked George if he'd bring them some dinner.

As we serpentined toward the Town Hall on the Town Center Road, the mayor momentarily regained his old spark. "Joe," he said with enthusiasm, "we got a chance to make a model city in America, if we don't blow it."

But the line itself made me wince. It sounded hollow.

As election day neared, in his paid advertisements in the Spring Hill *Morning Sun,* Pete Boyd insisted he had no conflicts of interest and wasn't threatening to fire Police Chief Lovell, as rumors claimed. In a full-page ad in the same weekly, Mayor Jones reminded the voters he had negotiated their favorable in-lieu-of-tax agreement, built the new Town Hall, and repaired the streets, all the while lowering property taxes by twenty percent. A poll conducted by the *Morning Sun* just before the election, with a hundred voters participating, or approximately fifteen percent of the checklist, gave Jones a two-to-one edge over Boyd. The poll also put most of the incumbent alderpersons, including Naomi Derryberry, back in office.

The day before the election I found Pete Boyd campaigning in front of the Spring Hill Post Office, then still on Main Street. It was a sunny, crisp morning, and Boyd, a solid, short, gray-haired man in his fifties, had on a short-sleeve white shirt and a tie. He was chewing a toothpick. Removing the toothpick, he encouraged a woman he intercepted by the door to the post office to cast her vote tomorrow. "Bring your husband with you," Boyd urged.

Once she went inside, Boyd drifted my way. I asked what he thought the biggest changes were in Spring Hill since Saturn had arrived.

"This election," he replied. "Before, if Spring Hill had an election, you'd see it in the back pages." Now he was going to be interviewed by Channel 5 in one hour, he said.

"Bubba, don't forget tomorrow!"

A black man was about to enter the post office.

Boyd removed his toothpick. "I don't want to have to come git you out of bed," he said.

"You won't have to," the fellow said jovially.

A blast of air buffeted us. It was followed by three more blasts in succession. Tires singing, eighteen wheelers were leaving the village in tight formation. Boyd glanced through the wake of the last one. Across U. S. 31 sat the white board-and-batten Episcopal Church. Staring at it, chewing his toothpick, he began reminiscing about the days when Spring Hill had only one cop walking the streets rather than seven in cruisers, all heavily armed. In those days it had been a big deal to come into town on Saturday night, he said. He looked at me, intent. That poll in the *Morning Sun* the other day, he interjected, don't take that seriously—the paper supported Jones.

"Hey, how's it going?" the campaigning coach said suddenly, moving laterally toward some action by the door. To one lady he must have thought was in his opponent's camp, he explained his stand on the garbage fees. The fees didn't bother her, she replied. So Boyd explained why he didn't like the sign ordinance, concluding with, "I think a man should be able to advertise his business." When the woman asked about the future direction of the town, Boyd waved his arms around, the toothpick in his mouth, and said that was for the people to decide. She started to sound exasperated. She said she felt that Spring Hill village was being ignored, that new businesses and shops should have opened by now, that they should have an attractive, historic village, not this.

I followed her glance up the street. John Campbell's deLaval dealership in its worn cinderblock building was still functioning, but the McKissack place looked worn, its "For Sale" sign tilting on the narrow scrap of lawn. The Cedar Inn was long gone and the bank at the main intersection would soon be moving. As would the post office into which the woman slipped.

Walking away from the door Boyd assumed his more relaxed manner. He said the police force had just gotten way ahead of what was needed and that Jones and his ideas were too far ahead of reality. "Maybe I'm too easygoing to be a politician," he reflected. "People say you've got to get mad and throw some rocks."

"You going to go door-to-door this afternoon?" I asked.

"No, I'm going home," he said, grinning. "Getting out my weed whacker and doing my lawn."

There had been some rock throwing in the campaign, which George Jones had initiated. Apparently worried, he had made the mistake of throwing the rocks at the wrong targets, however. In this case, at Pete Boyd's wife, whom he claimed was mad because the town wouldn't give her a raise (Mrs. Boyd had worked for the town), and at Pete Boyd's son-in-law, whom the mayor said was spiteful because he used to have the town gasoline account but had recently lost it. What hurt the incumbent more than these personal swipes, though, and more than his support of the controversial police department, garbage fees, and sign ordinance, was his complete lack of any kind of political organization. George Jones campaigned the way he ran his business, as a kind of one-man band. He entertained, dispensed wisdom, made mistakes, negotiated, fired from the hip. But he never gathered about him a coalition of supporters, periodically soliciting their views, getting their opinions, respecting their advice. He didn't draw his constituents into his decision-making process or demonstrate that he could lead in a nonpartisan manner. So as election day approached he found himself pretty much alone. Being alone, and seen most often in the company of his police offices and a few alderpersons, a lot of citizens decided that George no longer cared for them, that all he cared about was George Jones and power. With his hillbilly twang, country boy wit, and nouveau-suburban vision, which did in some ways seem to ally itself more with the developers than the people, Jones had created a complicated persona. Very possibly too complicated for those he represented. He had established Spring Hill's presence vis-à-vis Saturn to a degree no other local politician had managed for his or her community, and had become a media personality. But he had become distant to many, aloof.

Even the blacks in Spring Hill, previously supportive, seemed to have doubts about him. Elbow, an eighty-four-year-old black man in Newtown, told me just before the election, "He's gonna get beat. Powerful white folks don't like what he's been doing."

Elbow's shack, with its little porch, sat up the lane from the house that sheltered a goat. I was in the neighborhood with George who was nervously toying with some quarters in one hand while overseeing the cleanup of a cafe that had burned. The cafe had been a place where black people rendezvoused, gambled, and sold drugs out back. As Elbow watched the bulldozer bashing in the charred remains of the cafe, he recalled how realtors had come around and offered him

$30 thousand for his little place a couple years ago. "I'm eighty-four years old," he said, eyes bright, weight on his cane. "What I'm gonna do—kick my ass out in the street? I said no."

A short while later Chief Lovell drove up in a cruiser and got out in civilian clothes. Arms out to his sides, he stalked around the bulldozer.

"He's fixin' to go marijuana hunting," George told me, now swinging a set of keys in one hand.

The bulldozer was making an awful racket, corkscrewing tin roofing into the ground before burying it. A few days ago the chief had found fifty-odd marijuana plants around here, George said. Now he hoped to discover some more.

Minutes later, out of the blue, the mayor assured me, "The solid people, I'll git their votes. The riffraff, I won't; I been on their ass."

Hand on his cane, Elbow was wobbling back toward his front porch; he didn't seem to hear or heed the mayor.

We ate lunch in the restaurant adjacent to the Steeplechase Inn. George told several inquisitive people that the election "is either this Saturday or next." Back in his truck, however, he was tense. "If I dropped this thing on them now," he said, "it'd be a damned disaster. And they don't even realize it."

"Why do you want to run again?" I asked.

"Why?" He glanced where the temporary Town Hall used to be, spit some chewing tobacco in a cup. "I think that I've accomplished something for the town that some people will realize and appreciate. I feel like I've put something together. Without me, I don't think it would have been done. I intend to run for county executive, possibly. And I wanted to keep my feet in the limelight for the time being. If I'm going to do that I had to stay in office. Say if I'd have got out, things would have started falling through, and I would have been blamed."

"What do you have to do to run for county executive?"

"Circulate a petition and get twenty-five signatures. That job does pay $45 thousand a year. With nothing but a high school education, where can a man go get a job for $45 thousand a year, unless he busts his ass, like I'm doing now?"

Naomi Derryberry, realizing her political career was on the line, too, had some political flyers printed and distributed around the fourth ward. Both she and Billy Kinnard, the two incumbents, were being seriously challenged by Boyd supporters.

Election day, May 13, 1989, the opposing camps set up their lawn chairs well apart from each other along the sidewalk leading from the parking lot in the front of the new Town Hall around to the community room in the rear, where the voting booths were located. Side bets on the election ranged from $5 to $100, I heard. At twilight, just before the polls closed, a poker-faced Larry Atema showed up. He had told me a few days earlier that he'd been worried about George losing until about three weeks ago. But no longer. "Boyd's a do nothing," Adema had said. "He doesn't have any idea what it takes to run the town government now."

Now the developer joined seventy or eighty other citizens gathered around a fellow in a green sport jacket who was reading the results. George, in a brown shirt, brown slacks, and hushpuppies, looked as if he was in a relaxed trance. Naomi Derryberry, wearing a jacket with a big brooch on it, gradually looked mortified, then on the verge of tears. Pete Boyd had beaten George Jones, 225 to 147. It wasn't even a contest. She had been reelected, but just barely. Billy Kinnard had gotten beat.

Looking dazed but not without a plan B, Larry Atema wandered over and introduced himself to Pete Boyd, whom apparently he had never met. When I got close to George, he was smiling but with his teeth tight together. "I'm a winner for losin', Joe," he said, not sounding very convincing.

Atema returned to the deflated group of Jones's supporters. He borrowed my pencil and hastily jotted down the full election results from a posted tally sheet. His young son, by his shoulder, kept whispering, "Can we go, Dad? Can we go?"

"It's a changing of the guard," Atema muttered, returning the pencil.

Walking to my car, I stopped by a recently attached bronze plaque at the front of the ponderous Town Hall. On it were the names of the defeated mayor and several defeated aldermen. I asked two weathered older men—former farmers, I guessed, from their leathery complexions and go-to-town jeans—if the outcome of the vote was what they'd expected.

"Just about," the dark-haired one said. "Two to one. It was just about two to one."

"About three to two," his friend corrected.

The first man didn't seem to hear, concentrating as he was on the numbers he had in hand. "That's just about two to one."

"Three to two," his friend insisted.

17

Learning to Be Teams

During the summer of 1989 U-Hauls carrying Michigan tags were a common sight in Maury County. So were tour buses—circling courthouse square in Columbia, slowing by the mansions in Ashwood, unloading in Spring Hill so passengers could look at one of the places where some of them would soon be registering kids for school, paying taxes, voting.

"They talk funny," not a few Saturnites said about Maurians.

The talk funny thing worked both ways.

Saturn's RASS established a Newcomer Center, a Saturn buddy system, and served lunches at Haynes Haven for spouses to get to know each other. Children were a little shortchanged in the relocation effort until two teenagers ran away, heading north. Then RASS shifted some money and attention from employees and spouses to their kids. Teen dances were organized, support groups met. Jim Wheatley, the UAW rep, told the press, "The real cornerstone of the whole thing is the teenager. I found out if you can make the teenagers happy, the Mamma's happy. If Mamma's happy, Daddy's happy. You blow this whole thing if he comes home to an argument every night." It was the kind of public utterance, partially true but out of touch with the times, that expedited Wheatley's transfer back to Detroit.

The average age of a Saturn employee was thirty-six. Families had 2.8 children, one above the American norm. They learned that the cost of living in the dimple of the universe was higher than expected. Racial tensions seemed lower than in Flint and Detroit. Local schools, though short on resources, were not as bad as some had been led to believe. In fact, many new students discovered they were behind their Southern peers in select subjects. To their parents' dismay, report cards soon reflected that.

As a group the newcomers were highly motivated. After all, that was what much of the job testing had been about: will, desire, eagerness to change. Most were also anxious to fit in. As they pointed out to the Maurians who cared to listen, they had left behind job seniority, established homes, old friends, family networks (especially crucial to single parents, of which there were many) to move to a new place and earn less money. Don Hitko, a mechanical technician who gave up his job at the Fisher Guide hardware plant in Flint after twenty-eight years, summed up how many viewed the change. "I like to compare Saturn to a pretty young lady," he told a reporter in the language a country songwriter might admire. "I first met Saturn and there was an enchantment, an attraction, a newness, a challenge, the publicity. After being in one place for so long, there's an appeal. I had some early interviews. I was impressed, and the more I talked it over with my wife and heard more about this pretty young lady and what her intentions were, the more I became enticed. One day something just clicked and I said, 'Why not just go for it? Go for the challenge. The change might do you good.' "

That August, Saturn donated fifty acres of the former Elizabeth Love farm to the Maury County School Board, ending the site hunt for the new Spring Hill High School. The Saturn Parkway opened and Governor Ned Ray McWherter showed up to cut the ribbon. Even Roger Smith finally visited, riding around Saturn in a golf cart with Skip LeFauve. "He's made a special effort not to give us direction," LeFauve said.

Of the hundreds of strangers arriving in Maury County late that summer one was a thirty-two-year-old black man from Flint named Al Burris. A former Marine with a wife and four kids, Burris had not applied to Saturn for the challenge or the philosophy or the team concept, although those things interested him. Foremost, Burris wanted to get closer to his roots, which were in Tunica, Mississippi, in the Mississippi Delta. A lanky guy with an easy smile, fluid brown eyes, and a quick laugh, Burris had first heard about Saturn back in 1986. A spot welder at GM Truck and Bus in Flint, Burris, having been laid off for ten months, had just returned to work. But he wasn't blind. "Flint had hit rock bottom," he recalled. "Nothing was making it in Flint." Burris geared up his application to Saturn in early 1988, once RASS opened the official recruitment campaign. But then he heard nothing for twelve months. Finally, he got a call and a forty-five-minute phone interview. Its purpose, the spot welder deduced, was to determine "where your mind was at."

His mind being eager to learn and change and to get out of Flint and down South, Burris passed the phone interview. He received two airline tickets via certified mail. He and his wife Catha flew to Nashville and rode a bus to the Steeplechase Inn in Town Center. Burris took a quick tour of the plant. Machinery was going in everywhere. He was interviewed by two WUMAs, or work unit module advisors, one representing the UAW, the other GM. He took tests in math, reading, and problem solving. He and his wife returned to Flint. A few days later the phone rang. It was RASS personnel.

"When can you start?"

In early September 1989 Burris moved into an apartment in Columbia with Dennis Muse, an engineer and friend of his from Flint. On Burris's first day on the job, though, Muse should have done him a favor and sketched a map. "I really didn't even know how to get back and forth to work," Burris told me much later, laughing about the incident. "I got lost."

Burris's situation was not untypical: the hiring process, the quick move, the sense of physical and cultural dislocation combined to make him a little disoriented. In addition, the training was intense and demanding, like nothing Burris had ever experienced. It started with an introductory week of Saturn Awareness Training, which everyone received and which emphasized the company's mission and philosophy, and had a heavy indoctrination flavor. Then Burris entered the standard three-week training rotation: a week of classroom instruction followed by a week of job training followed by a week of hiring future members of the marriage work unit, of which he was the charter team member.

Intense training was at the heart of Saturn's newness. It was benchmarked from established and successful programs at such companies as Motorola and IBM. Underlying the training program was the conviction that it had to transform the way a person felt about his or her job, redefine the relationship between labor and the leadership, and be ongoing even after Saturn started making cars. The initial training for CTMs, as well as for the op techs and trade techs, varied from 300 to 350 hours, depending on their future jobs. Operators had to learn not only their assigned tasks, but how to be familiar enough with those of the entire team in order to see the bigger picture and be able to step in and take over another job temporarily. Few of the new Saturnites could recall a job where training had exceeded fifty hours. In fact, for some jobs the training had been pathetic or counterproductive, or both. Nancy Laatz, who would join the crankshaft machining team in the powertrain building in early 1991, remembered a brief and ridiculous stint she had put in at Fisher

Autobody, a GM subsidiary. Experienced as a machine operator, Laatz had found herself installing wiring harnesses in dashboards. "A harness has about a million wires," she said. "I didn't know what in the hell I was doing. So about the third day the foreman says, 'So, you ready to work by yourself?' I said, 'Hey, I don't know what I'm doing.' He made me work by myself. I'm sure every car I worked on they had to fix later on."

Training at Saturn intended to alleviate such blatant disregard for the customer—both the customer who would buy the car as well as the next person down the assembly line making it—in Laatz's anecdote, the person who had to fix her mistakes. Saturn also did not want its people burdened with the poor self-image inherent in feeling they didn't know what they were doing.

With its emphasis on almost Biblical precepts, such as trust, respect, and listening, training at Saturn took on a kind of sacred aura. If the South was "haunted by God," as popular mythology claimed, Saturn was haunted by a resurrection of worker self-esteem. If new business systems were at the heart of transforming the way business got done, people training was the crux of transformation for the individual. It was going to be the bridge of learning from the old and mundane to the new and radiant. It was a bridge that every Saturnite had to cross because the company was not going to make a new kind of car without a new kind of work force. A work force, figuratively, that had arrived in the promised land.

Toward that end there were classes in team building and team dynamics. Instructors taught principle-centered leadership ("keep the end in mind," "plan," "develop an emotional bank account," being three of its dicta), and stressed the relationship between responsibility and accountability ("You have to be responsible to be accountable"). A consensus decision-making model was unveiled and memorized. A working understanding of the model was imperative if consensus was eventually going to steer the teams and be the fulcrum between them, and between the teams and the leadership. The model resolved conflicts, determined direction, gave teams the key to self-management.

In total, before one car was built, upwards of a million hours were invested in the training of the original three thousand Saturnites. Once the plant was running, five percent of each forty-hour week—from the president on down—was earmarked for ongoing training. That compared to three percent at even the more progressive American firms.

At its most optimistic, the training promised to help Saturnites see their jobs in a new light, view their relationships with their teammates synergistically, and realize how their own personal visions and the vision of the company were often one and the same. Viewed cynically, it was jargon-heavy, soft-sided skill building that cost a fortune, created individual expectations that could never be met in a factory, and irked the hell out of traditional managers. Some of them asked Joy Rodes, a former educator and consultant for GM's retraining center in Flint, and the woman responsible for much of the design of Saturn's training program, "Why do we need all of this crap?" Rodes' answer was, "Because the competition is doing it." In the competitive global market place, she added, "The need to train and retrain people is going to be tremendous."

All the training certainly was new to the recipients. If their Saturn awareness training could be characterized as "why I'm here and how this is different," team dynamics could be summarized as "how I'm going to grow as a person and how people create a great team."

Ideally, Saturn wanted an enlightened work force that ran on the consensus of the membership. It was democracy at work in the factory—that was the theory. Each little group, each team, was to run its show, assuming such responsibilities as producing to schedule, creating a quality product, performing to budget, housekeeping, inventory control, repairs, scrap control, and controlling absenteeism. And each team was to communicate and cooperate with adjacent teams. Every team had to hold meetings, keep good records, constantly make improvements. And each team was to be self-directed. That is, individually, each team via consensus was supposed to initiate action. Then, collectively, a majority of teams could initiate some action in order to make Saturn more of a bottom-up organization, a rarity in American industry.

Would it work?

The training, by its very nature subjective, lacked definitive yardsticks. That was both its strength, because it emphasized intangibles such as will and spirit and shared desires, and its weakness because big business wasn't yet in the business of stroking such intangibles in lowly blue-collar workers. There was also the hard question about the caliber of the workers themselves. Could they take in a flood of new information, assimilate it individually, integrate it into their teams, and really change? A second, complementary question was: if the work force did shift, did get a taste for bottom-up leadership potential, would the leadership really want to share power? Would the leadership accept a flat leadership pyramid? It was a change roughly equivalent in its degree of difficulty as transforming tough-minded managers into tender-hearted ones.

Al Burris said he liked the training. But even more he liked being part of the hiring process. That was really foreign. Spot welders had *never* hired anybody at GM Truck and Bus. Now every third week Burris pored over applications in a RASS trailer with other CTMs doing the same. Burris conducted phone interviews of good prospects according to a script RASS had written. Each interview was graded. If it produced a "fully effective" candidate, the person flew to Tennessee, was interviewed by the tandem WUMAs, and took the "start" tests. About one in three applicants passed the phone interview, Burris said. Then one in five passed the Spring Hill interviews and tests and was offered a job.

"It was something I'll never forget," Burris said about those initial months at Saturn. "First time I ever been in an environment where everybody was concerned about quality."

Other elements of the new world were also strange and stimulating. For instance, there had been no teams focused on particular tasks, such as his marriage work unit team, which married (bolted) the powertrain to the chassis, at Truck and Bus. No all-encompassing chassis work unit module existed either, with its nine separate teams, each one a customer of the team preceding it. There had been no WUMAs, or BUCs, (Business Unit Coordinators) or CTMs at Truck and Bus. No slogans such as "Keep the end in mind," and "Stop, challenge, and choose." In the old world there had been departments: paint, body, and so on. At Truck and Bus, Al Burris had clocked in, done his job, clocked out. Now he had to think, learn, hire. He had to get a grip on the elusive concept of quality. He had to help lay out the marriage area, relate it to pre-marriage and button up, which were upstream and downstream of marriage in the chassis work unit module. He had to develop an ITP, or individual training plan, as did all new hires. As his team grew, he attended team meetings about leadership, safety, costs. All the time he had to stay focused; WUMAs, BUCs, and trainers were always talking about it. "At Saturn they preached focus," he said.

Yet Burris was a little scared, a little confused once in a while. He didn't know anybody really. The newcomers were beginning to be his teammates but they weren't yet his friends. They were strangers in the new world, a fluid and at times frustratingly vague world where, as Burris recalled, "no one was telling you what to do."

The sense of freedom and learning at Saturn in 1989 was unprecedented for GM and significant for American industry. The training was linked to risk and rewards, to the presumption that long-conditioned union workers could rise to the occasion, could not only absorb a flow of new information but integrate it into their character and act with heightened awareness and understanding. Of course the training also had to improve productivity and lower costs, making Saturn lean and competitive. This wasn't Esalen or a New Age boot camp. This was big business in a new paradigm, the horizontal team paradigm, as contrasted to the traditional vertical one. If the new world was too much for some of the hirees—they needed a foreman, more rigid authority—they had the option to "de-select," forgetting all this new lingo, brainwashing, and team building, and returning to the old world. Some did.

Settling into Maury, Williamson, and other surrounding counties, the newcomers found most of the locals hospitable, if reserved. Burris said folks were friendly. They waved to him, spoke to him on the streets in Columbia. A few blacks he met even chided him: "When am I going to get a job out there?"

He laughed the question off because he knew it wasn't going to be for quite a while.

In late November, Burris's wife and kids moved down. He had rented one of Eugene Heller's Columbia Garden Apartments, which George Jones had built in the early 1980s. Rent for the apartment was $499 a month. The year before, the rent had been $349 a month. Catha Burris soon found a job at Weather Tamer, a clothing factory, but the children—predictably, the teenagers were the most difficult—did not adapt to Columbia quickly. Shopping for a house, Burris found prices in Columbia "outrageous." His house in Flint was on the market for a paltry $32,000, so the $70,000 to $90,000 asking prices in the city were out of his reach. The Burrises settled into the apartment. Over the next two years only one person in Burris's team managed to buy a place. Many workers he knew had some adjustment problems in Maury County. They were offended by the higher prices asked of Saturn workers only, and though they understood the local resentment about the lack of jobs available at the plant they got tired of being scapegoats. Some of Burris's friends simply missed city living. "They feel lost without their city structure," he said. "Many of them are moving to Nashville. For some reason they like to be around the shiny lights."

Bob Courtemanche, a big, red-bearded third-generation autoworker, didn't miss Flint's shiny lights. In late 1988 Courtemanche moved down from Flint and bought what he called a "hobby farm," twenty acres with a tractor, near the Alabama state line, in Cornersville. His wife Cathy landed a job at the local Wal-Mart. "Made her almost a celebrity," Courtemanche said. Two of his three boys made the high school football team. Having done a lot of soul searching before moving, and having given up almost twenty years of seniority at the Flint Engine Plant, where he had been an ace grinder operator on the crankshaft machining lines, Courtemanche was thankful to his dad for having kept the pressure on to get out of Flint; otherwise, he just might have stayed.

A retired dynamometer operator for Buick, Bob Courtemanche, Sr., had, in his words, "seen Flint go from vacant fields to new homes in those fields to vacant stores downtown." So when Bob, Jr., had come to him for some advice about joining the new Saturn division in late 1987, he'd said, "You're crazy if you don't look at it. What are your boys going to do in Flint?"

Some folks thought giving up twenty years of seniority would qualify a person for being labeled crazy. Sometimes, as he mulled Saturn over, Bob Courtemanche felt that way. His roots were in Flint. His grandfather, as well as his father, had worked for GM there. Family picnics were mini-GM reunions, with salaried and hourly types knocking down beers and eating hot dogs together. Bob Courtemanche had first applied at Flint V-8 Engine, as it had been called in the 1960s, on his father's recommendation, been hired, served a tour in Vietnam, returned home, and went straight back into the plant. At Flint V-8 three machining lines turned out crankshafts, two lines for eight-cylinder engines and one for V-4s. A total of six hundred people worked on the lines, two hundred on each of three shifts. A crank product handler, a nice name for a laborer who lifted the seventy-pound engine parts from one work station to the next, Courtemanche didn't mind lifting a few tons of iron each day, but he wasn't excited about doing it all his life. Looking around he decided that being an equipment operator was a step up. He took it and was soon running a lathe, then a main bearing grinder. In the late 1970s he sat in as a UAW committeeman, drunkenness having gotten the better of the elected committeeman. Eventually, Courtemanche was elected in the fellow's place.

At Flint Engine, as the plant was then called (in the never-ending reorganizations at GM, it went from V-8 Engine to Flint Engine to C-P-C Flint Engine during Courtemanche's years), the late 1970s and early 1980s were not good years. Automation came in, sales went down, and the labor squeeze was on. As a union committeeman, a bridge position between the shop floor and management, Courtemanche found himself in the middle of a lot of anger, layoffs, and jaw grinding. Unhappy with his job, he switched to third shift, where the tension was less, and enrolled in college part-time. He first became intrigued by Saturn when the company tried to hire his brother. His brother told the recruiters that he didn't want to leave Flint. When they shifted their attention to Bob, he replied, "Let me think about it."

At the time—it was late 1987—Saturn's product development teams, or PDTs, were handpicking members. Being wanted stroked Courtemanche's ego and he decided he'd give Saturn a look see. He was interviewed and took some tests. Shown the Saturn Engineering and Preproduction Build Center in Madison Heights, he was "a little dazzled by the engineering," he recalled. Back in Flint, he was suddenly afflicted by a severe attack of ambiguity. On pins and needles about being offered a job at Saturn, he still was debating whether to say yes if one was offered. He'd never been to Tennessee, he had his seniority in the engine plant—but his old man maintained the pressure, kept asking that depressing question about the boys' future around Flint. His wife was encouraging. Courtemanche found himself daydreaming about a front porch somewhere in the green hills of Tennessee. When the call from Troy finally came, he thought, Ah, what the hell.

"What I brought to the party was twenty years experience as a machine operator," he told me three years later, in Northfield, where Saturn Communications arranged for us to talk. The product development teams in the "sandbox," the name he gave the Saturn Engineering and Preproduction Build Center, had needed his input in order to design user-friendly machines and equipment, Courtemanche recalled. He'd joined the crankshaft machining line team, focusing on product and process together, in harmony. On the team were four engineers, a team business leader, and two UAW members, himself and a skilled tradesman. Initially, the atmosphere in the sandbox was alarmingly old world, he remembered. The engineers had reservations about the union guys, the union guys weren't that eager to be buddy buddy with the engineers. There was that same old distance, that same old distrust. But as they worked side by side, rolling up their sleeves, loosening ties (not a big problem with Courtemanche who tended not to wear one), the barriers started to come down. A shared vision began to emerge. The team had to design the line, order the machinery, qualify it, hire seven operators and three trade technicians. Instead of status and power, they focused on the shared vision. It was enervating, even exhilarating for the big-handed machine operator with the red hair and freckled smile. Nevertheless, he still thought he was going to be fighting with Bob Davis, the team's business leader. "We did have a couple of scuffles," Courtemanche recalled. But Davis, a whip-thin, bespectacled guy who at first glance looked like the stereotypical computer nerd, gained the machine operator's respect when, evidently sensing Courtemanche's feelings, he confronted him and said, "Don't ever hold anything back; let's get it out."

Davis, whose job included cost control of the line, had previously worked for Ford. He had been awarded a chrome-plated crankshaft for performance. That chrome crank kept catching Courtemanche's eye until finally, having wholeheartedly adopted the Saturn spirit, he challenged Davis (he was the team business leader for crankshaft and head machining in powertrain, too) to give chrome-plated parts to whichever machining line made the first part once they all moved down to Spring Hill. Davis accepted.

In September 1988 the team's focus shifted from the sandbox in Michigan to Spring Hill itself. Courtemanche packed up his family and moved to Cornersville. At work the interior of the powertrain building was still rock; the building itself was mostly a vast shell of automotive potential. In November, just after Thanksgiving, Courtemanche boarded a plane and flew to Japan, another first for him. In Komatsu, with two engineers and two technicians, he qualified the Komatsu Company's rough-end equipment for the crank line. Qualifying machinery was standard procedure to insure, as Courtemanche put it, "the machine did what they told us it would do."

Courtemanche stayed in Komatsu for a month, running crankshafts. The huge, complex machine measured each crankshaft's geometry and started refining the journals, pins, and bearings along its spine. It had an enclosed mill and extensive electronic controls. Courtemanche was impressed by the machine, though he didn't much care for Japanese food. "I'm a big beef eater," he once told me with a laugh, cradling his girth. "I like my beef. You get over there, and there's a lot of seafood. Japanese-style seafood. That's not my way to live."

Back in Tennessee, throughout early 1989, machinery, robots, and electronics arrived at powertrain for the crankshaft machining line, as well as for the head and block machining lines, the foundries, the transmission and engine assembly lines. Mechanical systems were being installed in the concrete. Wires literally snaked everywhere. Amid the trucks, the superintendents, the contractors, and the sub-contractors, one heard the constant beeps of trucks backing up, and the occasional chatter of Japanese engineers. They had flown over to make sure machinery, including the Komatsu rough end, went in right.

That the installation of the entire 525-foot, $25 million crank line, which included four robots, eight machines, and well over a hundred feet of eight-foot-tall panel boxes that communicated with everything electronically, not to mention a network of traces for coolants and fluids beneath the floor, went in smoothly, amazed Courtemanche. Engineers, vendors, contractors, the Japanese team, the nucleus of the future crank team that would actually be making crankshafts—all co-operated.

Recalling that heady time, Courtemanche said, "We had come far enough in our relationship that we trusted each other. I was amazed at what we accomplished because I know what would have happened trying to install one piece of equipment in my old place. It would have been a big fiasco. I've seen it before. The service guy can't touch anything because you got some other guy saying, 'He's stepping on my territory.' Then you've got the supervisor saying, 'I don't care; he's got to get the machine in.' Down here you didn't have all that to deal with."

As the line's CTM, Courtemanche had been hiring his teammates through the RASS system. The nucleus of the future team that would be responsible for the operation and maintenance of the line was a high-spirited, skilled quintet: Courtemanche, operator Scott Prins, electrical tech Danny Lentz, mechanical techs John Plourd and Gary Harvey. Their collective machining experience was broad, deep, and hands on. The team was given unheard-of flexibility to get the line up and running as the members saw fit. It was another example of a shared vision moving a group to a higher level of performance than any of them as individuals had ever experienced. It was a high.

Lentz, an outspoken, on-the-edge-of-genius electrical whiz kid, remembered 1989 and early 1990 at Saturn as a rarefied atmosphere. Particularly for a skeptic, as he was. "I didn't trust the place before I came," he once told me. "I was afraid there were too many idealists and too few technicians. But I came because I was desperate for a job.

When we started up this crank line, we did things that I don't think have ever been done before." Yet afterwards he had been disappointed; the engineers and business leadership in the powertrain building had stopped listening to this top team, just kind of letting its talent and enthusiasm wilt. That had gone counter to the Saturn philosophy and, according to Lentz, knuckled under to the GM corporate philosophy: "We got to save money." To him it was the first sign of the old world reluctance to share decision making with blue-collar technicians and operators beyond the task at hand.

Throughout the installation period, Courtemanche had often found himself thinking about Bob Davis's chrome crank and the bet they had made back in the sandbox. The friendly competition in the machining lines between heads, blocks, and cranks reminded Courtemanche of a giant game of chess—one he knew his team was winning.

In March 1990, Cortemanche told Davis to have vice president of manufacturing Guy Briggs on hand because the team was going to run Saturn's first machined part. The five men did, painted the crank gold, and handed it to Briggs and Mike Bennett, who attended the mini-celebration for the union. "Okay guys," Courtemanche told the big wigs, "let's get Saturn going!"

Later, he said, "I nailed Bob Davis on the chrome crank. I've got one at home on my fireplace mantle. That was a big day; it made you forget you had twenty years in at the old place."

Four months later, on July 31, 1990, as scheduled, the rollout of the first Saturn occurred, with outgoing GM chairman Roger Smith at the wheel. By then the foundries were pouring cast iron and aluminum engine parts, the presses were banging out hoods, trunks, and spaceframes, the paint shop was coating everything using state-of-the-art technology, and the conveyors overhead were clicking from one building to the next, carrying subassemblies toward final assembly. New people were still joining their teams, however, and bottlenecks were an everyday occurrence. In the final assembly building, for instance, CTM Burris and his marriage team spent a lot of time waiting for the line to go after it had temporarily stopped.

Saturn had not managed to get tuned yet. Rather than a symphony with all sections harmonized, it remained more like a high school band still trying to learn the music. Because of that the rollout—unlike Nissan's unveiling of its first Sentra in Smyrna in 1985, with

Lamar there smiling, with bands playing, with the media attending—was a private affair. For the Saturn family only. "Roger and No Me," one disgruntled journalist called it.

Down at the plant security was tight. Frustrated journalists rode the roads in a much diminished version of the whirlwind weekend of five years ago, almost to the day, when Saturn had been announced. Inside, bleachers had been erected in a big, open area of final assembly. Practically all the three thousand Saturnites hired to date packed in the space. Some sat, others stood. A few, like Scott Prins, a member of the crankshaft machining team, climbed into the red steel rafters overhead.

For Prins, looking down at Smith driving, chairman-to-be Stempel in the passenger seat, LeFauve in the backseat with UAW president Owen Bieber, emotions were mixed. Prins felt good about the car, but he couldn't stand Roger Smith and what he'd done to GM. In fact, on a nationally televised TV program about the competitiveness of the American work force, called *Work Force 2000* and broadcast in early 1992, Prins would say, "I loathed Roger Smith. Yet [for the Saturn rollout] I clapped and cheered for ten minutes for the man."

As did his Saturn teammates. Swept up by the emotion and momentum of eight years, they clapped, hooted, cheered in a prolonged standing ovation for the little flush-faced man who the next day was handing GM over to Robert Stempel and joining the board of directors. Smith's retirement pension was $1.2 million a year, or the annual payroll of 428 of the cheering op techs, roughly fifteen percent of Saturn's start-up work force.

Saturn's real launch came two months later, in October. It was heralded by ads on national TV and in magazines and newspapers coast to coast. Hal Riney & Partners' ads were a blend of testimonials by the engineers and workers who had brought Saturn together and soft-focus little dramas about relocating to rural Tennessee, complete with dogs, newspaper boys, and tractors in the sunset. None of the first round of ads showed a car. The intent was to reawaken Americans to Saturn as a new company of somewhat mysterious origins but committed to that nebulous cluster of traditional American values: the land, the family, the farm, the paper route. The phantom car also had to compete with the recession that had a grip on the economy and the war threatening to explode in the Persian Gulf.

In the fall of 1990 Saturn, whatever it looked like, was not something most Americans could have bought even if they had seen or wanted one. Although the plant had been finished on time and on budget ($1.9 billion for the complex only, an estimated $1.1 billion for all the rest), if the facility had a motto, it was "We're still debugging." Production was plagued with problems, with the worst concentrated in the lost-foam foundry and the state-of-the-art paint shop. The industrial symphony was not in harmony. *Kanban,* or just-in-time inventory, was proving difficult to put into action. Some modules in the plant stockpiled parts while others worked overtime and still couldn't keep up.

"You can sit there in a classroom and talk about that job all day," Al Burris said about the rough start-up. But being on the line was totally different. Much of the training, he realized, had been "for attitude." Now every job had an operation description that had to be followed. Tools and machines had to be used correctly. Coordination between team members and between the upstream and downstream teams had to be practiced. In the chassis work module, for instance, the nine teams had well over one hundred members. All of them were working things out, Burris said, discovering what it was like to be a customer, have a customer, aspire for continuous improvement, stay focused on quality, *and* attend training classes.

Where Burris worked, first a spaceframe floated down from overhead and met the powertrain, which moved into place horizontally. The powertrain went up into the spaceframe of the chassis. Parts were bolted, brake lines and a master cylinder attached, as the vehicle moved along. "Every person checks the work of the person in front of him," Burris explained. They used electric tools, which were more sensitive than the air tools most team members had worked with in older plants. Team members took breaks, spelling each other at their jobs, then rotated to other jobs on their team. If Saturn had been tuned, Burris's team would have been completing one marriage a minute. It wasn't. Sometimes minutes would lapse between the bolting together of a chassis floating down lazily from above and a powertrain trundling in along the floor.

The consequences showed in the stores. That fall many opened with an embarrassing lack of cars. Some stores had only one. You could kick the tires, stroll around it, take home some literature. Saturn soothed the dismay of store owners, who had invested a couple million each to sell the little import fighter, by compensating them for the lack of product.

In the real world Saturn was greeted with a blend of polite applause, muted enthusiasm, and outright skepticism. *Automotive News,* the auto industry's weekly, awarded Saturn its "story of the year."

Time magazine put the car on its cover and summarized the eight-year drama. The automotive magazines were restrained but encouraging. Their reporters seemed a little gun-shy. With GM stumbling toward a terrible year, with yellow-ribbon patriotism in high gear over the impending War in the Gulf, and with most economic indicators down, bashing Mother Motors' new baby smacked of overkill. Besides, the car itself—especially the SC, the coupe—wasn't bad, most test drivers concluded. It handled well, was laid out sensibly, looked pretty good. If the engineers had only taken their ear plugs out and listened to the Osterizer-loud engine, *Car & Driver's* Rich Ceppos lamented.

Financial analysts were less kind. Even if Saturn did sell, they tended to agree, it wouldn't make any profit for a long time. First there was the need to amortize the $3 billion in start-up costs. Second, GM had seldom made money on low-volume operations. And third, the selling price for Saturn's three models was extremely low, from $8,200 to $12,000, which eliminated high profit margins, margins that traditionally helped distribute dividends to stockholders. The relentless GM watchdog, analyst and author Maryann Keller, said she didn't see how Saturn could help General Motors. Eight years from conception to launch "is simply too long," Keller claimed. "Nobody can get away with a product program that has that kind of gestation. It is simply ridiculous in today's world."

That fall three hundred new students swelled Columbia Central High School. Downtown, the Magnolia House, a restaurant featuring fancy cuisine and candlelight, reopened in an historic house. "This is something Northerners are used to, and we don't have down here," boasted the owner. You still couldn't get a martini. Liquor by the drink remained illegal in Maury County. On Saturdays, though, you could catch the University of Michigan's football games once a bar in Franklin started receiving them via satellite.

Inside the plant increasing production without lowering quality was the number one challenge. There were more than 150 teams, with each team numbering between six and fifteen members. Teams were continuing to define their roles, learning their machinery, training. If there were problems, and there were plenty, a team's CTM went to his or her WUMAs. If the WUMAs, who were resource people and problem solvers, couldn't help, the CTM went to the BUC, or Business Unit Coordinator, who was in charge of an integrated number of work unit modules. If the BUC got stumped, all of them went to the SAC, the Saturn Action Council, which included LeFauve,

Bennett, all the vice presidents, and some advisory members for training and strategy. "Those were the BUC's bosses," Burris said. "They were the big guys."

That first fall there was a "rebalance." Heavy teams got trimmed. Burris's team was cut back to twelve but remained an ethnic and gender mix: two black men, one Hispanic, two black women, a white woman, six white males. They became the A-crew once a second shift was started. RASS continued to hire. So training was continuing, with new people coming aboard. Weekly, A-crews and B-crews alternated working days and nights, which was hard on single parents and families.

When Burris came to work the first thing he did was put on his safety glasses. He read the log book to see how the last shift had left things. He took attendance. If the marriage work unit was short-handed by a member or two before the line started (it stopped between shifts), the team could still operate. If three team members were absent, however, the team needed to borrow from another team, or else report the shortage to the WUMAs—ASAP. Because chassis, cradle, and brake master cylinder systems, all three the marriage work unit's responsibilities, were crucial components of each car, they were classified as "MVSS" items. That is, they had to meet federal Motor Vehicle Safety Standards. So, focus and quality in the marriage work unit module were exceptionally important.

Sometime in early 1991, Burris recalled, he first noticed a decline in the hospitality of the locals. He attributed some of it to the jobs issue, but most of it to the bad economy in Maury County and across America. His wife lost her job at Weather Tamer. Their house in Flint still hadn't sold. Burris was pleased with his job, though. He did miss one thing he had enjoyed at GM Truck and Bus. There had been more camaraderie in the old world, he recalled, more interaction. At Saturn every main building was sort of like its own world, and even in that world you tended to spend most of your time with your team. You could get a little sick of your team.

Each building at Saturn had its own cafeteria. The food service jobs did go to locals. Whether that assuaged some of the growing resentment about the job situation was doubtful. Even Burris said, "They were working for free" because the cafeteria jobs paid minimum wage.

That first year, Burris's son Timothy, who was in high school, struggled academically. His grades dropped to Cs. The family started attending the Baptist Mount Cavalry Church in Columbia. The congregation was all black. "The only time I seen whites there was when it came to election time," Burris said.

At St. Catherine of Siena, the Catholic Church on the white side of town, the congregation grew so large that Father Rudisill held three Masses on Sunday and one on Saturday night. "You get more Indians than chiefs here," Father Rudisill said, describing the make-up of his congregation. "Of course, they claim to not have chiefs any more," he added, sounding skeptical.

Meetings before and after shifts, focusing on leadership, productivity, safety, and other issues, were a way of life at Saturn. Team members who weren't "buying in at 70%," which was the commitment necessary to be a partner in any decision, were shifted to consultation. Consultation put you in a green, then a yellow, and finally, if you were only buying in at twenty to thirty percent, say, or not buying in at all, into a red zone. If you landed there, the WUMAs sent you home for a few days to think if Saturn really was the right place for you.

Saturn Communications published a Saturn daily *Newsline* that carried plant-wide information. Each building had a news bulletin, such as the *Powertrain News*. Each team had a team center room with a TV tuned regularly to the Saturn Channel, 33. A Saturn Communications video team ranged throughout the plant. Its shorts—on problems, successes, updates, people, and on keeping everything they heard confidential and in the Saturn family—ran repeatedly on the Saturn Channel. But if there was one thing at Saturn that stood out in practically every newcomer's mind, it was the EXEL course.

"The pole was tough," Al Burris said, recalling the course in the comfort of his living room.

"How come?" I asked.

He grinned. He had done the EXEL course three months ago, in March 1991, so it was fresh in his mind. "The pole is, first of all, forty-seven feet in height," he said. "And just like a regular telephone pole. It had little steps. You climb on up those steps. And they had a little round disc on the top. The circumference of the disc was something like eight inches. Once you reach the top of the pole, you make a three hundred and sixty degree turn on that little old disc. An eight-inch disc. You got to *stand* and *turn*—forty-seven feet up in the air! Believe me, it wasn't easy. Once you turn—"

"Have you got a belt on or something?" I interrupted.

"You got what you call a safety harness on, the same thing the paratroopers use," Burris explained, laughing. "But once you're up there, you never know you got your harness on. Your mind keeps telling you you don't have this harness on. You is up there with the trees! You can look over the treetops. The height really was fearsome; it feared some people. But the hardest thing for me was letting go. For me, climbing the pole was easy."

Burris compared letting go on top of the pole to making the adjustment at Saturn from the old world of GM. "It's like people being leaders, and CTMs," he said. "After team members come on board, you don't want to let go some of the functions, cause you say, 'I been here two years.' You wanted to feel like you were in control, but the purpose of the pole was to let go. Let go of some of the things you had learned to share with your new team members. And it wasn't easy for most of these people to let some of this stuff go. That was the purpose of the pole. Once you get up on the pole, you got to jump. That was my biggest feeling: I was afraid to jump off the pole."

"Why would you leap from a forty-seven-foot pole above the trees?" I asked.

"To ring the bell!" Burris exclaimed. "They had a bell about eight feet from the pole. You had to jump from the pole and try to ring the bell."

"So, did you hit the bell?"

"No, I didn't hit the bell. I was afraid to jump. I jumped." He shook his head, chuckled. "But I missed the bell. To hit the bell is easy— but you can't be afraid to jump."

It had been an unseasonable March day, windy and snowy, Burris remembered. His teammates in the marriage work unit, along with team members from button up, tire and wheel, pre-marriage, and brake, had their eyes on him up there. They were cheering him on, he said, shouting: "Come on, Al, you can do it! You can do it!"

But, he repeated, "It wasn't easy to let go." Never mind ring that bell.

"Another event was the high-Y," he continued. "It was shaped just like a Y. The purpose of this was teamwork."

The way Burris described it, the high-Y involved a thirty-five-foot climb to the opposing top branches of the Y, then a walk down a sloping steel cable. Each partner edged down a branch of the Y toward the apex. Each wore a harness. Once they clasped hands at the apex, movement down the bottom branch of the Y was easier because they helped each other. The lesson? Two people were better at a task than one.

"The high-Y was the hardest event there was," Burris declared. It left him exhausted. He'd done the high-Y with a teammate named Mary. "She was saying, 'Al, will you help me?' We got up there and she just got so scared that her legs were shaking. She shook for about five minutes. I was coaching her all the way through it. I was saying, 'Mary, stop shaking; don't even think about it; close your eyes.' And she went to shaking worse."

They had been taught what to do. But, Burris said, "Once you get on the high-Y, your mind keep telling you you ain't got nothing on. All you can see is those people down there hollering at you. And they confusing you."

The next obstacle was the wall. "It was high, it was high," Burris remembered. "Something like what—fifty-three feet in the air? The wall has got something like pegs on it." With one hand Al Burris stuck the pegs in an imaginary wall between us. "Here, here, here. You start off, three of you, and you have to grab these pegs." Harnessed together, of course. "That means these three people got to go up together. One guy can't get ahead of another guy. And one guy fall, they all three fall."

Finally, there was the trust fall. You walked out on a ledge eight feet high and fell over backwards, into the arms of your teammates. Burris smiled with his recollection of the trust fall. He said, "Once you falls backwards, some of them takes you and rocks you from side-to-side, and sings you a little old song. What they call the *Baby Rock,* for two or three minutes. Ease your mind. Ease you down real slow."

The EXEL program lasted three days. The course, tackled on day two, was behind Rippavilla. While standing on the eight-inch disc or the high-Y, you could see the mansion's chimneys. Not that Burris was looking at them. He kept his eyes mostly on the ground. The freezing rain and snow on day two of his team's program had made the course particularly memorable. The purpose of the learning adventure was to foster teamwork, as the lectures the first day of the program emphasized. Here was a chance to better know yourself, to improve relationships with teammates. Dealers went through EXEL, as did sales consultants. So had management. Even new GM CEO Robert Stempel, when he visited the plant in the fall of 1990, had done some of the course, together with his wife.

On his third day, Burris said, they played games. One game was a version of blind man's bluff, with the seeing partner leading the blindfolded one. Another involved passing a ball around forty people gathered in a circle, cutting the time down from over a minute the first pass to less than a second five tries later through discussion and innovation and cooperation. Finally there was a cookout: hamburgers, hot dogs, soft drinks, congratulations. "Some people think it's sick, you know," Burris said about EXEL. Not him. "It reminded me of being in the Marines."

New World
Old World

18

The Chairman

In late July 1991 I went to Detroit for a week. I had not spent much time there since my undergraduate days at the University of Michigan in Ann Arbor, forty miles farther west. Detroit had been on the road to ruin even then, but now, over twenty years later, it had no rival in America for the quality of those ruins. Square block after square block of ragged brick, sagging metal, tilting towers whose wondrous shapes would make an imaginative child smile and a retired autoworker cry were scattered here and there. Detroit was worse than it had been, yet also beautiful, or so it seemed to me, in an odd way. Its downtown, in particular, retained a certain grace. It was a forgotten, somewhat forlorn, but undeniably marvelous architectural monument to the decades that had opened the American Century, decades during which Detroit had been a power hub, its automotive factories belching smoke, its jobs luring immigrants, its swagger and industry epitomizing that high-octane blend of the utilitarian and the sublime that had washed over the roots of the American Century like a magic elixir. An elixir that had totally dried up during the century's fourth quarter, leaving downtown Detroit to rot.

Ever since Saturn had been announced there had been scattered mutterings—usually casually brushed off as nonsense—that the fate of Detroit, and of Flint to the north, awaited Spring Hill, Smyrna, Georgetown, all the new car culture locations. Of course, it took a giant leap of the imagination to envision a post-Saturn Maury County with the homeless panhandling you whenever you parked, with windows smashed in the plant, with weeds waving where corn and soybeans now were cultivated. Yet if history was a guide—and there was little evidence in the history of American automobile manufacturing to refute the bleak prognosis—a particularly virulent and mean future was out there in the early twenty-first century for the dimple of the universe because the car industry threw away places as cavalierly as drivers junked cars.

Driving eastward on West Grand Boulevard one morning, with the red neon GENERAL MOTORS sign, like a tiara, on a roofline in the distance, I was thinking about this when I again had a sudden appreciation for Detroit's era of great prosperity, along with a shuddering realization of how dead and distant that era now was. Once-elegant homes with Art Deco flourishes lined both sides of the potholed boulevard, their doors heavily shielded, their lawns littered, their rooftiles dangling. It was an exercise in redundancy, a kind of intellectual cliché, to remind myself that the cars that had made downtown Detroit during the first half of the twentieth century had also become the means by which people had vacated the city, gradually swelling the suburbs and spawning growth patterns that emphasized the grid and the shopping mall bathed in stoplight glow.

After I passed the Henry Ford Hospital, the GM Building materialized in all its might and glory. It was a classical hulk suggestive of Gotham City, of Superman. It was broad and solid, with a touch of elegance, yet also oddly working class; the building's repetitive H-patterns suggested, at least to me, the shifting sequence for an eight-speed gearbox. Across the boulevard, towering like a ziggurat and more visually exciting, stood the second anchor of this once elite neighborhood, the Fisher Building. Pink granite in its lowest stories, then buffed marble above in a stepback pattern, the "cathedral of commerce," as it had been dubbed decades ago, had been erected as a twenty-eight-story monument to the freespending vision of the seven Fisher brothers who made a fortune manufacturing car bodies.

Both buildings were by Albert Kahn. Kahn had also been the architect of factories for Henry Joy at Packard Motor Company, for Henry Ford a number of places, for the Dodge Brothers, for Chrysler. Though less well known than the giants of twentieth-century architecture—the Wrights, Van der Rohes, and Peis—Kahn's contributions to the field in some ways dwarfed those of his better-known successors. He was the father of the modern American factory. He had formalized his concepts at Ford's Highland Park plant, which opened New Years Day in 1910. Assembly-line production originated there in 1913. Kahn refined his design concepts at dozens of other factories, and optimized them at "the Rouge," Ford's sprawling automotive facility built in the 1920s. Kahn's factories were different because they used steel and reinforced concrete instead of the bulky wooden beams of traditional plants. Steel and concrete, coupled with long runs of

218

windows to let in natural light, set the industrial stage for the creation of long, uninterrupted assembly lines.

Inside the GM Building, despite the Gotham City look of the exterior and the Beirut-like sense of much of the neighborhood, the lobby had the feel of yet another era, the self-confident America of the 1950s. Executives in dark suits and white shirts carried rectangular briefcases, wore wingtips, had newspapers folded beneath their arms. The women wore dresses and heels, had their hair coiffed. Everyone seemed to be moving purposely, confidently. I signed in with the security guard, a kindly older fellow with a pistol on his hip. He called upstairs to tell the director of news relations that I was here.

Given my frustrated wanderings through Saturn Communication's procedural labyrinth to date, the ease with which I arranged this interview with GM chairman Robert Stempel struck me as fortunate, if not downright lucky. I had called the fellow Stempel had named that hot afternoon the previous May, and everything had just fallen in place. Now, waiting to go up to the fourteenth floor, I wandered into a ground-level showroom. A white Saturn SC, with a $13,650 sticker price, was on display. Extras, which had upped the base price of $11,775, included a/c, cruise, power locks and windows, and an AM/FM stereo cassette player. Nearby was a bright red Geo Storm GS 2 + 2 sport coupe with a 1.6-liter DOHC engine. The Geo, manufactured by NUMMI, seemed not terribly different from the Saturn. On the wall of the showroom I noticed something rare: Saturn's banner in line with those of Chevrolet, Oldsmobile, Buick, Cadillac, and GMC truck.

A few minutes later I was with John Mueller, the director of news relations, walking down a corridor, heading toward Stempel's corner office. Mueller was friendly and upbeat. I, on the other hand, was experiencing a slight wave of panic. I felt a little disreputable in this crisp, buttoned-up environment, as though my shirt wasn't white enough, my hair too long, my shoes not shiny enough. At the same time I was at the top ("Is he the top?" Dr. Deming often asked). I had hopes that by getting to the top I might find it easier subsequently getting to the bottom, which, in truth, was where I wanted to be: in the Saturn plant, on the crankshaft line, witnessing teamwork in action.

Mueller led me into an office. Two secretaries glanced up. We continued into the inner sanctum of the chairman, a Spartan-looking room with a clean desk. Stempel suddenly stalked toward us from a door to my right, thrust out his hand and smiled, putting me immediately at ease. With his slicked back hair, scrubbed skin, broad shoulders, and dark suit, the chairman struck me, oddly enough, as having the look of a gangster from the 1920s. We sat at a small round table near a wind tunnel model of an Opel. Stempel had a yellow pad. He took the first notes. Mueller switched on his tape recorder.

If the eras evoked here—the 1920s, the 1950s, 1980s Beirut— seem to clash, they clashed in my mind, too. Maybe when all was said and done, *that* was GM's top dilemma: the leadership of the company didn't know what era it was in. As a result GM was wasting a tremendous amount of energy in a doomed quest to cover all eras. Be all things to all people.

Allotted half an hour, I got an hour with Stempel. Almost instantaneous shifts—a veritable four-speed verbal transmission—linked his responses, asides, digressions, and comments. He spoke in management-eze, a language barren of any emotion; he descended into the popular idiom of the factory rat; he adopted the personal tone of the faintly remorseful confessor; he boomed with the confidence of a general anticipating a rout; he backed up, a seasoned man reflecting on personal vicessitudes. All in all the interview was like a ride in a finely tuned touring sedan, a convertible cruising over human, organizational, and historic terrain. Stempel's hands seemed constantly to be in motion, as though steering or adjusting dials. Occasionaly he leaned back and glanced at Mueller as though checking out the scenery. We speeded across the concept of teamwork ("The best teams today are still those that understand *win!*"). He nostalgically recalled his favorite car (the front-wheel-drive 1966 Olds Tornado). He distinguished between the soft and hard issues of business ("If you're just nice to people, you're going to lose your ass; I can't say it any clearer than that").

The chairman wore large gold cufflinks decorated with the astrological sign of Cancer, the crab, and took it as a good sign I had come today, a year from the day of the Saturn rolloff. "It was going to be Roger Smith's last day," Stempel remembered, getting excited. "And the next day was going to be my first day. We pulled the car in and it was like pulling into a coliseum with a football team or something. I'll tell you, they went wild! They had done something, and they were proud of what they had done. . . . . You couldn't help but feel the emotion."

Stempel admitted that Saturn's had a rough time since then. He leaned close to me across a quadrant of the table. Through his bifocals his eyes took on a dual cast. "Everybody in the world is looking at them under a microscope," he said. "Every time they lift a finger," and he lifted a finger, "somebody says, 'Got a hang nail there!"

From Detroit, with all of GM to worry about, how did he get good information about Saturn, I asked.

He kept informed through GM president Reuss to whom Skip LeFauve reported. "Not on the [organizational] chart are a number of people I know at Saturn, engineers working for Jay Wetzel, guys in the powertrain. Then of course I have a Saturn, so I get all of the literature." Stempel laughed, a basso echoing around the office, which was not that big. "I should say, correctly, my wife owns a Saturn. We're the wrong demographics, of course."

When I said that teamsmanship had been around GM in other guises for years, but with less rhetoric and hype than the concept evoked lately, Stempel started tapping the table impatiently with a finger. "The best teams today are still those that understand *win*," he insisted. "Work together!" He tapped the table. "Play together!" He tapped the table. "Win. Don't ever forget win! And I'm telling you I'd rather be on the Pittsburgh Steelers than I would be on a group that went out and said, 'Gee, don't get your pads dirty today—we got a game tomorrow.'

"The soft issues are there to bring in more people to help your understanding, but a team has to be mean, lean, tough—a team has to want to do, it has to be driven.

"The difference about today's team is that when you were working on the car back in the sixties, you went over to the shop and you were a little guarded. You weren't too sure about the guys who worked for the UAW. You worried a little bit about them. 'I don't know if I'm going to tell them everything,' [you'd say to yourself]."

"Has teamsmanship been the main learning experience of Saturn?"

"No," Stempel answered without hesitation. "The main learning piece has been trust. Why didn't you let a guy who was building an engine up in Flint—why didn't you let him stop the line and say, 'Hey, Foreman, we got an oil leak problem and here's why.' Instead of just saying, 'Your job is to put those rings in and don't look up until five o'clock.'

"If team means being polite, being civil and so forth—that's fine. But the key issues are trust one another, work together, understand what that objective is, and don't deviate from winning, if that is your objective. You find that the best teams are usually pretty hard on themselves."

In 1985 Roger Smith had declared that Saturn "was going to be the key to General Motors long-term competitiveness, survival and success in the domestic market,' " I read from my notes. "Do you still feel that's true?"

"Absolutely. What Roger said is absolutely true. What's behind that is if we can't build a car the size of Saturn and sell it successfully in North America for a profit, they'll eat us alive. They'll just walk right on up the ladder: next thing it's the Cavalier; next thing it's the mid-sized Lumina; next thing it's our full-sized Park Avenue. And you better be able to build a competitive small car profitably in North America—otherwise, you're not going to be in business." Tapping his yellow pad, Stempel said, "Roger challenged the organization. We absolutely want to be profitable on the cars we make."

I reminded him of Saturn's multibillion dollar start-up costs, which had to be amortized, and its production problems. Given those factors, could Saturn be expected to make a profit?

"We're on track," Stempel insisted. "We're going to do it. It isn't that far away."

"Was there much thought given to the fact there would be some backlash in Maury County from the UAW getting all the jobs?" I asked.

"I think that aspect has been a bit overworked," he replied. "We had an agreement with the UAW. They wanted to prove something, we wanted to prove something. You can always do something with a new work force—that's easy." As for the locals expectations of jobs, he said, "Short-term wise, we were careful not to promise golden chariots in the sky."

Toward the end of the interview I mentioned the black/white tensions, Baptist belt mentality, large percentage of Catholic Saturnites in a county where there were sixty-eight Protestant churches, one Jewish synagogue, and only one Catholic Church.

"Yeah, we should have paid more attention to that going in," Stempel admitted. "So it's been an assimilation process."

"The people seem to be very comfortable in the plant, and they like what's going on there," I said. "But one of the questions I have is, are they able to establish the same level of comfort in the community? Because if you're not comfortable where you are, you're going to take that anxiety to work with you."

"There's a reverse to that, too," Stempel countered. "You may stay at work longer than you should, you may bring your family into work more frequently than you would other places. You may find your comfort in the plant. Well, you got to transfer that back into the community: that's the thing that has to happen."

He recounted the exodus of thousands of southerners to the promised land of Detroit after World War II. There had been friction between groups as a by-product of that. Likewise, friction was now a consequence of northerners being uprooted and sent South.

As I left Stempel made one last allusion to football. Apparently, he had been pondering a question I asked early in the interview: was GM so vast that it really needed to be run by a three-man team at the top, rather than one individual? He reminded me that when all was said and done a football team still only had one quarterback.

"Did you ever play football?"

"Oh yeah, in high school, in New Jersey. When you go out there on Saturday," Stempel said, raising his voice, "you want to win."

19

The Engineer

"Mr. Wetzel!"

Wearing a dark suit and looking at a low-slung red race car on display in the lobby of the design studio at the GM Tech Center in Warren, Michigan, Jay J. Wetzel, II, Saturn's vice president of engineering, the guy who had first been stopped for speeding in a Saturn prototype in 1985, heard the security guard call his name and turned. Wetzel strolled in my direction, briefcase swinging from his hands, a grin flickering at the corners of his lips.

Of all the Saturn executives I interviewed over several years Wetzel was consistently the most forthright and cooperative. He also returned my calls. All in all, in a Deming-esque way, he made me a satisfied customer. Why Wetzel dealt with me directly, talked to me at length alone, and opened doors so I could talk to Saturnites who otherwise would not have seen me, I wasn't exactly sure. But my intuition told me it was his self-confidence.

Today he led me up to the second floor and in a small conference room we were soon circling a touchy topic, Saturn's public relation's distance from its troubled parent. The ailing giant's coffers had absorbed Saturn's first year losses, estimated by most analysts to be in the vicinity of $700 million for the twelve months just ended in mid-July. Meanwhile, GM's troubles had reached staggering proportions. The core of its business, North American automobile operations, was on the way to losing $8 billion this year. In the bleak picture Saturn, despite its losses, two recalls, and production headaches, remained a shining star. Sales were strong, new stores opened monthly, and a groundswell of enthusiasm for the mostly-made-in-America car seemed to be spreading.

Defending GM, Wetzel reminded me that whether Saturn stayed at arm's length from its parent or not, it was still GM. "I'm GM," he emphasized. Everyone at Saturn was GM. The ads were a marketing strategy that recognized GM had a perception problem among import car buyers. And the strategy was working. Customer enthusiasm for the car was just incredible, Wetzel continued, shaking his head. "I've never seen anything like it. Our customers want to become sales people for Saturn."

He'd been receiving dozens of testimonials, many of them from older drivers who had spotted his name in the sales literature handed out at the Saturn stores. Just the other day, for instance, a ten-page letter had arrived filled with all kinds of futuristic suggestions. An eighty-three year old wrote in to ask if an assist strap might not be installed on the driver's side of his coupe. The man had arthritis, Wetzel said, so he arranged for a dealer to put a strap in for him. But that wasn't the point. The point was that the car was connecting with buyers. They cared enough about their new Saturns to get in touch. As for the fact older drivers liked the car, from an engineering point of view, Wetzel said, it made good sense to broaden the marketing profile, with its emphasis on single professional women and young families, and to include seniors as well. Insuring "easy in, easy out" did that. One senior he was personally trying to get into a Saturn coupe, he added with a chuckle, was seventy-nine and driving a Pontiac Trans-Am, a muscle car. The driver was his father.

Given several ads scheduled for the fall, the idea of broadening the market to include senior citizens had been discussed with Hal Riney & Partners. One of Saturn's more eye-catching print ads of the coming season would feature Velma Willarson, a seventy-six year old with a beatific smile standing by the raised trunk of her SC, from which she had just removed several large bags of bird seed. Bird houses hovered in the image. The colors in the ad were liquidy, with the most liquid of all being Velma's blue coupe. If you were thumbing magazine pages, at a glance it almost seemed to be floating. Like the copy for practically all the ads, Velma's was personal, told a little story, had a touch of humor. It said that Velma Willarson liked to feed nuthatches and rose-breasted grosbeaks around the town of Winchester and that her SC had plenty of trunk space for her bags of birdseed, as well as ample pep to spirit her out to her feeding stations in good time. All of which, presumably, made her happy.

Although production problems still plagued the plant, Wetzel sounded satisfied with the first year's numbers: 50 thousand cars: 35 thousand sold, 15 thousand still in the distribution pipeline. Nevertheless, Saturn had taken some pounding from the Detroit automotive press. The press saw itself as car-tuned, he explained, and a center-of-the-universe mentality prevailed here. Saturn was neither a Detroit company nor a far-out design. Saturn was not conservative, either, he said. It was affordable, built with quality foremost in mind, and fun to drive. Those factors were helping Saturn establish its own reputation in the marketplace. "We're only a little sixty-car-an-hour company," Wetzel claimed, somewhat wishfully since Saturn was at the time only a thirty-car-an-hour company doing everything in its power to become a sixty-car-an-hour company, "but we're trying to get the attention of a Chrysler or a Ford."

He reminded me of the themes behind the project's development: unity of purpose, a single design voice through teamwork, and the blending of product and process into a synergistic partnership. As Saturn was growing and expanding, it was proving harder to keep a grip on the themes, especially unity of purpose, which had fractured a little since the launch. Sitting up and raising his voice, as though talking to a team, Wetzel said, "Now we're working hard on recapturing that. Don't let that unity of purpose, that teamwork, slip away." At the same time, "Don't let technology and business systems get in the way of street smarts and common sense."

Toward that end he and several product development teams, totaling around seventy-five people, would be spending a few weeks in Spring Hill soon, focusing exclusively on increasing production. They would fly down, stay in hotels, and work with their counterparts in manufacturing. Fine-tuning production to increase the numbers often sounded orchestral, the way Wetzel described it: "You get the cadence, the music going, keep it going. When you keep stopping and starting, the musicians can't get harmonized."

Returning to the GM/Saturn linkage, Wetzel brought up something I had not heard mentioned for a while: Saturn as a learning laboratory for GM where new discoveries could be made and then disseminated back through the divisions. Wetzel said he wanted that to work. "One thing about technical people, they really network well," he elaborated. "My guys know everything going on in GM. They're bouncing their ideas off their peers; their peers are bouncing ideas off Saturn.

"One of the visions I have is that the technical community, if they have an idea that they think is really going to be strategically important to General Motors, but that the scale of GM is too big to try it on, that they ought to try the idea on Saturn." That way Saturn could stay small, family-like, yet be strategically important. "You can't run

226

General Motors on a family basis," he went on. "You can't run General Motors sitting around the dining-room table, like you run your personal life—although we try to do that at Saturn. Okay, but what you can do is you can think that way. You can force yourself to think that you're a smaller entity than you really are, then channel your focus in that way."

I mentioned that big business seemed to go back and forth between the philosophies of centralization and de-centralization, with the smaller-is-better concept he was describing in favor now. He agreed. "We're in this period right now, industry-wide, not just automotive, that everyone needs to be involved," he said. It was the era of "the team participatory approach to managing the business." And participative teamwork was extremely important to success, "but where some people get confused is that they think that means everyone involved in everything. You need leaders. You cannot let your leadership let go. Leadership can never let go. The task is to continually get unity of purpose and focus the team. Then what you do is break the elements apart, just like we do with our little car. I only have one guy I have to deal with about the interior of the car.

"I think big companies need to learn how to think like they were small companies, and channel their participation strategically, so they can be more effective. I try to do that every day. I have the opportunity to be an expert in people systems. I need to be able to stand up and to be able to explain most anything to my team, or to you, or to the public. But you know I found that I'm more effective when I put my thrust behind the product, have a good, very broad understanding about the people, the initiatives at Saturn. Apply them. But don't sit and debate them. I leave that to the people experts."

"Did you have any real trouble changing from an engineering focus to a managerial focus?" I asked.

"No."

"Isn't that traditionally a bridge that engineers have trouble crossing?"

Wetzel thought a moment. "Yes . . . I've heard that. But I don't see that very often. You have many technical people who are generalists. You have many technical people who have laser-sharp focus on a specific element of expertise. The interesting thing there is that that laser-sharp specialist probably couldn't do three things. And that generalist, who knows a lot of everything, but not much of anything, couldn't get you there either. So, when you're starting up a new car company, or you're trying to change General Motors, or whatever, the generalist you can't rely on because he has to rely on other people to get things done. And the specialist, you can't rely on because he can't work with the big picture. Now you need them both. What we really need," and he paused a moment, shifting around and looking pleased as though he'd thought about this a lot, "what we really need are people that have the total grasp of the business, and also have damn good knowledge of all the elements within the business. We need people who understand the working of all the elements, but are very broad based."

I asked where that training would come from.

"It has to be in the real world."

Wetzel recalled how important "words of wisdom from his grandfather and his father" had been for him at a young age to grasp the big picture in the automotive business. "Then I was on a good program early in my career, with lots of varying assignments. I'm doing that with my children. I've got three daughters—all instilled with the same kind of philosophy. All three developed a love for the automobile because of my interest. All had good working assignments during the summer. Not at Kroger's, or at the grocery store, but in the automobile industry. Two of them have graduated now from college and have good jobs because of their skill sets." Returning to my original statement about engineers having trouble cross training into managerial leadership roles, Wetzel concluded, "When you say, 'There aren't many of them,' I've heard that some people are born natural leaders. I don't think so. I think somewhere in their formative years they got the right stuff. The bottom line is, the generalist won't work, and the specialist won't work. You need people that really understand the subject, and are broad based to a deep depth."

At the outset of the interview Wetzel put his watch on the table so he could keep an eye on the time since he had an important appointment that afternoon. Now, leaning sideways in his chair again and checking the time, he announced with a wry grin that he had to go. "I've got to finish this little talk I've got to give."

On the way down to the lobby Wetzel described a somewhat bizarre safety exercise he had conceived. All too often, he said, whenever they talked about safety, people's eyes glazed over, they yawned, they might as well have been asleep. So today, in a little while, a bus was going to pick up thirty-five or so of his team leaders and members, none of whom had any idea of what was going on, and take them to a nearby cemetery. "We've rented the chapel. In fact, the guy who runs the cemetery said, 'This is so unique, I'm going to donate the chapel.' "

Wetzel had written a long, elaborate script for the macabre but effective fake funeral. "It's bizarre," he said, "but in this business, as in life, you tend to let something happen. Then you go back and fix it." A fatality didn't give you that luxury, a truth he intended to reemphasize that afternoon.

After Wetzel, sunglasses on, left for his safety sermon at the cemetery, I checked out the race car he had been looking at earlier. Low slung, fat tired, and bright red, the Lola was powered by the 1.9-liter performance engine found in both the SC and the SL2, coupled to a Hewland five-speed gear box. Fitted with high performance cams, special injectors and headers, along with a crafted fiberglass body, the Lola's top speed was 167 miles per hour, well over the coupe's maximum, which was around 115. The Saturn-powered Lola had recently beaten a field of sixty-two racers at a four-hour event at the Sears Point International Raceway in Sonoma, California.

Outside, in front of the design studio, an eight-to-ten-acre rectangular lake had a pebble beach and willows waving down both shores. To the left, its aluminum roof gleaming brightly in the sunlight, sat the design dome, inside which LeFauve had been rather unceremoniously put in charge of Saturn over five years ago. I walked over, but the doors to the dome were locked. I stood in the arc of shade cast by the roof. Most of the Tech Center buildings I could see were horizontal, glassy, three and four stories. They reminded me of the U.S. Air Force Academy north of Colorado Springs. Finnish architect Eero Saarinen had been responsible for the Tech Center's modernist touches, including this wok-like design dome and its taller counterpoint, a perfectly round 132-foot water tower covered with aluminum and gleaming like a buffed airplane wing.

In the 1950s the Tech Center had been the prototype rural corporate research headquarters. Lavishly praised and written about, it was part of the post-World War Two land-buying pattern that staked out territory just beyond the exploding suburban fringe where growth was sweeping aside the remaining silos and barns, leaving in their stead subdivisions, shopping complexes, industrial parks, and a paved grid of streets, boulevards, and roads. Driving to work here in the 1950s must have felt a little like being Buck Rogers off to the office, I thought. Of course, this was also where designers' and engineers' dreams had run head-on into economic and manufacturing realities. But in those days dreams often gained the upper hand. Pre-OPEC, mid-Cold War, and relatively carefree, the period nursed heavy chrome, pastel fins, and big-bore V-8s into appealing auto elements as American cars ruled the world's roads.

Back in 1950, of course, three-quarters of the world's passenger cars were found on America's roads. Most of those cars were built in and around Detroit. But the competition to satisfy the world's hunger for cars geared up as worldwide production of cars climbed steadily throughout the next four decades, from about 7 million cars a year in the early 1950s to 32 million in 1990. In 1990 cars were being manufactured in more than a dozen countries, from Brazil to Malaysia, from Russia to England, from Canada to Mexico, with China and India just getting into the car game. Since the early 1950s America's market share had dropped from seventy-five percent of world car sales to about twenty-five percent. In 1990, only one-third of the world's cars were found on America's roads and the dreamy 1950s—back when American industry had been the model for the world—had become the survival 1990s, with American industry wondering if it could compete globally. Many observers argued it could not. A fixation on short-term profits, outdated corporate strategies in manufacturing and sales, a long-term neglect of people, and slow-motion technological change put America "in serious trouble with respect to our industrial performance," wrote co-authors Robert Solow, a Nobel laureate in economics, Michael Dertouzos, chairman of MIT's Commission on Economic Productivity, and Richard K. Lester, a professor of nuclear engineering, in *Made in America*. Predicting harsh and wrenching change unless America responded before a financial crisis, they urged industry to start processes from scratch, to accept that it was sometimes good to bounce back from a big loss, to work steadily on improvements rather than rushing, to consider suppliers allies rather than enemies, to better understand foreign cultures and business practices, to make labor a partner in innovation, and to lobby government to reduce military spending and soften labor laws and tighten restrictions on corporate takeovers. Saturn had started from scratch, was leading GM in its rebound, and was progressing, if not steadily at least forward. But it had not made suppliers its allies yet or made an effort to know or adapt to rural southern culture, never mind influence national domestic policy.

I left the Tech Center and headed downtown. At Eight Mile and Mound Roads I passed Chrysler's Dodge City complex. "Home of Ram trucks," a sign declared. The plant sprawled alongside rough-surfaced Mound Road, which was littered brightly with throwaway packaging and an occasional consumer durable. Given the plant's closeness to heavy traffic and an apron of security fences, it was not hard to imagine the logistics and security headaches at Dodge City, headaches that Saturn had avoided, at least for a while. The traffic thinned and I passed several soul food catering establishments, barbed-wire-topped fences, and litter that rivaled, in depth, color, and variety, that found alongside highways in Mexico. On the edge of downtown, along West Grand Boulevard, I came to a vast ruin, the multistoried hulk of one-time auto king, the Packard Motor Car Company. A large worn sign hung on the side of one of the buildings: "For Sale."

Like Studebaker and Hudson, Packard had been a dying breed during my youth. The land yacht of land yachts, Packards were bought by the well-to-do and had the power to evoke boyish fantasies about gangsters and Prohibition Era night rides along dirt roads, the trunk and back seat crammed with cases of Scotch. Once I had been shown little flower vases crafted into the interior windows supports of an old Packard, an amenity even the Japanese didn't bother with any more. During the 1950s Packard had been absorbed briefly by Studebaker, before the South Bend, Indiana, legendary firm collapsed. That decade had witnessed the disappearance of practically all the independent automakers in Detroit, together with the independent body companies and parts suppliers. Dozens of huge industrial complexes had closed, eliminating 70 thousand jobs and devastating the city as cheap suburban sites had become popular.

I drove around the Packard complex, which stood isolated in sun-warmed decay. There was broken glass everywhere, rust, and dangling cables. The Packard ruins reminded me of the textile factories that had once lined rivers in New England. Stopping and checking my map, I realized I was on the edge of Hamtramck, where the City of Detroit had razed Poletown in the early 1980s so GM could build its new Cadillac plant. A few minutes later, I pulled over between a high wire fence and a former nightclub, now bombed out, left my car, scrambled up a short knoll, and peered across acres of mowed grass toward the plant. Somewhere out there had been the Church of the Immaculate Conception, which people in the neighborhood had made such a fuss over when the wrecker had come to knock it down a decade ago. The Polish community had not accepted the razing of its stores, homes, apartment buildings, and churches lying down. The racket and protest had lacked political punch, however. As an attempt at inner city renewal the plan here had not looked bad on paper, but the paper hadn't paid much attention to the human heart. General

Motors brought a wrath of bad publicity down on its head because a vocal community was razed so Cadillacs, declassé and out of touch with the wants of the affluent Americans who could afford them (they were buying Mercedes and BMWs), could be manufactured.

Why hadn't they knocked down the Packard ruins and built there instead, I wondered, looking through the security fence.

Subsequently, partially because of the negative publicity about Poletown, GM management turned away from the idea that it might be a major force in Detroit's economic comeback. "Green field site," "rural America," "anywhere away from this damn place," became the criteria for new plant sites. Saturn fit all three.

At the Cadillac plant, even after it opened in the mid-1980s, there had been problems. The plant had rejected the idea that technology was not the solution to GM's carmaking woes. Two hundred and fifty robots, together with new stamping presses to hammer out parts faster and automated guided vehicles to deliver parts throughout the factory quicker, were supposed to cut costs and increase quality. The robots were called "turn-key operatives." You turned the key, they did the job. At Cadillac, though, you turned the key and some of the robots did things like position windshields, then smash them, or load up with paint, then spray it all over. In a way the robots acted like an unpredictable generation of adolescents with a destructive sense of humor rather than mature cooperative machines that did exactly what was expected of them. Although the automation headaches were not as bad as the press made them out, it took several years for the plant to get on track.

Now, over five years later, as an article in *The Economist* pointed out this week, Cadillac had gone from "the most troubled car plant in America," to "a showcase." Last October, Cadillac had received the coveted Malcolm Baldrige National Quality Prize. Teary-eyed production workers attended the ceremony. Now *that* was change.

But why had the turnaround taken so long, *The Economist* asked. While NUMMI had "provided a golden opportunity for GM to discover that it was charging down an automated blind-alley," the article said, "robots certainly were not the key" to finding a way out of that alley. Yet it had taken years for NUMMI's lessons to sink in at Cadillac. Skip LeFauve would explain the time lag to me some months later as being an example of the fact that GM people simply were not adequately trained to observe. Besides, he would say, at NUMMI, they had not even known what they were looking at, which were new people systems, not high-tech ones.

Eventually, at Hamtramck, some of NUMMI's lessons had sunken in. Several robots and automated guided vehicles had been removed, control of decisions had been returned to workers in teams, and teams had been harmonized. Today Cadillac remained highly robotized and automated, but it was also more human.

Saturn and its "unique form of teamwork and consensus management," as *The Economist* described it, paralleled the NUMMI experience. Thus it also raised again the issue of GM and change, the issue of whether you could teach an old giant new tricks quickly enough for it to survive, and whether systems were in place for the transfer of knowledge to facilitate the survival. The magazine concluded that it was too early to draw any conclusions about Saturn's success or whether "a Saturn-type transformation is already under way in other parts of GM."

20

"Talk About a Woman Who's Smart"

For the next few days the weather in Motor City was spectacular. "Zephyr-fresh," one reporter at the Detroit *Free Press* called it, "with a sky the color of infinity." Air conditioning was not necessary because, as the reporter added poetically, "Breezes twirl through the house like phantom ballerinas."

Of course, when most folks think of Detroit in the summertime, phantom ballerinas and skies the color of infinity are not what spring to mind. They think Detroit, they think urban black hole, they think outhouse of the Rust Belt, they think cesspool of crime, crack, and despair thriving in a grayish world inhabited mostly by blacks. Or they think Detroit Tigers. The morning I drove north on the Chrysler Freeway, whether to rebuild Tiger Stadium in the Brigg's neighborhood where it presently stood, or to build a new stadium downtown, was the topic of conversation on a popular FM station. Although down, battered, and neglected, Detroit, the home of the most powerful force unleashed during the American Century—the car—was flirting with the idea of rising from its ruins. Or at least getting to its knees. Moving the Tigers near the old theater district, some callers felt, would generate more of what was desperately needed to accomplish the task: pride and money. Others said the whole idea was folly. Listening to the commentary, I passed by Hamtramck, new home of the once mighty Cadillac, passed through Highland Park, former home of Ford's Model T and the inspiration for Charlie Chaplin's *Modern Times,* drove past Madison Heights where Saturn's Engineering and Preproduction Build Center was located, and exited at Troy, about fifteen miles north of Cadillac Square, which was downtown's ground zero.

Saturn's headquarters occupied a two-building complex of little design distinction next to the four-lane Stephenson Highway, parking lots fore and aft. Inside, though, it was the new world: silver-gray and maroon offices, open-style cubicles, paper plates in a spartan cafeteria. It was a world where, an article in *Fortune* had said, "consensus and teamwork are the management bywords."

A security guard behind a counter in the small lobby called Beth Miakinin for me. I had first noticed Miakinin in one of the Saturn prelaunch ads the previous fall. She had angular features, the thoroughbred good looks that used to be ascribed to fine blood lines and breeding. When I mentioned her name to Wetzel in the design studio the other day, he had said, "She's one of our fast trackers—talk about a woman who's smart!"

Miakinin strolled up in pink flats. Softer-featured and easier going than the ad suggested, she had green eyes and shoulder-length hair. Her Saturn ID was pinned to the bottom of a blue sweater over a loose pink dress. We went into the cafeteria and found a table in the corner. It was a few minutes before lunch.

Beth Miakinin was as forthright as Jay Wetzel. When I asked about the ad, she said it "didn't even come close to capturing what I said." Hal Riney & Partners had paraphrased what she meant; they captured her message, Miakinin said, but not what she had said despite the quotation marks.

A series of long phone interviews had resulted in her being selected as a Saturn spokesperson. Her first interview had been for something called a "customer enthusiasm brochure" back in mid-1989. The brochure informed suppliers and other internal customers about the company through the voices of people like herself, the engineer-in-charge of the interior. While helping with the brochure, Miakinin had told the interviewer about the "Saturn spirit," or what she felt distinguished this company from others she had worked for. "When I first came to Saturn," Miakinin said, recapping the story, "most of the interior packaging was done on the car. So it wasn't like I was starting out with a fresh slate. What I saw I didn't think was real competitive, based on what was out there and what I knew about Saturn customers. I met a lot of resistance up front about Saturn's initial push, which was to go for a sporty sedan. Part of what some people termed sporty was a very tight interior package.

"It was a real battle," she continued. "I was doing a lot of soul searching about working on a car that I just really didn't buy into what the interior packaging was."

Miakinin learned she was not alone. A number of people were saying, "This doesn't feel right."

"But we were long past the point where all of that should have been locked in," she said. "Finally, there was a group of about thir-

teen of us which, after many, many late-night conversations discuss-
ing this—would you sign your name to this car? Would you be proud
to put your name on this car when it goes out?—we all decided no,
we couldn't. We ended up going over to talk to Skip. In most companies, this does not happen.

"We sat down one afternoon with Skip," Miakinin continued, "and
laid it on the line. None of us was willing to sign our name to this
thing, given where we were at."

Coincidentally, a car clinic, one of many that attempted to gauge
reactions of imported car owners to the phantom Saturn before it
went into production, happened to be going on that same week. The
results confirmed what Miakinin and the others were saying: the car
was too cramped inside for driver comfort; the interior was definitely
too tight.

"Basically, at that point in time, Saturn's top management made the
decision we would go back and redo it—even though it was late in
the game to start redoing it. That was a really big step, to admit we
had made a mistake early on about how tight was too tight for a
sporty sedan.

"We went around the clock for about six weeks, completely rede-
signing and repackaging the interior of the car. We raised the roof
about an inch. There was a lot of engineering work making that come
together. We repackaged the entire interior—door panels, instrument
panel console—to make the interior more open."

Design staff from the GM Tech Center were totally at their dis-
posal. As changes were visualized, they were modeled in various materials: wood, fiberglass, styrofoam. A more open, competitive, and
comfortable interior emerged. One of the blessings of the pressure
they were under, Miakinin thought, was that it forced the bureaucracy associated with making changes at GM to get out of the way
and let this makeshift team gather speed and momentum. "It was
really a neat time," she said, smiling, "because, I think, of probably
all the times that I've been here, it embodies the spirit of what Saturn
was all about—everybody kind of working together and breaking out
of that formal bureaucracy of 'Gee, you need to give me a formal
drawing and something that says you really need this.' You could
actually sit down with someone who was modeling and sketch something up and say, 'This is what I need, and this is what is important
about it. Give it a shot and I'll stop by in an hour.' The traditional
differences just melted away. Everybody came in with blue jeans and
their grubbiest clothes. You'd go home and grab a couple hours of

sleep and come back. Nobody bothered getting dressed up. All the trappings of corporate America kind of fell away."

Having gotten what they wanted by pushing the system, Miakinin said, everyone involved wanted future crises and dilemmas resolved the same way.

A year ago, in July 1990, Hal Riney & Partners called Miakinin again, picking up on the Saturn spirit theme in anticipation of packaging it for promotion. By this time Hal Riney & Partners had been Saturn's communications partner for a little over two years. In San Francisco the agency was busy making the crucial prelaunch print ads and about a dozen TV commercials, with about a hundred staffers working on the Saturn campaign. A cloak of secrecy surrounded the car redesign, which the competition and the press desperately wanted to describe and photograph, so shooting locations for commercials that included a car were confidential and often secluded. Although Hal Riney did not set up an operations center reminiscent of Tennessee's Department of Economic and Community Development's coterie under Bill Long five years before, the aura of a special, hidden operation prevailed. As the launch date approached, though, a certain uneasiness about Saturn crept into the high-flying ad agency. "We were skeptical the dealers could meet our ad's expectations about a different kind of customer experience," recalled Melinda Gonzales, one of the account executives. "The early spots came from what Saturn hoped it would be."

Troubling some of the Hal Riney people was the thought that their firm might be a victim of that old nemesis, the Big Three credibility gap. Bad cars and hype had made the gap into an abyss, as far as many prospective buyers were concerned, and it was going to be Hal Riney's job to get Americans to believe in a domestic car company again. If the first Saturns were not well-made small cars, the task might prove impossible. And really, all Hal Riney had to go on were verbal reassurances that Saturn really was a darn good little car.

The initial ads worked well, drawing strong responses. The prelaunch print series in which Miakinin's ad appeared resulted in 100 thousand people calling Saturn's 800 number and asking for more information. In the fall of 1990, the national and regional ad campaigns shifted into high gear despite a shortage of cars and worries that the stores couldn't live up to the promises. At the agency fingers stayed crossed that the plant would soon come through with more good product and that the stores would come on line and have that product for sale.

Once Saturns started rolling into showrooms, seemingly one car at a time, Hal Riney's gauzy, nostalgic style did communicate a consistent message: Saturn is a common-sense car for the future and buying one isn't going to be a hassle. Whether viewers believed that or not, they generally liked the commercials, which had a look, a recognizable style, and told brief stories. The ads didn't play on the made-in-America theme, nor did they emphasize Saturn as a last chance to stop the dreaded foreign invaders from undermining the national economy. Yet, by not stating those sentiments, the ads' subliminal effects seemed heightened—by the Americana images, by the focus on people doing their jobs, by the absence of any identifiable competition.

Following the launch, new print ads and TV commercials were constantly being created. The brand-building campaign intended to imprint Saturn the company, Saturn the car, on America's collective cortex. Typically, seven or eight print ads, and a similar number of TV spots, were in circulation at any one time. The most effective would remain in circulation for upwards of two years. The others disappeared after six to twelve months. As soon as positive feedback from new Saturn owners became available, Hal Riney's creative team used it, for after all customer satisfaction was Saturn's holy grail. Ads focusing on the customer documented positive experiences, including Robin Millage of Petersburg, Alaska, ordering an SL2 and having it delivered to an island where she lived off the coast of British Columbia; Dave Rosenblum and his partner, Peter Farrell, recruiting "car nuts from drug-plagued neighborhoods" and winning races in SCs with their Inner City Youth Racing Team; and Judith Reusswig writing a letter full of optimism and nostalgia (Saturn "reminded me a little bit of a mom-and-pop operation of the old days," the third grade teacher said, referencing a cover story in *Time*), and getting it back in the glove box of her new Saturn when she picked it up at the dealer.

Beth Miakinin's ad preceded these. It had been conceived and shot during the prelaunch period of nervousness and anticipation. "There was a lot of back and forth," Miakinin recalled about the copywriting process. A woman whose career focused on details, Miakinin wanted Hal Riney's people to print exactly what she said, so when paraphrasing toned her down she felt a little disillusioned. "They read exactly what I said," she told me earnestly. "Then they said, 'Here's what we want to try to convey. Here's how we paraphrased this.' In the end I don't have any grudges against what they did."

Soft focus, name-building advertising did not want *edge*. Color, thoroughbred looks, the Gibson Girl look, yes. But not edge. Miaki-nin's innocence about how marketing worked had a certain charm, I thought. It probably had played into her selection by Hal Riney's scouts in the first place.

The ad had been shot upstairs, in one of the design rooms. The shoot took five hours, about five times as long as she anticipated. The director had an image in mind of what a female engineer should look like and, in service of the image, Miakinin's long hair was tucked in a bob and secured with rubber bands. There had been considerable debate about where she should sit, Miakinin recalled, and about the background, the foreground. Eventually, Miakinin's left arm rested on a brown bucket seat. Over her shoulder glowed a CAD diagram of the seat, the outline of a passenger's torso in it. Practically surround-ing Miakinin were upright engineering drawings rolled into tubes. By her right hand, spread flat on an unrolled blueprint, was a small red car, a paperweight one of the crew had spotted in a nearby office and thought was cute.

To millions of readers of such national magazines as *Cosmopolitan, Elle,* and *Runner's World,* when the ad ran in mid- and late-1990, Beth Miakinin looked assertive, attractive, brainy. At the top of the double-page spread was some biographical information: she had attended engineering school, her father had been in the auto business for thirty-seven years, she'd come to Saturn as a product development engineer. The copy, in quotes, said basically that it was smarter to design a car's interior based on conversations with human beings who actually had to drive and sit in the car than by using all the stuff in this photograph.

21

Prototypes

After lunch I followed Beth Miakinin's bright red Pontiac Sunbird south a few miles to the Saturn Engineering and Preproduction Build Center in Madison Heights. After checking through security, which was tight because prototypes were pieced together here and new body styles given three dimensions in a business exceptionally paranoid about spies, Miakinin led me inside. She introduced me to Rick Youngblood, thirty-nine, a personality "A"-type engineer wearing a striped shirt and glasses with little plastic protective skirts attached to the bows, and to Maurice Bobo, forty-two, a relaxed fellow with a beard who had worked with Jay Wetzel at Pontiac. Youngblood was the manufacturing team leader at the build center, and Bobo was team leader for product development. With their counterparts from the UAW, who were not in today, they managed the facility.

After Miakinin went off to a meeting, Youngblood and Bobo showed me around, as per Jay Wetzel's request. The 130-thousand-square-foot building was divided into an engineering and car-building area that was a miniature version of the plant in Spring Hill. Several dozen engineers were chatting and pecking away at computer terminals in the engineering room. Rolled drawings were everywhere.

I slipped into a red shop frock and put on protective glasses. We entered the car-building area. The "sandbox," as the facility was nick-named, was a compact version of the mammoth complex, distilled and without robots or presses. Body parts were trucked here from foundries. There were distinct body fab, powertrain, vehicle interiors, and final assembly areas. In effect, this was the learning laboratory of the learning laboratory, the crucible of Saturn's new car technology and processes. Here was where thousands of hours and millions of dollars got funneled into prototypes that determined each model's technological fate.

The life of a prototype was usually short and abusive, I learned.

Fabricated from drawings and models, the typical prototype got measured, analyzed, and tested to death. Tests included mass analyses of engine components before and after long-term running to determine wear and tear, emission control tests to comply with federal environmental regulations, thermal shock tests that were the equivalent of driving from the Arctic to the Sahara in a couple of minutes to insure that head gaskets did not blow from abrupt temperature changes, coordinate measurement sequences to determine specifications, and corporate durability engine tests to simulate a four-hundred-hour drive at varying engine rpms. There were also visual inspections and road simulations. One simulation put a prototype on the long road to hell. It came complete with potholes, soft shoulders, cracks, dips, and frost heaves, all without any horizontal movement.

Bobo directed my attention to the simulator, which sat on the other side of a large wall of glass. The machine gripped a car and shook it like some gigantic nasty spider with a big red bug in its clutches, yellow arms and legs moving every which way at once: ramming the shocks, tilting the car to the right, whamming one wheel. The sedan bucked to and fro, fore and aft; it pitched and yawed.

"Sort of like driving in Detroit," I suggested to Bobo.

"You bet," he replied, laughing.

Bobo said this prototype-build facility was GM's most sophisticated. "We build the entire vehicle here, outside of making parts," he told me. "It is extremely expensive, but cheap compared to repairing problems during production, which is not the time to be fixin'."

"At one point in time, before we got up and running in Spring Hill, we were building everything that got built," Youngblood added.

Hundreds of the first op techs and trade techs had received their introduction to both Saturn's engineering and philosophy here. The first people "were part of the whole process," Bobo said. "They were involved in putting the vehicle together, and putting all those processes and procedures in place. A lot of them went to Spring Hill. They were responsible for training those who subsequently came on." The biggest difference between the center and the factory now, obviously, was that in the factory two thousand or so Saturns were being manufactured each week, while here, if pushed, seventy-five or so technicians, with the support of several hundred engineers, the design people at Saturn's headquarters, and the design staff of GM at the Tech Center, could make five or six prototypes.

Bobo and Youngblood showed me the coating technology center, a small shop in which spaceframes were covered with corrosion-resistant paint by a crew of three. They pointed out the coordinate measuring machine, which was similar to the one Miakinin used to experiment with interior design changes.

"Programs are developed for various configurations of the body," Youngblood said, gesturing at the machine. "They automatically check various points, checking the dimensions."

Bobo directed my attention to its mechanical arms, which could trace a hood, a fender, a seat like two fingers lightly going over your head, shoulder, butt. "They can work independent of one another," he said, "they can work simultaneously."

"They can take something in free space," added Youngblood, "and go up and check it. Or in this particular case, on the wagon, they would have a program. They put it in and it automatically starts checking points. If you had a rocker panel, say, that was way out of spec, you would want to find out why. Each particular component— if you're out of spec right there, you start tracking back. Your ultimate goal is to bring your body into specification."

"This operation is isolated," Bobo said. "It sets on about 700 thousand pounds of mass that totally eliminates vibration. It's a hermetically controlled room as well, because you want to be able to maintain your metal at a certain temperature so you don't have expansion and contraction."

Engines stacked in wooden boxes filled a corner of the powertrain area. Engines were assembled on one side of the room, transmissions on the other. About twenty technicians worked here regularly, though only a few were at their stations today. I spotted a pair of camshafts by a red tool box and asked if Saturn would be offering high-performance cams in the future for racing buffs.

"We won't be doing it," Bobo said.

"They're so fast now," added Youngblood, "you wouldn't need it."

Recalling my ride with Dexter Riffe in Charlotte six weeks ago, I said I had been impressed by the SC's torque curve. "You can wind that sucker right up to six thousand rpms," I said. "It doesn't drop off at five thousand. That is an attribute of the cam, isn't it?"

"Cam, induction combustion chamber—"

"Transmission," added Bobo.

The dynanometer testing area is where engines are run hard and long. Entering it, I heard the loud hum of high rpms. On the other side of a glass partition sat an operating engine. On this side sprawled a bank of measuring devices. Youngblood leaned over and checked the variables listed on a computer screen: fuel use, coolant temperature, spark advance, a dozen others. The engine's rpms increased and a certain shrillness rent the hum. One irksome problem with Saturn to date was engine noise. Since the launch last fall auto writers had jumped all over its high pitch. Only two months ago, in May's *Car & Driver,* "Saturn is close. Really close," a writer said. Except for "The Flaw," as he called it, "a rushing, whining, whirling howl."

A friendly young guy wearing a white lab jacket introduced himself as engine dynamometer durability engineer Martin Murray. Murray explained that we had walked in on "a corporate durability test," which would last four hundred hours. "We run it at wide-open throttle through an average rpm range," Murray said, staring intently at the engine in its cell. "The test assesses general durability of the components: crank rod, piston, etc. It takes about a month.

"We do a power run, make sure the power's there," Murray continued, looking at the engine in its cell. "We change the oil. Put it back in. Let it run." Glancing at the numbers on the computer screen, he said, "These things run automated tests. They run with a lot of parameters being monitored at a time. In the old days, guys would actually sit all day and watch the cell run. Today, it's electronically monitored."

Murray looked pleased watching the engine run, as though he might not have minded sitting here all day and doing just that. In the next few minutes the dynamometer durability engineer made the analysis of dirty oil sound like a doctor doing a urine analysis. He and his associates checked for impurities, he said, for signs of internal illnesses, for contaminants in the engine's life fluid. "We can evaluate and make a judgment on this engine's ability to last ten years and a hundred thousand miles," he said proudly.

As Youngblood and Bobo led us from dynamometer testing, Murray insisted I see one final thing. He pointed me toward an empty cell adjacent to the one in use. "That's where we do thermal shock tests. We run the engine very hard, wide open throttle. We'll bring it up to maximum operating temperature, where you see the hot light come on. Then we'll change the valves and flood the engine with cold coolant, about fifteen degrees C. It just puts the motor through hell. That's why we call it a thermal shock test. The object is to cycle the head gasket. It's primarily a head gasket thing. When you're running aluminum engines and iron bores, the shrink and bimetal characteristics tend to really be aggressive on head gaskets." He grinned, his thick mustache lifting. "Seeing as we don't want to be another Vega, this is one of our key tests in the early stages."

In the hallway, having been struck by Martin Murray's Saturn spirit, I asked Bobo if he still found his job exciting. He stopped and thought a moment.

"It's a lot of fun still. No two days are alike." A few moments later he expanded on that. "What makes this a real joy to me is that I don't come to work expecting a lot of confrontation. We work together."

Youngblood nodded in agreement. Then the higher strung of the two engineers checked his watch and darted to a nearby wall phone to make a quick call.

"Fast trackers from other GM divisions seem to have been drawn to Saturn," I said when Youngblood returned to his partner's side. "Is that still happening?"

"There's no way for us to have a real pulse on that," Bobo said.

"I think that human nature would say you're right," Youngblood threw in.

I asked the engineers if they had participated in Jay Wetzel's mock funeral at the cemetery the other day. Both nodded yes.

"What did you think about it?"

"It created an emotional vector, and got everyone's attention," Youngblood said. "I don't think they'll forget about it. I know I won't."

My tour of the sandbox ended in front of the windows of the mass analysis room, where components got weighed and tested before and after hard use. Normally, I surmised, health-aware patriots ran the tests in there. A large Operation Desert Storm poster—"These Colors Don't Run!"—hung from the ceiling close to a "Wellness" sign. An American flag and a Navy flag also caught my eye. Taped to a window was a cartoon strip in which Charlie Brown lamented, "Work is the crabgrass in the lawn of life."

The talk turned briefly to Saturn's competition. Even though the entry level cars numbered in the dozens, for benchmarking purposes the Honda Civic, Toyota Corolla, and Mitsubishi Eclipse were the vehicles for Saturn to beat. Since it was crucial to keep up on the three main competitors' innovations, I asked how they did that.

"We filet 'em out," Bobo said with a toothy grin.

"Who gets to go out and buy the cars?" I asked.

Neither engineer answered. They glanced at each other, then chuckled as though sharing a private joke. Did they buy the cars, I wondered, from Motor City's mean streets as part of a subversive you-better-buy-American campaign? Before I asked for more details Beth Miakinin strolled up, briefcase in hand, pink flats scuffing the cement floor. She asked how my tour had gone with these two guys. I told her I was suffering from information overload. Youngblood and Bobo smiled, as though they had accomplished their mission. Moments later, Miakinin buttonholed Youngblood. As the two fast trackers drifted off, locked in conversation, she was reminding him that they needed to get together so he could bring her up to speed on a few things.

Maurice Bobo led me back to the lobby. I gave him my red frock and protective glasses, then asked how he had adapted to Saturn after working at Pontiac.

"Initially, I didn't like it." He mentioned the open cubicles here, the lack of privacy. "Now it's no big deal."

In the lobby by a scale model of the Spring Hill plant, I sat down to study my notes. Some technicians strolled out, across the carpet, and headed outside. An older security guard called after a blonde guy in his mid-twenties. "You just started smoking," he joked, "so you can go out in the sunshine and get a tan."

22

Twentysomething Sales Consultant

West of Detroit, Saturn of Plymouth was located off a busy highway out behind Don Massey Cadillac. Don Massey, who owned the store, happened to have delivered newspapers to Haynes Haven as a boy, which may have spurred his interest in the subsidiary. His store had the Saturn look, with an extra long portico and a raised, circular display area out front.

The afternoon I stopped there, I walked beneath the portico and into the showroom where sunlight was pouring through a lot of glass and skylights. I told the receptionist I was here to see Karen Tibus, the president of the store, then sat in the small waiting area near a middle-aged man who kept glancing distractedly over one shoulder at a blue cutaway of a Saturn. His son, who looked eleven or twelve, wore a Michael Jordan sweatshirt. Compared to his dad, the boy was a model of relaxed resignation.

"I'm not really happy right now," the man soon told me. "Ordered a car. Supposed to be ready at one. Now it's approaching four." He tapped his shoe on the floor. His son glanced at the Saturn sales display: twelve pictures flanked by fake plants, a video screen in their center. "It's usually not the car that's a problem," the man said. "It's the dealer."

Saturn of Plymouth was supposed to have installed a right-hand mirror, but hadn't; his a/c didn't work; cruise control, which he had wanted, was out of stock. "When we wrote up the order a few days ago, they should have worked that stuff out," he complained.

"New car sales, please," came over the intercom, interrupting the mood music. "Customer in the showroom."

A customer stood alone in the sunny interior. Looking a little lost, she wandered toward the cutaway. As a Saturn automotive consultant appeared and intercepted her, the man by me said he lived in Lansing, over an hour's drive from here. "Now I got to come back again," he said. He glanced at his watch and muttered something to his son. The two of them stood and walked purposely past the cutaway, heading toward the offices at the back of the store. I got up and went to the eight-by-ten-foot sales display and scrutinized one of the twelve pictures. In eight colors it revealed the complexities of Saturn's electronically controlled 4-speed automatic transmission with lockup torque converter and a performance/normal shift switch. Beside it was an aerial shot of the factory complex in Spring Hill.

I punched several buttons in a console. Short videos gave model overviews, then information about Saturn's powertrain, ride and handling, low ownership costs, safety considerations, and dent/corrosion-resistant body side panels.

The disgruntled new Saturn owner reappeared with his son. They stood together, staring mutely at the engine of the cutaway. I walked over.

The dealership was prepping him a loaner, the fellow said, and would deliver the car later. He still wasn't smiling, but admitted, "I'm impressed."

Karen Tibus, president of Saturn of Plymouth, a short, intense lady with teased hair and long red fingernails, soon led me into her office. Tibus's Saturn story echoed those I heard from other store managers. An experienced car dealer, she had worked for Don Massey for years, she said. They had broken ground here the day Roger Smith had driven the first car off the assembly line, July 31, 1991, and opened in late November. "There we were, up and running—with no cars," she recalled.

Tibus and her first automotive consultant, Don Page—twenty-three, energetic, clean cut: "he fit the image," she said—sold Saturns for three weeks from brochures. They had one SC on the lot for customers to scrutinize, kick the tires, drive. Finally, cars started arriving. "We'd get a truck load and people would be standing out there," Tibus said. " 'I'll take that blue one, I'll take that red one.' It was exciting, but frustrating."

These days she was very short of cars; she'd just been on the phone about it. Tibus said that Saturn of Plymouth ranked number one or two just about every month in total sales in the organization. July's sales had been around 180 cars and she needed inventory. Initially, she added, Saturn marketing had told her she'd sell 950 cars a year, but Saturn marketing had been way off.

When I asked about training, Tibus said she had not sent her sales crew of five, plus a manager, to Spring Hill as was strongly encour-

aged. The training, which included Saturn awareness and team dynamics since the consultants were in fact the point team in the marketplace, wasn't necessary when you were already selling more cars
than the factory could supply you with, she said. Besides, her sales
team, on its own, had developed "an incredible amount of teamwork." What helped, she continued, was that she went light on rules
and gave her consultants a lot of slack. But she expected them to sell
a lot of cars. "A guy who feels good about selling ten cars a month,"
she said, "won't make it here."

Was everyone still motivated, I asked.

"They're still pumped; it's very, very fun."

Pumped most of all was twenty-three-year-old Don Page. In July,
Tibus said, Page had sold thirty-six cars in a recession that was hitting
Detroit hard. As a yardstick, she said that in the car business, eighteen
new car sales in a month usually put you in the top one percent of
sales people nationwide.

"What kind of car do you drive?" I asked.

Poker-faced the whole interview, Tibus faintly smiled. "A black
Saturn sports coupe."

I joined Don Page in his cubicle, an L-shaped partition with a view
of the showroom floor. He had on a crisp white shirt and a tie smat-
tered with bright flowers. His hair was stylishly clipped close on the
sides and left long on top. As we talked, his big brown eyes radiated
an almost bovine sincerity. His twentysomething patois was sprinkled
with the word "fantastic" and he confessed that his paramount goal
when he first met a prospect was, in his words, "to make a friend."

Sitting in the customer's chair, it wasn't hard to imagine a lot of
twenty-five to thirty-five year olds buying a Saturn from Don Page.
But he had buyers all over the demographic spectrum. He'd sold a
car to a seventeen year old whose parents had to sign for him. He'd
sold a coupe to an eighty-seven-year-old man.

"How much actual selling do you have to do?" I asked.

"Not a lot, to be honest with you. Mainly what I'll do when we get
really busy is I'll find out if they want a stick shift or an automatic.
Which style car. Then I'll stick them in a car until I have time to
properly handle them."

"They just take the car out by themselves?"

"Yeah. The car will sell itself. They'll come back and say how much
they love the car. I mean, a lot of times it's pretty easy."

"Do you have an intuitive sense about who you're going to sell?"

"You always do, but it's not right." Page grinned. "You never know. I always try to read 'em, but you never know who's going to buy."

Saturns sold particularly well, he thought, because there was set pricing and no pressure. "Set pricing's fantastic, great. Couldn't ask for anything better. I've had people tell me, 'This is fantastic, I really like this.'" Page leaned forward on his desk, looked straight at me with his sincere brown eyes. "You know, they're not arguing with me. I'm a stranger to them. They don't have to sit down here and argue with me about a car. It makes it a lot easier for both of us."

A fellow professional automotive consultant stood listening to us in the open-court Saturn way of doing things. "They concentrate more on the car than they do the price," he tossed in. "So they get what they want."

"If you've got a lot of tension, they're worried you're going to rip them off," Page said. "Normally customers hate buying a car."

But not from Don Page. Not from Saturn of Plymouth. "This dealership compares to no other," he said. "It's way better. We're a family group. My boss never tells me to do something I don't want to do."

"Sounds like heaven."

"It's not bad. I don't mind coming to work."

Page laughed.

"When do people buy cars?"

"Monday nights are always our busiest."

"Even in the rain?" I asked, remembering it had rained last night, a Monday.

"In the rain I sold four cars. I've sold seven cars on a Monday before."

The best sale of all, however, was what he called a "lay down." "I get at least one lay down a week," Page said. "They come in and just want that car." All he had to do was lay down the keys.

Saturn
Takes Off

23

The Crank Team A-Crew

Teamsmanship was the hue and cry of Saturn. In a way, the entire enterprise strove to be one big winning team in order to recapture a substantial share of the small-car business from the Japanese. The suppliers, retailers, machinery manufacturers, and new-car haulers were members of the big team. The plant itself was the team's center—its body, so to speak, with Troy as its brains and the retailers its fingers actually shaking buyers' hands. As the body, the plant was where quality began, in teams, inside an integrated and complex facility. Here consensus was supposed to be guiding decisions, teams were refining lean production, bottom-up leadership was a password, trust and communication replaced time clocks and grievances.

Yet determining how close to the ideals Saturn had gotten had been a frustrated goal of mine since June, when I received LeFauve's tentative go-ahead to join a team and observe teamwork in action in the powertrain building. Finally, in December 1991, after more requests, Saturn Communications vice president Bruce McDonald called, nudged into action by LeFauve and made confident by the fact Saturns were selling well across the Republic. I could come in—no provisos. Plans were arranged for me to spend a week on the crankshaft-machining line under the wing of Bob Courtemanche, the former ace grinder operator with a chrome crank on the mantle of his little hobby farm down in Cornersville, Tennessee.

I had last seen Courtemanche in August. For two hours we talked in a vacant Communications' cubicle on the second floor of Northfield. Courtemanche told me about his recent promotion to WUMA, or "work unit module advisor," and about his team.

"I like to brag about the crankshaft team," he said.

Cut figuratively from a bolt of blue-collar cloth, Courtemanche used clear, honest, working-man language that sliced through all the rhetoric. But he would rather show me stuff than talk about it. He

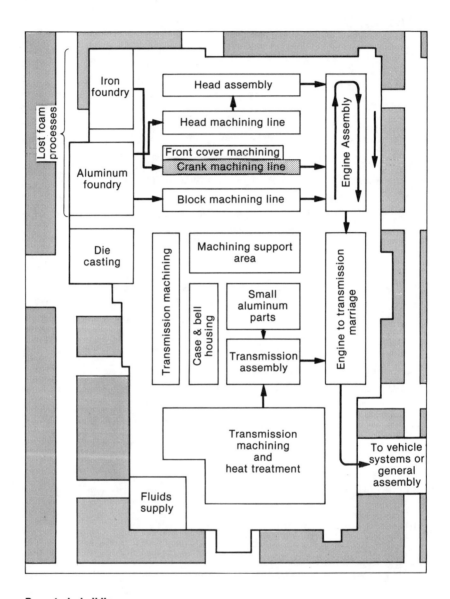

Powertrain building

said he wished communication's Jennifer Schettler was there, as she was supposed to have been, monitoring the interview. He would have urged her to let him take me down to the powertrain building, he said, so I could see what he was talking about in action.

Courtemanche had been promoted to WUMA last spring. It was a position of responsibility that he had only previously dreamed about, the first level at Saturn where the labor/management partnership was physical as well as philosophical. He was partners with Marv O'Gorman, a management WUMA, and in charge of the crankshaft machining line A-crew along with the foundry A-crew who poured the rough crankshafts and the differential cases.

Given the go-ahead to observe the crankshaft team, I met with Courtemanche a second time on a chilly December morning at 5 A.M. in the parking lot of the Holiday Inn in Columbia. We headed north on U.S. 31 in his old Plymouth Fury, soon cleared security at the plant's southern gate, and circled the southwest corner of powertrain, the bag houses dim in the dark and dawn just tinting the sky to the east. In the faint light, the powertrain building looked more monolithic than ever. Dozens of exhaust vents jutted off the roof. At the time Saturn was running two shifts, A-crew and B-crew. Each crew worked four days a week, ten hours a day, and rotated shifts, nights and days, every other week. On Monday mornings, like this one, Courtemanche usually got to the shop—that's what he still called it— a little early to make sure things were going right.

We parked in a mostly empty lot, walked several hundred feet, went up some stairs and inside. The building was oddly quiet. There wasn't a soul in sight. Partially assembled engines stood still on the engine assembly line, which stretched hundreds of feet down one side of the cement floor. We walked for a couple hundred feet, passed beneath a *Teamwork Builds Quality* sign and turned down a long corridor. The crank line, all 525 feet of it, was on our right, block machining on our left. The machines of the crank line looked calm— robots resting: gantries, which move parts from one operation to the next, coiled. Once we reached the foundry, though, the plant was awake. Buzzers were blaring, fans whirring overhead. An alarm behind the smoky furnaces rang shrilly every minute or so. From a steel catwalk we watched a little train network transporting crankshaft molds toward a ladle bubbling with hot iron. Leaning close to my ear so I could hear, Courtemanche explained that "iron melt," as he called this area of the foundry, started early because it had to be pouring cranks before the machining lines crews arrived at 6 A.M.

Below our feet, steel flasks holding the crankshaft molds moved along the miniature track. A woman op tech lowered four crankshaft molds made of styrofoam, and a three-foot tall pour cup made of white ceramic, into each flask. At the next station black sand was blown into the flask, packing tightly in and around the four molds and the gating connecting them. By hand, excess sand was brushed away from the trumpet-bell mouth of the pour cup, which jutted above the flask like a white flower. Once a flask reached the furnace area on the far side of the track, molten iron flowed from a hand-operated ladle into the pour cup in a two-foot tongue of golden light. Out of sight the iron tongue probed its way through the four styrofoam molds, creating liquid crankshafts that were cooling even as they took shape. The iron vaporized, or lost, the foam, thus giving the process its name, lost foam. Originally, the ladle operation had been automated, Courtemanche said, but the foundry team had gotten better pours, more consistent and with fewer defects, pouring by hand.

Handling the ladle was a hot, dangerous job, one teammates share. From our safe distance away on the catwalk you could feel smooth blasts of heat rolling off the molten iron. The ladle held several hundred pounds of iron and was refilled by a transfer vessel that trundled back and forth between the ladle and two electric-arc furnaces. Each furnace could hold six thousand pounds of iron. As one furnace was emptied, the other melted fresh scrap. Behind the furnaces was a large pile of scrap iron. A magnet plunged from a crane, picked up forty, fifty pounds worth, lifted it thirty feet, and dropped the scrap into a furnace. A refractory lining kept each furnace from melting once the electrodes, inserted from above, started zapping the scrap iron with tremendous jolts of electricity. When a "melt" was ready, the temperature stood between 2800 and 2900 degrees F.

The foundry had a hard, smoky, metallic smell. At the end of each circuit of the little rail network, the flasks, into which the iron had been poured, were dumped onto a shaker. A vibrator jarred the black sand from warm oil passages, knocked it loose from cooling journals and pins. The sand circulated outside to the bag houses, was filtered, came back inside, and was used again. The crankshafts were stacked on pallets and transferred to the head of the crank machining line.

Although I spent only a few hours in the foundry during my visit, I found it fascinating. It had the dusty, noisy, people-heavy ambiance of an industrial age factory, and seemed not only physically on the edge of Saturn but figuratively far removed from soft-side skill building. At the same time, as I learned, it had the most people problems in powertrain, as well as the need for the most process refinement. The success of the foundry team was crucial because they created rough product. And without good rough product all the process refinement in the world would not produce quality. Because the crankshaft machining line team was a customer of the foundry team, it needed to trust the team, communicate with it, lend a hand at times. Toward that end, Courtemanche said, "We've been moving some machinery folks back into the foundry when needed; they learn what it's like, get out of that fingerpointing."

The crankshaft itself— or "crank" for short—is the strange-looking piece found at the heart of the internal combustion engine. Few drivers have ever seen one, which is a shame because a crankshaft possesses its own quirky beauty. A completely machined crankshaft is sculptural, with counterweights jutting off its spine to assure balance, and with gleaming pins and journals. The pins on a crankshaft connect it to the piston rods, which grip the pins like tight bracelets and pump the pistons up and down. The journals ride in bearings and oil; they secure the crankshaft to the engine block without actually touching metal. If the metal starts touching, your engine is soon going to seize.

As crankshafts go, Saturn's is small. It's about twenty inches long, has five main journals, four counterweights, four pins, and a reluctor wheel. It weighs twenty-six pounds when it starts down the crank machining line and is skinned in a refractory wash, a residue of the lost-foam process. At the end of the line, after the machining process, each crank weighs twenty-two pounds.

The crank line, which Courtemanche walked me down shortly after 6 A.M., includes machines, computers, flashing video screens, overhead gantries that uncoil like giant scorpions, splashing coolants that look and sound like dirty shower water, and constant noise. At eight-five decibels, the noise almost sounds alive; it's a chorus that embraces you. The noise was the single constant companion of the seven op techs who ran the equipment—watching it, fussing over it—and the three trade techs, two electrical and one mechanical, who fixed and fine-tuned everything.

Courtemanche was their boss. Of course at Saturn the word "boss," like the words "foreman" and "supervisor," had been banished from the vocabulary. So Courtemanche was a teamleader, a WUMA, a labor resource person for machine operators and technicians to turn to. In Courtemanche's case, a resource with a red beard, a gait like a bear, and an endearing straightforwardness. His management credo, a natural extension of his personality, was pretty simple. "Basically, I like to hand off things," he told me. "I prod them and guide them. It's like raising kids; they're going to make mistakes. You try to guide them through it."

Ultimately, Courtemanche's job was to make sure enough cranks, defect-free, made the trip from the pile of scrap in the foundry to the end of the crank line. That way he kept the customer, engine assembly, happy.

People-wise, the crank team A-crew suggested a cross section of working America: eight men and four women, two blacks and ten whites, ages thirty-one to forty-seven. A-crew included a gay, bachelors, divorcées, single parents, traditional family types.

Machine-wise, at the head of the line stood a robot surrounded by a seven-foot fence. One rough crank at a time, the robot placed the product on a conveyor that carried it to the Komatsu machine Courtemanche had qualified three years ago in Japan. The machine performed "op 10" and "op 20," milling the rough geometry, cutting off excess iron, and testing for preliminary tolerances. The operators were Joe McKean, forty-four, and Tom Reinhard, thirty-two. Both men had been at Saturn less than a year. Reinhard came from a Cadillac plant and McKean from a moonlighting job he had taken in Narrow Lake, Michigan, at a little non-union stamping plant where he'd worked for $4.75/hour. "They could hire quality people for that," McKean recalled bitterly. "I saw my best friend get his hand stamped off, and I decided to get out of Dodge."

"Op 30" was a rolling machine whose "whole purpose in life," Courtemanche said, "is to harden the iron."

"Op 40" drilled oil holes.

"Op 50" drilled bolt holes in the ends of each crankshaft.

"Op 60–70" was the grinders. There tolerances started getting tight. The operator was Pam Saint. Thirty-five, with braces on her teeth, her hair in a spiral perm, Saint was a single mom with a teenage son in Columbia Academy. Her grinders (actually five grinders in one machine) massaged twenty-eight different dimensions in a bath of coolant. Slouched in her chair Saint watched cranks go by in front of her while a steady stream of men seemed to sidle up behind her and talk to her from the side through all that hair.

"Op 80" notched the reluctor ring. Via a sensor the notch would communicate with the engine, telling it when to fire. William Jenkins, thirty-six, was the operator. Jenkins, like Saint, had come to Saturn from Saginaw Steering in Alabama. A Tennessean from Pulaski, south of Columbia, Jenkins had a Fu Manchu mustache and a warm smile—when he extended it. He didn't extend it much and stayed apart from the rest of A-crew, taking his breaks at his station and eating lunch with friends on other teams. When I asked him why he had come to Saturn, Jenkins replied bluntly: job security. When I asked him about racism, he said Saturn was no different than "being out on the street; you feel other races are against you because you're black."

"Op 90's" two robots "picked the buggers" out of the oil holes, as several operators informed me. Our first time down the line Courtemanche got a kick out of introducing me to Op 90. "This is Darryl and Darryl," he said, smirking, his hairy fingers gripping the fence surrounding the robots. "From Vermont—'The Newhart Show.'" He was referring to two bumbling rubes on the popular weekly TV sitcom, which starred comedian Bob Newhart as an innkeeper in rural Vermont.

We watched the robots for a while. I found myself vaguely hypnotized by the combination of the noise and the movement of Darryl and Darryl, who were almost humanly gentle. When, for instance, one eased down and plucked up an air-dried crank from the end of a conveyor, moved, and then lowered it slowly onto a twirling probe, the robot's motion seemed almost tender. Finally, Courtemanche said into my ear, "I like watching robots; they just mesmerize me for some reason."

"Op 100" was the balancer; it drilled holes in the ends of each counterweight.

"Op 110," the finish polishing machine, "is probably the nastiest job we do," according to Courtemanche. A large, complicated affair with hundreds of moving parts, long strips of abrasive sandpaper, called microfilm, and a habit of breaking down, the polisher looked like a Rube Goldberg contraption. Nancy Laatz, thirty-one, and Seaborn Powell, thirty-five, were the operators. Laatz, a solid, good-natured woman with a quick wit wore T-shirts advertising groups like the "Bad Boys." Like Pam Saint, Laatz was divorced. Her eight-year-old son lived up in Michigan with her ex and she missed him a lot. "He's scared to fly," she told me one day, so he wouldn't be with her in Columbia on Christmas. Seaborn Powell moved with the lightness of an athlete. He had white teeth and a wedge haircut. Having just joined the crank team, Powell sounded genuinely happy to be here, although before he had left Detroit, "I heard Saturn was a lot of bull," he said. Powell also suggested to me early on how thin the Saturn training

Darryl and Darryl

was being stretched when, in response to my question, "What did you think of the EXEL course?" he stared blankly at me and replied, "Never heard of it."

"Op 120" was a washer that cleaned each crankshaft.

"Op 130" took fifty-eight measurements on each crankshaft in twenty seconds. If the product did not pass, the machine rolled it out to the side to a reject bin. The operator for the measuring machine, Leanne Schipani, did not return from sick leave until the third day I joined the team. Schipani, thirty-one, had just had her fourth child, but Saturn was not so New Age that it granted maternity leave. You had a baby, you were sick. Before she applied to Saturn, Schipani had been on layoff at Cadillac for three years. "I was just about to lose my house," she told me. "Things were bad." Once in Tennessee, she and her husband initially lived in Spring Hill, but the other kids in school had called their son "Yankee" all the time, taunted him to fight. Now in Pulaski, the Schipanis liked it much better. Butch Schipani stayed home, taking care of the infant and their three other children.

"Op 140" was the end of the line. Steve Sherman, thirty-one, a shy fellow who had come from Chevrolet Truck and Bus where he road tested trucks, sat hunched over in a chair, visually inspecting each crankshaft. It struck me as rather ironic that it took an attentive guy wearing white gloves and yellow ear plugs to give each crank the final yes or no.

On a little stand Sherman rotated each crank on its milled journals. With the finger of a dirty glove, he pointed out the most common flaw: porosity in the number one journal. Porosity meant a tiny hole, an absence of cast iron, a defect. The flaw hid in each crank, like a cavity in a tooth, from the moment it was poured in the foundry, gradually being uncovered by the milling and cutting operations that removed four pounds of iron.

My first day on the line I asked Sherman how many cranks he inspected in a shift.

"I probably go through five hundred crankshafts a day," he said, glancing up. Over his head was a *Committed to Quality* sticker on a vertical beam. "It's got to be done right," he said. "If it's not, I'm not going to have a job." Today, he went on, defects were running high, around twenty-five percent. Most days, they stayed around twenty percent; the goal was ten percent.

"What's causing the twenty-five percent?" I asked.

"If I knew what the problem is, we'd have it solved."

The number three crank in every pour of four seemed to be the culprit right now. Sherman kept notes to pass along to the foundry to improve pours. He lifted defects in an old world product handler kind of way—using both hands—and dropped them, with a clang, into a reject bin. When full, the bin would go straight back to the foundry and the defects were melted over again. The quality cranks were loaded on pallets by a six-axis robot. Talked to by a computer in the engine assembly line, the robot them lifted, swiveled, and lowered one crankshaft at a time onto a lowerator. Each crankshaft descended beneath the floor, and rose about thirty feet away, where, after a shower of oil, it was lowered into an aluminum engine block before the pistons.

My first day with Courtemanche he jokingly told me, "It takes a tough guy to make a crank." That was old world talk, however, macho nostalgia for the Flint V-8 plant where human hands drilled the buggers out instead of Darryl and Darryl, where cranks weighed seventy pounds rather than twenty-six, and where tolerances were measured by go-and-no-go gauges instead of by sophisticated mechanisms wired to computers. Here, by contrast, a single machining line with no backup did everything, so if there was a major breakdown, it had to be fixed by the trade techs quickly or the entire powertrain building would malfunction and not pass engines along to final assembly. In this new world, Courtemanche said, "The operators are more sitters than actual operators."

It took me a couple days to figure out exactly what he meant by that. No one actually *worked* on the crankshaft machining line. Worked, as in moving weight through a distance in the old world benchmark of blue-collar toil. The operators mostly sat and watched. Periodically, they did things such as replace worn grinder wheels the size of huge manhole covers, or replace reluctor wheel cutters the size of door knobs. They also tested a certain number of cranks, measuring seven-micron tolerances (a micron is .000039 inches and numerous posters along the machining lines graphically demonstrated how a micron is a fraction of the diameter of a human hair). But neither the op techs nor the trade techs actually worked cranks. Fanuc GMC Robotics, Komatsu Ltd., Landis Machine Tool Company, ASEA, Marposs Gauges, IMPCO, and a human inspector wearing white gloves and looking for porosity at the very end of the line did the work, in the old-fashioned sense of the word. The people waited for the machines to give them opportunities to do their thing—which could happen quite a lot.

As Scott Prins, the CTM of the line, put it, "We have a saying around here: 'We're knee-deep in opportunities.'"

In Saturn speak an "opportunity" was in truth a headache, a dilemma, a problem. "Knee deep" had a more rural flavor; it was farmer talk, having to do mostly with manure.

In the ideal new world A-crew was a happy customer of rough cranks from the foundry, defective cranks moving down the machining line never exceeded ten percent, and engine assembly, to which the heart of the internal combustion engine traveled via a robot and a lowerator, was a pleased customer because it received quality parts. In the real world, however, things often went awry. This happened for one of three reasons: the foundry team supplied its customer, the crank team, with low quality cranks; the crank line machinery and/or robots went a little haywire; or the crank team let some opportunity get the best of them despite all the training and started feuding and grumbling.

My second day on the line, for instance, proved less than a great day for teamsmanship. On the other hand, it was knee deep in opportunities.

"It was supposed to be calm," Courtemanche said sarcastically a little before nine that morning. He sat in the team center, a small room roughly ten by fifteen feet with a low ceiling and a closet-sized office attached. A kind of sanctuary, a place to take breaks, eat lunch, and gossip away from the noisy machinery, the team center contained several tables, a TV perched high in one corner, white boards for messages and training sessions, a list of Saturn's Thirty Work Unit Functions (number one, "Consensus Decision-Making," had been crossed out by B-crew's electrical technician Danny Lentz, who had scribbled in its place, "Make it happen!"), a photo of UAW legend Walter Reuther, and Glenn. Glenn Gingrich, fifty-six, was a short, chain-smoking service technician on loan from Landis Machine Company. His job was to keep Pam Saint's grinders working well. Mostly though Glenn joked and smoked, or stared into space and smoked. He struck me as being as much a fixture in the team center as the Mr. Coffee, and along with caffeine and nicotine, a third touchstone for team members seeking a break from technology's efficient monotony.

For the last five minutes Courtemanche has been telling Glenn how he'd arranged for a red-zone consultation for a team member in the foundry this morning. The guy skipped work again, leaving the iron-melt team shorthanded and angry. Iron melt already had more than its share of Saturn-style opportunities, due in part to the new technology of lost-foam casting, so absenteeism, which upset morale, it could do without. Earlier, Courtemanche had told me that during the hiring process he felt the foundry "abandoned the method. I think they goofed around on hiring for so long that they just hired for the sake of hiring." Now he and Dennis Dowers, CTM of the foundry's A-crew, were constantly dealing with the consequences. "We don't discipline them like in the old place," Courtemanche said of folks who mistook the new freedom at Saturn for liberty to do what they wanted. "We try to correct the problem rather than pushing it off to the side." Today, Courtemanche and his partner O'Gorman had shifted the unresponsive team member into consultation's red zone from the amber zone, or warning zone. The red zone was the final warning: you went home for three days, with pay, to think about if you wanted to work for Saturn. Could you change your behavior? If the answer was no, the UAW and management could cooperate in terminating you. The lifetime job guarantee at Saturn did not mean you couldn't be released. It might take six months, but that was less than the two years typical at other GM divisions. And here the union and management cooperated over this crucial issue of when to terminate somebody rather than fighting about it while the employee stayed on the job.

Machining opportunities proved plentiful this morning as well. One involved Pam Saint's reaction to what Courtemanche called "a funky coolant." While Courtemanche and Glenn were sitting quietly in the team center, Saint swept into the little room on a wave of sound, her bleached perm bouncing.

"There is something wrong with that coolant," she told her WUMA, sounding a little hoarse. "I'm all plugged up. It's like I'm fixin' to break out with the flu."

As the WUMA blinked a couple of times, apparently mulling over this new opportunity, Saint went to the Mr. Coffee. She wore a cranberry-colored blouse with her ID card attached to it, tight jeans, and stylish, pointy black shoes with steel toes inconspicuously designed into them. A Snoopy watch hung loosely on her wrist. "Yesterday I broke out all in welts," she said, pouring herself a cup of coffee.

Evidently, the bacteria level of the coolant, one of the liquids that looked a lot like dirty bath water and recirculated in the grinders, had gotten high. Usually changed every six months, and periodically tested in the plant laboratory, the coolant was going to be renewed during the holiday shutdown, which began in a few days. Meanwhile, Pam Saint wanted her WUMA to do something about it now.

"You didn't go out drinking last night?" he asked.

"No." She grinned. "If I did, I'd been sick this morning."

Saint had a syrupy Southern accent pitched a little high by her braces. The metal flashed when she grinned, which she did a lot. She sat at the end of the table, Courtemanche to one side, Glenn to the other.

Glenn lifted his weary eyes and exhaled. Pam did have a real problem, he knew. Not in the service technician's department, however. Maybe the mole people, who worked in a subterranean chamber beneath the powertrain building, filtering sludge and filings from various coolants, could come up with something short term for her, he suggested. An additive, maybe. Something to quell the bacterial funkiness until shutdown.

Courtemanche also knew Saint had a legitimate gripe. Although he would not have phrased it this way, her brain-body system had a health need caused by the working environment. And the working environment was the WUMA's bailiwick. One of Saturn's guiding principles was a willingness to grant priority to brain-body systems. These systems were vulnerable, highly trained, and emotional. Courtemanche stubbed out his Merit, stood, and ambled out of the team center. Pam Saint smiled, sipped her coffee.

"Bob got promoted," she told me, "I don't think he realized all that was involved."

Not five minutes later, Courtemanche came back into the team center. Saint still sat there, talking with Glenn. Another opportunity had arisen for the WUMA, and since I had been privy to enough opportunities for one morning he suggested it might be a good time for the writer to spend a little time with Dennis Dowers in iron melt. I followed him out into the noise.

Entering the foundry we passed an op tech with long red fingernails and short blonde hair dipping styrofoam cranks into a refractory wash and hanging them on a rack. Once the rack was filled, it would roll into the baking oven, drying the wash into a skin that could withstand the high temperatures of the molten iron during the pour.

Courtemanche halted by the oven and peered around for Dowers. Two engineers were inspecting the styrofoam molding machine. The warning alarm behind the furnaces rang loudly, alerting everyone that scrap iron was riding upward on the magnet. Courtemanche stood there, arms hanging loosely by his sides, something resembled a scowl starting to form on his freckled face. He wore his usual uniform: scuffed cowboy boots, jeans, a T-shirt, with a flannel shirt over it, unbuttoned and the tails out. He squeezed between several racks of dipped crankshaft molds.

Dennis Dowers, a tall fellow in his late thirties, was talking earnestly with one of his team members by the catwalk overlooking the iron pouring area. Courtemanche told Dowers he could send me back to the crank line when he was through with me. "I got to go back and smooth Nancy's feathers," he said by way of explanation, turned on a boot heel and strolled off, lighting up as he walked.

The foundry seemed noisier than yesterday. I could hear the electrodes sparking in a scrap stew in the overhead furnace area. Smoke hovered up there. Bells and buzzers were ringing away, red lights flashing from the vicinity of the train track. Dowers was busy but had time to stand calmly amid the activity for a few minutes and answer a few questions.

Dowers had previously worked at GM's Central Foundry Division in Danville, Illinois, a dark, gloomy place where the ventilation had been terrible and where "you'd spit dark stuff out of your nose and throat for days," he said. Now he lived in a little community of six families, all of whom worked for Saturn, outside of Lewisburg, in Marshall County, and was convinced he had made the right career decision by coming here. "It's given me the chance to really deal with problems," he said.

From what I had heard, the opportunities in iron melt runneth over: the lost-foam process itself was weak, there was too much American machinery here, the team had too many clashing personalities, the team had blown its budget on overtime rather than on process refinement. Courtemanche had told me about the "nightmare of the furnaces," as he called it, a horrendous few weeks during which molten iron broke right through the furnaces and ran on the floor, creating an explosive situation and an awful mess to clean up. The nightmare took weeks to resolve. And it had not been a matter of a trusting relationship with a supplier working toward a mutually satisfactory solution. The foundry had switched to another supplier, whose refractories didn't fail after only a few melts. In defense of the foundry, lost foam was new and risky, it had never been tried on this scale, and, once perfected, promised substantial cost savings. That was why Jay Wetzel and Guy Briggs had intuitively gone for it way back in 1985.

Presently, the foundry cast forty crankshafts an hour, four hundred a shift, Dowers said. That was just enough, with a ten percent defect rate, for the 730 cars the plant was averaging per day. The foundry's goal was sixty cranks an hour, which would satisfy the 1,000 cars per day production goal the entire plant was focused on. Porosity—"a nasty word around here"—remained the technical opportunity of the moment. It was an expensive and exasperating one because porosity was seldom detected before Steve Sherman visually inspected each crank almost a thousand feet from where it had been poured. But an even bigger opportunity, as Courtemanche had implied, was absenteeism.

"It gives me heartburn," Dowers said. "A few individuals are trying to push the system as far as they can."

We walked past twenty-six-pound rough cranks bobbing and turning and shedding black sand. The silo-like sand containers were bolted to an interior wall and ducted to the bag houses outside. One of the biggest challenges for the foundry, Dowers explained, was the lack of benchmarks for the lost-foam casting process. He couldn't just call up the GM Tech Center or Central Foundry for answers because they didn't have them. No one knew much about lost foam on this scale. So the team, with the help of the WUMAs and other Saturn resources, had to find solutions on its own. And right now, Dowers said, "No one knows why the gas bubbles tend to collect near the surface of the number one journal."

On my way out of the foundry area I talked to the red-nailed op tech. Wearing protective gloves, she was dipping more foam cranks in a refractory wash. Her name was Sharon East. She was thirty-two, single, living in Franklin and loving it. "I'm having the time of my life," she declared. She whipped a dripping crank mold out of the dip with a motion I associated with the making of a soft ice cream twirl and hung it on a hook. "Opportunity knocked and I answered."

I asked East about her team.

"We have our share of problems," she confessed. "I think we'll pull together. But it may take a while."

Back on the crank line I soon got the scuttlebutt about the WUMA's latest opportunity: CTM Prins and op tech Laatz had gotten into it. Apparently Prins, on the urging of some members of B-crew, had told Laatz how to run the polishing machine—the complicated behemoth for which mechanical tech John Plourd's advice was, "Don't touch nothing!" Along with the other female op techs of A-crew, Laatz did not take kindly to B-crew telling her much of anything. B-crew's opportunity, Laatz felt, was in the touchy area of respecting women. In fact, a female member of B-crew had recently been transferred to final assembly because of the men hassling her. Now one woman remained on B-crew, feeling alone and as distant from its members as William Jenkins apparently felt from most of the white members of A-crew.

A-crew's three female op techs all told me at different times that there was a gender gap on the team, although A-crew's gap was normal, run-of-the-mill stuff, compared to the abyss on B-crew. Laatz and Saint also said they wished they could communicate better with CTM Prins, whom they consulted as a team resource. Prins, thirty-two, was a heavyset man with a peculiar pigment condition about his eyes that gave him the look of a raccoon. Erudite, inquisitive, and always eager to talk about Saturn, both pro and con, he was the intellectual of A-crew. Prins was interested in the broader ramifications of Saturn as an industrial model, and criticized the gap between the Saturn philosophy and shop-floor realities. He had become an autoworker after his professor father had gone off to teach in Beirut, Lebanon, in the late 1970s. Scott had refused to go, stayed in Michigan, and married his girlfriend before either of them turned twenty. He had gone to work at the Fisher Body plant in Flint ("The one in *Roger & Me,*" he said, "the one where the white watertower comes crashing down at the end"). His marriage had failed. He'd remarried and now lived with his second wife, Joni, a schoolteacher in Maury County, and two children, on a street in Columbia populated mostly with Saturn families. "We all lift our garages up together in the morning," he noted wryly. His wit, though, could also be sarcastic and cutting. He was moody at times. Pam Saint, the most outspoken of the three women for whom Prins was a primary resource, said bluntly, "You can't get together with Scott; he gets P.M.S."

Toward noon I passed Saint, whose mind-body system opportunity had been temporarily relieved. A member of some other team leaned his lips near her hair, chatting. Nearby, William Jenkins tested a crank with Marposs gauges at his bench. Darryl and Darryl were bobbing and weaving. Then I saw Laatz and Prins, staring at a row of pistons in the polishing machine. A white ribbon held Laatz's dark hair back. Prins wore a striped work shirt with a UAW/Saturn insignia on the pocket. The smell of mineral seal, the lubricant for the operation, permeated the air. The CTM and the operator kept talking, getting along, smiling and joking with each other.

What had happened was that A-crew had a lot of scrap and less production from the polisher than B-crew. Prins had talked to B-crew's more experienced operator about how he calibrated the machine to avoid scrap, then passed along the information to Laatz who didn't care to hear it. She didn't respect B-crew's operator.

"It was another case of people wanting to reach the same goal," Prins said. "But don't dare tell them how to get there."

He and Laatz did iron the nagging problem out—people-wise and production-wise (A-crew had been losing a half-hour production off the polisher every day they started it up). Prins claimed, "This incident is half the fun of being at Saturn!"

In theory, however, Prins and Laatz should not have gotten into a head-to-head in which his authority exceeded hers. By now, eighteen months into production, the CTMs were supposed to have been integrated into the teams and the teams were to have assumed their functions and responsibilities, becoming their own resources. Consensus was supposed to be running things. That had not happened. Instead, the CTMs had become like foremen, but with less authority. As of January 1992 all the CTMs were going to be replaced by WUCs, or "work unit counselors." But the only significant difference between a WUC and a CTM was that each WUC was going to be elected by his or her team rather than appointed by the higher-ups. On the crank line A-crew Nancy Laatz was joking about challenging Scott Prins for WUC. That might have aggravated their conflict.

The retention of what were supposed to have been temporary positions of authority, which, like candles of light, should have melted away once they had made things clear, was an example of how making Saturn a lean horizontal organization, instead of a more traditional hierarchy, was proceeding less than ideally. At the work unit level strong teams with a lot of power had proven too radical a concept, both for the plant leadership and for the teams.

Putting ideas into action is the test of both their practicality and the willingness of their creators to have the patience for those ideas to be practiced, refined, and to mature. The team ideal at Saturn—team-oriented people using consensus decision making in a self-directed manner in order to establish a distinct bottom-up voice—had been implemented, practiced some, but not refined. There were several reasons for the diminution of team power. First and foremost, if least acknowledged, was that management was threatened by team power. Second, and blamed the most, was consensus decision making; a version of democracy in the workplace, it was said to have proven too slow and cumbersome a process to refine, especially with Saturn's ongoing production problems and with a tottering corporate parent now figuratively hanging from Saturn's youthful shoulders and breathing down its neck, saying, "Can't you make more cars?" And third, the teams themselves had not been assertive enough; many members simply had not made the personal stretch necessary for strong teams to emerge.

That stretch required not only a shared vision between the leadership and the teams in a plant constantly in flux, but serious long-term motivation by the leadership and constant self-assessment by the teams. The bottom line for the teams was that taking charge of functions was hard, despite constant training, and that the motivation to take charge was weak. Pay and perks were pretty good already. The collective will necessary to challenge the leadership wouldn't come from sitting in classes, or listening to speakers on the Saturn channel in team centers. It required learning, then transforming learning into action on the floor, in the team center, during the day-to-day operations. A good team shifted its level of competence, its self-confidence, its conflict-resolution abilities up a notch at a time, accepting new members and integrating them into the group, always staying focused. A good team was not simply a group of people working together and absorbing information.

With certain exceptions, epitomized by the concentration of skilled personnel first working in the plant in 1989 and 1990, the work force demonstrated that it could not transform into good teams. Fair teams sometimes, poor teams a lot. But rarely into good teams.

One reason was that the work force as a whole couldn't seem to shake the old world need for clearly identified voices of authority giving the orders. Maybe it was the pressures of production which, as Don Ephlin once told me, "Makes you turn back to what you know," that made the teams look to the higher-ups. Or maybe it was the changing nature of each successive generation of Saturnites. The Saturn spirit had thinned by late 1991. And the subsidiary kept growing at a fast clip. Lured less by the Saturn spirit and the promise of a different kind of job than pushed here by layoffs throughout GM, successive generations of newcomers cared less about the company. Recently, the UAW had also changed Saturn's hiring policy. All hiring now had to be done from GM's pool of laid-off workers. As the point man for hiring on the crank team, which was looking for another operator, CTM Prins told me, "The labor pool is garbage." Al Burris seconded that. "We hired most all of the good peoples," he said. Two years ago, he added, sounding perplexed, "It sounded like there were thousands of good applications. At one time, when I first came—I don't know what happened after that—there were sixty thousand aps. I guess we just went through all of them, and out of sixty thousand we only came up with just a little over four thousand good ones."

Finding good Saturnites with high skill levels, experience, and motivation had suddenly become a plant-wide challenge. The hiring complications cast a long shadow over the future of quality teams-manship at Saturn. Whether a third shift was eventually added, or one of GM's mothballed plants converted into a Saturn factory—two ideas being discussed as alternatives for increasing production—good people had to staff and run the teams. Where would they come from? How would they be trained? With tremendous pressures on Saturn to make more cars right now, could growth be accommodated with-out affecting quality? One thing was definite: without good people from a healthy labor pool, future teams would never be self-assertive and present ones might be weakened.

Meanwhile, several newcomers longed for foremen, no matter whether the person was called a WUC, a CTM, or whatever. As Joe McKean put it, and not without good reason, "Sometimes we need a foreman, sometimes people need discipline."

Few teams were confident or willing enough to deal with conflict, never mind resolve it by disciplining someone. When push came to shove, "We're still in the polite stage," Laatz told me about A-crew, one of the more together groups in the plant, attested to by the fact that management was letting me observe them.

Courtemanche seconded Laatz's observation. "The team likes to make the easy decisions," he said. For the tough ones they came to him, to Marv O'Gorman, to the BUCs. Taking responsibility for the hard decisions, for being the bad guy—something absolutely neces-sary for a team to become self-assertive—remained with the higher-ups, with the WUMAs and above.

There was also a new team policy being formulated at the top that would fundamentally alter how the teams worked. So-called "self-managed" teams, SAC had decided, would replace the "self-directed" team, which had been the ideal as defined in the original 1985 labor contract. A self-managed team would accept more direction from above, though it would still decide how to carry the direction out. In con-trast, the former self-directed teams theoretically had a voice in cer-tain decisions about the future of the plant and then were also sup-posed to have carried them out. LeFauve called the change "one of those shifting lines" that kept the balance between the teams and the leadership. A few Saturnites I talked to were more blunt; they called it "a loss of power."

Some team members objected to the change; they had not come to Saturn to drift back toward the GM way of doing things. Yet there had been no collective union reaction against the top assuming more power and the teams giving it up. And the decision to alter the nature of the teams and their potential to direct change had not been made by management alone. LeFauve and the vice presidents weren't diluting the potential of teamsmanship by themselves—the UAW leadership was a partner in the decision. Yet no team members I talked to mentioned having been polled by their leadership, or by the Saturn/ UAW partnership leaders, about giving up what they had never really attained.

The newest Saturnites, meanwhile, had little sense of what was being lost. They knew the Saturn story, or a version of it. Few were getting a strong taste of the Saturn spirit, at least not in the intoxicating dosage those who had brought the vision into being had received. The benchmarks these newcomers brought with them to Saturn were their old jobs. By those benchmarks, Saturn still seemed like a new and fresh experience because it was: no time clocks, few work rules, and five-percent training. Yet Saturn hoped to create a new breed of worker, a new world of bottom-up teamsmanship, not a breed simply happy to have a little better job than before in a world ruled from the top down.

Little attention was paid to the rift between Saturn's vision of its future and its present reality. Production worries obscured philosophical shortfalls. Yet now new team members such as Seborn Powell entered an environment of ambivalence about team authority and direction. The team ideal seemed unclear, adrift. A gap existed between what the teams were supposed to be and what they were. "It's loose around here," Courtemanche said to me one afternoon. "People have so much freedom when they first come from the old world, they don't know what to do." Most of them gradually did what they had done before, which was look to management to tell them what to do.

At its top the UAW reacted favorably to the watering down of teamsmanship at Saturn. Within the twenty-six-member UAW International board, Saturn continued to be viewed as a black sheep, a departure from the status quo. Don Ephlin's successor, Stephen Yokich, shared little of the enthusiasm about Saturn that Ephlin had brought to it. In the fall of 1991, Saturn's labor contract had been renegotiated, and the production bonus provision, conceived as a means of stimulating Saturn's competitiveness by linking rewards to production, had been weakened. In the new contract, only five percent of wages, instead of twenty percent, were at risk. Even then, the risk was linked not with production, where it should have been, but with training hours. There was no provision to evaluate the effectiveness of the training, which seemed to go hand in hand with the absence of clearly identified channels through which to transfer knowledge from Saturn to GM. Wages, however, went up. Op techs would soon be making $38 thousand annually, without overtime, and trade techs around $44 thousand.

Finally, there was Saturn's management. With their company on the verge of national success (sales were already taking off), they too lacked sufficient motivation to push teamsmanship, as originally envisioned, into a new world reality. This was somewhat understandable. Management at Saturn was in a kind of Catch-22: do a good job empowering teams and maybe lose your job as a consequence. If the avenues for passing along Saturn's lessons throughout GM, for connecting the learning laboratory with its parent, had been clearly established and well nourished, the managers and engineers and crew chiefs and WUMAs one saw everywhere might have been more disturbed by the shortcomings of Saturn's teams. For after Saturn they would have had places to go—out into the GM hinterland, spreading the Saturn gospel to enthusiastic audiences. As things stood, that was a learning laboratory pipedream. Division chiefs at GM despised Saturn and were still bitter about losing capital to the subsidiary, capital that had been needed to modernize their plants and make them competitive. In other words, Saturn was often being blamed in many offices of GM's scattered North American operations rather than praised.

What all this distilled down to was not a simple truth, such as wages, after various adjustments, had risen significantly while production lagged and costs were high. But a complex interplay of factors: high wages and low production, team redefinition and leadership assertion, a learning laboratory with a less-than-enthused audience and ill-defined avenues of knowledge transfer.

Nevertheless, and this was no small feat, out in the marketplace, Saturn maintained its vision of giving Americans a good cheap car they were starting to buy with more and more enthusiasm and pleasure. That was good news. The quality car, the improved cooperation between union and management, the partnerships with suppliers, with Hal Riney & Partners, with the stores—all seemed to be having a synergistic effect. Yet like porosity in journal number one, which needed resources and creativity to be solved, teamsmanship, which lay at the heart of Saturn's long-term success, required prolonged scrutiny, refinement, and a big dose of creativity. For despite all the clapping in the marketplace in late 1991 for Saturn, the plant still wasn't in tune. And the teams still weren't good teams.

In the near future, no matter how well all the partners outside the plant got along, the teams at the heart of the enterprise had to harmonize, had to think and sing, had to be given their promised voice. Or else Saturn was not going to remain an entry-level vehicle for very long. Presently, each car was losing several thousand dollars.

Lean production, touted so highly before and during the start-up, had been partly achieved. There were also fewer layers of management at Saturn than at many competitors' plants. Yet the partnership of union and management meant two people where there often was one in a traditional plant. The result was that at Saturn fewer layers did not always translate into significantly fewer people between the top and the floor. *Kanban,* or just-in-time-inventory, remained elusive as well. Some processes stored parts, others worked long hours of overtime just to provide the minimum number needed without defects. In final assembly, getting a rhythm some days seemed impossible because the parts from body systems, powertrain, and vehicle interiors arrived in a stop-and-go fashion rather than in three smooth currents.

My assessment was that Saturn had stepped out mightily toward the concept of the empowered team, but in late 1991 had shortened its stride to a worried shuffle. The teams themselves shared the blame for that since most of them lacked a critical mass of dynamic people. And now, complicating things further, management had undermined the team concept in a subtle but effective way with the self-managed team, which was the equivalent of a team on a leash as opposed to roaming free, and the UAW had diluted the hiring pool. Worried that the teams might just flounder, and blame would be placed on it, the top had dropped back, huddled, and called a very traditional play: "We're taking over."

Money was one obvious cause for this end run of the teams by the top. General Motors was losing billions. Time had simply run out earlier than anticipated on the great experiment in horizontal teamsmanship. Now Saturn had to make more cars. Make them faster. Get costs down. Self-directed or not, the teams remained in the spotlight. Their partnership with the leadership, that shifting line of balance LeFauve alluded to, was trying to discover an equilibrium that worked, that didn't drift too far back toward the old world. But finding the equilibrium was not going to be easy, especially with Saturn's parent tottering perilously close to bankruptcy.

B-crew's electrical tech Danny Lentz had a reputation. If mechanic John Plourd could, as Nancy Laatz put it, "fix anything but a broken heart," Lentz was his counterpart in the wires and circuits department. Lentz was also a lapsed member of Mensa, the high-IQ club. I was repeatedly told that he was irascible, a renegade, and wouldn't talk to me. All were true but the last.

Bald, cherub-faced, wearing a blue work shirt and greasy boots, Danny Lentz led me out of the team center at the start of the B-crew shift, when I introduced myself, up and over the line, and into the electricians' repair room where he said we could talk undisturbed. A partially dismantled robot stood in the middle of the floor like an electronic scarecrow. Lentz took a chair by it and smiled. "What do you want to know?" he asked.

He laughed when I said others called him a renegade electrician.

He wasn't a renegade, he insisted. He was a skilled tradesman. An underappreciated, underpaid, and often frustrated skilled tradesman who—it increasingly became clear—had no love loss for "spider-chart drawers," as he called engineers who had too much power and not enough knowledge.

Lentz swiveled in his chair and pointed to the one-foot mark of a six-foot-long shelf of manuals to his rear. "From this point over are basically manuals for this line," he said. "These suckers are hard to read."

He had long sideburns. His name tag hung from his shirt collar. He shook his head, smiling woefully. Through the thin metal walls came the powertrain chorus.

"Engineers don't fix machines!" Lentz declared. "Electricians and machine repairmen do. Some engineers are capable, but we are also saddled with an awful lot of very young engineers who think they know everything. They haven't got to the point in knowledge—" and he smiled even harder, twisting his face and squinting his eyes, "where they realize what they don't know yet."

Two years ago, Lentz said, the crank team had tremendous freedom. It performed at a high level, as high as he had seen in more than twenty years on various machining jobs. But once they got their chrome cranks, the encouragement to perform at high standards disappeared. Nowadays, for him, the leadership was blurry, hard to define. Some of it was "very good," he said. "But our leadership is still in the paper-shuffling mode. With a few exceptions—and there are exceptions to this—people do not get promoted unless they are 'yes, sir; yes, sir.' There are very few people around here who are willing to have an opinion, or are technically skilled enough to have an opinion.

"The last class I went to in Northfield there was a lady teaching who didn't know a thing about building cars, and she said the whole problem was we didn't have enough people skills, that we had all the technical skills that we needed because we had all these oodles and oodles of engineers."

I asked what he thought about lean production, and he said, "We are lean in some ways." He went on, "Under the original concept we had this dream—and there were some people who came later who had this dream—that we were going to get rewarded for running lean." He repeated the fact that the original crank line had called for seven operators, not nine as it now had. "We know damn well that if we were paid for it, if there was any *reward* for it, we could do it with six. But we don't make that decision." More money didn't have to be the carrot. "If we could just control it," he said, looking past me and sounding pained, "it probably could be done. But right now all you can do is get in trouble by going against the system and saying we got more people than we need."

In the second year of production, Lentz said he found Saturn "not that much different from the old world."

"Do you find that very disappointing?" I asked.

"Oh," he winced, "extremely disappointing. It depresses the hell out of me."

Honesty was eroding too, he added. It was becoming popular to conduct plant-wide surveys to confirm what the leadership had already decided ought to happen, just to go through the motions.

The earlier successes of some teams, Lentz felt, was due to their smallness, their technical skills, and, in the case of the crank team, to their leader, Bob Davis, "who didn't do much of anything—he wasn't a very popular man." Yet under him the team had clicked. The business leader who replaced Davis "did not trust the team with anything," Lentz said.

He talked briefly about the ascent of the working man up the ladder to a management slot, a climb which not that long ago was routine but now was rare. America devalued skilled hands was a truth that hurt, he seemed to be saying. "Because I don't have a degree and wear a blue shirt," he said, but trailed off into a burst of sour laughter that nearly shut his eyes. A minute later he was remembering the Japanese installation crews that had been here for Komatsu and others. "What was shocking was the level of people who were here starting up their machines," he recalled. "Their project engineer was out there with the big wrenches; nobody looked down on him for that."

Now the Komatsu machines were the best running ones on the crank line. The wrench-using engineer had obviously been their leader. "They didn't look down on working," Lentz continued. "When you start out as a tradesman at GM, unless you change your outlook and life, unless you decide you're going to have the people skills and learn how to draw spider charts and play other games, you're going to end up your career as a tradesman."

He shrugged, reached for a cigarette, thought twice about it, and slid it back into the pack. "Things have to change radically before we can stay in business," he said. "And GM lacks the will to execute radical change." Pausing a moment, he asked a rhetorical question, "Is it GM or everybody here? Is it an engineer who was taught in college that he was a superior being? Does our whole system allow for this?"

On a larger scale, Lentz said, "Two things have cost us our competitiveness. One's our educational system. And the other is the fact that we never promote from the bottom anymore. The Japanese— their whole system is based on education. Our learning skills have shrunk. TV's done that; it's burnt a lot of brains."

Nowadays Lentz lacked the initiative to go the extra yard for Saturn. "You don't believe the extra effort is going to accomplish anything," he said. He heard too much phony cheering from the sidelines, too much propaganda. He recalled seeing a professor from MIT, a consultant, on the Saturn channel a few weeks ago. The fellow told the audience, " 'you have to believe that you can do it, even if you know you can't, before it can be successful.' " How could he do that when he didn't even feel the crank team was really a team any longer? The group lacked common goals, Lentz added, wasn't striving hard to be efficient. "We're all real nice to each other and go our own way. I criticize because I'm a bitcher."

He smiled.

I asked about other teams in the plant.

"I don't know that much about other teams. We're so isolated. I only know that I hear from other people that there is much more turmoil on other teams than on ours." Which, he admitted, was leading him to conclude that the team idea might never work well at Saturn because it conflicted with the culture of individualism. "We're still Americans, and I question how effective the teams can really be." He laughed again, a short burst. "I question everything."

He pulled his cigarette pack out of his shirt pocket, fingered a cigarette, lit up, and began reminiscing about his years at John Deere in Dubuque, Iowa. That company had respected tradesman, he recalled, had few managers. Management here was going through a transformation, he said, by way of comparison. Originally, there had been three distinct layers, with certain powers at each layer. "Now it's very vague—it's a real sloppy pyramid. And some people don't know where they fit on that pyramid. They're actually establishing their position in that pyramid. And then there are people who aren't effective and they're left inside the pyramid. They're inside that pyramid still trying to create something to make them important."

"And it all goes into the cost of this low-cost car," I said.

"Yes."

24

Surviving the Cut

Wednesday, December 18, at 11 A.M., Stempel was scheduled to talk to the entire GM family, 700 thousand plus people scattered around the globe. It was not going to be an "I wish you a Merry Christmas" chat, but rather a "Honey, I shrunk the corps" broadside.

For weeks the media had been speculating: which plants would be closed? How many thousands of blue-collar workers would be laid off? Would GM finally trim at the top? Critics had been pointing there with renewed vigor as the giant had slid first to its knees in 1990, and now, to stretch a metaphor, was sprawled flat on the world's playing field, bleeding capital at the rate of $15 million a day, an outflow even GM could not sustain for long.

In the media guessing game Saturn had been spared much attention, despite its significant contribution to losses. But given GM's unpredictability, that was less than reassuring to the crank team members who seemed to be lingering around the team center more than usual this morning. They knew their different kind of company had lost $700 million the first year, that production was low, teams less than lean, the total manufacturing cost per vehicle way too high. As this day approached, questioned about Saturn's status, Communications spokespersons, along with the executives led by LeFauve, have been a chorus: Saturn is about quality, not quantity; we're still debugging; we're on track and will turn a profit in the future.

The company line was true, but getting old. Somewhere down the road, with the road shortening by the day, Saturn needed to go into the black, turn a profit, demonstrate its economic viability. Looking at the positive side, something Saturn still managed with aplomb, buyers liked their new SCs, SL1s, and SL2s a lot, stores were clamoring for more inventory, and sales kept climbing despite America's being mired in a nagging recession.

Could Saturn increase production and lower the cost per car without nickel and diming quality to death? Because, if that happened, the whole multibillion dollar experiment, the eight-year development time, the commitment to a bumber-to-bumper showdown with Toyota, Nissan, Honda, et al. on various level-playing fields was over, and the little car that was going to demonstrate that American industry could make good stuff at a competitive price would be just one more example that in fact it couldn't.

With the tough question in the background and doomsday forecasts in the air, the crank team was understandably less than cheery and relaxed this December morning, with Christmas six days away. So, presumably, were the other Saturn teams, not to mention the entire GM family. Heads were definitely going to roll. But whose?

For the past few days CTM Scott Prins and other members of A-crew had been picking on two junior powertrain engineers, Tom Brittingham and Ricardo Martinez. The engineers' jobs were at peril because they were members of the middle-management fraternity that included Danny Lentz's spider-chart drawers. This morning there was a lot of playful yet serious banter about which one, Tom or Ricardo, was going to get canned as a steady stream of people circulated in and out of the team center for a cigarette, coffee, or some anxiety-reducing conversation about whether Tom or Ricardo ought to go. On several occasions eight or ten bodies crowded in, talking and smoking. Hovering at about eye level, the smoke suggested a miniature cirrus cloud, with the TV, switched to the Saturn channel, glowing above it. The TV announcer was counting down how many minutes were left until GM Constituency Communications brought the GM family Chairman Robert Stempel's speech. Every time the door to the team center opened, the smoke undulated, like a magic carpet put in motion by a wave of sound.

A story came on the Saturn channel about four teenagers recently flipping a SL2 seven times. It was their lucky number because the spaceframe held and none of the boys died. A cop appeared and said they had been speeding. Prins, sprawled listlessly in a chair, his eyes encircled by big black circles, said to no one in particular, "They had the speedometer pegged; it goes up to 130."

Pam Saint swept in, sound pouring in the open door behind her almost like a liquid. She lit up, glanced at Glenn, said, "It's chilly in here," and briskly rubbed her shoulders.

"They're chilling us out before the announcement," Nancy Laatz told Saint over one shoulder.

Laatz, wearing her *Bad Boys* T-shirt, and Michelle Mullenhour, a short, stocky electrical technician in a striped Saturn shirt, with a yellow voltmeter hooked to the back of her belt, were talking about babies with Leanne Schipani, who was just back from having her fourth.

"If Bob asks us," Saint told the women, "we're unwinding."

Glenn grinned, exhaled. Laatz and Mullenhour returned their attention to Schipani who was seated. Prins eyed the tube. John Plourd strolled in and sat by the water cooler. Plourd tugged off his boot, located a small stone in it, pulled the boot back on and glanced around at the others. He removed his ballcap, ran a hand through his long hair, and asked, "What is this, a union meeting?"

A couple minutes later, bored, Prins rolled two chairs directly beneath the TV after pinning hand-lettered "reserved" signs to their backs. The chairs were for Brittingham, now sitting across from Glenn and trying to act nonplussed about possibly being unemployed, and Martinez, who was not in the room. Two styrofoam cups were taped to the wall, one labeled "Tom," the other "Ricardo." They were for collections.

I left the team center with Mullenhour. A short, articulate woman, she had told me earlier that she loved living in Maury County. "If Saturn falls apart, I'm staying," she said. Mullenhour was, like hundreds of Saturnites, from the bleak set of *Roger & Me*. She worked at Buick City on hydromatic transmissions. Union seniority kept her from training programs she needed. At Saturn, she said, "Every time I go out on a job I'm getting trained."

We climbed a steel catwalk, a gantry flexing to one side. On the far side of the line, using a large screwdriver, Mullenhour opened a tall gray cabinet. Colored wires, fuses, and chips, the electronic brains of the Komatsu machine, filled the interior. Every machine on the line had its own electrical system, Mullenhour said. The machines drilled, milled, and cut according to commands, moving each crank from one operation to the next. "They all seem to communicate better than the people," she noted.

Suddenly, I spotted something I recognized: two large fuses, each one the size of a small flashlight. I asked the electrician if she ever got shocked.

"The third day on the job."

The big stuff isn't what most electricians worry about, however, she told me. It's the smaller stuff. "Old electricians always say they'd rather be hit by the big stuff—you'll get some burns, but it'll blow you away." The smaller lines, on the other hand "contract your muscles, make you hold on. If it goes through the heart, there's where it kills you. Any of the power will kill you if it goes through the heart."

Mullenhour pointed at some of the big stuff: 250 amp/600 volt fuses, three of them, each about eight inches long and three inches in diameter. I imagined how much power was surging through them right now, heading toward Op 10 of the Komatsu rough ender.

"I'm still trying to figure out why I'm an electrician," Mullenhour said. "I freak out from static cling."

"What's static cling?"

"You know, stuff sticking to your clothes."

She chuckled and I laughed nervously.

Opening one metal door after another in the wall of panel boxes, she came to a programmable part of the hardware. She said she had a plug-in hand-held device that could program the memory boards that operated the gantries and transfer bars of the machine. She could change the speed and accuracy of cuts, the time between transfers. She pointed at a unit she called "the big boy."

"He communicates all the information and interprets what everybody's doing."

"What's the technical term for that?" I asked.

"The PLC . . . the programmable logic controller. It's got a memory. It holds programs, has a power supply. Some of them do arithmetic."

"And this whole thing," I swept my arm back toward the other electrical panels we scrutinized, upwards of fifteen feet of them, "is just for the Komatsu machine's op 10?"

"Yes."

As we passed more panel boxes Mullenhour said she spent hardly any time down at this end of the line because everything runs great. "All the problems were down there." She gestured down the line. "The rough end was perfect. I said why didn't we buy Komatsu for the whole line."

"Who was the manufacturer of the equipment that hasn't worked so well?" I asked.

She grimaced. "American."

We soon stood at the head of the line, watching the robot swivel and pick up refractory-skinned crankshafts from a pallet, swivel back and set each one gently on the conveyor.

"Do you find your job challenging?" I asked Mullenhour.

"Yeah . . . more so than where I left."

"How much of the day are you really busy, really occupied?"

"Lately?"

"Yeah."

She puffed out her cheeks, thinking. She had on glasses, with side protectors attached to the bows. The robot bent over and the air sounded vaguely alive. "An hour?" she said, quizzically. "A good day is when you don't have to do anything. I'm basically—I was told, and I believe it—I'm an insurance policy. If I'm working, they're losing money." Not that she didn't try to stay busy, fine-tuning things. "If you can make things run smoother, go for it," Mullenhour said.

We walked down along the line. Lights flashed on the panel boxes. Joe McKean, a smear of oil on his forehead, was gauging a crank on a bench. Nearby, on a video screen, colorful images in red, purple, and blue, like balls of string traveling in arcs, traced the geometry of the crank, telling him where it still had excess iron so he could reprogram the mill, reload the crank, and correct the defect.

"I don't know," Mullenhour said above the noise. "Sometimes I think if it ain't broken, don't fix it. Some people, they can always find a way of improving something. I give them credit for that."

"What do you think of the whole Saturn philosophy: teamwork and partnerships and CTMs and all the rest? How do you think it works?"

"For the most part I think it works pretty good. Sometimes you could feel pressured in the old world. Here, I feel pressured when something goes down. But as a whole I don't feel somebody's watching me all the time."

In the team center both junior engineers were in their assigned seats, eyes on the screen. Prins was ribbing them good-naturedly. Most of the team milled around. The countdown clock showed five minutes until Stempel's talk.

"Saturn's going to shut down for five years," Tom Reinhard speculated loudly, drawing a couple of angry glances.

Minutes later trumpets and drums in a triumphant processional march played on and on in a kind of "Hail to the Chief" bit of fanfare, then Stempel's grim face filled the screen. "Speculation in the press has made many of you nervous," he said as an opening. Hair slicked back, wearing a dark suit, he briefly touched on GM's need to cut costs and boost productivity, then skipped to the substance of his talk: "We don't see significant changes in the future . . . must make fundamental changes . . . can't blame everything on the economy."

I counted twelve people in the hushed room. Then Seaborn Powell hustled in. The only missing A-crew member was William Jenkins.

Stempel began outlining a corporate downsizing, the largest in GM's history. Twenty-one facilities would be closed, he said, including six assembly plants. Seventy-four thousand people would be laid off, twenty thousand of them salaried employees. Stempel sounded deadpan, his voice void of any of the sparkle I had enjoyed in his office. Masking the savagery of the cuts was the fact that specific plants were not named but listed in pairs, one of the two to be mothballed or closed after additional analysis; in effect, the plants would be competing for a while to see which survived. Added up, the changes were sobering and telling: by 1995, GM's total work force would be half the size it had been in 1985. Stempel closed his talk by dutifully bashing the press and the stringent fuel economy standards.

Since nothing had been said about Saturn, the grim mood in the team center lifted. Backhanded compliments for Martinez and Brittingham, both smiling broadly, flew around as the collection cups were ceremoniously untaped. Prins presented the men with some change. The talk switched to folks team members knew in the targeted plants. They commiserated about how they must be feeling. Awful, not knowing if they did or did not have jobs.

One positive aspect of the downsizing, Prins told me, was that the labor pool would be deeper for Saturn to draw from. Good union people would be needing jobs.

Stempel soon appeared back on the tube. At a nationally broadcast press conference he repeated the details of the downsizing, then fielded questions from the media. In the audience sat reporters I recognized from the media day in Northfield seven months ago. The chairman defended what he euphemistically called "consolidations," or the closing of one of each of the plant pairings listed. He emphasized the "lean" future of GM. Sitting in the team center, thinking about what I had learned about Saturn's leanness, I wondered if he knew what he was talking about.

Team members, all in good moods, started exiting. Their machines needed observing. Shattering the surface of the mood, exposing its tenuousness, someone suddenly shouted angrily at the TV, "Speak English!" A Japanese reporter was asking Stempel a question.

Later that afternoon LeFauve appeared on the Saturn channel, responding to Stempel's speech. LeFauve looked drained, with bags under his eyes. His cheeks were sallow. Specifically how the downsizing would impact Saturn would be taken up tomorrow, he said, at a presentation to be given by the leadership to all the teams. Late in the afternoon Saturn Communications' Jennifer Schettler, making a rare trip to powertrain from "the Taj Mahal," the name derisively given to Northfield by some team members, found me scribbling notes between the foundry and the crank line. Schettler, in buffed leather boots and a dark suit, wanted to know if everything was going ok. I said everything was going fine. When I mentioned how wane LeFauve had looked on the broadcast, she brushed it off. "Skip's got TV pallor," she said.

The next day, as scheduled, the Saturn leadership appeared on the Saturn channel. Vice president of manufacturing Bob Boroff told the audience gathered in team centers around the facility that the leadership had discussed many alternatives for Saturn's future. They had narrowed them down to four. He went through them one by one, after emphasizing that everyone would be voting on which one he or she wanted in January. It quickly became obvious to everyone in the crank team center, however, that there really were no alternatives being presented. The first three Boroff sketched were simply preludes for alternative four: shifting to five days a week, ten hours a day, plus a minimum of nine Saturdays, to boost production to 217 thousand cars next year.

Contemplating the tentative schedule's impact on his life, Prins said loudly, so the others could hear, "This is a question of survival. We've got to realize we've had it too good for too long." Nevertheless, it was going to be tough on people, he added. Even on the forty-hour-a-week rotation, "I need a day to sit around like a zombie and regroup," he said.

Joe McKean said, "I'd work a fifth ten-hour day for no overtime."

Ken Baker, the team's second electrical trade tech, said, "I came down here for one reason: I don't want to get laid off any more."

No doubt, Danny Lentz wouldn't like it. Although the outspoken electrician had said, "We're not stressed at all—until you get into where you got to struggle to get those parts through, you're not stressed," he had been very critical of the rotation's effect on his blood pressure. "I already told them," he said, "I'm not dying for the job!"

No one on A-crew grumbled openly about the increase in overtime, or about the rotation putting greater demands on biorhythms, not to mention families. For single parents, it sounded like a nightmare. In the aftermath of yesterday's announcement, a sense of positive resignation reigned. Tom Reinhard seemed to sum up the consensus when he said, "You gotta do what you gotta do."

Boroff's talk encouraged that sentiment. "The battle for survival has reached a feverish pitch," he warned. The present output of 730 cars a day "clearly spells disaster." The teams had to get up to a 1,000 cars a day and more soon, he said.

Then, in the Saturn partnership style, Boroff's partner, UAW representative Joe Rypkowski, reviewed the alternatives and reached the same conclusion Boroff had: alternative four was the way to go. When Rypkowski mentioned a goal of 217 thousand cars for 1992, Leanne Schipani spoke up. "I'll bet quality drops with these numbers," she said.

"How close are those guys on TV to the floor?" I asked her.

"They can't be too close," she replied.

Rypkowski urged team members not to blame each other for not having reached earlier production quotas. He sounded reassuring. The teams could do it, he insisted, the plant could produce more cars. While listening to him, Schipani talked about the tension between A-crew and B-crew. She mentioned fingerpointing, blame. There was a gap between the leadership's view of what was going on inside the the plant, she said, and what was going on.

I asked her about a sexual harassment incident I heard about on B-crew. Schipani said the woman complained about being hassled, but got the runaround from the WUMAs. She finally had to go over their heads and was transferred to engine assembly.

Pam Saint came into the team center for a smoke.

"How do you feel about going on five days?" I asked.

"Go on five days?" the single parent rejoiced, laughing. "I've been working six!"

Wearing stonewashed jeans and a Saturn shirt, Seborn Powell bounced in like a lightweight boxer. Soon even William Jenkins entered the team center. He was there to eat. Since this was the final work day before the Christmas shut down, the crank team was having a spread for lunch: cold cut platters garnished with home-made pickles, chocolate dessert balls from Tom Rinehard's wife ("I gave her a hand," he boasted), beans, deviled eggs, potato salad, dips, soft drinks, pecan pie, and a Merry Christmas cake. Prins brought in a video, *National Lampoon's Christmas*. The team members ate from styrofoam plates while watching the cutting of the huge tree, the decorating of the house with ten thousand lights, the arrival of Uncle Eddie—penniless, in a rusty recreational vehicle, with his wife and kids and rottweiler that kept slurping the water out of the Christmas tree stand.

I thanked the team members for allowing me in their midst. Before I left, John Plourd talked to me briefly about Richard Quin, to whom

I had introduced him the evening before at the Rebel Grill in Columbia, where Quin had joined me, along with Plourd, Glenn, McKean, and Prins, for a few beers and burgers. Plourd had been impressed by Quin's easy grip on local history, and Quin, doing his part to redeem local hospitality, had told the men he hoped none of their loved ones were getting pink slips in the massive layoff.

Late that afternoon, I had a drink with Al Burris at the Holiday Inn outside Columbia. He was in high spirits. He had taken an informal survey of the marriage team about the proposed five-days-a-week, ten-hours-a-day work schedule, he said, and only one of fifteen people didn't want to work the overtime. As for the rotation, Burris acknowledged most of his teammates felt it would be hard. "Your body's got to get acquainted with the proper sleeping cycle," he said.

I told Burris I had read some graffiti in one of the Saturn bathrooms that afternoon. Scratched into a toilet paper holder, it said: "If you wood [sic] hire more Southern boys, you wood [sic] run more cars off the line."

"We probably would," he agreed. "You look at it like this. It's a small area. People already got a home and their kids are already in school. Plus you probably going to cut out a whole lot of bad feuds, too, because people are sort of jealous. Sat-ur-en moved down here, and they's not benefiting from Sat-ur-en."

For Christmas his family might go to Flint, Burris told me, after ordering another drink. When the family went North now, they couldn't wait to come back South, he added, laughing a little, then sipping out of his swizzle stick. "Time will heal everything," he mused. The healing nature of time was also true in the chassis module, he added, segueing nicely. "At first we feuded," Burris recalled. "Now we're reaching our goals. The team running everything. Scheduling. Budgeting." But the bosses weren't asking for team input, which was the same complaint I had heard on the crank line. And rumors of more WUMAs being added to final assembly were circulating. "You don't need another middleman boss," Burris went on. "Most teams call them deadweight. When we are short of help, they don't fall in line."

I asked Burris, a CTM, if he would like to be a WUMA.

Sipping his drink, he thought a moment, then leaned back and flashed a grin. "No," he said, "but I is thinking about running for WUC."

25

Feeling Cheated by Change

The next day was mild. The air smelled crisp and clean, the sky was light blue. Driving along Cleburne Road to the west of Saturn, on the mowed field to the other side of the road I saw round hay bales. They were on property once part of the Doctor Black Place. The Black family's gravestones had been tossed around by the tornado of 1963. I recalled with a sudden awareness of time, which startled me, how I had stood up there four years ago, by the wind-scourged gravestone of Jane Black ("Then rise unchanged and be an angel still," the faded inscription read), and looked across at yellow trucks, churning bulldozers, dusty drilling rigs. Now I saw a mile-long sprawl of building, a hundred acres under roof, a company believing it would survive the turmoil besetting its parent organization.

Not that the Maurians who lived out here in the rolling fields surrounding Saturn, and for miles around, cared much if it did or not. For if Saturn was becoming a much longed for American success story on the national level, it was a protracted tragedy closer to home. Many Maurians resented Saturn and the Saturnites—not so much individually, but collectively, as a force that had come to this place with great promises that were turning to dust.

The Kmart incident of just a couple weeks ago demonstrated how much resentment toward Saturn boiled just below the surface. "It was savage," Richard Quin said. "The locals went ballistic."

It had started innocently enough. Kmart printed a flyer offering a special sale for Saturn employees on December 1, after hours. It received a hundred calls in response—all complaints. A few callers told Robin Dockery, the manager, he was going to die. Meanwhile, as a nasty prelude, accusatory letters were appearing in the Columbia *Daily Herald*. Writers attacked and defended Saturn. In one letter, the native Tennessean and now retired Saturnite Billy Joe Horan confessed he was "fed up with all the anti-Saturn feeling here." He said he'd moved North to work in auto plants in the 1950s, then returned home three years ago, when Saturn was still welcome here. Now the atmosphere had soured. "They called us rednecks then," Horan wrote about his early years up North. "And now I come back to my home state to work and I'm called worse things. The Yankees up North treated us better."

Over Thanksgiving weekend a dozen protesters had picketed Kmart, even though the sale had been canceled and manager Dockery transferred out of town. Driving by the store, supporters of the picketers honked their horns.

During the next weeks the *Daily Herald* printed letters that were a Ping-Pong match of sentiments: proud to work for Saturn; your politicians brought Saturn here; Kmart stop your favoritism; "Saturnians . . . behave as newly arrived citizens rather than coming as conquerors." Then the paper cut off the repetitious debate, claiming that continuing it simply stoked hostilities.

Quin told me, "It's kind of embarrassing to me to see this breakdown in Southern manners."

Rubbing the situation in was the fact that more than anywhere else in America you saw slope-nosed Saturn sedans and metallic-bright Saturn coupes all over the roads of Maury County. Saturnites got a good deal from the company, but they also seemed to genuinely like the cars they were making. To those who had bought into the Saturn philosophy at seventy, eighty, even ninety percent, what better way to start and end the work day than by wearing your Saturn T-shirt, or Saturn ballcap, and driving your Saturn down the Saturn Parkway? At the same time, with the local job outlook worse than it had been since the early 1980s, despite America's biggest industrial success story of the last few years located right here, native Maurians were not exactly buying the small cars in record numbers.

To keep answering the question, "Why aren't we getting any jobs out there?" press releases from Saturn reminded locals about the in-lieu-of-taxes payment *their* leaders had negotiated for them in 1985. And refreshed memories that the whole deal from Day One had guaranteed jobs for United Auto Workers until "a full complement" was hired. A full complement, if you could get anyone at Saturn to discuss that slippery term, meant at least enough workers to run three shifts. In December 1991 there were only two shifts and a work force of just over five thousand.

The last year Occidental Chemical Company and Rhône-Poulenc AG Company, two phosphate plants, had completely shut down, adding about six hundred more people to the unemployment rolls. If that wasn't bad enough, Resolution Trust Corporation, the federal authority created to deal with the savings and loan swindle, was now holding paper on a thousand acres in Maury County because of bankrupt land speculators. The only new business that had recently opened in Columbia was a Displaced Workers Center, staffed by six. There the unemployed could sign up for counseling and retraining, or for help relocating.

"Real estate prices might go below what they were before Saturn," Cyril Evers told me one afternoon, sitting in his windowless office, three rifles on a rack over his bald head. "That's what scares me."

Even Robin Courtney, the affable, usually smiling, information-rich lawyer who had represented Spring Hill for years and who tended to see things on the brighter side, acknowledged, "We're really hurting." Rather ironically, Courtney was now working for Waller, Lansden, Dortch & Davis in their Columbia branch office. Not only had "the bustle bustled off elsewhere," the white-haired attorney said, "and the development everybody envisioned still not materialized," but now people were indignant. They were making jokes about the car, saying the doors wouldn't shut and sniggering about how noisy it was. They seemed to want Saturn to fail, Courtney said, had lost respect for it at some deep level.

Simply framed, in Maury County the boomtown development model had gone bust, the traditional economy was limping, and any leadership to do much about it had not emerged. It seemed that the little new blood and vision that had materialized briefly between 1985 and 1988—with the now much-maligned George Jones and the out-of-office Delilah Speed, two conspicuous representatives—had lost their hold on people's hopes. The ultimate irony was that both Maurians and Saturnites resented the situation they found themselves in. Maurians were muttering, "We're paying for this and getting no jobs." Saturnites were saying, "We gave up everything we had, and what we knew, to come down here and not be welcomed."

The burning question was, who gets the blame?

In Spring Hill one scapegoat was the sign ordinance. Rather than keeping the village scenic and free of billboards, Mayor Boyd and the mostly new alderman board concluded, the sign ordinance had in fact ruined development. Pete Boyd's vice mayor declared the ordinance had to go. "Unless you have a tape ruler," he told a reporter, "there's no way you can enforce that." It was a statement that invited the suggestion he visit a hardware store. It also brought to my mind the day George Jones had propped himself up on the Coke cooler in the temporary Town Hall, back in late 1987, plucked his twenty-five-foot Stanley from his belt, and extended the tip to identify the place where a gas line T had to go. Even the editor of the Columbia *Times,* a paper not known for being critical, and itself about to fold in the moribund economy where county unemployment was pushing fifteen percent, labeled the attack on the sign ordinance "weak kneed."

Naomi Derryberry, who had lost her seat on the Spring Hill board in May 1990 by thirty-one votes and joined George Jones on the political sidelines, was not bemused by the local changes in leadership. She had been a strong supporter of the sign ordinance, hoping to keep the town free of visual litter in the form of billboards. But what bothered her more than that was a recent homicide investigation in Spring Hill. "We had a body dump last February," she told me. "Probably a prostitute. She had no shoes on, and her feet were clean." Chief Lovell and his officers hadn't been able to find any good leads, Derryberry said. Mayor Pete Boyd and the aldermen had told them to drop the investigation and no one had picked it up.

Although Derryberry had lost her bid for reelection, her political ambition still burned. She wanted to be mayor and was going to run again for the board. As for the new Saturnites, they surprised her. "At first, there was a lot of talk about how different they were going to be," she said. "Ironically, there was never a lot of talk about how much alike we were all going to be."

Joe Max Williams, executive director of the South Central Tennessee Development District, tried to put a little positive spin on what he agreed could be perceived as a negative situation. "Turn a negative to their advantage," was how he put it. One way to do that was to recognize that Saturn wasn't competing for the skilled labor force that was laid off, so any industry moving in would have them all to itself. The country could use that for recruitment leverage, Joe Max Williams said. First, though, he conceded, it would help if they could get out of the bottom of this recession and convince different groups— the Columbia City Council, the Maury County Chamber of Commerce, and the Maury County Commission—to stop "playing against each other. We've had a lot of squabbling going on. You got a community squabbling, they're not going to bring prospects in. They want a community that shows good, that's got its act together."

Maury County did not have its act together. As Delilah Speed had put it the previous June, the neglectful past had caught up with the needful present and was threatening to swamp the future.

It seemed, Joe Max Williams went on, that despite the county's industrial and agricultural past, it was going to have to restructure, going to have to shift more to a service-based economy, to tourism, to high-tech industries. A new economic development commission was encouraging the expansion of existing businesses. The strategy of pulling northern companies South because labor here was cheaper, taxes lower, and officials more compliant was history, Joe Max Williams said, even if many voters still thought it was what officials like himself ought to be doing.

Much of this sounded dreamily hypothetical, having something to do with the distant future when most Maurians would probably have been more cheered by economist John Maynard Keynes' adage, the one that says that as far as long-term economic solutions are concerned, in the long run we're all dead. The still popular questions, "Where are the jobs we've been promised?" and "Why'd you let these Yankees move in here to begin with?" were beside the point. Another issue bothering folks, Joe Max Williams said, was that some planners and bureaucrats were holding onto their created positions to deal with the kind of rapid growth that even the diehards no longer expected would materialize. The media, Joe Max Williams added, wasn't helping things one bit. The Nashville papers, in particular, had been running stories last summer about irate locals and favoritism shown Saturnites.

One of the vocal locals was a fellow named Roger Sears. A Maury County native and laid-off furnace man from Rhône-Poulenc AG Company in Mt. Pleasant, Sears lived in Porters Chapel, a settlement south of historic Ashwood. I had visited Sears in August 1991, and he sounded both proud he had spoken out, yet perplexed over the response his angry denunciations of Saturn generated. Dozens of folks had called Sears after he had lambasted local, state, and Saturn corporation officials and the story ran on the front page of the *Tennessean*.

"We don't hold no grudge against the workers of Saturn," Sears had told me in his southern drawl. "The people who come down here—I haven't got nothing against those people. As far as that's concerned, I would have done the same thing. A man's got to do what's best for his family. The people I hold it against is Saturn itself and our own local politicians for letting it happen to us."

Pam Sears, a nurse in Columbia, and two children, ages nine and twelve, sat on a sofa, listening. Roger Sears went on, "I don't feel bad about not working at Saturn. I feel bad about having to pay the price for it and not getting to work there." One argument he didn't buy, he said, was that someone like himself, thirty-two and strapping, wouldn't make a damn good autoworker because he didn't know how to build a car. "Well, that's right," he said, rolling upright, and glancing at his two kids and their serious faces, "I don't know the first damn thing about building a car. But it don't take me long to learn. I didn't know nothing about operating a furnace when I went to Rhône-Poulenc, but I was pretty good at it once I had five weeks training." And heck, he added, sarcastically, weren't a lot of those UAW people retrained with Tennesseans' tax money?

Sears eased backward into his chair. He said there was a lot of talk lately about eliminating busing from the county school budget, of passing a privilege tax on construction, of increasing the hotel and meals tax. Although taxes hadn't gone up much in the last few years, discounting for inflation, now they were going to take a big leap "after things had gone sour," Sears said, all to pay for things Saturn wasn't paying for and that local officials had not been foresighted enough to see and do something about.

I asked Sears what he thought about George Jones.

Shifting a little in his lounge chair, he replied, "Everybody thought George Jones was crazy. Turned out he was the smart man in Maury County. But no one listened. What you got to understand is that we couldn't comprehend General Motors: the size of it, the magnitude of it." He recalled having been laid off briefly in 1986, yet there had been alternatives then, other jobs. He said, "That gave you some kind of hope."

Now was different. The unemployment people had confirmed for Sears what he already knew: there were no jobs here. "They told us if there was any way you could afford to go to school and get some kind of education, some kind of trade, do it. Because there's nothing here to do. And there's not."

As for doing something about the injustice of the situation, Sears said he thought about that all the time. "This is just like anything else. You gonna have a lot of people sit around and bitch about it and do nothing. Then you're going to have a few people that's gonna do something. Well, I'm one of the ones that set around and bitch about it. But I'll do something, too! Cause a little stink here and there."

A moment later, he said, "I can visualize being on the square, in downtown Columbia, with a thousand, fifteen hundred people out there with signs. That would get somebody's attention. Nobody likes bad publicity." Until then, he'd keep talking. "I'm very bitter about this—it leaves a bad taste in my mouth every time Saturn comes across my tongue."

Now that their economic world was crumbling and Saturn was less a life raft to most Maurians than a deadweight, the politics of resentment rose to the fore. The dilemma for the angry, like Roger Sears, was where did you direct your hurt, your disappointment? Many major players from the middle and late 1980s were gone. The one vocal outcast, George Jones, had been tossed out as Mayor of Spring Hill and soundly defeated by a hands-off conservative for county executive. In Columbia a new City Council of mostly freshmen politicos had been sworn in. In Spring Hill, the biggest item on the alderman agenda was the elimination of the sign ordinance.

Some of the blame for the bad economic situation fell, by default more than by reason, on those least responsible: the Saturnites. Not that Maurians, as Sears had said, acted openly hostile. But the hostility lurked there, even in Sears who said about the newcomers, "They think they can stay apart from the local people, and they can't." Being conspicuous, with their kids overcrowding the schools, their cars overcrowding the roads, their resentment at being resented overflowing into the *Letters to the Editor* columns in both Columbia papers, the newcomers, whether called "Michiganders" or "Saturnarians," or even "Yankees," became scapegoats. The better adjusted could chalk it up as paying the price for being part of history.

Had much really changed here since 1989, when Richard Quin had told me "the honeymoon is over between Maury County and Saturn," I wondered. Now there seemed to be more grumbling about a divorce, but that wasn't possible, warned Judy Langsdon, director of community development for Maury County. "We're in a marriage we can't get out of."

If the Saturn/Maury County relationship created a marriage—and that seemed as good a metaphor as any—Maury County suffered a severe case of the economic abandonments while Saturn claimed it had fulfilling its responsibilities in a way the region was accustomed to. Communication, the balm for feuding couples, gave way to blame and denial, the next step down the ladder of accommodation. Extensive counseling before the wedding might have saved a lot of heartache and pain, but given the circumstances behind this shotgun affair of corporation and place, that kind of old-fashioned guidance was out of the question.

A troubling truth Maury County at last accepted was that it had been jilted rather than presented with a carefree and prosperous future, one in which the county didn't have to lead, didn't have to forge an identity. Now the county was waking up to reality: its traditional manufacturing jobs, with their higher wages, were drying up; Saturn was no panacea; and low-paying service jobs were practically all that rippled through the regional economy.

Here, Saturn's presence was supposed to have made things different. It had; they were worse. The political expediency of cutting a few bureaucrats from payrolls and rolling back what planning had been voted in place and claiming that this might shake the county free of its economic lethargy was thinly reasoned. Cooperation between Saturn and the county was no closer to being a reality that it had been in 1985.

Maury County had gotten to where it was to some extent by blindly charging in with a Rebel yell that had turned to a whimper. The challenges of organizing, of finding common ground that ended feuds, of leveraging Saturn any way possible once it became clear no other methods would work, had not been met. Maury County leaders still rejected a simple truth: they had let their constituents down. Having watched the chapters unfold here for five years, I had to give up on my expectations that dissent would finally show its angry face. There had been no dissent—no public dissent, anyway—since farmer John Campbell had formed a concerned citizens group in Spring Hill in 1985. Now there was Roger Sears. What bothered me most about the situation was that the South I had so admired in legend had proven a Yankee's romantic pipedream. Not that the burden of a new Southern identity should, I guessed, have been placed on the shoulders of Maurians. Nor should I have expected some kind of mythical strength and sense of injustice to have roiled up from the dark roots of the Old South. But given all the ballyhoo about this age of information and about advances in education, one had to ask if history meant anything at all here in this backwater so draped in it. There seemed to have been little thought given to what had been going on across the South for the last thirty years. That evolution from the agrarian to the industrial, from yesterday's values to tomorrow's jobs, "has already leveled many of the old monuments of regional distinctiveness," as historian C. Vann Woodward wrote in *The Search for Southern Identity*. It had leveled them here in an accelerated mode as surely as Saturn had leveled the rolling fields behind Haynes Haven. And seemed well on its way, again in Woodward's words, of "erasing the very consciousness of a distinctive tradition along with the will to sustain it." Like Northerners, Westerners, and Midwesterners before him, the Southerner, as Woodward observed so presciently, would "yield to the impulse to suppress the identifying idiom, to avoid the awkward subject, and to blend inconspicuously into the national pattern—to act the role of the standard American."

Was that "standard American" a grumbler who just muttered and took it?

There seemed to be some hope that another model might emerge in place of the failed boomtown one to guide Maury County toward its twenty-first-century future. What the model looked like, and how it might work, remained murky. There was now an additional hurdle, again one that few officials wanted to talk about. Saturn, which had never attracted suppliers, now hampered diversified development. The plant discouraged potential investors for two reasons. First, the inflated prices for county land, despite some downward movement, remained in place, and put the county at a disadvantage in relation to adjoining counties. And, second, many companies simply didn't care to relocate to what they perceived, rightly or wrongly, as an automobile manufacturing region. So the failure of the boomtown model was a double whammy: no Saturn jobs and little attraction for high-paying alternatives.

26

A Nationwide Hit

In April 1992, in its annual auto issue, the buyer's bible for millions, *Consumer Reports,* awarded Saturn its highest rating for mechanical reliability and claimed it was "a breakthrough for a car designed and built in the United States." J. D. Powers, the rating people, soon ranked Saturn third in its "customer satisfaction" category, after Lexus and Infiniti, luxury cars made in Japan. Attending the huge auto show in New York, Ruth Ann Leach, a columnist for the Nashville *Banner,* praised Saturn's low-key, real-people approach compared to the competition's use of what she called "tart marketing." Leach wrote, "Cleavage must sell cars; otherwise, why would so many car companies use cinched-in, pushed-up, bleached blonde babes to extol the virtues of automotive products?" She said she thought Saturn's marketing appealed strongly to women.

The "Buy American" mentality affecting much of the country was not hurting Saturn one bit either. National attention on the widening trade deficit with Japan ($65 billion in 1991, much of it attributable to car imports), a trip taken by President George Bush and the CEOs of the Big Three to Japan in an effort to relax import barriers, some out-of-character bashing of American workers by Japanese officials who called them lazy and badly trained, and the still lagging economy all brought out the flags. But instead of waving a flag, or in addition to waving one, many folks began reconsidering American cars for the first time in decades, with Saturn high on their "look-see" list.

Buoyed by the ratings, materialistic nationalism, and coast-to-coast magazine and TV ads, by mid-1992 Saturn was becoming a hit across much of America—not the home run Stempel had claimed at the previous year's annual meeting, but a good solid standup double at least. The sales climb was impressive: 10,204 in January, 13,035 in February, over 16,000 in both March and April, then 18,031 in May. More than 150 stores (plans called for 250 by year's end) sold almost

20,000 Saturns in June. Now the question was, could the plant keep up with demand? Down in Spring Hill the teams were now building about 1,000 cars a day.

Saturn vice president of marketing and sales Don Hudler told the media, "We've kind of almost developed a cult, if you will. We actually have Saturn owners volunteering to work for us on our behalf, manning auto shows." A cover story in *Business Week* lauded the retailer training program, which brought sales consultants to Northfield for a few days of Saturn awareness, team dynamics classes, and the no haggling with the customer philosophy. "To ensure that dealers make a profit selling small cars without haggling," the article said, "Saturn built a gross margin of 17% into sticker prices versus an average 12% for competing models."

The excitement over sales (a few stores were doing phenomenally well: Saturn of Rivergate, in Nashville, was averaging 340 sales a month until "we ran out of cars," said the store manager) obscured the nagging question about profitability. And despite articles, including the one in *Business Week,* commending the low turnover of consultants in the stores, some of the stores were being less than reverent about the Saturn sales philosophy. One such store was Saturn of Charlotte, which I visited the previous summer.

"You can't take someone who's been baptized in the old-time car religion," Al Hendershot, former sales team leader in the store, told me over the phone, "and move them into the New Testament." Hendershot had quit the Saturn store and was now a marketing consultant in Charlotte. He said only one of the original twelve sales consultants remained at the store. And it was not Dexter Riffe.

Riffe, who had laid such an enviable strip of rubber in a red coupe the previous summer while smoking the Mitsubishi Eclipse, had also quit Saturn of Charlotte. Dexter Riffe started getting stomach aches and headaches, Hendershot said, after the general manager began giving the team regular two-hour lectures on how to sell. Ironically, Hendershot went on, the store management had already forsaken the Saturn system, stopped trusting the sales people, and started "milking Saturn a little because it's a popular commodity." The situation made him feel like a hypocrite. A newly instituted Saturn cheer hadn't gone over real big, either.

As Hendershot described it, the Saturn cheer involved gathering all the consultants in the store at the time of a sale, ushering them out beneath the portico, then orchestrating a loud cheer for the buyer.

Nice idea, he said, but try it when your sales consultants despised one another. You created a farce. "We had two salesmen fight in the showroom," Hendershot recalled. "One coldcocked the other. We had six guys in the showroom talking about the Saturn philosophy, and these two guys fighting."

Nonetheless, Hendershot still stopped by the store frequently and was a fan of the car. "It'll be like the VW beetle," he said. "The cars are built to last; you'll see them on the road for years."

Sales manager Linda Penland acknowledged her store had consultant turnover, but the team was still selling its allotment of cars, about a hundred a month. And satellite stores were in the works in Wake Forest and Hickory, North Carolina.

For the first quarter of 1992, surprising almost everyone, GM eked out a small profit: $179 million on sales of $32 billion. The performance did not satisfy the board of directors, however, and they finally shook up the top. The directors removed Stempel as chairman of the board's executive committee, gave his good friend, GM president Lloyd Reuss ("Lloyd's my man," Stempel had declared only two months earlier in an attempt to dampen the clamor for a human sacrifice) his walking papers, and named yet another Smith—John, head of European operations, where GM was making money—to take Reuss's place. Bill Hoglund, Saturn's second president, was promoted to GM's chief financial officer, suggesting that experience at Saturn might not cost you your career at GM after all.

Meanwhile, Saturn, the twentieth-century flagship, could be seen almost blithely sailing along, quite removed from GM's ongoing turmoil, luffing its sails with Buy American discontent and demonstrated quality. Meanwhile, financial analysts were putting forward various hypotheses: Saturn needed to sell 16,500 cars a month to make a profit, Saturn needed to sell 500 thousand cars a year to make a profit, Saturn needed to add a third shift to make a profit or expand the plant in Spring Hill or take one of GM's plants out of mothballs and convert it into Saturn plant #2.

An emergency meeting was called at the plant before Memorial Day to talk about profit, or of the lack thereof; WUCs, BUCs, WUMAs, and grim-faced SAC bigshots all attended. LeFauve cheered them up by reminding everyone that the public loved the car, the sales organization loved no-haggle pricing. Yet the costs of overtime, continuing bottlenecks ("Once you run into a bottleneck," one Saturnite said, "everything comes to a screeching halt"), glitches in the *kanban* just-in-time inventory system, and other factors painted a dark financial picture. For Saturn to stay viable, LeFauve said, they had to get $1,600 out of manufacturing costs per car.

This *was* an emergency. Recall that thirty years ago Corvair, to transform a well-received car into a safety hazard and public relations disaster, had only trimmed between $15 and $20 in parts against the advice of the engineers. "In the Information Age," as Marshall Thurber, a Dr. Deming acolyte, often said at workshops preaching the doctor's philosophy, "you don't have to kill many kids to dampen a quality image." Now the character of the fun-to-drive car, its quality, and its very feasibility were being called into question.

Manufacturing head Bob Boroff ran down the worn ladder of possible improvement: reducing scrap, achieving quality the first time, reducing overtime, improving attendance, involving each team in performance improvements. He invoked the old saws: everyone had to buy in at seventy percent, a crisis existed, each employee had to become part of the solution. Union president Mike Bennett, a sleepy-eyed workaholic whose uninspiring speaking style belied his passion for Saturn, told everyone they had a voice, that Saturn was building a better GM and a better UAW, but that they had to make a quality car at a competitive cost. Ultimately, quality, performance, and cost, Bennett said, passing the weight onto the shoulders of the teams, were the responsibility of each work unit.

There lay the rub. The gradual shift in the balance of power away from the teams and toward the top had cost the teams much of their confidence—a scarce commodity to begin with—that they could significantly change Saturn.

In June, a few weeks after the emergency meeting, over beers at Betty's, a watering hole by the Duck River in Columbia, I met with several members of the crank line A-crew. I got the impression they didn't believe that everybody taking a nickel out of the car, which was being pushed as a good way to cut costs, would work. Definitely not with the blurry authority system presently in place.

"The frustrating part is they throw the issue out for the team," Prins declared, referring to the leadership. "Then when the team starts on the issue, they take the authority away from you." A moment later, he added, "We choose a course, then they say you went the wrong way."

John Plourd insisted it wasn't that bad. "This isn't Buick!" he snapped.

Empties littered our table. Country music—laments, heartbreak, too much alcohol—played on the jukebox. Nancy Laatz and Joe McKean had joined Plourd and Prins to talk with me. They expressed concerns about the team, about efficiency, about production realities. They sounded as though they felt helpless about affecting much of anything. Plourd mentioned one positive change. As of June 15 all the trade techs on the four machining lines in powertrain were forming a single maintenance pool, which would cut overtime and reduce costs. Presently, Plourd said, block machining stalled production way too often; in fact a BUC had gone into consultation because of the problems there, and that would have never happened in the old world.

The foundry had finally gotten porosity licked, which improved crankshaft production. Slowdowns elsewhere were hard to predict; sometimes they occurred in one building, other times in another. The more he thought about it, Plourd reflected, leaning back and lifting his ballcap, running a hand through his hair, the more he realized the problems weren't in the manufacturing processes though—they were in the people systems.

"The more time you spend in that place," Prins seconded, "the more people problems rise up."

"We're still in the polite stage," Laatz repeated about A-crew. Conflicts were avoided rather than resolved.

McKean said he had been surprised to learn during training sessions just how together the crank team was and how well they communicated relative to most other teams. Mutterings about going back to the old world way of doing things were increasing, as were questions such as, "Where are our paid absences?" "Where are our time clocks?"

Danny Lentz told me months earlier that revised scheduling alone was not going to relieve Saturn's production and cost headaches. "If you're intimate with the lines," he explained, "you know that by working fifty hours a week you're not going to get twenty-five percent more cars, due to the fact that some places are already working seven days a week to get forty hours production. They need to go on a five-day operation, eight-hours-a-day, and have enough time to catch up in the places they're behind. But because people have committed to this in the union and in the company they will never change to the direction we need to go."

A-crew agreed that a change in direction now seemed unlikely.

I interviewed Skip LeFauve for the last time that June. He sat behind his desk in Northfield. Sunlight streamed in the windows. Schettler, sitting to one side, didn't even turn on her recorder. Since Saturn had started being a hit, paranoia had slackened. LeFauve held up a news-clip and said that Chevrolet dealers claimed Saturn was stealing their customers. In a rare break of corporate unity, LeFauve dismissed Chevy's gripes, insisting that Chevy's problems were pervasive and that Saturn had nothing to do with them. Although accusations of stealing one another's customers in a tight market were common, LeFauve seemed unusually sensitive to Chevy's claim. Rumors that Saturn might expand its model line in order to appeal to more Americans driving tastes, rumors that Saturn Communications did not deny, may have had something to do with Chevy's aggravation.

The division sold fifty percent of GM's cars, with many of them entry-level vehicles, and Saturn definitely was luring some of its customers. As for the expansion rumors at Saturn, one line of reasoning, the pro-expansion line, argued that Saturn prospects should not walk out of a store because they could not buy an SL2 with leather seats, say, or a roomier model, maybe something designated the SL3. A second line of reasoning, one the Chevy dealers apparently supported, was that Saturn's mission in life was not to compete with Chevrolet, or with Pontiac, Buick, Oldsmobile, or Cadillac. Saturn ought to stick just with entry-level cars, make a profit, and reestablish GM's quality image, which would help all the divisions. This line of reasoning said that if Saturn intended to be a learning laboratory, the leadership in the other divisions had to trust Saturn to help them, not resent it for stealing customers.

"People have not been trained to observe," LeFauve said, rather regretfully, when I asked about the success of the learning laboratory concept. He recalled how the lessons at NUMMI five years ago had been fresh, unexpected, and simple. Here, on the other hand, the lessons were more complex, couched in a new language, and taught in hard economic times. Presently, what was attracting attention within the GM family was the Saturn sales strategy, the fixed price/no-haggling approach. Saturn's marketing people were meeting with their counterparts at Pontiac, Oldsmobile, and Buick about it, LeFauve said.

Was he going to remain here as Saturn's president, I asked, noting that six years in one position was a long time for a GM executive.

He nodded. "Yes."

LeFauve looked tired. He still spent about half his time in Troy. His travel schedule mapped his face, bagged his eyes. The one-time Navy pilot was getting as much air time as he used to off carriers.

"When is Saturn going to make a profit?" I asked.

302

"I can't tell you." He grinned slightly. "As soon as possible."

I asked how he felt having sales exceeding the plant's production capability.

"It's a positive discomfort. It makes you feel good to know what you're doing makes sense."

My final question—the old one about hiring locals—evoked a blunt response, one void of game playing. Maurians weren't going to be hired soon—not with seventy-five thousand folks being laid off at GM, LeFauve said.

Before leaving Northfield I stopped with Schettler by the Communications cubicles. Riffling through some files, she gave me a sheet listing regional demographic variables. When added to LeFauve's final comment, they made things look even less promising for Maurians. The average age of a Saturnite, union or management, was thirty-eight, the sheet said, so they had a long way to go before retirement.

"Have things relaxed around here at all since sales have taken off?" I asked Schettler.

"I don't know if we can ever relax," she replied.

"Life here did not calm down after the launch," added Sue Holmgren, editor of *Saturn Visions,* a good news bimonthly distributed free to Saturn's families. Holmgren was hunched over in a cubicle adjoining Schettler's.

"They said it would, didn't they?" Schettler said.

Holmgren nodded. "The public thinks our baby's cute."

With the American public thinking Saturn was cute, queuing up for the 1993 models, and putting tremendous pressure on the plant to expand, it seemed fitting to ask, what would Dr. Deming have thought? Would the irascible perfectionist have scowled and chewed LeFauve's ass, in a Deming sort of way, pointing critically at the top? Or would he have been complimentary, assuring LeFauve and SAC, "You *are* getting it."

Surely, no better example of *not getting it* was readily available than GM's pre-Saturn blindness to the need for a good cheap car in a resource-scarce world. Once the blindness had been acknowledged in 1982 by the skunk works that eventually became Saturn, the subsidiary attempted to stand on its own with new business systems, new technology, and with a new attitude: people first. To its credit, Saturn created the new systems, married process with product, put people first, built the integrated plant, emphasized customer satisfaction and better labor relations, and stressed the lean manufacturing process based on *zaizan* and *kanban*. Maintaining a vision for five years in the face of constant criticism about the length of the start-up was a feat. I think Deming would have appreciated all of that.

But actually making cars had dramatically altered the equations, as had GM's financial distress. Dr. Deming probably would have asked if the top had adapted Saturn's systems to changing realities, thinking about what was happening and refining everything, without upsetting the whole.

I thought Dr. Deming would have told the top they had gotten it with their partners and customers, but not with the help or the locals. Since the launch the top had partially abandoned bottom-up team leadership and lean production, two bulwarks of Saturn's initial vision for creating a different kind of company, to deal with the exigencies of production. Now, with GM limping and struggling, forced into a painful recognition of its neglected past and constantly asking the upstart division, "Where are more cars?" the pressures to retreat to old conditioned responses exerted more force than ever. There was a threat that teamsmanship might become a victim of the very system it was designed to displace. Saturn's partnerships insured good suppliers, provocative ads, happy store owners, yet teamsmanship in the plant had the core responsibility to build quality cars at costs low enough to compete in the global marketplace.

To successfully compete with Honda, Toyota, Nissan, and all the rest, Saturn had to get horizontal and lean and keep caring. That was the bottom line. The intensity of the competition was not going to diminish, despite a brief respite (an article in the August 1992 issue of *Autoweek* noted that "Japanese automakers are losing market share to Detroit's Big Three for the first time in a dog's age"). In fact, just the opposite was true; the competition was going to get tougher, it was going to validate the often heard statement, "If you didn't like the eighties and thought they were tough, you'll hate the nineties." For how long would it be until Russia and the Eastern European countries started exporting small cars? Or Malaysia, India, and Mexico, where cars were already being manufactured, entered the global market? In late 1992 BMW announced plans to build an assembly plant just outside Spartanburg, North Carolina. Ironically, one of the few places Saturn felt less competition was the level playing field in Tennessee. The Sentra, so high flying in 1985, had lost its cachet in the marketplace, and Nissan Motor Company "may be as weak as it's been since it exported its first Bluebird to the States in 1958," the *Autoweek* article claimed. By flattening the management pyramid inexorably lifting inside the organization, by recharging everyone in the company with a second jolt of the Saturn spirit, and by maintaining its small-company integrity, Saturn might emerge as the industrial phenomenon it kept intimating it wanted to be.

Dr. Deming taught that integrity is the essence of everything successful. And that integrity is built on trust. Trust in turn is the plinth on which teamwork stands. The quality Deming sought is a result of continually maximizing customer appreciation and minimizing the variation in a product. Inside Saturn, teams had become skeptical about where authority truly lay and were wondering how much power they could exert without getting into jeopardy. Training had come to a kind of abyss—that is, to a place where its promise and potential were encouraging workers to step beyond the authority restrictions being handed down from the top.

In *The Fifth Discipline,* Peter Senge writes about good leaders being able to step up to the next level, to leap across an abyss. They can see the world's movement, for instance, toward small, efficient cars. They can feel the crucial importance of regional integrity. For such leaders making Saturn the best small car in the world, as well as the pride of the neighborhood, would be a sensible goal.

No leather seats! Make that an ad slogan.

We revitalized a rural county! Make that a truth.

A visionary company can step up to the next level, to the twenty-first-century level. Saturn's leadership could see that level; they certainly talked about it. But maybe all of them needed a few days on the EXEL course every twelve months or so, up there at treetop level out behind Rippavilla.

"Jump!" the five thousand Saturnites could have hollered up in unison. "Jump! Let go! Ring the bell!"

That fall, as Saturn entered the third year of production, the company was many of the cliches attached to it over the years: "a new start," "a learning laboratory," albeit a misunderstood and underappreciated one, "one more chance." But, as I hope I have made clear, it was potentially so much more. The largest one-time investment in the history of America, even downsized, was still pretty potent as a model for future growth, especially in that tender zone where ever precious farm land gives way to the spread of the multiringed, twenty-first-century city.

Yet what the average American wanted from Saturn was not a runaway GM success story, or the reassertion of General Motors' might, but rather a believable signal that big business could make something good that the ordinary family or young person trying to make it could afford and feel good about—and not screw up the landscape.

Was it worth it—this tremendous exercise in nineteenth-century land buying, early twentieth-century political/industrial/legal chicanery, and late twentieth-century New Age industrialism? All for a good little car with *Made in America* stamped all over it?

General Motors thought so, although given the corporation's tottering economic position, there was the possibility the parent organization might collapse on its prodigal child before it reached maturity. The thousand of Saturnites with tomorrow's jobs in a county still holding on to yesterday's values were winners, even if they did bristle at the resentment of the locals. Native Maurians, on the other hand, were taking what they could get.

"A man can find something like this, he's lucky," former furnace man Roger Sears told me from behind the counter of the Maury Package Store. Working part-time for $5/hour instead of leading anti-Saturn rallies by the courthouse was a necessity since Sears had recently enrolled at Columbia State College.

Fifty-odd dairy farms still operated in Maury County, Randy Lochridge told me, and a handful of row crop operations like his dad's. Now executive director of the U.S. Department of Agriculture's Agriculture Stabilization and Conservation Service, Lochridge claimed, "I have the best of both worlds." He helped farmers, but only had to work fifty hours a week, managing a staff of four, doling out federal money, and doing compliance flight checks to make sure farmers planted what they said they would. Thirty-two, single, his hair gray, his blue eyes big and still sad, Randy Lochridge kept three hundred acres of soybeans and a hundred brood cows near his dad's place in Spring Hill. Like his father James, he remained philosophical about Saturn's transformation of his world, a transformation he had come to accept. "What can be done can," he said. "What can't be done cain't."

By late 1992, as Saturn became as much an economic force field as it was a car—a force field of change in the way America thinned its past and seeded future industry in its pristine countryside still attached visually, socially, economically, and spiritually to that past— it wasn't a question whether this was right or wrong, but by what standards should it be judged. Who had gained and who had lost? What had been learned from the billions spent, the millions of hours worked, the great dreams and deep depressions, the heart attacks and the personal attacks, the great corkscrewing of energy that sprayed all around this massive story? Here, American capitalism's competitiveness in auto manufacturing was at stake—no small prize.

Don Ephlin had said back at the outset, "If Saturn fails, America is in big trouble."

Saturn had not failed.

But here too was a place. Did *place* have a place in such gargantuan economic gamesmanship? Why haven't we learned to respect place in partnership with progress? Is the decline in the quality of American goods related to the ruin of place? Are people disconnected from place able to work at their fullest?

That America's largest company could come to its senses and start treating people as the solution to its business headaches rather than as the problem was good news. And not only to the Saturnites, but to those companies that looked toward Mother Motors for a model. That Saturn and the State of Tennessee collaborated to drop a $3-billion investment in a rural backwater with a leadership vacuum was nineteenth-century powerbroking at its more opportunistic. Even granting the difficulties of buying a large tract of land and allowing some duplicity to accomplish that formidable task, the screw job of no jobs in Maury County, where the state paid for the Saturn Parkway and for much of the initial Saturn job training was compounded by both Saturn's and the state's duplicity. Ultimately, the dimple of the universe became less a garden spot for America's newest auto plant than a pawn sacrificed for economic and political gamesmanship.

As a model for building a quality product, Saturn set high standards internally. As a model for rural development, it did not. America had gotten a good little car, but Maury County had lost its rural soul. Some will argue that the forced transformation of the backwater was for its own good, and a small tradeoff for Saturn. I'm not one of them. This story could have been more win/win.

The future awaits an example of a rural development project of near equal size that takes as its partners not only those who stand to benefit financially and politically but those who are being forced to give up, as George Jones said of his constituency, "the most." A place not as a pawn to be exploited but seen as sacred as training was initially at Saturn. Then maybe those who work there won't be forced to say, as Scott Prins does nowadays, "I may never be accepted around here, but my kids will be."

Epilogue

In late September 1992 an article in *Business Week* praising recent market-share gains by American car makers was headlined "The Big Three Think They Smell Blood." A month later, however, the smell of blood was seeping not from the Japanese competition, but from the fourteenth floor of the GM building in Detroit. CEO Robert Stempel, in trouble since April when the board of directors usurped much of his power, had been axed. Officially, the car guy resigned. In fact, the revamped board figuratively slit the car guy's throat and tossed him to the critics—stockholders, lending institutions, analysts. Stempel's demise was a clear signal the old regime was changing things too slowly and had to go. The board, now steered by John Smale, former head of Proctor and Gamble Corporation, which he had thinned of executive bloat, next went after Roger B. Smith. Smith retained his seat on the board, but he too was soon shown the door to the inner sanctum, a bastion of power he had ruled like a despot only three years earlier. Somewhere in America Michael Moore, maker of *Roger & Me,* must have celebrated.

"The radicals are in power at GM." That was the post-shakeup assessment of David Cole, director of the Transportation Research Institute at the University of Michigan in Ann Arbor, a nationally known and highly respected auto think-tank. As for Saturn being swallowed by the changes rippling down from the top, Cole saw little threat of that. "Saturn is less likely to be subverted by General Motors' tradition," he told me, "because General Motors' tradition is disappearing very rapidly."

When I called Scott Prins in Spring Hill to get the crank team reaction to the changes at the top, Prins said, "You kind of got two camps down here: this is the end for Saturn; and no, it means bigger and better things." The teams were told that there would be some reorganization in Saturn's upper ranks, and that engineering and marketing would answer more to GM. "But basically," Prins added, "right now we're not feeling anything; it's business as usual."

Production held steady at 1,130 or so cars a day. Teams remained on fifty-hour weeks, with weekly rotations. A few team members from each team throughout the plant were training to interview applicants for C-crew, a third shift to begin in June 1993. C-crew would boost next year's production to 300,000 cars.

"How are people holding up working long hours, with the rotation?" I asked Prins. Dozens of normally healthy op and trade techs were on prescription drugs for high blood pressure or stress, I had heard.

"They're tired," Prins said. "They're grumpy."

A *Time* cover story a few days later asked, "Can GM survive in today's world?" It recapped the coup, named the new and younger cast of key players replacing Stempel and his dishonored lieutenants (two of the new guys, William Hoglund, now executive vice president and a member of the board, and Bruce McDonald, promoted to vice president of GM Communications, were Saturn veterans), and noted that new CEO, Jack Smith, fifty-four, better be harder hearted than the old softy Bob Stempel because the human costs facing GM were brutal. In yet another metaphor of death and dismemberment, the magazine said, "The bloodletting promises to be deep and wide and painful."

In subsequent reports, relying on the classic metaphor of automotive confrontation, the new leadership asserted that it intended to "play hard ball" with the union.

Or try. From the looks of things the union had already taken a quick lead while Smale, Smith, Hoglund et al. were jockeying for positions. A strike at a Lordstown, Ohio, parts plant just before the coup had hobbled North American operations. Ostensibly about job security, the week-long strike demonstrated the union's muscle and showed the weakness of Saturn's just-in-time inventory that lacked Japan's *keiretsu,* or interlinking supplier-manufacturer network.

Without Lordstown, even though its labor contract was separate and much different from that of all other GM divisions, Saturn couldn't build cars. The trusting harmonious partnership fostering long-term trust, which Saturn was supposed to epitomize, played second fiddle to UAW worries about approaching contract negotiations with GM. There was no *keiretsu* here. Just old-fashioned muscle flexing, intimidation, and power. And with Saturn powerless to act independently.

September 1992 was a bad time for Saturn's assembly line to sit idle, even if only for a week. Stores nationwide—now numbering over two hundred—were clamoring for cars. Summer business had set records, with many stores averaging more than two hundred sales a month. The new models were out, including the well-received station wagon, the SW. Saturn had raised prices nine percent but that didn't dampen demand. The SW and the strike intensified production pressures in the plant when work resumed. Saturn spokespersons insisted that quality remained priority number one. Since the plant couldn't supply the stores open already, new openings tapered off, however.

That fall, in the marketplace, Saturn's continuing success created an odd situation. GM seemed to lurch from one crisis to another, and the loose alliance of auto writers and analysts whose lifeblood is the car business weighed in steadily with conflicting free advice on how the giant could regain its balance. Yet they also urged: "Leave Saturn alone." They agreed that the subsidiary had in spades what most other GM products lacked: prestige.

Down in Spring Hill though, despite high production figures, morale was low. Neither the new guys running GM nor the old guys commanding the UAW International in Chicago could bring themselves to openly embrace Saturn. As GM rebounded a little, drawing energy from its reorganization, regaining some semblance of balance, the ambivalence about Saturn was hard to fathom. Was it the subsidiary's continuing defiance of the status quo? A defiance, I must add, substantially softened from that of the original Saturn vision of an arms-length division charting a path toward the next century. At the top there was little rejoicing over Saturn's "conquest sales," sales to buyers who had given up on American-made cars, or over the demonstrated success of Saturn's common-sense philosophy—that people cooperating, rather than fighting, can make a better car. There was some enthusiasm for sure, with Oldsmobile in particular cozying up to Saturn marketing. But overall GM, as well as the UAW, procrastinated about clarifying Saturn's place in its future. And in the crucial area of partnerships and cooperation, management and labor seemed to be retreating to old positions. They sounded as restless to butt heads as they were eager to shake hands.

This put Saturn in a sort of limbo. Blurry, ill-defined relationships exacerbated existing divisions within Saturn itself. Dissidents in the plant were given unspoken encouragement to rally and consolidate, for if neither GM, which had at least publicly endorsed Saturn, or the UAW, whose GM department head Stephen Yokich did not, supported the subsidiary, an easy conclusion to draw was that they wanted it changed but not by direct order.

In January 1993 the dissidents forced a referendum to test support of the Saturn contract. One key issue was the selection of WUMAs. The dissidents wanted WUMAs elected, whereas management and Saturn contract supporters argued that electing WUMAs would make them old-world committeemen. The plant-wide vote upheld the contract two to one. But the friction in the rank-and-file, in the very teams at the center of change, again flared to the flash point in March. At its hot blue tip was the embattled, somewhat burnt out, philosophical Mike Bennett, president of Saturn Local 1853. Bennett, a true believer in Saturn, found himself seriously contested for reelection.

His opponents attacked Bennett, a workaholic, for steering his energy the wrong way. He was too buddy-buddy with management, they said, spent far too little time on the plant floor, was defensive of criticism. Rallying his Vision Team, Bennett shook off the image of being burnt out (for months he'd hemmed and hawed about running) and counterattacked. He insisted the days of table-pounding grievances were over, that the partnership between labor and management worked. Bennett failed to win a majority in the March election, then barely defeated challenger Bob Hoskins, fifty-two percent to forty-eight percent in a runoff. Hoskins headed a group called Members for a Democratic Union, which questioned elements of Saturn's people-first, realize-your-human potential, pay-should-be-linked-to-performance vision. Slim victory margins by most members of the Vision Team assured Bennett support for the next three years. Yet the opposition, empowered by its strong showing, was probably going to make it tough for Bennett and the Vision Team to be happy seventy percent of the time.

During the campaign, which featured in-plant broadsides and lots of mudslinging, the usually tight-lipped Bennett begrudgingly told the press that Saturn remained distant from the hearts of both GM and the UAW. Everything he'd worked for, Bennett conceded, including the labor/management partnership and a conciliatory atmosphere that eschews grievances, felt threatened. Lessons learned at Saturn had not sunk in. He said woefully, "There's a reluctance of leaders in the union and management to change." By this date the new leadership at GM had been in power for five months.

It struck me as ironic that Mike Bennett, in a desperate move during a dirty campaign, spilled his feelings to the press and opened

Saturn's phony solidarity up to much needed light. Not that he was happy about doing it. Defending his actions, Bennett accused his critics of hanging Saturn's dirty laundry out for everyone to see. In that way Bennett remained a hardcore traditionalist. Heaven help us if a big company simply told the truth that transformation is hard and people get mad and not everyone is going to remain happy, that anger and bitter infighting are as crucial to change at a certain point as trust and risk are at other points.

Newcomers arriving at Saturn and training for C-crew were understandably a bit confused about how Saturn was much different from the rest of GM, what with all the heated debate, posters slapped on walls supporting this side and that, and leadership questions. Following the election a plant-wide refresher course, *Yesterday, Today, and Tomorrow,* attempted to cool things down and provide common ground and a sense of harmony. Every Saturnite, newcomer and old-timer alike, attended for twenty hours; the course reviewed the company's short and tumultuous history, attempted to revive sagging spirits, and plotted Saturn's immediate future. That future might include an expansion of the plant, conversion of Corvette's Bowling Green, Kentucky, plant into a Saturn facility because of its location, or even the reopening of a mothballed GM facility under Saturn's banner. But no matter what happened, Saturn spelled growth and opportunity in a corporation shrinking in most of its automotive operations.

With these latest events in Spring Hill, the big question was not whether Saturn would continue to explore teamwork and cooperation between labor and management, because with Bennett and LeFauve still in charge it would, but rather how far it could push its explorations given its short leash held jointly by GM and the UAW. Without the understanding and support of both forces, Saturn would figuratively stay in second gear, never achieving its vision or even testing its possibilities. That was Saturn's restraint. Like a young thoroughbred now at the crucial age of three, its managers didn't know what to do with it—to let it run, rein it in, to cheer or jeer. Their ambivalence was eased because expectations of Saturn transforming GM had cooled considerably. The question now was not could Saturn change GM, but could it integrate into the parent company.

Analyst Maryann Keller didn't think it could.

"Saturn has nothing to teach GM that it doesn't already know," she told me during a phone interview. "Except to stop haggling over prices in showrooms." Labeling Saturn a "no brainer," Keller said the design already looked "a little tired." "The plant is grossly inefficient," she went on. "It's not world class—this is not lean manufacturing. Saturn is a win for the consumer, not the corporation. I think it proves the obvious: the public has no bias against a good car made in America."

Interestingly enough, Keller felt GM would turn itself around. Not because of Saturn—rather, in spite of it.

Predictably, Bill Hoglund disagreed with Keller's assessment. Organizational changes at the top had resulted in Saturn and Skip LeFauve reporting to LeFauve's predecessor, a man familiar with the company's beginnings and attuned to its philosophy. I interviewed Hoglund in late April in Detroit (Jack Smith was too busy getting GM straightened out to give interviews, I was told), and he said that Saturn has been "an outstanding success." When I asked if Saturn was being integrated into GM, he replied, "We're very sensitive about the image of Saturn being apart." In the public's eye the division remained independent, he explained. Out of sight, however, "There are tentacles going all over the place. Integration is occurring under the water, but not where the customer can see it."

Lanky and casual, in his late fifties, Hoglund leaned back and sipped coffee from a styrofoam cup as we talked. He was a striking contrast to Stempel, not only in his cool and detached manner, and with his striped shirt and red tie, but in the way he disassociated the new GM from Roger Smith's regime and how he recognized Saturn's problems, problems he dealt with almost day to day (Skip LeFauve had left his office just moments before I walked in). Hoglund expressed personal "reservations" about the speed at which Saturn was transferring knowledge to GM, even out of sight. But it *was* happening, he insisted. He remembered how surprised he had been, back at Saturn's start-up period in 1985, when he and Wetzel and the other vice presidents were running Saturn by the seat of their pants, that Roger Smith had initiated such a project. Why? Because Roger Smith was not good at empowering people who worked for GM, Hoglund said, adding, "He never understood Saturn very well." Then, shining a fresh ray of light on Saturn's origins, Hoglund recalled that pressures to close the 1984 labor negotiations with the UAW had more to do with the company's beginnings than was commonly recognized. At the time Smith had gone along with Don Ephlin, then head of the GM branch of the UAW, less because of his enthusiasm for some idealistic human relations system (Ephlin too had called Saturn rather "utopian"), but to get the 1984 labor contract signed.

Now, just short of a decade later, Saturn was no utopia, though Hoglund kept referring to it as "a fair-haired organization." It takes tremendous stamina to follow through on a vision, a resoluteness Saturn no longer possessed, fair haired or not. The retreat from the original ideals, the absence of clear channels for transferring knowledge (underground channels nowadays, according to Hoglund), the misunderstandings between the UAW leadership and the Saturn local—all combined to put Saturn on shaky ground. Dave Cole, director of the Transportation Institute, put a positive spin on the shortcomings and insisted that Saturn remained an experiment and that all the ripples "are part of the experiment." But so many ripples also muddied the waters. Specific improvements, failures, lessons became harder to identify.

Murkiest of all were the present misunderstandings about the union's role at Saturn. Hoglund recalled that back in 1985 there had been talk of bringing Ephlin's designated successor, Stephen Yokich, into the loop, indoctrinating him into the Saturn philosophy, making him part of the creative process. But they hadn't done that—in retrospect, a big mistake. According to Hoglund, Yokich's attitude now was: "Whether Saturn is good or bad is immaterial; it's not his."

I asked where Owen Beiber fit into this puzzle. Beiber was president of the UAW International when Saturn was announced in 1985 ("We have made vast strides here," he'd said). He still was. Why wasn't Beiber putting pressure on Yokich to cooperate with Saturn, I asked Hoglund.

Beiber let his endorsement slide, he replied. "I may have to sit down and talk with Owen."

Hoglund acknowledged that without more harmony and understanding between GM and UAW over Saturn's future course, that course would go nowhere. Not to Bowling Green, not into a new facility. What he was saying, it seemed to me, was that if they couldn't work as a team to expand Saturn, why continue with the charade of being a team inside it?

"So where is Saturn going vis-à-vis GM's other divisions?" I asked.

"Saturn's product plan has to fit into the General Motors' portfolio," Hoglund stressed. For instance, Saturn was not going to compete with Chevrolet. The focus would remain on entry-level buyers. John Rock, general manager at Oldsmobile, understood the GM/Saturn linkage as well as anyone, Hoglund said.

Oldsmobile, routinely called GM's "sickest division" by the press, had definitely hooked its wobbly future to Saturn's rising star. John Rock seemed to be defining how the other divisions could learn from

Saturn, or at least take some advantage of its success. Oldsmobile's strategy was to inherit Saturn's second generation of buyers. In other words, go to an Oldsmobile showroom for the bigger engine, the leather seats, the bulkmobile. There, Rock claimed, Saturn owners would enjoy a Saturn-like buying experience.

But what about a quality car? Could Oldsmobile, a marketing entity without its own plants, duplicate the substance of Saturn or just the surface buying experience? At least the division was copying the retail partnership concept. Time would tell if it worked, if greater expectations in the showroom filtered back through the division and resulted in higher quality cars. When and if Saturn ironed out its labor troubles and expanded its facilities, maybe it would start making Oldsmobile powertrains and chassis but with more luxurious interiors and different skins.

In early 1993 GM announced its largest loss ever, $23.5 billion (much of it attributable to health cost writeoffs for 594 thousand retirees and their families), but then posted a $513 million profit in the first quarter of 1993. The corporation also savored a rare public relations victory. It exposed an NBC-TV faked documentary about exploding side-saddle gas tanks in GMC pickups, a vehicle haunting the giant with a possible massive national recall. NBC publicly apologized for rigging the tanks to blow up dramatically on impact. Nevertheless, a plaintiff's heirs were awarded over $100 million because of his death by fire in a side-saddle pickup. At this writing GM was holding fast to its defense that the trucks were okay.

Meanwhile, Skip LeFauve went public and said Saturn was going to make a small profit in 1993. In Spring Hill teams were breaking apart and realigning, spreading the experience and knowledge to C-crew. The last time I talked to Jay Wetzel, the vice president of engineering said, "We're now the leanest engineering division in the industry." In Troy he'd streamlined his department, cutting four hundred jobs and consolidating the remaining 1,250 engineers into one large room; it was laid out to resemble the processes in the plant. Wetzel said so many letters were coming in these days, a few of them critical, he couldn't keep up with them. But he did miss something. "Now we're established, we don't want to take risks; our cavalier attitude towards risk is gone."

Later Wetzel faxed me six pages of awards Saturn had won. One that caught my eye was the "Public Relations Society of America *Silver Anvil Award*" for internal communications and community relations.

Given the continuing slow burn of most Maurians toward Saturn, with the jobs issue as touchy as ever, I wondered what Orwellian criteria had been used.

Last year the American Advertising Federation recognized Hal Riney's Velma Willarson ad featuring the shimmering blue coupe and lots of birdseed as worthy of special recognition. I was pleased to read that.

Wetzel also included a note telling me Saturn had fifty new patents, with seventeen pending.

As this epilogue concludes, like a cornucopia the Saturn story grows and expands. On trips to Boston, Detroit, Seattle, and Montreal, I see the little cars everywhere. They remind me just how dramatically the car industry has changed since I started witnessing this story in 1986.

Back then Saturn was conceived in desperation, fertilized by hope and profits, and tended by both management and labor. In those days, with GM's market share plummeting, fuel economy very important to the average car buyer, and recent automotive history strewn with badly made American compacts—not to mention billions of dollars of technology and tens of thousands of laid-off workers—Saturn symbolized hope for a more competitive future. Hope conceived in a Detroit test tube, then transferred to rural Tennessee to grow, but without sharing its bounty with the locals. In 1993, although the Japanese imports were losing market share in America, at home they faced some of the same problems the Big Three grappled with throughout the eighties: high labor costs, excess manufacturing capacity, an overvalued currency. Combined with a gradual shift in American perceptions about the quality of domestic-made cars, a shift Saturn contributed to significantly, this added up to breathing room for the Big Three. And of course it eased up on the pressure to make Saturn truly become a different kind of company.

One mistaken presumption, though, was that the Japanese were in serious economic trouble, that competitively Toyota, Honda, Mazda, and the rest were falling apart. Presently, they had their troubles. But past patterns suggested the Japanese would not stay down for long. Doomsayers have been proclaiming the end of the Japanese economic miracle for years. Yet that economy, following such notable setbacks as the 1973 oil crisis, the 1985 devaluation of the dollar, and other blows to its momentum, invariably has bounced back stronger than ever, demonstrating an admirable flexibility to global forces out of its control. The Big Three could count on that happening again—in the mid-nineties. Meanwhile, they had momentarily leveled the playing field, with Saturn a star player in the protracted, strategic, and ongoing game of global car sales.

In May 1993, Saturn remained "the new chic in auto circles," as *Washington Post* columnist Mary McGrory called it. But she was a little off the mark when she said that inside the plant "people talk about 'philosophy' and 'mission' and never mention the bottom line, the profit the sleek little Yuppie delight is supposed to make." In truth the Yuppie age was behind us, surviving as a vague term of denigration attached to materialism led by the young. And few Saturnites mentioned mission anymore.

Down in the dimple of the universe upwards of seven thousand of them were too busy building a good small car. The times were changing, however. In 1993 a good small car wasn't what America needed as much as it had ten years before. America needed a great big example of how to do things right industrially, a more fully realized model of how to achieve the fine vision Saturn was at its inception—not as a product but as a process whose goal was quality. Quality in what it made, in how it made it, in how it treated the place where it was made, and, most important of all, in the human relationships that made change and growth and improvement possible. That is, a vision that integrates people, place, and quality in a bright shining example truly signaling the rebirth of American ingenuity.

Saturn pointed the way. But this different kind of company forging a different kind of America still has an uncertain destination.

Chronology

1950 The English small car invasion—MGs, Austins, Hillmans, Jaguars, and others—begins in America. Imports account for less than three-tenths of a percent of American car sales.

1955 The English small car invasion recedes. Volkswagen increases its exports to the U.S.

1957 Two Toyopet Crowns, made by Toyota, roll off a ship in Los Angeles. Miss Japan, dressed like a geisha, lays a wreath on one car's hood. The Crowns are a flop in the American marketplace.

1959 GM introduces its first "import fighter," the Corvair, which is joined by the Ford Falcon and the Dodge Valiant.

1960 Imports account for 6% of car sales in the U.S.

1961 Volkswagen sells 177, 000 cars in America, or 3% of car sales nationwide.

1965 Japanese car manufacturers sell 26,000 cars in the U.S.

1970 Japanese car manufacturers sell 381,000 cars in the U.S.

GM introduces the Chevrolet Vega, its second import fighter. Within 24 months 95% of all the Vegas manufactured are recalled for safety problems.

1973 U.S. car manufacturers sell a record 9.7 million cars in America.

Japanese manufacturers sell 625,000 cars in the U.S.

First oil crisis. Price of gasoline doubles.

1975 Japan accounts for half of cars imported into the U.S.

1979 GM introduces the first of a series of alphabet cars, the front-wheel-drive X-cars powered by V-6 engines, as their newest import fighters.

1980 U.S. car manufacturers lose $4.2 billion among them.

Japanese car sales in U.S. approach 2 million.

1981 In January Roger Smith becomes chairman of GM. Shortly thereafter, he kills Chevrolet's small-car project, called the S-car, because it cannot compete against Japanese imports.

1982   In June, at the GM Technical Center a "skunk works" starts to explore the feasibility of a radically different small car made a new way.

That September the skunk works becomes the "no name project."

1983   In March GM and Toyota announce they have formed a partnership to build small cars in Fremont, California. The partnership is called NUMMI, for New United Motor Manufacturing, Inc.

That November the new small-car project, now called Saturn, is first made public.

In December GM and the UAW establish a Saturn Study Center to work more cooperatively.

1984   Between February and April, the Group of 99, a mix of GM and UAW people from throughout the corporation, tour 49 GM plants, visit 60 non-GM facilities, and travel more than two million miles, asking "What if?" Their findings become the groundwork for the design of the Saturn Corporation.

That September, the first Saturn prototype is completed.

1985   On January 7, Roger Smith announces the formation of Saturn Corporation, a wholly owned subsidiary of General Motors, and the search for a site for the future plant. Smith drives the first prototype.

Three weeks later Joseph Sanchez, Saturn's first president, unexpectedly dies. William Hoglund succeeds him.

In March at the Peabody Hotel in Memphis, Tennessee, governor Lamar Alexander urges Roger Smith to locate the Saturn plant in his state.

A week later Tennessee joins several dozen states eagerly pursuing Saturn.

In May, George Jones is elected mayor of Spring Hill, TN.

Meanwhile the Saturn site hunt has focused exclusively on Tennessee.

By late July two historic mansions, several farms, and a total of 2,450 acres have been optioned in Spring Hill by a mystery client.

On July 26 the GM/UAW Saturn labor contract, which gives workers a say in the future of the company, is announced. Within a week the National Right to Work Committee challenges the contract as illegal under Tennessee's right to work laws.

On the weekend of July 27, as word gets out that Saturn will be located in Spring Hill, a land speculation whirlwind hits the village and the surrounding region.

On July 30, Spring Hill is officially declared Saturn's future home.

In August a Maury County Planning Commission is formed.

On September 4, Spring Hill rezones the Saturn property from agricultural to industrial usage.

On September 11 the state of Tennessee announces it plans to build the Saturn Parkway, which will connect the plant with I-65, for $29.3 million.

On September 12, the Spring Hill Area Concerned Citizens Group meets for the first time.

On September 19 the newly formed Maury County Planning Commission meets and freezes all development in the county until zoning ordinances are written and passed.

That October, in Michigan, Saturn moves its northern headquarters into new offices in Troy.

In November the Saturn in-lieu-of-tax agreement is announced. It says the plant will pay about one-third the normal industrial property taxes for the next 40 years, along with several million dollars for city improvements in Maury County. Consumer advocate Ralph Nader labels the tax agreement "peanuts."

1986 In February, Richard "Skip" LeFauve is named the third president of Saturn.

The same month, despite lobbying by Saturn, a proposed Scenic Preservation Corridor to restrict development near the plant is left out of the proposed county zoning ordinances by the Maury County Planning Commission.

In April a land annexation battle between Columbia and Spring Hill begins. Tennessee law allows a larger municipality to supersede a smaller one in order to expand its boundaries and provide orderly growth. Spring Hill eventually loses the battle.

That May site work begins on the 200-acre construction zone.

In June the National Labor Relations Board dismisses the complaint filed against Saturn for violating Tennessee's right-to-work laws.

The same month Citizens for Progress in Maury County, an organization of developers, organize to lobby for more favorable zoning.

In July the second phase of plant construction begins. It includes moving 2.8 million cubic yards of dirt over the next ten months.

In October Saturn announces a cutback, which will reduce the work force to 3,000 the first year, and trim the investment down to $3.5 billion from an original estimate of $5 billion.

In November growth consultants hired by Maury County report that the county will need up to $33 million to meet projected expenses for improvements in water, sewage, schools, law enforcement, and roads over the next 15 years. Population is expected to increase from 54,000 to 75,000 by the year 2000, a jump of 38%.

1987 In April Spring Hill initiates the construction of a new $1.25 million Town Hall on three acres donated by the developer of Town Center Development, adjacent the village. The construction funds will come from the in-lieu-of-tax agreement with Saturn.

In December Spring Hill celebrates its 150th anniversary.

1988 In January steel erection is completed for the powertrain building, the first in the complex.

In February the recruitment campaign begins for 3,000 Saturn team members, all of whom will come from GM.

That March the first machinery arrives at the plant.

In December the plant construction work is at its peak, with 2,500 workers on the site.

1989 During the first six months of the year GM's new car/truck sales drop 23% from the previous year.

During the same time Japanese-made cars and trucks account for 31% of sales in the U.S.

In April the Saturn Training and Development Center opens at the Northfield administration center on the site.

In May Spring Hill mayor George Jones is voted out of office.

Throughout the summer months a large number of UAW transferees begin moving into Maury County.

By the fall all the Saturn buildings are enclosed. Machinery is being moved in and tuned. Teams are being trained.

1990 In January, ground is broken for Saturn's first store in Memphis.

On July 31, the first Saturn rolls off the assembly line. Roger Smith, who retires the next day, is at the wheel.

By October, with a national advertising campaign in full swing, only a trickle of Saturns are in the stores.

In its December issue *Automotive News* names Saturn the "story of the year."

GM loses $2 billion for the year.

1991 In May at the GM annual meeting, Saturn is a "home run," according to GM chairman Robert Stempel, despite the recall a week before of 1,800 cars for a coolant problem.

In July Saturn's first year production ends. The plant made 55 thousand cars and lost an estimated $700 million.

In November, in Columbia, locals picket the Kmart store after it offers Saturn employees a special pre-Christmas sale.

In December GM announces the largest downscaling in its history. Seventy-four thousand people will be laid off and 21 plants closed. Saturn escapes the cuts.

For December production at Saturn averages 800 cars a day.

During 1991 GM loses a record $8 billion in its North American car-making operations.

At year's end Japanese-made cars command 36% of U.S. market.

1992   That January, in hopes of increasing production above 200,000 cars for the coming year, Saturn shifts to a 50-hour work week.

In April *Consumer Reports* gives Saturn its highest rating for mechanical reliability. J. D. Powers ranks Saturn third in "customer satisfaction," behind Infiniti and Lexus, two luxury cars made in Japan.

That April former Saturn's second president, William Hoglund, is promoted to chief financial officer at GM.

In May 150 Saturn stores sell 18,031 cars. Sales per dealership for Saturn are the best in the nation and have been for several months.

At an emergency meeting Saturn team leaders hear they must cut $1,600 from the manufacturing costs per car.

By July production averages 1,050 cars a day.

That September a strike at a GM Lordstown, Ohio, parts plant shuts the Saturn plant assembly line down for a week.

Second-year loses are estimated at $1 billion.

In November GM chairman Stempel is removed by the board of directors.

By December nationwide sales of Saturns far exceed production, which remains at 1,050 cars a day. Customers wait as long as a month for a car.

Hiring begins for Saturn's third shift. All the hiring will be done from the pool of laid off GM/UAW workers. No production workers are to be hired locally.

For 1992 GM loses $23.5 billion dollars, most of it attributable to pension plan health insurance costs. Saturn's losses, which were running at about $100 million a month in January, have been reduced to a quarter of that. Total losses for 1992 are $620 million.

1993   In January a plant-wide referendum is held on the future of the Saturn labor contract. Seventy-three percent of the union membership vote to keep the contract as is.

After a long lawsuit the family of a 17-year-old killed in a GMC pickup, one of the so-called "firebomb" models with side-saddle gas tanks, is awarded $104 million in total damages. A recall of all GMC pickups, which would cost GM estimated $500 million, might be a consequence.

To GM's relief, NBC publicly admits it tampered with a television documentary that showed a pickup with side-saddle tanks exploding.

Saturn president LeFauve announces this "is our break-even year. We'll earn as much as we spend."

In March, in a run-off, Saturn union president Mike Bennett is narrowly re-elected, keeping the Saturn vision in power.

In May, Saturn posted an operating profit for the first time on sales of a record 22,697 cars. As a reward, each Saturnite got a $1,000 bonus.

Bibliography

Books, Journals, and Magazines

Andrews, Wayne. *Architecture in Chicago & Mid-America.* New York: Atheneum, 1968.

Chappell, Lindsey. "Get lean, warns MIT book, but Ford already has." *Automotive News* 5373 (1990): 1, 26–27.

———. "Japan's 'lean production' called a must for all automakers." *Automotive News* 5373 (1990): 26–27.

Dobyns, Lloyd. "Ed Deming wants big changes, and he wants them fast." *Smithsonian* August 1990: 74–82.

Ferguson, Marilyn. *The Aquarian Conspiracy.* Los Angeles: J.P. Tarcher, 1980.

Fisher, David. "Spring Hill on the brink." *Automobile Magazine* September 1986: 63–69.

Gitlow, Shelly J. and Howard S. *The Deming Guide to Quality and Competitive Position.* Englewood Cliffs: Prentice-Hall, 1987.

Greenwald, John. "Can GM survive in today's world?" *Time* 9 November 1992: 42–51.

Gwynne, S.C. "The right stuff. *Time* 29 October 1990: 74–84.

Hildebrand, Grant. *The Architecture of Albert Kahn.* Cambridge: MIT Press, 1974.

Hiss, Tony. *The Experience of Place.* New York: Vintage Books, 1990.

Hyde, Charles K. *Detroit: An Industrial History Guide.* Detroit: Detroit Historical Society, 1980.

Jacobs, Jane. *Cities and the Wealth of Nations.* New York: Vintage Books, 1984.

Keller, Maryanne. *Rude Awakening.* New York: HarperCollins Publishers, 1990.

Kerwin, Kathleen. "The Big Three think they smell blood." *Business Week* 28 September 1992: 35–35.

LeFauve, Richard G. and Arnoldo C. Hax. "Managerial and technological innovations at Saturn Corporation." *MIT Management,* Spring (1992): 8–19.

Lee, Albert. *Call Me Roger.* Chicago: Contemporary Books, 1988.

Lemann, Nicholas. *The Promised Land.* New York: Alfred A. Knopf, 1991.

Lienert, Paul. "Saturn two years on: in a sea of red ink, a pinpoint of passion." *Automobile Magazine* July 1992: 47.

Mangelsdorf, Martha E. "Broken promises." *INC.* July 1991: 25–28.

Pirsig, Robert M. *Zen and the Art of Motorcycle Maintenance.* New York: William Morrow and Company, 1974.

Bibliography

Rothschild, Emma. *Paradise Lost: The Decline of the Auto-Industrial Age.* New York: Random House, 1973.

Servan-Schreiber, J.-J. *The American Challenge.* New York: Atheneum, 1969.

───── **and Michel Albert.** *The Radical Alternative.* New York: W.W. Norton & Company, 1971.

Senge, Peter M. *The Fifth Discipline.* New York: Bantam, 1990.

Sobel, Robert. *Car Wars.* New York: E.P. Dutton, 1984.

Taylor, Alex III. "Back to the future at Saturn." *Fortune* 1 August 1988: 63–72.

Vettraino, J.P. "Myth identified." *Autoweek* 27 July 1992:14–17.

Wilson, Charles R., and William Ferris, eds. *Encyclopedia of Southern Culture.* Chapel Hill: University of North Carolina Press, 1989.

Wright, Gavin. *Old South, New South: Revolutions in the Southern Economy Since the Civil War.* New York: Basic Books, 1986.

Womack, James P. Daniel T. Jones, and Daniel Roos. *The Machine That Changed the World.* New York: Rawson Associates, 1990.

Select Newspaper Articles

Battle, Bob. "Secret's out! Nashville lawyers held key to Saturn site options." *Nashville Banner* 8 August 1985: A1+.

Baxter, Emme Nelson. "Saturn Growing." *Tennessean* 24 July 1988, D1+.

─────. "Greater power, less pay are issues for Saturn applicants." *Tennessean* 5 September 1988, E2.

─────. "My, how Spring Hill has changed." *Tennessean* 13 May 1990: D1+.

Boruff, David. "Spring Hill still awaiting big boom." *Nashville Banner* 27 July 1988: C1+.

Eisenstadt, Todd. "Spring Hill planners embrace Saturn site area, beyond." *Tennessean* 30 July 1985: 1.

Fox, David A. "Car worth waiting and waiting for . . ." *Tennessean* 16 August 1992: E1+.

Frazier, Gary. "Controlling traffic concern for Spring Hill police force." *Daily Herald* 22 January 1989: 7.

─────. "Differences blemish Saturn relocation. *Columbia Daily Herald* 2 March 1989: 1.

Henry, Jim. "Saturn Corp. president drops hints on new car." *Nashville Banner* 3 December 1987: C6.

─────. "Saturn workers in Michigan gear up for Spring Hill move." *Nashville Banner* 23 March 1988: C5.

─────. "Saturn complex impresses lawmakers." *Nashville Banner* 31 March 1988: C10.

─────. "Machine goes in at Saturn." *Nashville Banner* 14 April 1988: C17.

Higgins, James V. "Saturn—'They're saying they can compete.'" *Tennessean* 13 May 1990: D1+.

Hilman, Randy. "UAW to represent Nissan by Saturn opening: organizer." *Tennessean* 17 July 1988: D1+.

Hudgins, Bill. "Spring Hill landowners' dilemma: To sell or not to sell." *Nashville Banner* 31 July 1985: 1.

Keel, Beverly. "Teens key to success for Saturn move." *Nashville Banner* 24 July 1989: A1+.

———. "Saturn set for flood of workers." *Nashville Banner* 24 October 1989: A1+.

———. "Expert predicts Saturn profits doubtful." *Nashville Banner* 12 February 1990: B10.

———. "Spring Hill won't be new Flint: GM chief." *Nashville Banner* 28 March 1990: B1+.

———. "1st Saturn leaves launch pad." *Nashville Banner* 30 July 1990: A1+.

———. "Saturn mission 'like a religion' for employees." *Nashville Banner* 9 October 1990: A1+.

———. "Nation watches as curtain rises for Saturn." *Nashville Banner* 11 October 1990: A1+.

———. "Auto dealers finally have Saturns to sell." *Nashville Banner* 1 February 1991: D1.

Kennedy, Tonnya. "GM chief Smith tours Saturn plant." Nashville Banner 14 April 1989: B1.

———. "Saturn supply system called worth the risk." *Nashville Banner* 28 August 1992: D1+.

Lippert, John. "Ahead for Saturn? Station wagons, convertibles, vans." Nashville Banner 26 January 1991: D1+.

McCampbell, Candy. "1st Saturn just Roger and no me." *Tennessean* 29 July 1990: D1.

———. "Drivers give Saturn high marks." *Tennessean* 15 October 1990: E1+.

———. "Saturn recalling cars to fix seats." *Tennessean* 14 February 1991: E1+.

Maynard, Micheline. "Resignation unlikely to end GM troubles." *Burlington Free Press* 27 October 1992: A6.

Nader, Ralph. "Spring Hill, take lesson from Flint." *Tennessean* 15 December 1985: H5.

Nelson, Emme. "Saturn to install die-casting unit." *Tennessean* 7 March 1988: E3.

Paine, Anne. "Spring Hill: One year after Saturn landed." *Tennessean* 27 July 1986: A1+.

———. "Town's pulse slows to pre-Saturn rate." *Nashville Tennessean* 22 July 1990: A1+.

Patterson, Gregory A. "Two GM auto plants illustrate major role of workers' attitudes." *The Wall Street Journal* 29 August 1984, sec a: 1+.

Pollock, Andrew. "A lower gear for Japan's auto makers." *New York Times* 30 August 1992, sec 3: 1+.

Pratt, James. "GM may build in Maury." *Tennessean* 13 June 1985: 1+.

———. "GM makes Saturn site official." *Tennessean* 30 July 1985: 1+

Richie, L. Carol. "Saturn migration stirs cultures together." *Nashville Banner* 10 October 1990: A1+.

Stein, Beth. "Piloting a planet." *Nashville Banner* 11 October 1990: D1+.

Stertz, Bradley A. "Our cars are alive with the sound of (irksome) music." *The Wall Street Journal* 12 September 1991: A1+.

Thomas, Steve. "Dueling speculators bid Poplar House to $450,000." *Nashville Banner* 9 August 1985: 1.

White, Joseph B. "Japanese auto makers help U.S. suppliers become more efficient." *The Wall Street Journal* 9 September 1991: A1+.

Bibliography

White, Joseph, and Paul Ingrassia. "Determined to change, General Motors is said to pick new chairman." 26 October 1992: A1+.

White, Joseph B., and Paul Ingrassia. "GM outside directors seek removal of ex-chairman." *Wall Street Journal* 30 October 1992: A1+.

————. "At once-stodgy GM, management change is a generational one." *Wall Street Journal* 3 November 1992: A1+.

Williard, J. Patrick. "New route vital link for Saturn production." *Tennessean* 5 August 1989: D1.

Wissner, Sheila. "Schools not measuring up: Saturn chief." *Tennessean* 17 November 1989: A1+.

Pamphlet

Saturn Update. Spring Hill: First Topping Out. January 1988.

328

Acknowledgments

For helping me a great deal with this book I want to thank Richard Quin, George Jones, Trish Rasbury, and Jay Wetzel.

Grateful acknowledgments also go out to the following Maurians: Randy and James Lochridge, John Campbell, Naomi Derryberry, Delilah A. Speed, Mrs. Blair Jackson, Robin Courtney, Eugene Heller, Phil Lovell, Joe Max Williams, David Holdenfield, Cyril Evers, Judy Langsdon, P.D. Boyd, Bobby Ingram, Clint and Freeda Brown, Bill Fryer, Peter Frierson, Charlene and Rose Ogilvie, Roy Caruthers, Roger Sears, Waymon Hickman, Joy and Victor Rasbury, and Elmer Holt.

And to the following Saturnites: Ed Killgore, Skip LeFauve, Donald Ephlin, Reid Rundell, Billy Joe Horan, Jim Wheatley, Beth Miakinin, Rick Youngblood, Maurice Bobo, Joy Rodes, Laurie Kay, Jennifer Schettler, Bob Courtemanche Jr. and Sr., Marvin O'Gorman, and to the crank line A-crew: Scott Prins, Steve Sherman, Michelle Mullenhour, Ken Baker, John Plourd, Tom Reinhard, Joe McKean, Pam Saint, William Jenkins, Seborn Powell, Leanne Schipani, and Nancy Laatz. And to B-crew's Danny Lentz, the assembly line's Al Burris, and foundry team members Dennis Dowers and Sharon East. Thanks also to Dexter Riffe, Al Hendershot, Don Page, Linda Penland, Karen Tibus, and Gary Porter for their cooperation in the Saturn stores.

I gratefully acknowledge the input of professionals Ron Cooper, Mort Stein, Judy Daniels, and John Costonis. And the time, encouragement, and information shared by my colleagues in the press: Beverly Keel, Randy Hillman, James Pratt, Elizabeth Murray, Gary Fraiser, and Lindsay Chappell. For the bits and pieces fleshing out the narrative supplied by numerous reporters' articles in the *Tennessean* and the Nashville *Banner* over the years, I express my gratitude.

Others I am indebted to in no small degree include Maclin Davis, J. Ross Cheshire, Jr., Mrs. Lawrence Dortch, Jack Brandon, Dinning Love, Vance Berry, Roger Boelio, Alden Smith, James Huhta, Bill Long,

Acknowledgments

Ted Von Cannon, Claudia Dunavant, Robert Stempel, William Hoglund, and David Cole.

For his support, and guidance of this project, I owe much to Herb Addison, my editor at Oxford University Press, and to Mary Sutherland, his assistant editor, for her reliable help.

During my research Bea and Percy Cohen tolerated me at their home in Nashville far beyond any reasonable stay by an itinerant son-in-law, and I thank them for their generosity. Their neighbor Libby Fryer provided me invaluable leads at the outset of this book.

Last but not least I wish to thank Jeff Colin, former editor of *Historic Preservation* magazine, for first sending me to Spring Hill in 1986 and introducing me to the potential of this story. And to the many Maurians I talked to in bars, on the streets, in churches, and along the back roads of the dimple of the universe—hats off for your contributions that are woven between the lines of this story, giving it, I hope, the ring of truth.

Index